Optimal Parenting

Optimal Parenting

*Using Natural Learning Rhythms
to Nurture the Whole Child*

Ba Luvmour

SENTIENT PUBLICATIONS

First Sentient Publications edition 2006
Copyright © 2006 by Ba Luvmour

A paperback original

Printed in the United States of America

Cover design by Kim Johansen, Black Dog Design
Book design by Nicholas Cummings

Library of Congress Cataloging-in-Publication Data

Luvmour, Ba, 1947-
  Optimal parenting : using natural learning rhythms to nurture the whole child / by Ba Luvmour.— 1st ed.
      p. cm.
  Includes bibliographical references.
  ISBN 1-59181-041-8
  1. Parenting. 2. Child development. I. Title.
  HQ755.8.L89 2006
  305.231—dc22

SENTIENT PUBLICATIONS
A Limited Liability Company
1113 Spruce Street
Boulder, CO 80302
www.sentientpublications.com

To all the grandchildren—born and unborn

CONTENTS

ACKNOWLEDGEMENTS

First, I am happily indebted to all the families who have trusted me over the years. There has been no greater reward in my work than participating in programs and learning with you. Your courage and dedication to meet life's challenges and your willingness to grow and accept that all people are our mutual responsibility have opened my heart. Second, I wish to thank the many generous people who donated to EnCompass as a way to support and further the vision of optimal well-being, and of whole families learning together. Last, and so important for this book, I offer deep appreciation to the readers of this manuscript for their excellent critiques, especially Susan, Trudi, Ron, Nita, Josette, Mary Clare, Albee, and Amber. Connie Shaw, and Sentient Publications, have been impeccable in their handling of me—no easy task—and this book.

William Blake said it best: *Gratitude is heaven itself.*

SECTION I

The
Ground

By aesthetic, I mean responsive to the pattern which connects. So you see, I was lucky. Perhaps by coincidence, I
faced them with what was (though I knew it not) an aesthetic question: How are you related to this creature?
What pattern connects you to it?
    —Gregory Bateson, *Mind and Nature: A Necessary Unity*

Chapter One

AUTHOR'S VOICE

Natural Learning Rhythms is inspired by the greatness in each of us. Two frontline workers in the fields of family dynamics and child development have revealed what so many of our family learning partners have intuited for years: Focusing on optimal health and well-being is much more valuable than focusing on pathology. Almost every family has experienced joy in their intimate relationships. Almost every teacher has been dazzled at the moment when "the penny drops"—when a student knows, and knows that she knows. The goal of Natural Learning Rhythms is helping others to live this joy, this learning, this place where shared vision and action come together in a moment of mutual growth and care. Life with their children is often good, but they have tasted greatness and know there is no comparison. Greatness is the human birthright, the human destiny. We are so extraordinarily gifted! Look around—we have transformed our environment. Recall the love you experienced at the birth of your child. Think about mathematics and the arts; you can use symbols to create and communicate meaning. Feel the fear of your enemy; you can empathize and have compassion. Become intoxicated with the scent of the rose; you can connect to all that is beautiful in life.

Natural Learning Rhythms does not deny the pain and suffering in life. It does not deny the conditioning and the social pressures that inhibit great relationships. It does not deny the litany of problems that fill our newscasts and trouble our hearts and minds. But we ask: Is just reducing symptoms sufficient? Aren't we caught in a downward spiral of expensive symptom reduction with no clear vision of transformation?

Natural Learning Rhythms focuses on emerging greatness rather than the pathology that inevitably results when greatness is ignored. Natural Learning Rhythms states that without health and well-being inexorably expressing themselves, there would be no conflict, no stress, and no pathology. Indeed, there would be no recognition that there was a problem. After all, how could a problem be recognized if there were not a deep-seated knowing of human greatness? We would have no basis of comparison. Inflicted pain, unnecessary suffering, and mindlessness would go unnoticed.

Looking through the lens of well-being brings forth a vision of transformation that can be actualized by most families. It is a well-founded vision based on research in child development, family dynamics, and other disciplines, such as anthropology, quantum mechanics, and spiritual philosophy. It is a well-tested vision used in more than a thousand experiential programs with whole families and children of all ages. Above all, it is a practical vision that can be applied to all interactions with children and within families.

As family greatness awakens, many of the common problems that beset families fall away. Our experience of twenty-three years suggests that about 66 percent of adversarial confrontations go the way of the dinosaur—extinct, gone forever. At the same time, this vision helps families develop responses to most chronic problems—responses that can be applied at little cost, impose no stigma, and make no one the "identified problem." Amazingly, pathology does not exist side-by-side with well-being. Well-being accepts pathology and transforms it; in that transformation everyone is enriched, people grow, and the families experience joy.

Natural Learning Rhythms restores genuineness to parenting and teaching. Indeed, one of the most common evaluations of our seminars is, "I already knew most of that. I just never put it together." Natural Learning Rhythms marks a clear path for:

- Nourishing optimal well-being in each family member
- Helping parents and teachers build confidence
- Breaking the stranglehold of focusing on pathology—on what is wrong and bad and substandard
- Restoring nonsectarian spirituality
- Putting adults in touch with critically important events in their children's development, such as their perception of personal mortality, the growth of interpersonal relationships, the devel-

opment of the ability to understand abstract concepts, and their increasing exploration of the physical world

- Treating children as integral members of the family—they are wise and worthwhile, and they continuously make important contributions to family well-being

Natural Learning Rhythms holds a vision that is constantly emerging and continually teaching. It is open and available. It shows the nature of child-rearing in understandable detail yet leaves its actualization to its practitioners. As many program participants have commented, "It treats the parent like an intelligent person and not a dummy who needs to fill up on techniques from an expert who never met my family." Therefore, it is eminently respectful.

I often feel inadequate in my attempts to articulate Natural Learning Rhythms. At the same time, there are spectacular successes and the programs enjoy high participant approval. But it is the learning that draws, the ever-deepening self-knowledge that awakens, the privilege of participating in a social endeavor that can lead to optimal well-being for so many that compels.

I invite you to step into the field of family well-being. Deepen your experience of intimacy, enjoyment, and family learning. You will have to be playful as well as serious and sober. Effort is required to go from good to great. Some beliefs will have to be shed, others adopted and experimented with before they can be fully accepted. Nevertheless, we assure you that the time and effort invested in seeking well-being will pay off many times over. Familial relationships will have greater depth and meaning, problems will turn into challenges and learning, and, best of all, children will want to communicate with the adults in their life. I ask only that you experiment with any insight or suggestion that appeals to you. Direct experience through participation is necessary for the fullest appreciation of the program.

On Josette

In our twenty-three years at home together, Josette and I have sat in silence for thousands of hours, co-pioneered Natural Learning Rhythms, and created transformational retreats for families. We parented Amber and built a house from the ground up (though neither of us had carpentry skills). We have led numerous meditation retreats, co-facilitated hundreds of Natural Learning Rhythms seminars, co-authored four books and numerous articles, and raised a couple million dollars for a nonprofit to build an integrated learning center. We skirted bankruptcy while the learning center was sold. We have made many friends and some enemies, made many mistakes and had some extraordinary successes, faced the challenges of committed marriage without flinching, and experienced joyful intimacy. We saw the likely implications of Natural Learning Rhythms for our personal lives immediately: lots of contact with people, learning how to be sensitive to the crucial importance parents attach to their relationships with their children, immersion in the suffering of others, and the challenge of learning how to be a public couple during high-powered programs. Our lifestyle at that time, twenty-three years ago, centered on quiet and study, so the changes, were we to accept them, seemed dramatic. For a year we sat with it, then realized we had no choice. A vocation is a vocation is a vocation. While I am writing this book, you can perhaps understand if I do not see myself as the only author. There are times when it is Josette's words that you are reading, though they come through my hand. I would dedicate the book to her, but in a real sense she is writing it too.

In addition to her activities of creating and facilitating programs, gardening, and creating fabric arts, Josette has decided to work toward her doctorate. Her research has been an invaluable source as I have written this book.

On Pronouns and Imperatives

She and he are used interchangeably throughout the book unless the reference is to a specific person or to a topic about one of the genders. One is used sparingly as it fails to carry the necessary intimacy. Optimal Parenting is about children, parents, and families; about people and relationships; and about she, he, you, us, we, and me.

On occasion, I write that something should be done; these are not moral injunctions. No one is bad or wrong if these things are not done. Should refers only to a necessary condition. If something is to happen, this is what must be done. If, for instance, you eat, you should open your mouth and chew. Natural Learning Rhythms is an invitation to optimal well-being, not an imperative from which censure "should" follow if a standard is not met. That use of should has no place in optimal well-being.

On References

Natural Learning Rhythms has always been dedicated to parents, teachers, and others who interact directly with children. For this reason, I have minimized the use of references. For a long time, this decision left us with tension, because I hoped—and continue to hope—that academicians will appreciate our efforts. Also, references equal validity in the eyes of many. In this book I will take a new path. Where I am indebted to others, I will reference them in an endnote. If there is additional useful information, I will include it in the endnote. In this way, I hope not only to leave the flow of the text unimpeded but also to provide sources for further inquiry for those who are interested. When I quote others, it is to explicate Natural Learning Rhythms, not to attempt to explain what they might have meant or to demonstrate kinship. Quotes are used only where someone has written something that will help us to deepen appreciation of children. Our intention is for NLR to be easily understandable and to provide the references that create the bridge with academics and professionals.

I must be clear that I have not made an exhaustive study of each and every author cited. I have, however, tried to capture the essence of their work as it applies to Natural Learning Rhythms. I make no claim to have captured every nuance or modification the author may have made in subsequent works. Also, while I have looked carefully at the way children are treated in other cultures, I have refrained from using anthropological research. I am cautioned by the words of Anne Cameron, the insightful Native American author of *Daughters of Copper Woman* and other books. She states that even her writing, which is obviously authentic, cannot be adequately represented in the writings of others. The only redemption I can offer is that participants in NLR programs have come from all segments of the American population and no one has ever found it inconsistent with their culture.

Any mistakes in this book are mine, for which I apologize in advance. But the point is not intellectual debate, which I will never enter, but appreciating development. The conclusions in this book rely as much on twenty-three years of working with children and families as they do on supportive research.

Chapter Two A BRIEF OVERVIEW OF NATURAL LEARNING RHYTHMS

Capacities are innate; development occurs in relationship. The connections among the people in the child's life, and primarily between parent and child, determine the degree of excellence and well-being in the maturation of the capacities. What are the capacities of children of different ages? How can they be recognized? And critically, what kinds of environments nourish optimal development of each capacity? These are questions that every parent, teacher, and child-oriented professional yearns to answer. They wish to be able to recognize the child's capacities and respond to them to ensure optimal well-being. Is this possible? Yes! When we ask the right questions, the door opens. But do the answers require complex academic training to understand? Does their implementation require professional skills? No! Remarkably, the door opens to an intuitively satisfying appreciation of children that requires no extensive training to understand and act on. This appreciation—this world that lies beyond the open door—is described by Natural Learning Rhythms. Succinctly stated, NLR maps the development of the innate capacities in children and offers guidelines to creating relationships that lead to optimal well-being. Natural Learning Rhythms goes beyond just safeguarding the child and making sure they become productive or creative members of society. The program helps each family member hit their notes at just the right time, so that the family and the community can be creative and inspiring.

It is important for the parent and teacher to value and understand the developmental stages of childhood—to know a child's capacities and potentialities at his level of development. To truly understand the child, we must consider not only her cognitive attributes but also her emotional, physical, and spiritual development; that is, development of the whole person.

Along with its appreciation of the various levels of child development, NLR brings extraordinary clarity and simplicity to the subject by emphasizing the way children organize their world. Natural Learning Rhythms helps participants create environments and relationships with children that honor the organizing principle toward well-being as it expresses within the child and throughout childhood.

By *organizing principle*, we mean an innate capacity to receive, organize, and respond to the psychological and physical environments in ways that promote well-being. In each of the four sequential stages of childhood recognized by NLR, as well as in all life, there is an organizing principle that determines the general ways in which human energy, capacities, inclinations, and interactions are structured and act.

Natural Learning Rhythms describes in detail the psychological, emotional, and physical components of health and well-being that emerge during each stage of childhood. We call these components nourishments, because they nourish the whole being.

When an adult intentionally nourishes a child, well-being is available to both the child and the adult. Many of the blocks to the adult's health may be dissolved. The family system flourishes. Natural Learning Rhythms specifies the dynamics by which the whole family can be served by nourishing developmental capacities.

Natural Learning Rhythms offers considerable information on each developmental stage. For instance:

- Creating environments that support (or poison) well-being in the child
- Clear, simple descriptions of the special qualities, nature, phases, and characteristics of each stage
- An in-depth appreciation of how a child moves from one developmental stage to another—often the most difficult times for parents and teachers
- The importance of the language of each stage—key to successful communication
- The development of meaning within each stage
- Shifts in the perceptions of time and space during the stages and their implications for intellectual, social, emotional, and spiritual learning

- Identification of developmental malnourishment and of remedies that restore well-being in the child and the family

Approaching child development from the perspectives of health and well-being rather than pathology or cultural standards of normalcy yields many surprises. For instance:

- Development occurs in the matrix of relationship, not in the individual child.
- Many behaviors viewed as pathological are natural expressions of health, especially during critical transition years around eight, thirteen, and seventeen.
- A child's personality is not solely determined in the early years of life, but forms and re-forms throughout childhood.
- Children seek boundaries and thrive when boundaries are created with sensitivity.
- Gender and racial prejudice do not arise in developmentally nourished children.
- Nonsectarian spirituality is implicit in each stage.
- Teens yearn for guidance from trusted family members.
- Most childhood dysfunction can be remedied with proper developmental nourishment (and without professional interventions).
- Primary learning of the importance of community and environment occurs between the ages of eight and twelve.

Amazingly, almost every family can nourish the well-being of a child. This means that Natural Learning Rhythms has value for parents, teachers, education administrators, counselors, therapists, and grandparents. We have proved this in the many experiential learning programs that we have facilitated—for whole families, for children, for schools, and for social service agencies. In the vast majority of participants, socioeconomic status or ethnic/religious background has not inhibited learning. Generally speaking, Natural Learning Rhythms has stimulated ideas about how to glean the best from the culture to boost family well-being.

In response to many requests, we have created a brief definition of Natural Learning Rhythms. We offer it here to summarize this introduction and to set the stage for the rest of the book.

Definition of Natural Learning Rhythms

Natural simply means that which we are born with. It has taken on the additional meaning of "the essential properties of a thing." Natural Learning Rhythms uses both definitions. That which is not acquired, which is inherent, is necessarily an essential quality of every living organism.

Learning means to gain knowledge, comprehension, or mastery through experience or study. Learning describes the way we operate in the world, while nature refers to our inborn qualities. Learning depends on relationship.

Rhythm means movement that has regularly recurs; for example, the rhythm of the tides, the progression of the seasons, or the stages of life.

Thus, Natural Learning Rhythms describes our inherent capacities (natural) to move through life to gain knowledge, comprehension, or mastery (learning) in recognizable and recurring patterns (rhythms).

In addition, Natural Learning Rhythms recognizes two meanings of *natural*. There are two aspects to nature: the natural world as we perceive it through our senses—nature with a small *n*. Then there is the life force imbued with meaning, power, and mystery. This life force is inherent in all natural objects—Nature with a capital *N*.

Natural Learning Rhythms makes this claim: When we connect to a child's Natural Learning Rhythms we can see through his eyes and feel through his heart.

Chapter Three

ONTOLOGICAL
EPISTEMOLOGY

Man demonstrates in his own nature a pressure toward fuller and fuller Being, more and more perfect actualization of his humanness in exactly the same, naturalistic scientific senses that an acorn many be said to "pressing toward" being an oak tree or that a tiger can be observe to "push towards" being tigerish...The environment does not give him potentialities and capacities; he has them in inchoate or embryonic form, just exactly as he has embryonic arms and legs. And creativeness, spontaneity, selfhood, authenticity, caring for others, being able to love, yearning for truth are embryonic potentialities belonging to his species-membership as much as his arms and legs and brain and eyes.

—Abraham Maslow, Humanistic Psychologist

Now, do not be intimidated by the phrase *ontological epistemology*. *Ontology* is the inquiry into being, into the essence of who we are. It is the commitment to appreciate human nature—its capacities, potentials, and behaviors. *Epistemology* is the inquiry into how we know. It describes both the method of knowing and the ground of knowledge. An *ontological epistemology* thus elucidates our essential human qualities and describes how we come to know them. It is the field of self-knowledge.

Everyone lives by an ontological epistemology, whether it is deliberately articulated or not. Every time a person steps into a house of religious worship, they are saying that God is the essence of being and that what we can know of God comes through prayer, study, and good works. Every time a parent states that they want the best for their child because they love her, they are stating that love is an essential human quality that can be known through their feelings in the presence of that child.

Poetically, ontology is what is in our bones, in our deepest understanding of ourselves. Philosophically, ontology is what we mean by the word *being*. It is our existence, our wholeness, in which nothing essential is missing. Every time that we name ourselves as a human being, we make an ontological statement. Every time we talk of inalienable rights, we are making an ontological statement. In each of these instances, we are pointing to an enduring, unalterable aspect of our humanity. And each time we justify our ontological statement with how we know it to be true, we are expressing our epistemology. For instance, we hold inalienable rights to be self evident. It is as if we are saying to others, "Don't you get it? These rights are our humanness, the very essence of our being."

Natural Learning Rhythms is an ontological epistemology for children. It explores, examines, and describes the essential nature of children. It elucidates how children know. It answers these questions: How do children organize their world? What are the innate capacities of children and why do they appear when they do, and to what purpose? What is the nature of optimal well-being in children? Which kinds of environments allow well-being to thrive and which cause it to shrivel? How and when do children make meaning from their world?

As an ontological epistemology, Natural Learning Rhythms applies to all interactions with children. Ontology demands it. I cannot describe the essential nature of a child and leave out any aspect of their lives. Over the past twenty-three years, thousands of parents, child-oriented professionals, and educators—from day care providers to K–12 teachers to university professors—have been able to understand and apply Natural Learning Rhythms in their lives with children.

In other words, Natural Learning Rhythms offers profound insights and tools for families, educators, counselors, therapists, and social service workers—to anyone interacting with children. It offers responses to the most pressing concerns that adults have about children, including helping teens make responsible choices, dealing with sibling rivalry, mitigating the problems of divorce, creating healthy boundaries for children of all ages, remedying dysfunction, supporting different learning styles and abilities, helping them achieve work-life balance, and encouraging academic excellence and much more.

But primarily, Natural Learning Rhythms offers operating instructions for achieving optimal well-being in children and families. It reaches deeply into family dynamics and shows how nourishing the organizing principle of each stage in childhood is key to realizing optimal well-being for all family members. In this sense, Natural Learning Rhythms can be seen as an epistemology of families—as a description of how family members come to know themselves and one another.

The knowledge base for an ontological epistemology necessarily ranges far and wide. Accordingly, we have investigated many discourses about children—psychological, pedagogical, and spiritual. We also have made extensive forays into neurobiology, anthropology, and the sciences of quantum mechanics, relativity, chaos, and complexity as they relate to children.

As a source of information for Natural Learning Rhythms, this valuable research is secondary to the hundreds of experiential learning programs we have run over the past twenty-three years. Creating the programs and facilitating them has served as a crucible for us to field test and refine NLR time and again. Insights gained from experiential learning have stimulated deepening inquiries into the discourses mentioned above. An exciting synergy has developed between work in NLR and other research that continues to this day.

One should expect that an ontological epistemology centered in optimal well-being would yield some surprises about children, families, and education. Natural Learning Rhythms does not disappoint. A brief mention of a few of them provides a taste of what is to come in this book.

To take just one example from child development, Natural Learning Rhythms finds that development occurs in relationship. Capacities are innate, but the quality of their expression depends upon the child's environment. Understanding this concept leads to appreciation of knowledge as emergent—not fixed. This appreciation in turn opens the door to optimal parenting, for it is in the relationships among family members that innate capacities can be fully nurtured. Parents and educators can concentrate on developing those relationships rather than on the dull tasks of avoiding pathology and trying to maintain normalcy.

Natural Learning Rhythms also describes how parents can heal their own childhood wounds by meeting the developmental needs of their children. Moreover, they can grow in self-knowledge—in increasing awareness of themselves and their world—through participating in developmentally appropriate relationships. Natural Learning Rhythms calls this the *dance*. Well-being is a family dynamic—entirely interdependent and mutually beneficial for each family member. More than a few NLR practitioners have rejoiced when they realized that connecting with the child's developmental imperatives connected them with their own profound well-being.

Natural Learning Rhythms also undermines many cultural myths. For example, boys and girls do like to play with one another; sibling rivalry is not natural; a child's personality is not formed in the womb, birth canal, first year of life, first three years of life, or even the first six years of life; teens do not seek to rebel or wish to discount familial relationships; and neither physical nor cognitive development is the best indicator of a child's life stage.

At the same time, Natural Learning Rhythms provides fresh insights into areas heretofore ignored or marginalized by developmentalists. Matters such as spiritual awareness, the process of interpersonal learning, the blending of freedom and responsibility, the value of words in the various stages, the critical importance of transitions between stages, and the changing roles of extended family and community are some important examples.

Natural Learning Rhythms offers new opportunities for education as well. Perhaps more than other child-centered disciplines, education has tried to bring developmental information to its practice. Very few educators have developed a curriculum for interpersonal learning, however. Also, while there is a new trend to service-based learning for teens, no school has tied it to the development of freedom and responsibility and its importance for constructing the identity. Without these things, there is but momentary value to the exercises and the deeper attributes of well-being remain untouched. No one has examined how didactic teaching (teaching that is overburdened with instruction and the proprieties [from *Webster's Collegiate Dictionary*]) is received by children at different ages. This speaks to how education and learning occur, a field of abiding interest to Natural Learning Rhythms.

I have spoken to a wide variety of audiences about NLR and have found that it can be described from several perspectives. It has been presented from the perspective of its rich intellectual foundations, abundant case histories, many applications, responses to dysfunction, emphasis on family dynamics and, of course, epistemology. One would expect nothing less from an ontological approach.

Genetic Epistemology

It helps to briefly compare Natural Learning Rhythms with another epistemology for children—genetic epistemology, as pioneered by the brilliant Jean Piaget. As the name implies, genetic epistemology studies the innate human capacities by which we know. These innate capacities determine the mode of knowing available and by extension the information a child can assimilate.

To illustrate the approach, consider one of the most famous experiments from Piaget's laboratory. Using two vessels of different shapes but holding the same volume of liquid, Piaget poured water from one to the other while children of different ages watched. He then asked if the vessels held the same amount of liquid. Children below the age of seven believed that the taller vessel held more; children older than seven knew that they held the same volume. From this and many similar experiments, Piaget described biological cognitive schemas that appear at different ages in childhood. He gave these schemas unique names, as all developmentalists do, to serve as placeholders for the central idea of his theory. He said children aged three to seven were in the *preoperational phase*, and those aged eight to eleven were in the *concrete operational phase* of thought. *Formal operational thought* occurs from age eleven onwards; *sensorimotor* is his descriptor for the years zero to two.

Piaget, in accord with the zeitgeist of his time, equated knowledge with cognitive structures and primarily with thought. He saw thought as the measure of intelligence and the ability to articulate thought as the indicator of the quality of thought. He argued continually for the scientific validity of his approach. Scientific validity meant a logical positivist approach; that is, only that which can be observed, measured, and categorized is real. Children gain knowledge by assimilating the data in their environment, accommodating that data with innate cognitive schemas, and then skillfully manufacturing adaptations. The capabilities of children to assimilate, accommodate, and adapt change with age. These changes can be measured through laboratory experiments and field observations. In Piaget's genetic epistemology, knowledge implies acquiring, storing, and retrieving, and it is currency used to solve problems.

Piaget's seminal work has been revised, criticized, and deconstructed since the late 1960s when it was introduced, and this book happily leaves that work to others. My purpose is to compare ontological epistemology with genetic epistemology and to clarify the field that Natural Learning Rhythms occupies.

At the heart of the comparison, in Natural Learning Rhythms knowledge is used in the sense of its ancient derivation, from which we also have the words *kin* and *ken*. It refers to an intimacy, a familiarity that is natural and responsive. It sees knowledge as emergent, needing context and relationship to come to life.

Natural Learning Rhythms is an ontological epistemology. The epistemology—the way the child knows—is ontological—through her whole being. Piaget is correct to include the child's ability to process data for a purpose and to attempt to show how this changes in each of the life stages he considers. However, he fails to include other abilities such as spirituality, interpersonal and community relationships, and the creation of values.

Natural Learning Rhythms is an ontological epistemology. The epistemology—the way the child knows—is ontological—through her whole being. Piaget is correct to include the child's ability to process data for a purpose and to attempt to show how this changes in each of the life stages he considers. However, he fails to include other abilities such as spirituality, interpersonal and community relationships, and the creation of values.

In Natural Learning Rhythms, a developmental stage is defined by the way the child organizes the world for a certain time of their lives. The child is always remembered as whole and worthwhile. Nothing essential is missing. Natural Learning Rhythms names its stages BodyBeing, FeelingBeing, IdealBeing, and ReasonableBeing. The suffix *being* means *one's basic or essential nature*. The prefix names the way the child organizes their world in that developmental stage.

Natural Learning Rhythms investigates all the developmental discourses, not just the cognitive. It turns to practitioners in education, psychology, philosophy, anthropology, sociology, and spirituality for guidance. It depends upon research conducted by Natural Learning Rhythms trained staff while in contact with the children as they are in their everyday lives. To genuinely appreciate a child's perception requires that we simultaneously enter their world and maintain our adult perspective.

It is well known that Piaget's work is extremely difficult to understand. It requires interpreters for most people, including for professionals in the field. Rarely does it make its way to the teachers, parents, and counselors who are in daily contact with the children. Natural Learning Rhythms, on the other hand, is easy to understand and easy to apply. It does not make the arcane information of Piaget, and other similar research, simpler. Rather, by focusing on the way a child organizes the world, it allows adults to reconnect with their own experience as a child and resonates with the intimacy they experience with their children. It makes sense. It indicates exactly where adults can interact with the child and to what benefit. It reawakens their deepest desire for their children, themselves, and their family—well-being for all. It reinstates children and family as sources of health, rejuvenation, and knowledge.

This intimacy—this knowledge—is a quality of being, not of cognition. It is the way we know our children; it is the way we know ourselves. It emerges; it is not constructed. The most eloquent statement about knowledge that I know of comes from the brilliant scientist and philosopher David Bohm. Bohm, a younger colleague of Einstein's and revered for his work in quantum mechanics, emphasized "the need to look on the world as an undivided whole, in which all parts of the universe, including the observer and his instruments, merge and unite in one totality...The new form of insight can perhaps best be called Undivided Wholeness in Flowing Movement."[1]

In other words, science alone cannot account for essential knowledge, just as the Uncertainty Principle[2] shows that it cannot account for the essence of matter. Something else is needed, which Bohm—in dialogues with the philosopher and educator Krishnamurti—called insight. These philosophers make it quite clear that insight is not an innate mental schema, but rather an aware participation in the totality of the moment.

For parents, there is no need for abstraction. We know our children intimately, as they know us. We know them in our bones, in our blood, in our hearts, and in our minds. We know them as whole beings and they know us as whole beings. Our relationships are ontological, not genetic; they are self-evident.

The paradigm shift toward an ontological epistemology for children has been incubating for a long time. The list of notables involved in this shift includes remarkable educators such as Johann Pestalozzi, Frederick Froebel, and Maria Montessori; spiritual adepts such as Sri Aurobindo, Rudolf Steiner, Thomas Merton, and Jiddhu Krishnamurti; psychologists such as Alfred Adler, Carl Jung, Abraham Maslow, and Carl Rogers; philosophers such as Gregory Bateson, Ken Wilber, and Aristotle; and educational historians such as Ron Miller and Johann Liebschner. True to the multidimensionality of ontological epistemology, most of these luminaries are impossible to categorize in a specific discipline. The inquiry into being and into the foundations of knowledge necessitates an interest in life and in the totality of being human.

Natural Learning Rhythms intends to make this paradigm shift unavoidable. To do so, it must dissolve significant problems and bring forth new questions that allow deeper, more complex inquiries into the nature of children. I will name a few significant principles of NLR here and elucidate them in the course of the book. These ideas will be easier to understand and apply when they are seen in the context of play, spirituality, and family dynamics.

From the perspective of ontological epistemology, then:

Spirituality is innate—a natural faculty of a human being—and it can be actualized in the ordinary course of life. It has little to do with extraordinary phenomena or lightning bolts of divine grace. It is present, and needs only to be appreciated in a child's developmental moment. Nourishing optimal well-being is all that is necessary for the spiritual faculty to flourish.

The archaic fascination with the differences between the genders takes its appropriate place in the backseat. Actualizing our human beingness reveals that most of the (mis)perceptions about gender tendencies and relationships are culturally driven and have little to do with the nature of boys and girls. This idea does not deny that gender prejudice stinks. It does, as does racial prejudice. Rather, ontological epistemology forms a response that is not rooted in society's exaggerations. It pinpoints how we know ourselves as a gender, as a race, and shows how to nourish that for optimal well-being. When this is achieved, we are left with cleaning up prejudices in society, but we are no longer creating them.

The supremacy of thought is undermined. From Descartes to Piaget, the arrogant belief in the supremacy of thought has contributed mightily to unnecessary suffering. The wider lens of ontological epistemology simply asks, if thought is more complex and richer than feeling or sensation, then why aren't there other modes of knowing that are more complex than thought? Or put another way, if cognitive processes are the synthesis and synergy of thought, feeling, and sensation, then why wouldn't there be synergistic processes that included intimacy, love, intuition, ethics, aesthetics, meaning, trust, insight, and wisdom? What about the peak experiences that the great humanistic psychologist Maslow talks about, or the fully functioning human of his equally respected colleague Carl Rogers? What about the consistent testimony of sages, saints, and philosophers from every culture that knowable realms of our minds lie beyond thought? What about the inspiration of artists, the bliss of loving sexual engagement, the freedom of loving a child? What about meaning? Ontological epistemology accounts for all these things effortlessly—as natural, as human beingness. Of course, it is thought that sees knowledge as data and currency and ontological epistemology that knows intimately.

In Natural Learning Rhythms, the idea that survival is the driving force behind evolution—with all its rationalization of violence and strife—finally is relegated to the competitive, industrial mind-set in which it was born. Seeing life as a struggle for survival describes what drives us; ontological epistemology describes what pulls us. That pull includes all that is necessary to satisfy the biological drives and adds that which is most important to humans—meaning and love. The family's physical resources, without the loss of necessary skills, become a way of supporting optimal well-being rather than of fabricating a false sense of security.

Human birth is no longer thought of as original sin or bad karma or a negative, harrowing event. The relationship between ego and spirit is ongoing; it is a fact of being. As the great poet William Blake said, "Eternity is in Love with the Productions of Time." We are not separate and never were. The dissolution of the illusion of separation becomes obvious from the perspective of optimal well-being. We are not sick and sinful, struggling to attain normalcy and goodness; we are vibrant and connected, full of wondrous capacities that allow us to participate in creation. The challenges in life are opportunities for greater intimacy, for creative engagement of emergent knowledge.

Adults are not doing the children a favor by "bringing them up." As we shall see in this book again and again, relationships with children are crucial for the adult's growth, happiness, and self-realization. It is a dance. Only when human beingness is reduced to a struggle for survival are adults superior to children, for children do depend on them for the physical necessities. From the ontological perspective, the relationship between parent and child is the medium in which they each awaken to self-knowledge. Adults do not know the purpose and destiny of a child's life. They are there to facilitate their emergence.

Family is a source of joy and rejuvenation, not a cost center. Parents are not police officers enforcing society's laws. Family relationships provide nourishment for ever deeper awakening of love, meaning, beauty, and truth.

Many so-called learning disorders are not disorders. When we stop seeing children as broken, then much of their apparent brokenness disappears. And those problems that require intervention approached with the goal of activating well-being so that remedies become part of the fabric of the child and the family—they are woven into beingness. Actually, it is as accurate to say that they are already in beingness and are just being actualized.

Natural Learning Rhythms emerges. Personally, I find its appreciation of the dance one of its most significant ontological insights. The dance shows how the awakening of the parent and child is mutual—that by meeting the conditions for optimal well-being in the child, the parent heals their own childhood wounds. The parent can then participate in spiritually pure service, devotion, compassion, and meaning; their being awakens to its true nature. Thus in the natural course of parenting, they can engage all the questions which bring forth joy that is beyond happiness and fun. They can achieve connections that are beyond desire and selfishness, and courage to face harmful cultural dictates.

Natural Learning Rhythms, and especially the dance, provides a way to minimize unnecessary suffering and to consciously participate in necessary suffering. Adult life doesn't have to be immersed in working through the wounds of childhood. Natural Learning Rhythms can be a way to freedom for all family members, in the profound ontological sense of freedom woven throughout this chapter. This freedom does not depend on social justice, economic status, or spiritual persuasion. It is a freedom that is natural, innate, available, and emergent in authentic relationships. This is freedom as true equality, built into the relationship of parent and child regardless of extenuating circumstances.

These are the promises of an ontological epistemology for children. Even if there is only a 25 percent chance that I am right, is it not worth the exploration?

SECTION II

The Child

What are the laws of development and formation? They are the laws of development and cultivation which have their cause and their source in [the Creation] of the world, by which and according to which Nature, being and life, goodness and love, reveal themselves and still make themselves known in humanity, in the human race, and in the individual human being, and which therefore appear in each newborn child, living and working anew as essence.

—Friedrich Froebel, *Education by Development*

Chapter Four   # PLAY

> We do not stop playing because we grow old. We grow old because we
> stop playing.
>
> —George Bernard Shaw

I begin the exploration of Natural Learning Rhythms with play because children begin with play. Children play first, and continue to play until they are forced to do otherwise. Play is the modus operandi of learning—the way to knowledge, to intimacy, and to relationships with the world and the people in it.

Natural Learning Rhythms maps childhood through the age of twenty-three; play is the primary mode of learning throughout. Play is not confined to the early years, nor is play to be equated with fun.

Johan Huizinga, the great cultural anthropologist who spent a lifetime studying play throughout the world, suggested that our species should be called *Homo ludens* rather than *Homo sapiens*, the being who plays rather than the being who knows.[3] He sees play as nothing less than the basis of civilization and as central to the way we establish order. Courts of law, for instance, have their roots in games. Contests that reflect spiritual awareness and thus confer spiritual authority, such as Zen riddles, are common. All the arts began as play. Fair play is the mark of a successful civilization; competition run amok, with much cheating, is the mark of an unsuccessful one.

The value of play changes from culture to culture, but there are some common themes. Play is a way to maintain honor and community. In traditional times, a debate or single combat was often sufficient for this purpose. Now athletic teams carry the banner. (Even these days, when players continually switch teams, the name of the uniform is sufficient to rally the locals.) *Prize* and *praise* are words that developed in the context of play. Play, as Piaget says, is for the pleasure of mastery. Margaret Lowenfeld, writing in 1967 as the psychological director of the Institute of Child Psychology in London, points out that play is critical to emotional maturity. Adults who lack this maturity often play in harsh and aggressive ways and most important, mistake the game for reality.[4]

It is of great importance that play allows us to represent ourselves and our deepest consciousness unbound by ordinary structures. Plato believed that humans were God's playthings and that made us good. Vedanta, the philosophical foundation of Hinduism, speaks of *lila*, meaning that life is God's play. Some philosophers, such as Immanuel Kant, saw the basic dynamics of the universe as a form of play. These are not meant as fatalistic or deterministic doctrines, but as invitations to participate in life without morbid earnestness. Play allows us to connect with the whole of ourselves and our world. It is the natural movement of non-alienated people, an expression of health and, given full support, a way to optimal well-being.

While play has numerous definitions in every culture, there are surprising similarities in the way it is understood. For example, play is often seen as a necessary contributor to the development of character. The act of playing is spontaneous, and play itself is an aesthetic expression. Play is never confined to a specific age group, although it is well recognized that age helps determine the way people play.

A Word about Froebel

Friedrich Froebel invented kindergarten. Before his time, children below the age of seven were given short shrift, most often being seen as neither intelligent nor valuable. Froebel is a founding sage of ontological epistemology, though he wouldn't have used the term, whose brilliant contributions connected education with the being of the child. He saw children as whole. Their destiny was to demonstrate their diversity, to comprehend the unity of their diversity, and so become aware of themselves and the totality of all relationships. He did not say that he knew what the destiny of a child was, nor did he measure intelligence objectively. Rather, Froebel demonstrated that learning succeeds when it is undertaken by an active mind with freedom to question. For young children, this means play.[5]

Froebel's gifts were toys designed to connect the child to the environment as an aid to learning, to remind the child of the connection between life and God, and to further the bond between parent and child. He emphasized time and again that parent and child learn together and that each grows in self-knowledge during play. These gifts were progressively more sophisticated, though always intended to stimulate the five senses (he knew that children through the age of eight evaluate the world through its sensory qualities). Play is active learning, an expression of creative freedom, and, echoing Huizinga, leads to discovery, poetry, and philosophy. The surprises that arise in play delight the child and keep him interested in his world. Play supports language; language supports play. Play promotes respect between child and elder. Play allows self-expression and then learning about the consequences of that expression. Play creates a constant feedback loop between the inner and outer worlds of the child. At no time is play frivolous or intended toward some trivial notion of fun.

Brilliantly, Maria Montessori refined Froebel's gifts so that they became the center of learning for the child. As has been reported in *The Absorbent Mind*, and has been repeated many times in my experience with Natural Learning Rhythms, children engaged in sensory-based, textured environments can concentrate for long periods of time and are more respectful and cooperative. They play with the utmost seriousness, absorbed but not obsessive, not so attached that their esteem depends on it.

Froebel changed the way educators perceive young children and the importance of their play. He's influenced every kindergarten and preschool in the Western world. Froebel legitimized investigation into early childhood education and psychology, an investigation that is rapidly becoming recognized as crucial for understanding ourselves and the world we have created.

Such is the value of an ontological epistemologist who stands his ground and points to the wholeness, the essence, the being of the child. Humbly, we offer Natural Learning Rhythms with the same intent. What Froebel did for our appreciation of the young child, Natural Learning Rhythms hopes to do for the whole twenty-three years of childhood.

For the moment, though, let's see how play develops in Natural Learning Rhythms. For sure, play will include connection to an expanding field of emergent knowledge, not an attempt to assimilate information to existing schemas.

Play and BodyBeing

Consider the classic situation of a dad attempting to teach his five-year-old daughter how to read. A bright man, he reads aloud to her; assigns her simple reading exercises from workbooks; and uses painting, crayons, and pencils to draw letters with her. These activities, he believes, should be sufficient to teach the task of reading. His mistake is that he has only thought about the task—reading—and not the perceptual world of the child. She, however, will observe his attitude, the place and time the lesson occurs, the importance of her learning to the rest of the family, the health of the dog, the intensity of the crayon colors (irrespective of the letters she is forming), and her physical condition. As she plays with any and all of these things, her dad might well say she is not concentrating. If an adult were correlating all these elements, it would probably be called multitasking.

Yet every one of these elements, as well as others that are not mentioned, are critical to the way the BodyBeing child establishes rightful place, the organizing principle of the life stage. As Froebel and Montessori demonstrated, when rightful place is actualized, the BodyBeing child often becomes absorbed in a single task such as reading. But rightful place is not a given and can never be assumed. To optimize learning, the dad must simultaneously maintain his adult role while entering the perspective of the child. He must remember rightful place as the priority. As we shall see throughout this book, this task can easily be accomplished. Certainly, the hit-and-miss approach he now takes and the frustrations that accompany the misses are a significant drain on him, his daughter, and the rest of the family. He has nothing to lose by seeing though his child's eyes, though it may seem unusual and awkward at first.

The BodyBeing child plays with the elements in her environment by exploring their sensory qualities. Where she meets a boundary, known by unmistakable sensations that say go no further, she stops and explores. As she plays at the boundary, learning deepens. She becomes more finely tuned to her world. Perhaps, for example, the delightful scent of freshly baked cookies entices her while she is reading with dad. She tells him she wants a cookie. He says she has to finish the lesson. She starts to wriggle. He insists. Mom overhears their struggle and with some ambivalence, suggests that she have one cookie and then return to the lesson. Dad reluctantly agrees. However, one cookie does not seem to do it. She wriggles. Dad reminds her of their agreement. She wriggles. She draws pictures, not letters. Dad insists. She reluctantly agrees to finish the lesson. To dad's surprise, she remains fully engaged for a half-hour.

Obviously, frustration could have erupted at several points in this process. The Natural Learning Rhythms response to conflict is described in chapter 10, "Reunification." In the example above it did not erupt.

This example portrays a situation that happens many days in many families. It is typical because similar dynamics appear around bedtime, manners, helping with chores, and many parent-driven tasks. Natural

Learning Rhythms pays great attention to the ordinary life of children. As an ontological epistemology, Natural Learning Rhythms sees the whole of the child's life as meaningful. Dedicated to social improvement, Natural Learning Rhythms always attempts to meet the actual situations that parents and teachers experience.

In our example the child was exploring her boundaries. Conflicting pleasant sensations flooded her being. Sensation is the language of BodyBeing—BodyBeing children move toward pleasant sensations and away from unpleasant ones. This simple way of assessing one's reality leads to sophisticated representations of the world and the people in it. Accurately decoding the sensations in oneself and in the environment provides a reliable basis for knowing one's rightful place.

The well-respected pediatrician Daniel Stern has synthesized insights from developmental psychology, psychoanalysis, and cognitive psychology. He is one of the few professionals who are able to enter the child's world and write about it. In his *Diary of a Baby*, Stern, speaking in the first person as the child, gives a phenomenological description of a four-year-old boy who accompanies his mother to a train station. We quote it at some length, for it captures the sensory texture of the moment and its effect on rightful place. Stern's description also shows how the BodyBeing child does not clearly demarcate their inner world and their environment. Natural Learning Rhythms combines this understanding with the egocentrism of the child and—also speaking as the child—states: "I am the center of the world and the world is an extension of my body."

Stern begins by detailing how the child keeps his mother in sight while he is moving to explore the vast terrain of the station. Then the child goes from safe space to the unknown.

Now I am father out in space, coasting, I design turns and sweeps. I balance forces to make stops. I command proper starts. I ride my own movements. Then I lose control over them, and they ride me. My movements and I take turns leading. But always as I move, the visible star [mother] and the invisible lines of force hold me steady in my wandering.

I approach people and pass around them. They bend space as my mother does, but in the opposite direction. They send out invisible lines of force that hold me away and guide me around them. I slip past them without even coming close.

Now I see something different. Another baby—one like me—is journeying out. She has the same special vitality I feel. But she doesn't bend space at all, there's no push away. I am free to come close and explore and touch. Suddenly someone picks her up and sweeps her away.

And suddenly I am lost. I can't find Mommy's star, and her line of force has grown weak. The space grows bigger and bigger. It becomes boundless. Nothing holds me, I am dissolving like grains of salt in the ocean of space. I panic.

Stern describes the child calling out. The child hears mother.

Her call back is a hammer blow on a block of clear ice. The blow leaves a lacy pattern whose white fault line and planes restructure the space. And with that, my world is transformed by her voice. Using the pattern of this new map, I can find my way back to point of the hammer blow.

The BodyBeing child organizes the world to completely inhabit rightful place. The primary information is received through the mode of sensation. Stern makes the point that the synthesis of the senses creates a perceptual mode that is beyond the value and meaning of any one sense.[6] As he attempts to describe the social and interpersonal world of the young child, he emphasizes that this unity of the senses is what allows affective (emotional) states to be commonly shared by parent and child. Children hone in on the underlying sensorial dimensions of intensity, time, and shape and then move toward pleasant sensations and away from unpleasant ones. These two qualities of sensory perception— that it occurs as a whole and that she seeks the pleasant and avoids the unpleasant—become the tools by which the child maps the world. In that map, rightful place is home. When rightful place is violated, mapmaking is a desperate attempt to find it. When it is nurtured, mapmaking is an event-filled exploration full of learning and wonder.

Rightful place requires boundaries, and children naturally seek knowledge of the boundaries of their world. Boundary creation is a secondary organizing principle of BodyBeing. Through sensory exploration of their world, BodyBeing children map the psychological and physical environment, learning the boundaries of both as they explore. As they develop a healthy relationship to these boundaries, they develop a sense of personal strength. They know that they belong and they know where they belong. This knowledge brings forth strength to explore and expand. Strength is in direct proportion to the support of safe sensorial exploration of themselves and their environment. Strength is also a secondary organizing principle for BodyBeing.

The secondary organizing principle provides the necessary conditions for the primary organizing principle to become viable. In the life stage of BodyBeing, there cannot be rightful place without boundary creation. There are secondary organizing principles for each of the four stages.

Children seek the boundaries, explore them, and learn to respect them according to their sensation content. Their land is one of color, texture, intensity, time, and shape. The forces that determine the specifics of their maps include the natural environment, the human-made environment, developmental capacities, and the responses and relationships of the people—primarily the family—in their lives. The boundaries define the map. In the map they come to place themselves. If that placement is right, optimal well-being becomes the ordinary mode of living for the child.

BodyBeing maps are topographical. They depict all the contours of the child's environment. It's as if they have a sophisticated version of the ability to echolocate found in dolphins and bats. As an analogy, they would send out a signal that would bounce back to their receptor site with a comprehensive description of the sensory world. This information would then be translated into topographical maps. The maps would be superimposed upon one another, which we have all seen computers do, and so create a well-defined image of the sensory landscape. It is my considered opinion that this may be more factual than analogous. There is no doubt that animals have used this tool to create richly complex lives.

Mapping their world is a delightful game for BodyBeing children. When we consider language development in the "Spirituality" chapter, we shall also see that words are often used for their mapping properties. BodyBeing children play with words to accomplish the very serious work of mapping boundaries and exploring their world.

The daughter learning to read is responding to the developmental imperative of playing with boundaries in order to live in her rightful place. She holds everyone at the boundary through the sensation of wriggling. She certainly receives and decodes the information that wriggling causes irritation in her dad. But what does it do to her mom? Where does baking cookies fit on her map? How does it reconcile with reading with dad? She is not communicating that reading is unpleasant—a conclusion adults are often too quick to accept. She has a fuzzy boundary. She wriggles—a sensory-based signal. Interesting events unfold. Mom appears. Dad and mom emanate confusing sensations as well. These sensations alert her to a rich learning opportunity. She wriggles again. Dad becomes like a mountain and holds the boundary. Mom agrees and leaves. The fuzziness dissipates. Rightful place is with dad now. The lesson becomes effortless.

Children's play reveals their blend of innate intelligences. According to the pioneering work of Howard Gardner and associates, intelligences fall into seven basic classifications: verbal-linguistic, logical-mathematical, spatial, musical, bodily-kinesthetic, interpersonal, and intrapersonal. Each child has a unique blend. Chapter 8 explores the intelligences and how they manifest in the developmental stages. It also describes how parents can noninvasively assess their child's intelligences and respond to promote optimal well-being. If mom and dad had a good working assessment of their daughter's blend, they could create a customized approach to reading that would result in accelerated learning and greater enjoyment. For the child, however, it would all be play.

This composite case history is derived from hundreds of similar cases in our experience. Unlike other studies of play, it does not emphasize play as practice to master life skills, to project schemas onto objects and then accommodate the similarities and differences, or to create order through learning rules after seven years of age. Nor does it pay much attention to play as a way to provide an outlet for frustration or to compensate for wounds. All of these are delightful aspects of play. None of them would be worth much if play did not bring forth optimal well-being by ensuring and furthering the organizing principle.

Natural Learning Rhythms takes this formal position: The organizing principle is a force that determines the general ways in which human energy, capacities, inclinations, and interactions are structured and act. The goal of the organizing principle is well-being, and the energy, capacities, inclinations, and interactions it has to work with are developmentally and contextually bound.

Play leads to optimal well-being in all developmental stages. For BodyBeing children, all actions are organized in order to ensure, further, and deepen their sense of rightful place. Here is an actual, not composite, case history[7] that illustrates how language and play are used to actualize rightful place, boundary creation, and strength in a BodyBeing child.

Every year EnCompass, the nonprofit organization of which I am executive director, runs two or three Natural Learning Rhythms–based family camps. Using cooperative games and activities, initiatives, and a ropes course, families play and learn together. There is little free time. Parents attend education blocks while staff engages the children in developmentally appropriate activities. Then whole families play together. Parents practice while they play. Parent circles provide opportunities for reflection and feedback. Trust builds, a community forms, and the children—with their organizing principles well nurtured—relax and open. Family camp consistently receives excellent evaluations from clients of all ages.

On the morning of the sixth day of camp, I happened to meet three-year-old Heidi near the water cooler at the end of breakfast. She greeted me with a smile and, as so many BodyBeings are wont to do, ran away with a giggle while looking back over her shoulder—an unmistakable invitation to chase her. I ran, she ran, and after three steps she stopped abruptly, raised her hand with the palm facing me, and commanded me to *stop*. I did. She turned to run, looking back invitingly, and I chased her again. This time she let me come much closer and then turned with the same voice command, but abandoned the hand gesture. I stopped. She ran far ahead and then repeated the game.

A cocoon seemed to envelop us. Her body was completely relaxed, her eyes were bright, and her attention was focused. We played many times, with Heidi varying the distances dramatically each time. She played with the boundaries continuously. Sometimes I could reach out and touch her; other times she was twenty yards away. She modulated the volume and intensity of her voice—sometimes it was loud and commanding, other times soft and insistent. She tried to talk as quietly as possible, barely mouthing the word, and was delighted when I stopped. Other times she shouted as loudly as she could, hardly stopping to notice if I responded.

We played for thirty minutes, and we both could have played longer had we not been interrupted. I was dancing; the energy sparking off was Heidi palpable and rejuvenating. She was shaping the space, creating boundaries with a carefree wisdom. Other parents were watching our antics, and several of them knew that in that moment Heidi realized the importance of words for defining her place. Knowledge had emerged that was supportive of her well-being. The components of this emergence were her innate capacities of language and boundary creation and a supportive relationship. The entire event was organized to optimize rightful place. The event was mediated within sensory perception. If her parents continue to play with words, they will likely facilitate a lifelong appreciation of the many uses of language.

From Heidi's perspective, nothing unusual or special occurred. She played, and the learning was effortless.

- BodyBeing Children Play with Words -

BodyBeing children play with words. This must be emphasized, for our society places arch importance on verbal-linguistic skills. So much unnecessary suffering is created when we hold BodyBeing children to the meaning and intent of their words. So, I repeat: BodyBeings play with words. In cognitive terms, Piaget stated that children between four and six cannot hold the narrative of a story. Lowenfeld believed that BodyBeing children use words to point to ideas but are scarcely concerned with their literal, definitive meaning. Reading comprehension tests show over and again that BodyBeing children do not grasp the contexts, subtleties, and nuances of words.

BodyBeing children play with words. That explains both the popularity and usefulness of Dr. Seuss. Words tumble—they roll over and through children. They are sharp, soft, colorful. Their true effect can be seen in the child's body, not in cognitive comprehension or resultant behavior. When verbally threatened, for example, a BodyBeing child will recoil in their body even if they act the way the parent desires. When words are toys, children enjoy them immensely.

Play and FeelingBeing

The knowledge that emerges during play deepens the child's actualization of the organizing principle. BodyBeing children organize the world to establish rightful place; FeelingBeing children organize the world to optimize trust.

BodyBeing children use specific objects as the locus for their play. They turn blocks of wood into ships, dolls into active families, stories into visceral adventures. They smear food; engage musical instruments through touch, sound, and rote; climb trees and imagine they are flying. Rules to specific games may make a convenient starting place, but they are often imperiously abandoned or amended. Goals have very little meaning. The time is now, the experience is sensory, the organizing principle is rightful place, and all the innate capacities are being nurtured and enriched. In most instances, optimal well-being is served by providing a sensory textured nonthreatening environment for BodyBeing play.

Chapter 6, "Transitions," details the exquisite chaos of the change from BodyBeing to FeelingBeing. For the present purposes, it is sufficient to note that the single most important psychological event for the child is the awareness of his own mortality. This awareness completely undermines BodyBeing's egocentric, body-oriented, sensation-mediated experience of themselves and their world. A new way of organizing the world appears, much to the surprise and consternation of both the child and the parents. The world must be played with in a new way, for a new order is called for.

As FeelingBeing dawns, the veil drops and the child realizes that older family members, friends, teachers, and community members also know they will die. Naturally, she is drawn to them. How do they do it? What are they really feeling? Do they know what I am feeling? These questions represent the concerns of the child. Some children will specifically ask them. For others, they will be implied in observations about others, such as their relationship with a teacher, relative, or friend. There is no single template for all children. Some might never mention it at all, yet their reactions to events reveal their concern with the feelings in relationships.

The aim of the FeelingBeing years is to learn how to decipher one's own feelings and the feelings of others. The child will spend the next five years playing in the rich, complex field of human emotions. The quality of her learning will be critical to her relationships with herself, members of the opposite gender, peers, family, community, society, other living creatures, the environment, and life itself. She will have the opportunity to feel the sacredness of relationships and of nature. She will learn how to trust and who to trust through direct experimentation and experience with her family, her community, and her teachers.

Awareness of Mortality

Very close to the age of nine, all children become aware of their own mortality. While this psychological fact has been known for a long time,[8] its significance in the development of children has been virtually ignored. There are many reasons for this oversight, but it is a credit to ontological epistemology that the child's perception of death is given the attention it deserves.

As humans, we are aware of our own death. Our response to this awareness shapes much of our life. We may defend against it by attempting to hold on to youth. We may deny it by pretending it is not important or that we can do nothing about it. We often turn to a form of religious belief about life after death, such as reincarnation or the heaven/hell model. Many believe that to die for one's country is considered the supreme sacrifice. The medical profession receives continued veneration as many of its resources are used to help delay death. Ethical concerns about euthanasia receive extensive media coverage. Considerable debate rages in the field of ethology as to whether elephants, dolphins, chimpanzees, or other animals are aware of their coming death, though they certainly express grief when death occurs. There are few advertisements for funeral homes or caskets on television, yet these are products almost everyone will need. Near-death experiences captivate our imagination. Entire philosophies are built upon proposed ethics of how individuals and societies should respond to the fact of death. Death is the way we come to define life, yet itself is utterly unknown. We are, in short, a species that is psychologically dominated by awareness of our coming death, yet we have paid scant attention to how this awareness affects our life and our development during childhood.

From the perspective of ontological epistemology, the value of the awareness of death for optimal well-being is inestimable. It calls forth humility and makes each of life's moments precious. It awakens the profound yearning to know what lies beyond death. It shakes out any foolishness that the body is immortal. It stirs the depths of our feelings as we seek to find what is genuinely trustworthy. It brings forth a new way of perceiving the world by midwifing the birth of the human capacity to deeply feel. Thus it demands that the child awaken to a new understanding of the values in relationships with the self, family, and community.

Many practitioners of other developmental and philosophical approaches see a human's awareness of death as a statement of separation, of our ultimate loneliness in the universe. They believe that people will die as isolated individuals and therefore are adrift and disconnected. This belief should be expected of a society weaned on separation—on individualism, conquests, and progress that inevitably attempt to ignore death. If one believes one is isolated, then one looks for, and finds, cause for the separation. Thus, perfectly natural events, such as awareness of personal mortality, are believed to be shattering. When a person is bounded by the fear of isolation, awareness of death is interpreted to rationalize that fear.

Natural Learning Rhythms suggests that adults who attempt to ignore death do so because of the isolation they felt when the awareness of personal mortality appeared at nine years of age. They were left on their own and so never learned to play with it. They did not learn to respect death and therefore didn't integrate it as part of life during the natural flow of development.

Unfortunately, this lack has resulted in widespread ignorance of the way children perceive death and of how to respond to the critical moment when awareness of death becomes a fact of life.

Death wipes the slate clean. Its importance has been well stated by David Bohm, the brilliant physicist and eminent philosopher:

> Death must be connected with questions of time and identity...Your whole definition of what you are will go. The whole sense of being separate from anything will go...Your whole sense of time must go. Is there anything that will exist beyond death? That is the question everybody has always asked...The past me is gone.[9]

Trust

Well-being is a dynamically balanced state of health that optimizes each individual's opportunity for self-knowledge. The organizing principle is the field where human energy, capacities, inclinations, and interactions are structured and act. The goal of the organizing principle is well-being, and everything it has to work with is developmentally and contextually bound. In each stage of life, the organizing principle takes the qualities, capacities, and talents of the child at a certain age and uses them to promote the well-being of the individual. Its nature changes with development.

Trust is the organizing principle for FeelingBeing children. All events in the child's life are organized to maximize trust, for when trust is felt, relationships can be safely created. The root of the word *trust* is the same as the root of the word *truth*, from which we also derive *troth* (as in betrothed) and *betray*. Thus the language follows the fact; we are most intimate with those who live truthfully. Trust is the core of genuine relationship. Genuine relationship allows the fullest exploration of feelings. It calls forth honesty, care, happiness, grief, longing, devotion, and the feeling of love.

When there is trust, the child plunges into the rich world of feelings wholeheartedly. When trust is lacking or absent, the child searches for it continuously. As always, development occurs in relationship. If the child's world is trustworthy, his innate capacity to trust and be trustworthy opens to becoming more complex. Therein lies optimal emotional, psychological, spiritual, interpersonal, and social well-being. Therein lies the greatest opportunity for an emergent self that knows itself as whole, relational, and spiritually attuned.

Reciprocal cooperation, the secondary organizing principle for FeelingBeing children, provides the field in which trust can emerge. Cooperation naturally arises when the adult and the child acknowledge that trust is the best possible way of being for each of them and for their relationship.

This is relationship-based cooperation, not one based on obligation or a family role. If trust is not there, the child feels no innate desire to cooperate. Reciprocal cooperation has little to do with becoming the good child, and everything to do with fidelity and reliability when with the child connects with himself and others. At times, the child's expression of reciprocal cooperation may be to act defiantly, as that is what the environment and relationships call forth. Life in FeelingBeing is organized to know trust. It is an act of pure cooperation to insist that we act in a trustworthy manner with one another.

Three anecdotes will help clarify the qualities of reciprocal cooperation.

⚬

The bright red berries were hanging from the many manzanita trees near our home, and ten-year-old Sarah had been collecting them all afternoon. At dinner, she turned to me and with an open smile presented me with a carefully crafted necklace she had made. "That's beautiful," I said. "I don't deserve this." Sarah looked perplexed. "Why not?" she asked softly.

Sarah's spontaneous action was simple and natural to her. We trusted one another, so why should I make an expression of that trust into something special? Isn't giving to one another what friends do? Is something wrong with the gift? Were the rules of relationship broken? Thank goodness the trust was strong enough so that Sarah was willing to cooperate by asking "why not?"

In that one moment, I learned a great deal. I had responded robotically, as I was a bit overwhelmed by the extraordinary nature of the seemingly ordinary act of a child. I received an additional gift of self-knowledge. This is one example of the dance, the mutual benefit that is always present in reciprocal cooperation. A description of the dance is presented in chapter 9.

⚬

"It's not fair," Joseph complained. "Steve was watching TV with Mike. I thought we all agreed to collectively pull the plug. It's not fair!" Eleven-year-old Joseph was having a difficult time at his cousin's birthday party. The extended family had read a report that TV arrested brain development in children below thirteen years of age.[10] As a community, they decided that they would experiment by putting their TVs away for six months. They agreed to support one another during the difficulties that might arise. The children went along, however reluctantly. At the birthday party, Joseph stumbled upon Steve and his seven-year-old son Mike watching the baseball game. Torn between wanting to stay and wanting to play by the rules, Joseph went to his mother, Eileen, for help. She told him that she would talk with Steve at another time, as she did not want anyone to be embarrassed at the party.

Joseph was not satisfied and said so to his mother. Eileen insisted that this was the best way for now. Joseph raised his voice and accused Eileen of not being fair and of not caring about his feelings. Eileen maintained her composure and her position until Joseph, frustrated, left.

When they were back home, Joseph was still upset and again used the magic word that so many FeelingBeing children favor: *fairness*. Often the cry "it's not fair" is the child's way of saying that trust is slipping away. Feelings of helplessness and frustration creep in. At this point, they are begging for reciprocal cooperation. Though their behavior often does not fit socially acceptable standards, it is nevertheless the language the child is capable of and an attempt to communicate a higher need.

Joseph knows his mother is becoming annoyed. He knows that he is risking her censure. Some might think that he is nagging her or being selfish. Actually, Joseph is exploring the dynamics of relationship. Social rules that were very difficult for Joseph to accept have been violated. Should he continue to trust the people in his dearest community, who made the rules? Should he trust his inner feelings of betrayal? Should he have just stayed with Mike and Steve and secretly share a lie, thus forming an inner clique? Joseph did the natural thing: He turned to his most dependable and trusted ally—his mother. This in itself is a profound request for reciprocal cooperation. When she chose social graces over fairness, he shut down, feeling betrayed.

⚒

The third anecdote seems to surprise many seminar participants. It involves a contrast between two teaching approaches. Its lesson can be summed up succinctly before it is told: Didactic teaching does not awaken trust, and those who teach didactically do not enjoy reciprocally cooperative relationships. This seems to be true irrespective of the subject.

FeelingBeing children love myth, drama, and stories they can learn from. They give the children an opportunity to engage an ocean of feelings, many of which would not be available to them in their everyday lives. Kristin is the head of The Ensemble, a group of professional actors who, as part of their livelihood, bring Shakespeare to fourth- and fifth-grade public school students. Slowly, over the course of three weeks, through questions and conversation, the members of The Ensemble help the children examine the meaning of the play. Using experiential theatre training exercises, these teaching artists, as they call themselves, help the children try on the various roles without having to commit to them. The Ensemble members often teach by example, as they experiment with roles they have never played before in front of the children. Of course, this activity mirrors the children's situation. Being with a mentor while they learn invites the children to engage and explore in an atmosphere of safety. Not surprisingly, the children often overachieve academically, doing far more for the ultimate production than is required. They have even, on occasion, defended the value of The Ensemble to their teacher and school administrators.

Many FeelingBeing children are also fascinated and inspired by nature. One community, on the edge of a national forest, has many politically active environmentalists. With the approval of the local school board, they hired a teacher specializing in environmental education for their elementary school students. Unfortunately, the teacher taught primarily ecological facts. Even when he took the children on outings, he was more concerned with classification than with relationship and concentrated on the names of things and their locations more than on their interactions with the other life forms and each other.

Although many FeelingBeing children do like to classify things, in private conversation most of these students could be accurately paraphrased as saying, "It's cool to know this stuff, but we don't know what to do with it." In this situation, the students responded well on tests and were able to recite many facts about their forest, but they were not inspired. Most of them did not want to continue in the class the following year. The students admired the teacher, but they admitted that they were often bored.

In the first case, children with little or no ethnic or historical relationship with their subject find meaning, are inspired, and engage in mutually beneficial relationships with their teachers and with one another. In the second case, although the subject came directly from their everyday experience and the community sponsored the class with parental support, it was not meaningful to the students. One would think that the children would be enthusiastic learners, yet all that happened was that they temporarily retained facts.

❧

These anecdotes illustrate the difference between learning and being taught, between knowing as intimacy and knowing as commodity. One teaching relationship acknowledged the necessity of trusting relationships and reciprocal cooperation, which allowed the learning to proceed as a mutual discovery. The other teacher, certainly well-intentioned, assumed the child's natural need to learn would be satisfied by supplying them with information that would stimulate understanding. Natural capacities are neither awakened nor nurtured. Even the seemingly most relevant material will not inspire a child or stimulate enthusiasm.

Reciprocal cooperation is not the sort of cooperation where the child accedes to the adult's wishes out of a sense of duty to tradition, imposed family values, or institutional rules—either tacit or explicit. It has nothing to do with obedience or with any hint of authoritarianism. That is not cooperation, but rather is acquiescence to real or implied rewards and punishments, bribes and coercion. These things have nothing to do with well-being for the child, parent, or teacher.

Rules and Play

Everyone from Piaget to Huizinga has noticed that children, beginning at about eight years of age, care deeply about the rules of a game. BodyBeing children, egocentric and assessing the world by its sensory qualities, hardly care at all. Parents who have tried to play a board game with BodyBeing and FeelingBeing children together know how difficult it can be. The younger child often likes the action of the dice, the color of the money, and the movement of the pieces. At some point, bored by the constraint of the rules, she will indulge her enjoyment of pleasant sensations such as scattering money, hogging and perhaps sucking on the dice, or moving the pieces haphazardly. The older child will cry, "Not fair!" Her feelings will be hurt. She was playing at learning rules through the medium of the game. She must take it personally. She is FeelingBeing, vulnerable and playing with any and all data in the service of the developmental imperative to find and engage trusting relationships.

FeelingBeing children love to play in social groups. Favorite activities include drama and the performing arts, team sports, and academic team learning. These activities become important for the camaraderie, not for winning and losing. FeelingBeing children play together. Friendships, identification with a team, wearing a uniform, and cooperating to achieve a common goal allow the safe space to experience and explore feelings and interpersonal dynamics. They show up for games enthusiastic and willing to follow instructions.

Through play, FeelingBeing children simultaneously create order in their social world and in their inner world. Play provides the field where they learn what is trustworthy in each. Rules provide the framework that supports this development. They make it safe to explore the new, vast realm of feelings and interpersonal dynamics.

Therefore, segregation in play of any sort subverts the development of FeelingBeing children. Boys and girls need to play together. Children of diverse backgrounds need to play together. FeelingBeing children need to play with people of all ages. Optimal well-being with trust demands it.

FeelingBeing children develop trust based on their interpersonal experiences. When they play in textured interpersonal environments, fear of others drops away. When they play in monotone interpersonal environments, fear of others is reinforced. Then cliques form and the values of the clique, naively determined and enforced through threat of excommunication, become a religion. Attitudes form and those who are not "in" are "stupid." The stupidity extends to parents and teachers. Life becomes adversarial. Prejudice flourishes.

Can it really be so easy for our children to avoid prejudice? Yes, a thousand times, yes. FeelingBeing is the age of character development. Our innate ethical capacity comes to the fore. Trust depends on ethics; it is the highest state of character. Relationship is built on the qualities of justice, fairness, morality, and caring, People of good character manifest these qualities. They feel them, they offer them, and they expect them in return. They develop trust by living in justice, fairness, and caring. It is a way of being—the essence of relationship with self, family, community, and the natural world. Where is the room for prejudice in this? None, when FeelingBeing children live in optimal well-being.

Friends, destroy the Mattel myth! Don't buy toys that promote gender separation. Don't buy toys that reinforce cultural stereotypes of children. Prejudice does not have to be eliminated; just take away the soil in which it grows.

One of my areas of expertise is cooperative games and activities, and I have co-authored two books on the subject. In addition, with the growing popularity of outdoor education, there are many other excellent resources for cooperative play. These enjoyable games allow children with varied degrees of proficiency to stay engaged and challenged. They enhance communication, build self-esteem, and can be used to support

- Rhythm Sticks—A Cooperative Activity for FeelingBeing Children [11] -

The sticks can be used for everything from learning academics to expressing ethnic heritage. They are just plain fun, yet used properly they invite the children to move together. Simple rhythms are sufficient for most purposes, but the children may also develop complex group movements that include everyone. Six to twelve players works best.

Rules of the Game:
Cut one-inch-diameter dowels into eighteen-inch lengths. These are the sticks.
Give each child two sticks. Let him or her decorate their sticks.
Sit in a circle, knees touching.
Begin tapping out simple rhythms. Develop routines that include tapping the floor and neighbor's sticks as well as their own.
Develop more complex rhythms.
Sing along.
Introduce a theme—it could be reciting the week's spelling words, math problems, or geography lessons in rhythm.
Give individual children a chance to lead. Allow them to introduce their own themes. Songs from their homes are especially welcome.

Hints:
Go slowly. Make sure the rhythmically challenged are cared for.
Vary themes regularly.
Give each child a chance to lead.
Use this activity to bring the physical energy of the group into balance.
Play along.
Many children learn the academics better when they say the material aloud. Also, those who do not know are not put on the spot and can learn along with the others.
Invite tricks and skill exhibitions but do not let any one child dominate. Let the more skilled teach the others.
BodyBeing children also love Rhythm Sticks, and so it is an excellent transition activity.

For more play ideas, visit baluvmour.com.

academic achievement. They emphasize our humanness and our strengths and so lead to greater appreciation of the greatness we share.

Everyday exchanges between you and your children provide the most important locus for play. Play with them as they sort through their impressions of people. Pause while reading to them or watching a video and try to guess what is going to happen to the characters. Sit it in a park and people watch. Take the time to talk about many of the interactions of the family, extended family, and community, not just the ones that are difficult. Bring light to relationships and let the feelings they are composed of become an acceptable and enjoyable subject. Open the family detective agency and try to ascertain both the explicit and implicit rules governing social interactions. Tell jokes and teaching stories that highlight the foibles of humanity.

Make up a game. For instance, tell a true story about your day and an interpersonal challenge that was in it. Then ask the child what they would have done. Present "what if" options. Have fun. Listen to the stories of their social life and ask the same kinds of questions. This can be spontaneous and freewheeling, not a contrived exercise.

Healthy FeelingBeing children accept nature as trustworthy. They feel the anguish of the rabbit in the clutches of the hawk, but they do not find it unfair. Sentimentality does not rule FeelingBeing children; it is merely one of the feelings available. The beauty of the soaring hawk and the anguish of the rabbit are each valued. Natural beauty sings of inspiration, of truth, of trustworthiness. Nature is not something you argue with; it is something you participate in. Nature is the field of play for FeelingBeing children.

The multitude of relationships of the natural world provides an excellent opportunity for FeelingBeing children to express and explore their ethics. I have had the privilege of many enlightening conversations with FeelingBeing children while we were in nature. For instance, we have considered loneliness while gazing into the endless vault of the night sky, death while observing a king snake fight a rattler, transformation while watching new redwoods grow out of fallen one, fairness while catching a fish for dinner, and prejudice while scraping the remains of a slug from my foot that I had accidentally stepped on when I was coming out of a lake in the forest.

In addition to playing together in inspirational natural surroundings—our most highly recommended play relationship with FeelingBeing children—many games are designed to be played in nature. I have included two as sidebars on the following pages.

Didactical teaching is slow and tedious for FeelingBeing children. It does not allow them to play. Learning loses its spontaneity, its free-roaming exploration of a territory, its field of interpersonal connection. Cooperative learning and team learning are better fields of play. For FeelingBeing children, knowing the data on the subject is not as important as the process by which it is engaged. Or it could be said that the process is the subject—is the main lesson learned. Group learning also removes the stigma of smart versus dumb, of exalted versus humiliated, of pride versus shame, of winner versus loser.

Play should not sting. If the game is competitive, great care should be taken to emphasize the relationships among team mates and opponents and to de-emphasize the glory of winning. Play is voluntary, not compulsory; it is an expression of freedom. Play allows mastery of self within certain boundaries. Children naturally impose those boundaries in order to actualize the moment's organizing principle. The natural boundaries for FeelingBeing children are rules and relationships, not individual achievement or proving oneself better than one's friends, for the organizing principle is trust.

Here are two case histories illustrating the importance of letting play be play and not imposing an agenda of victory or pleasing elders.

⁂

The first is from my own childhood. My dad enjoyed playing cards very much and so naturally, as part of my FeelingBeing connection to family and community, I learned to play poker and introduced it into my peer group, where it was enthusiastically adopted. During my ninth and tenth years, we played often, keeping the stakes very small and enjoying the game and the company.

As might be expected, winning soon became as important to us as it was to my dad and his friends. We raised the stakes. Players risked at the edge of their resources, and beyond. Debts grew. Winners banked losers and then resented it when the losers did not pay. A hierarchy formed and soon the poker games became exclusive. Best friends abandoned one another in order to join the desired game. I grew increasingly uncomfortable, as my best friend was a loser. He was also brilliant and funny and slightly out of focus with his world.

One day, my luck ran high and it seemed like I couldn't lose a hand. Near the end of the day, a particularly large pot developed and I sat with a hand that couldn't be beat. During the last bet, two guys, both of whom were friends, opposed me. I knew they were in over their heads and that they could not afford to lose. Nevertheless, I bet to beat them and I did, all within the rules of the game. As I gathered the money, I

- Two Nature Games for FeelingBeing Children -

What Does This Mean?

This activity builds trust and community. It calls for the children to state their values openly and plainly. It also helps as a diagnostic tool. Children who are interested in and rejoice in the meaning and values of other children generally are accessing developmental well-being.

Rules of the Game:

Gather the group together. If possible, have a brief group conversation about relationship and trust.

Ask the group to search the surrounding environment for an object that has a special value for him or her.

Invite them to take their time and try to feel why they are choosing their selected object.

Each child brings their object back to the circle. Taking turns, they explain why the object has meaning for them.

The others simply listen. The group may spontaneously converse about a particular value. Generally this discussion can be encouraged, but not at the expense of everyone having a turn.

Hints:

Do not discourage any expression, even if a child drags a tree branch to the circle or refers to something imaginary.

Teachers can create academic projects based on what the group offers. Creative expression, especially poetry and art, often deepens the experiences.

A natural or park setting works best, but surprisingly meaningful moments have occurred when the children were limited to a room or house.

Leave adequate time. Cooperative games and activities should never be hurried, and this game often takes more time than expected. Have a secondary activity such as reading or drawing available to those who are ready quickly.

Hug a Tree

Everyone loves this game. The blind trust walk catalyzes friendship. The intimacy with the forest heightens both sensory and feeling awareness. The mystery of finding the tree leads to great excitement. Any and all of these elements can provide an excellent forum for subsequent conversation.

Rules of the Game:
    Children pair off. One is blindfolded and the other, by a deliberate, circuitous route, leads that child through a forest area to a tree.
    The blindfolded person explores the tree completely, without using sight of course.
    The child is led back to where she started, again via a misleading route.
    She then has to go through the forest area until she finds her tree.
    Players switch roles.

Hints:
    Pair children who do not know each other well. The blindfold and the forest are great equalizers.
    Talk about how the children knew their tree. Many will refer to a particular physical characteristic. Invite them to go deeper and talk about the feel of the forest.
    Talk about the feelings of being blindfolded, the ensuing necessity of trust, and any attendant relationship insights.
    Play *Hug a Flower.*

For more play ideas, visit baluvmour.com.

chanced to look into their eyes. Their defeat and agony went right into me, without mitigation. The feelings were so intense that I could not decipher them in the moment.

I lost intimacy with those two friends. I lost passion for the game. Play, ruined, had become work. Poker became an obsession—something we had to do. Spontaneity and freedom evaporated. Learning went with them.

I know, and will explain why in the next chapter, that adventure is very important to FeelingBeing children. I also know that we were adventure starved and had to create what could only be crude substitutes. I also know that we lacked inspiration. Inspiration and adventure are crucial nourishments for optimal well-being in FeelingBeing individuals. Their absence prompted, in part, our desire to squeeze more and more out of poker. Talk about blood from a stone!

~

The second example tells the true tale of four FeelingBeing children who attended public school in the deprived and harsh world of East

Harlem. These four—two boys and two girls—found their inspiration in music and asked their teacher for special instruction. As East Harlem is a poor school district with few resources, the only way the children could be accommodated was by meeting with the teacher at seven in the morning and playing for an hour before school started. The children agreed. The teacher, skeptical that they could maintain this schedule given the cold, dark winter and their fragile home support, expected the children to stop in a short while.

Three months later, they had not missed a day. Word spread and a professor from a nearby university asked to run a social psychology experiment. Given his prestige and everyone's ignorance of the effects of what he proposed, the school gave him permission. His entire action was to meet the children each morning, shake their hands, thank them for coming, and hand each a gold star. You know the kind—one of those flimsy paper things.

After two months, he omitted the gold star and the handshake. The children would not play their music. Nothing could shake their resolve but receiving their gold star.

They would not play because it was no longer play. Their spontaneous, inspired expression of freedom had been subverted. They needed the approval of their mentors and they accepted the mentors' lead. The removal of the star signified a radical change in the relationship. Their social group lost coherence and with it the necessary support to play. Sacrilege occurred, a desecration of the connection with the essence of life. I mean that literally. I explain why in the next chapter, "Spirituality."

Heaven save us from indiscriminate use of rewards and punishment! They impose adult agendas, turn learning into work, and condition children to turn away from their innate knowing of right from wrong. Children then become dependent on the definitions of others. Relationship becomes authoritarian, no matter how subtle, and the stage is set for rebellion in the teen years.

There are times when rewards and punishments are necessary. If they are, then the situation has deteriorated for other reasons. Rewards and punishments may be used as a finger in a dyke, but they will soon give way and the dam will burst unless the underlying causes that inhibit the healthy behavior are remedied.

Also, relying on rewards and punishments turns the parent into the cop, the shrink, and the judge. She has to constantly meter behavior and hand out the right dose of reward or punishment. It is exhausting. Children resent it and soon learn to do the same to the parents. They will be "good" to get what they want and "bad" to annoy parents so that they are given what they want. It's a game, but it is not play. It is interaction, but it is not relationship. Trust vanishes when manipulation enters.

IdealBeing

Huizinga makes the point that play has an antagonistic element. Games encapsulate situations of life, which means that they include ambiguities, mystery, confusion, and unpredictability. Each of these is fraught with tensions. Will there be success or failure? A greatness of play is that players have the opportunity to participate in the tensions of the game, unencumbered by any boundaries except those that are accepted voluntarily. As Huizinga says, play occupies its own space. Players directly experience both sides of the dualism, the tension.[12]

This tense play is often very challenging. Huizinga calls it an ordeal and equates it with a spiritual journey—a process of self-actualization. Huizinga sees this ordeal played out time and again in the rites of passage many cultures have for their teens. Josette and I have facilitated and done extensive research in rites of passage and confirm Huizinga's observation. There are many other examples from every continent on the planet. In each instance, rites of passage can be seen as a nation celebrating a new birth in the child, a new way of organizing the world. But with or without these milestones, everyone recognizes the changes in the young teen.

Autonomy

A client, Craig, watched the last election with his fifteen-year-old son, Johan. Craig avidly supported one candidate and worked hard to get him elected. There was much excitement in the home as they watched. Then Johan asserted, "I don't believe in anything." Craig did not react, did not take it personally. He inquired. Johan made it clear that all his political values were those of his family and not necessarily his. His statement of non-belief was not intended to push his father away, but to inform him of the need for his self-discovery.

Craig played with his teen. He spontaneously enjoyed the moment of his teen's assertion of autonomy. Autonomy means self-government. It is the organizing principle of IdealBeing, which holds dominion from approximately thirteen through seventeen years of age. Autonomy does not mean isolation or separation. Eighty-five percent of all teens, a massive longitudinal study by the National Institute of Mental Health reports, value family relationships as extremely important. Eighty-five percent also state that they must learn to do things for themselves. Only a fractured perspective rooted in the belief in separation and finding it everywhere would confuse autonomy with a desire for individualistic separation. It is appalling to project separation, rebellion, and individualism on the teen when she is learning to navigate the complex terrain of self-government.

Autonomy includes governing oneself in relationship with others. When interactions support autonomy, adversaries disappear and mutual learning arises. Without Natural Learning Rhythms, Craig might have taken Johan's declaration as rebellious and lectured him on the virtues of his candidate, on the obligation to believe in something, and on the example he was setting for his younger sister. Johan would most likely have claimed that the lectures were a cover-up and that his dad just wanted him to pledge allegiance to the chosen candidate and the attendant values. Who knows the depths to which this spiral might have descended? Certainly, this would not have been optimal well-being.

The inquiry into Johan's ideals is play between father and son. It is spontaneous and voluntary, and it allows them to represent themselves without imposed constraint. Learning is free, easy, and enjoyable.

The shift from organizing the world for trust and within the matrix of family, friends, and community to organizing the world for autonomy within the matrix of self is monumental for both child and parent. The details of this shift are discussed in chapter 6, "Transitions."

The child entering the teen years has never asserted her self-governance before—she has always relied on the parent as the ultimate decision maker. Insecurity arises, an important ingredient for the health of the young teen. Insecurity has great value for developing autonomy, as the friction that arises when insecurity rubs against assertion burns off early childhood attitudes and behaviors that are no longer needed. It is the fuel for takeoff into the orbit of self-government. The thesis of assertion interacts with antithesis of insecurity, leading to the synthesis of self. Self then becomes the new thesis, the locus, the field in which the child plays on her journey of self-actualization.

No wonder it is tumultuous for parent, child, and the family. A wondrous human capacity is being born. To know the self and to be able to consider how to govern it implies a profound opportunity for freedom and responsibility. As Piaget shows, the innate capacities for abstraction and reversible thinking appear. From the perspective of ontological epistemology, these special human capacities are exactly what are needed to support self-government. Without the ability to think abstractly, it would be impossible to consider the self as an entity, as a locus of reference, as a participant in knowledge.

Naturally, the child plays with his newly discovered awareness of self. Needing to assert this self in order to gain experience—"to learn how to do it myself"—but insecure as to how to do this, the child projects his ideals onto the world. These ideals represent his self-perception. He then creates the identities that he believes will actualize the ideals. The goal is to find his core identity, to find out who he really is. This search, which can formulated as the question "Who am I?," is the essence of the onto-logical journey. It is the fundamental question for a human being to ask, for it accepts that all that we call reality begins with our own perceptions. Self-knowledge is the alpha and omega of existence.

Incredibly, this journey starts with the young teen's naive assertions of his ideals. You have to either laugh or cry. After being rooted in the body and communing with the world through the medium of sensa-tions, the child becomes aware of personal mortality. The bottom falls out of his world. He enters FeelingBeing. Vulnerable, having just lost that which he sensed was secure, the child now must find trust in rela-tionships with family, community, and environment. Okay, he takes five years to do that and now, fully embedded in trustworthy relationships, the child has to leave that and become self-referential on the journey to the core of his own nature. Obviously, titanic forces play through human beings. Either we open to them or spend a lifetime in conflict, living with less than optimal health.

Ideals are literally the stuff that aids and abets self-knowledge. To treat them with anything less than sensitive respect undermines the abil-ity to self-govern. They are the medium in which the child can play with identities and discover herself. This is no more selfish or inappropriate than the BodyBeing child playing with sensory textured toys or the FeelingBeing child playing with social rules and relationships. And it calls for the same kind of response—play with developmental sensitivity.

Most people find it more difficult to play with children as they grow older. By the time their children reach their teens, many parents have for-gotten play and try to turn to earnest work. But teens need to play. Teens willingly engage in games for the challenge and the opportunity for peer interaction. They relish the chance for self-definition. Winning is impor-tant, for it is triumphing in the ordeal and a way to affirm self-order.

But when teen game players become sought-after stars by college and professional recruiters, their self-exploration is subverted, not enhanced. They are told, "This is who you are and if you do everything to fulfill it you will be above the rest." The identity becomes fixed. The ideal does not progress into genuine reasonableness, which is the next developmental stage. The few who reach the top often abuse their privilege; others never leave the fantasy.

The crime is that the nobility has been destroyed. Discovering the honor and nobility of human nature is critical for healthy autonomy. They morally confirm the right to be free and to choose. They confirm the willingness and capability to be responsible. They confirm that the ordeal has been successfully met. The field of play is unimportant. Sports, academics, peer relations, problem solving, the arts, crafts, and many other challenging, focused endeavors can be fields of discovery. But when the honor and nobility are subverted, autonomy is thwarted. The enemy is taunted, not respected. Addiction to individual glory saturates the psyche and all that counts is the next fix. Teens never grow up. They are not stars burning brightly in the firmament but cheap imitations forgotten with tomorrow's headlines.

Parents in seminars often ask me how they can relate better with their teens. I always answer that the most important thing is to not take their actions personally. This advice brings a disturbed murmur and a few nervous laughs. A few wonder if I am serious. Then I say something like, "Pretty easy, huh?" The tension breaks; people laugh and ask if it is possible.

When parents feel personally challenged by the child's actions, play ceases. If BodyBeing sensory exploration is seen as a test of wills, then the enjoyment of mutually creating boundaries dissipates and each side amps up the sensory input. If FeelingBeing reciprocal cooperation is matched against social and familial notions of good and found wanting, each side slides down the slippery slope of mistrust. Defiance dominates. If IdealBeing identity explorations are taken as attacks on the parents and parental values, then alienation occurs, often attended by rebellion. Defiance, alienation, and rebellion infect every member of the family, not just the child.

Parents of teens justifiably find it difficult to avoid feeling personally attacked by their teen. Projecting ideals often seems naive and even ludicrous. At times, the ideal is simply to deny the parent's values and see what's left, as Johan did. At other times, the ideal can be more directly confrontational, as when the IdealBeing child challenges the political, religious, or social beliefs and behaviors of the parents. And there is a deeper, natural wrinkle that many are not aware of—the shadow.

Sarah, thirty-nine, and her daughter Alyssa, fourteen, had always been very close. They enjoyed their time together and were easily intimate while sharing their respective perspectives. One day at the video rental store, Alyssa chose *The Texas Chainsaw Massacre* and *Bride of*

Chucky. Sarah objected and expressed her annoyance to Alyssa who, she said, "knew that I hate horror movies." The annoyance met resistance and an intense argument flared, all the more unsettling to both of them as they rarely argued. Alyssa asserted that she had a right to pick out the movies and that her mother's "uptightness" shouldn't "run the show." Sarah boiled over, called Alyssa rude, and refused to pay for the movies. Alyssa stomped off and walked the mile to her house, refusing to ride with her mother.

All of this over a movie? Obviously something much more important was at stake here.

Sarah, who had been in family camp five years before, called, flummoxed. I reminded her of the shadow. She recalled that the shadow is a psychological term for a phenomenon observed throughout the history of both spiritual inquiry and psychology. The shadow consists of those aspects of ourselves that have been repressed in order for us to survive in the world. As a Jungian scholar, Dr. Charles Davis of Appalachian State University, puts it: "The Shadow is the personification of that part of human, psychic possibility that we deny in ourselves and project onto others. The goal of personality integration is to integrate the rejected, inferior side of our life into our total experience and to take responsibility for it." There are personal and universal shadows and they play out everywhere. Dr. Davis explains the dynamics of the shadow this way:

> We project our dark side onto others and thus interpret them as "enemies" or as "exotic" presences that fascinate. We see the Shadow everywhere in popular culture. He is Batman. She is Spider Woman. We see it in popular prejudice as well. We "imagine" that the Black Man is our enemy; that Communists are devils. We incline towards Hawaii as the "land of paradise." We accept people uncritically if we perceive them as "Fair Haired." Of course, Satan is the great Shadow image of popular religion. (Consider: the word only occurs fifty-four times in the entire Bible.)[13]

For many of us, violence is a good example of the shadow. Fear of the supernatural is another. Perhaps that's why 80 percent of all receipts for horror movies are from children between thirteen and eighteen.

For the IdealBeing child, the new, raw surge of idealism yearns to play out in the fields of freedom and personal power. Limits exist to be challenged. Established ethics and concepts have no strength simply because parents and society insist upon them. Nothing is sacrosanct.

Play with IdealBeing

At the EnCompass family camp, attention centers on the interactions among the family members. Staff, therefore, does not monitor softball games or swimming pools but rather observes and interacts with all members of the client families. There is also the grunt work of helping with luggage, cleaning bathrooms, and maintaining the facilities. It is a twelve-hour-per-day job for seven consecutive days. When family camp was held at the California campus temperatures often reached triple digits (the California campus has since been sold; family camp now takes place in Portland, Oregon). Yet IdealBeing children comprised at least half of the staff and there was always a waiting list of others wishing to help. It may look like work from the outside, but for the teens it is play. Helping families matches their ideals. Allocating responsibilities among themselves and determining their peer group social structure are opportunities to self-govern. Their participation is a never-ending delight and a source of wonder for the campers. All the stereotypes of teens as lazy, needing prodding, irresponsible, and insensitive to others die a quick and welcome death. It was, in the words of many teens, "all good."

Specifically, many IdealBeing children need to explore the shadow of both family and community. The idealistic assertion of freedom and personal power means that the child believes that they have the freedom to look anywhere and the power to win at any ordeal that may arise.

Freedom and personal power are the secondary organizing principles of IdealBeing. Genuine choice depends upon them. To govern the self implies a faculty for self-reflection, a faculty not matured in BodyBeing and FeelingBeing. The right to freedom is unalienable, is woven into being a human being. Yet freedom is an extraordinary capacity and needs power to be actualized. In properly empowered children, freedom of choice exists. With choice comes the opportunity to self-govern. The sidebar describes one example of how to play with IdealBeing children.

Of course, shadow exploration by teens gets subtler and leads to greater friction than simply disagreeing over movies. One young friend deliberately did poorly at tests in school even though he had easily mastered the work because he "hated the high-achievement trip my father laid on my sister." He was exploring his father's fear of failure.

The stakes get higher. Often, the child is not fully aware of what she is doing. A young man procrastinated about everything, which was the trait his father hated most about himself. A young woman wore sexually alluring clothes that made her Puritanical father seethe. He restricted her; she sneaked out; he hit her; she invested her ideals in sexual freedom; he threw her out and she became a teenage homeless child trying to finish high school. The family shadow, unacknowledged, has led to a great deal of unnecessary suffering.

The stakes get higher. So many inner city teens lack the proper developmental nourishment that they are forced to push their assertion to rebellion—to be overtly antagonistic about society's shadow. They have to use the powerful energy of their desire for freedom to force recognition of the fear, lies, and loathing that are not being admitted and which so severely restrict their lives.

Both psychology and spirituality agree that true freedom requires integrating the shadow elements of our personalities. Here, during IdealBeing, the sparkling natural capacities of development impel the child to make contact with the shadow. This serves her autonomy, her freedom. It also serves the freedom of her parents, for it invites them to examine and contact their own shadows. IdealBeing's exploration of the shadow provides a golden opportunity for parent and for child to grow in self-knowledge—to dance.

The argument that took place between Alyssa and Sarah breaks my heart in several ways. First, Alyssa was simply doing what came naturally and was ridiculed for it. She was not being confrontational, selfish, or rebellious. This type of confusion, where an elder misinterprets a natural expression of the child and than attempts to remedy what was never damaged, occurs in many family and school interactions. I will point it out throughout this book. This type of confusion is one of the reasons why my experience indicates that about two-thirds of family problems need only developmental sensitivity to disappear and never rise again. Second, mother and daughter could be learning together—could be dancing. Third, Alyssa must now either put her shadow exploration back in the shadow or become rebellious. Her identity experiment is undermined, for if she becomes rebellious than she may well concretize an identity she only intended to visit. Fourth, with a proper developmental response, the problem would disappear so fast it would seem magical. Their suffering is, in a word, unnecessary. Emergent knowledge is a very real possibility.

Fortunately, after reflecting on the situation, Sarah realized that she was taking it personally. Alyssa's action pinched her shadow. Sarah's parents had not allowed shadow exploration in her teen years, and she had stuffed much of her own freedom to choose. When her daughter played with her shadow, Sarah moved to suppress it, a habit she had learned long ago.

Shadows lose their grip when they are played with. Sarah can simply watch the movies with Alyssa. Better, she can use the pause button during the movie and ask Alyssa for a critique. She can share her perceptions. They can play with the sensations and feelings of horror movies together. They will probably find some humor in it.

The child's ideals and interests are the field of play. Some, like photography or computers, may be beyond the parent's expertise, but playing is still possible. Asking questions, escorting the child to conventions, becoming an impartial sounding board, and finding the humor in the moment are playful.

Many teens find challenging activities a dynamic field of play. Parents and teens can share these together. My daughter, for instance, taught me to downhill ski when I was forty-two. She applied a simple technique: Go to the top of the mountain and ski down. She stayed with me all the time, picking me up the many times I fell, and demonstrating the correct technique. With a devilish glint, she told me it wasn't much harder than learning to read.

Shared challenges do not have to be physical. Puzzles, guessing the endings of movies, friendly debates, and attending and analyzing controversial plays and events can be challengingly playful. Nothing can be taken personally; all interactions have to be seen as identity explorations. As the BodyBeing child fully engaged her senses to maximize rightful place and the FeelingBeing child fully engaged her feelings in interpersonal relationships to maximize trust, the IdealBeing child fully engages her newfound ability to play with identities to maximize autonomy. Any voluntary activity that occupies its own space and that provides the freedom to exercise personal power in the service of autonomy is play for IdealBeing children.

ReasonableBeing

Plato saw humans as God's playthings. It is this quality which ensures that we are ultimately good—that we are of God. The Sanskrit word *lila* refers to divine play, and it is often referred to as the reason for life by Vedantists. Parables, koans, question and answer tracts in spiritual texts, and even dialogue are play—voluntary, defining their own boundaries, and allowing each participant to freely identify themselves within the agreed-upon contexts.

Courts of law are play, too. The rules have been carefully created, the advocates are carefully trained, the outcome is uncertain, and the action is spontaneous. It is theater, and everyone dresses the part and plays their role. It is an ordeal to create order out of a sea of confusion, of civilization challenged. Only by playing with all the variables can something new emerge.

Play is always serious, always allows participation in emergent knowledge, and is always a way for players to know themselves—to know their world. What other way could we possibly find to respond to a life that reveals itself as ever more mysterious despite, or due to, ever more sophisticated ways of organizing the world? We can only hypothesize and then play with the variables. We might call this science, law, philosophy, or art, but if we play with it we will delight in the infinite creativity available. We might attain tremendous spiritual insight and then shrug and say that it's all divine play. We might lose ourselves in a muse or uncover a law of physics that startles. All of this and more can occur in the field of ReasonableBeing play.

Serious activity is not the opposite of play. That title belongs to obligatory work and imposed agendas. It belongs to being controlled and controlling others. It belongs to memorizing data, treating it as knowledge, and then being judged on data retention and regurgitation. It belongs to fortified boundaries so narrow as to create only a regulated path and not a field for explorative play. It belongs to interactions polluted with threat, hypocrisy, ridicule, or condescension.

ReasonableBeing children attempt to order time itself. It is this new capacity to play with time that allows dialogue with complex systems and concepts such as cosmology, physics, and law. Each stage, each organizing principle, has its own way of ordering time (see chapter 7). Only ReasonableBeing children literally play with time and thus take on ordering the entire universe.

An amazing evolution has occurred. Humans have gone from playing with a material object, such as a stick, to using that most unique abstraction, time, which cannot be seen or touched. Yet playing with a stick yields flights of fancy that matter only to the child, while playing with time fundamentally alters everything in our world. Playing with the material leads to localized abstraction; playing with the abstract leads to global material changes.

Alfred Korzybski, one of the great philosophers of the early twentieth century and the father of the highly influential discipline of general semantics, called this unique human capacity *time binding*.[14] He pointed out that time binding is everywhere—books, media, art, and even food preservatives are ubiquitous examples. Humans bind time with words, symbols, and signs. General semantics states that we do so according to the meaning we have attached to both the content of the message and the medium we use to make that message enduring—to make it last through time.

Perhaps the most renowned time player was Einstein. His game revealed that time is intimately connected with space, energy, and the speed of light. Time is neither absolute nor independent. It is simply a variable in a complex universe and can be bent, slowed down, and speeded up.[15]

Once the child can dialogue with time, she can dialogue with any system or concept. As the vast and ever-changing curricula in our universities show, ReasonableBeing children can play with most systems. Significantly, they can also see themselves as a system. They can examine their past and attempt to remedy those habits and conditionings that no longer have meaning. They can project a future and engage those disciplines that will lead to its actualization. They are no longer bound by ideals and the narrow choices they entail. Playing with time allows an unimagined freedom that will take the next six years to fully integrate.

Interconnectedness, Humor, and Humility

What developmental events brought this extraordinary stage to the fore? Awareness of mortality undermined BodyBeing and triggered FeelingBeing. Awareness of an autonomous self, with its attendant insecurities, precipitated IdealBeing. At approximately eighteen years of age, at the end of IdealBeing, asserted ideals prove inadequate to deal with the complexities of the world. IdealBeing asserts a self, projects ideals, and plays with identities for self-actualization. After five years that self finds that the world does not always bend to its assertions, that projected ideals fail to help it successfully comprehend complex realities. When that idealistic romance, which the self thought was going to last forever, crashes and burns, when the competitor meets his match, when the whiz math student faces differential calculus, when the foibles and limitations of heroes in sports, politics, and entertainment are seen, then the ideals fracture; they are revealed as a brittle shell held together only by the will of the child. A shattering occurs, as dramatic as any in the life of the child.

Doubt sets in. A moment of cognitive dissonance arises, in which the knowledge processes themselves are questioned. Doubt signals the onset of reason, for without doubt there would be no impetus to dialogue—to cut into the essence of meaning.

The organizing principles of ReasonableBeing are interconnectedness, humor, and humility. Doubt serves interconnectedness in the same way that insecurity served autonomy during IdealBeing. It provides the friction that energizes the child and keeps him open to new learning. With doubt, the child realizes that he has to use hypotheses for experimentation and examination and that conclusions further the dialogue, not end it.

The organizing principle is a force that determines the general ways in which human energy, capacities, inclinations, and interactions are structured and act. The goal of the organizing principle is optimal well-being, and the energy, capacities, inclinations, and interactions it has to work with are developmentally and contextually bound.

As ReasonableBeing dawns, the child discovers that life is an integrated, whole system in which they are interdependent with everyone and everything. This realization is synchronous with the arrival of humility, which is the ability to accept that one's own perspective is incomplete. Humility stimulates open dialogue and movement into another's perspective. With the expansion of the perception of time, the realization of interconnectedness, and the birth of humility comes the capacity for humor—the ability to laugh at oneself. Through the synergistic interplay of these three qualities, optimal well-being develops in the

- ReasonableBeing Humor -

"Laws as such do not make people better," said Nasrudin to the king. "They must practice certain things, in order to become more attuned to inner truth. This form of truth resembles apparent truth only slightly."

The king decided that he could, and would, make people observe the truth. He could make them practice truthfulness.

The city was entered by a bridge. On this he built a gallows. The following day, when the gates were opened at dawn, the Captain of the Guard was stationed with a squad of troops to examine all who entered.

An announcement was made: "Everyone will be questioned. If he tells the truth, he will be allowed to enter. If he lies, he will be hanged."

Nasrudin stepped forward.

"Where are you going?"

"I am on my way," said Nasrudin slowly, "to be hanged."

"We don't believe you!"

"Very well, if I have told a lie, hang me!"

"But if we hang you for lying, we will have made what you say come true!"

"That's right: now you know what truth is—YOUR truth!"[16]

ReasonableBeing child. See the sidebar for an example of ReasonableBeing humor.

The secondary organizing principles of incisiveness, intentionality, and systems creation allow the ReasonableBeing child to think and act with purpose, clarity, seriousness, and appreciation of the systems that compose the whole as well as the relationships between and among the systems. All of these qualities are necessary to maintain and further the organizing principles of interconnectedness, humility, and humor.

ReasonableBeing children thus recognize the inevitability of change. The worthiness of doubt, the varied perspectives, the realization of interconnectedness, the humor, and the expansiveness of space/time yield the indubitable knowledge that change is constant.

Society recognizes the precious human quality of reasonableness and does much to nurture and protect it. Accomplished reasonable people such as judges, academicians, and scientists enjoy many social privileges. Society also protects ReasonableBeing children who play with concepts and systems, as the ubiquitous existence of colleges and universities attests.

There is little research on child development for the ages of eighteen to twenty-three. Most people believe that all that can be said has been said by the time the child reaches fifteen or so. The child is grown up. Genetic epistemology drops the ball at the age of approximately twelve. The spiritual developmentalists see the years from thirteen to twenty-one as one long stage. They fail to see the differences between the projected, idealistic self and the one who can step back, consider variables, include herself without fear of identity dissolution, and be reasonable. Therefore, the material in this section is based upon years of fieldwork. In addition to observation and experimentation, many ReasonableBeing children have agreed with the Natural Learning Rhythms insights on the stage.

Playing with ReasonableBeing

Using the multifaceted tool of dialogue, ReasonableBeing children play with meaning. To dialogue is to slice into meaning and to know the interconnectedness between oneself and one's endeavor so that value and purpose are revealed. ReasonableBeing children live with "why?" and many of their actions are an attempt to answer the question. With their growing appreciation that they can, in part, influence their future by the lives they lead in the present, ReasonableBeing children yearn for meaning and purpose. They embrace change and they seek reasonable

values—values that endure and are not subject to the whims of momentary identities. What is real? How does change occur? What is subject to
erosion through time? Love? Truth? Beauty? For ReasonableBeing children, the statement that the only constant is change is not paradoxical; it
is a hypothesis to play with.

Dialogue is not only about words or concepts. The ReasonableBeing
child playing her violin is dialoguing with music as a medium of meaning. If you have the skill, play with her by playing music with her. If you
have only a bit of skill, play with her by asking her to teach you. If you are
like me and have no skill, play with her through verbal dialogue that is
open and authentic. *Open* means that you have no agenda but to comprehend the meaning and value of the music for her and to be connected
with her. *Authentic* means that you recognize that knowledge is emergent
and that you are there to learn—that you understand that the moment
has meaning for her and has meaning for you as well.

Play with all of it. Where is her concentration as she reads the music
and moves the bow? Does that ever become confusing? Does she think
about violin when she is not playing? How does violin affect the rest of
her life? What does she hear while she is playing? Is she concerned about
others' opinions of her playing? Which teachers does she respect and
why? Is it inspiring? These questions, and many others that you might
ask, are not a litany and certainly not an interrogation. Free-spirited and
originating in your own genuine curiosity, they deepen the spontaneous
dialogue—the field of play for ReasonableBeing children.

For me this is the most delightful play of all. It is subtle, for the play
does not depend upon the activity but only upon the perspective and disposition of the players. It is demanding, for to play I have to be willing to
expose and examine my meaning, purpose, and value. It is relational, for
without interconnectedness there is no optimal well-being. It is expansive, for I have to understand that dialogue and communication go
beyond verbal-linguistic constructs.

Finally, it is reflective, in that ReasonableBeing children can stand
outside of their actions and evaluate them; so we can look at our play
together, decide which aspects are valuable and which are not, and skillfully direct our play to create the greatest meaning.

Summary

Lev Vygotsky and his colleagues in Russia, who worked in relative
obscurity in the 1920s, deserve much credit for establishing that development occurs in relationship—in the context of family and environment
and not as an isolated, individualized event. Not surprisingly, they

looked closely at play. Considering this, Mary Belenky, author of *Women's Ways of Knowing: The Development of Self, Voice, and Mind,* says,

> They [the Vygotsky camp] argue that play itself is a precursor to symbolization and meaning making. Play provides children with their first experiences of creating metaphors, where an object and the children's actions combine to suggest other objects and events. Thus, when children saddle a stick and ride off on their imaginary horses, the stick becomes a symbol for the horse; and that symbol and the power of their own ideas govern their behavior. The physical stick becomes a tool that helps them dislodge the meaning of horse from its usual embodiment. In play, it is the meaning chosen by children that determines the significance of the stick. Play provides children with their first opportunities for adopting a pretend or hypothetical stance.
>
> In the ordinary course of development, the use of play metaphors gives way to language—a consensually validated symbol system—allowing for more precise communication of meaning between persons...Impulsive behavior gives way to behavior that is guided by the actor's own symbolic representation of hopes, plans and meaning. Without playing, conversing, listening to others, and drawing out their own voice, people fail to develop a sense that they can talk and think things through.

Cognitive psychologists see language as an extremely important aspect of self-definition. Play enhances language development. It encourages the use of the metaphor, or a word signifying something else, and so leads to language, as language itself is a signifier pointing to something else. The word *apple* is not the apple, but rather the signifier we use for the fruit itself.

Natural Learning Rhythms embraces the cognitive perspective and goes much further. Play leads to language, but then language becomes the field of play. Moreover, language cannot be restricted to words or verbal-linguistic intelligence. Communication is a totality—a sharing in common, an attempt at communion, at intimacy, at relational knowledge. It includes all noticeable aspects, such as context, dispositions of the communicators, culturally defined values ascribed to the sign, and the capacities of each communicator. The medium is the message, the content is the message, and the dispositions of the communicators are the message.

BodyBeing children play with words, develop language, and actualize a more complex self. Does the same happen in the other stages? Yes. Play remains the medium in which mastery develops. FeelingBeing children play with social relationships, IdealBeing children idealize a self and play with identities, and ReasonableBeing children—organizing their world to optimize interconnectedness—play with system creation.

Reasonableness implies a strong connection to self, developed in IdealBeing; a strong connection to others, developed in FeelingBeing; and a strong connection to one's place and belongingness in the world, developed in BodyBeing. These strong connections provide the freedom to fully embrace dialogue and to cut into the meaning of self and life. Perhaps this is why Plato believed dialogue, the favored communication mode for ReasonableBeing children, to be hypothetical and thus a field of play.

Chapter Five

SPIRITUALITY

Many have come to teach the holiness of God,
But still there is not peace in the world.
Many have come to teach the holiness of man,
And still there is not peace in the world.
When many come to teach the holiness of children,
Then there will be peace in the world.

—Rabbi Shlomo Carlebach

The work of child developmentalists spans many cultures and has added to my understanding of the way children organize their world. Most developmentalists believe that their approach can be applied to the whole child. A behaviorist, for example, presumes that the child's behavior reveals the nature of the child. They hold to the paradigm of logical positivism, which asserts that only that which is observable and measurable is real, and they defend their approach through quantifiable research methodologies. They then produce a valuable library of the behaviors of children.

Cognitive psychologists wonder about the workings of the mind. Keyed by the genetic epistemology of Jean Piaget, they probe the child's innate capacities to construct reality. As we have established, epistemology is the study of knowledge—the investigation of how we know what we know. In other words, Piaget attempted to answer the question, what are the innate cognitive capacities and how do they develop?

Piaget and his many colleagues over the years have extended the inquiry into human development far beyond behavior. Now a respectable cognitive psychologist must be current with brain research and the multitude of studies on language, perception, and emotions.

Cognitive psychologists have provided us with valuable information on the way humans develop mental constructions of their world.

However, there is much more to the way children construct reality than can be discerned just from their cognitive constructions. Three critical aspects of the child's reality do not receive their full measure of attention in either behaviorism or cognitive developmental psychology. First, children live within their family and community, which includes their school. Second, there is more to the mind than can be measured in experiments. Third, children learn through multiple modalities, including spirituality.

Fortunately, other schools of psychology have also investigated the way children organize their world. Social psychologists have established that the social relationships of the child have a profound effect of the child's organization of reality. Spiritually aware people, such as Sri Aurobindo, Hazrat Inayat Khan, Krishnamurti, and Goethe, have insisted that the child's spiritual development must be considered. Humanistic psychologists, such as Rogers and Maslow, have combined the two. Though not specifically developmentalists, they have insisted that children are innately drawn to greatness and health. They also reintroduced the importance of interpersonal relationships to the well-being of children. Transpersonal and integral psychologists, such as Alfred Adler, Carl Jung, Ken Wilber, Stan Grof, and Roberto Assagioli, have dabbled in child development while emphasizing the spiritual nature of children.

Educators also have made significant original contributions. Many of them, including Montessori, Steiner, and Froebel, have brought attention to the fact that optimal learning occurs when the learning environment nurtures the developmental capacities of children. They insist that the spiritual nature of the child be included. In fact, they claim, and I agree, that it is through nurturing innate developmental capacities that the spiritual breathes freely. The quality of learning, interpersonal relationships, social competence, and spiritual actualization depend on appreciation of the way children organize their world and, specifically, the development of the capacities of each life stage.

Benefiting from the work of colleagues past and present, Natural Learning Rhythms carefully assesses the information from these and many other sources. It also draws deeply from over twenty years of conscientious fieldwork, which refreshes and modifies its insights. From this perspective, the following is asserted.

- Children have innate capacities. These capacities have developmental trajectories.
- A child's organization of reality draws upon the available capacities.
- The development of the capacities is greatly dependent on the relationships with the people in the child's life.
- Every child attempts to optimize their capacities.

These points switch the focus for the way to appreciate children. Instead of their behaviors, cognitive development, learning modes, or spiritual qualities, the focus becomes their organization of their reality. The questions that come to mind are: What are the purpose, meaning, and goal of these capacities and qualities? What coordinates their timing?

Like the day dawning—like color added to a black-and-white world— the answers to these questions bring life, joy, meaning, connection, and compelling engagement to life with children. They allow us to see, feel, and be intimate with—to know—the child's reality. Once reality is shared, the odds of actualizing optimal well-being skyrocket. Parents and professionals are able to recognize and provide support for their innate capacities. Relationships evolve in which all family members grow, learn, and appreciate one another. Responses to conflict and dysfunction beyond symptom reduction or a return to "normalcy" appear that bring forth optimal well-being. Many problems disappear; others are approached with mutual respect and without antagonism.

What is this silver bullet? What is this "thing" we finally see that was there all the time and was implicit in so much of the study of children? What is this key that opens the door into the child's organization of reality?

It is the realization that each life stage has an organizing principle. The organizing principle is inherent and lives as a faculty in every human. There are no exceptions. It organizes all activities toward the best expression of health and wholeness available; i.e., optimal well-being. Like a vibrant river, well-being moves through the mind and body of the child. If thwarted, the mind and body bring attention to the problem, usually through conflict and dysfunction. Natural Learning Rhythms strongly suggests that we reinvigorate that which is well rather than focusing on pathology and spending precious resources on attempts to alleviate symptoms.

Focusing on the organizing principle accomplishes the important task of eliminating all terms with a religious connotation while still hon-

oring the inherent spirituality of the child. Providing environments for
the organizing principle to manifest optimal well-being *is* actualizing the
spiritual potential of the child. It is "beingness." It needs no reference to
esoteric terms or religious ideologies.

Each developmental stage has its own organizing principle. There
are secondary organizing principles as well. To live with a nourished
organizing principle allows the child the optimal circumstances for self-
knowledge to emerge. Again, this is optimal well-being. To support the
child to live in optimal well-being is the goal and purpose of parenting
and education. When the organizing principle receives the proper nourishment, all the capacities of the child—physical, emotional, cognitive,
and spiritual—flourish. Moreover, they flourish together, supporting one
another, emerging as a synergy in which the whole is greater than the
sum of its parts. And parents and professionals participate in this emergent whole—this self of the child—co-creating a reality that promises scin-
tillating growth for all.

The following table shows the organizing principle for each of the
life stages of childhood. The stages are named to provide placeholders
and reminders of the Natural Learning Rhythms approach. Naming
stages to reflect the intent of the developmental approach is a consistent
practice within the profession.

Table 5-1 The Four Principle Developmental Stages of Childhood

Stage	Age of Child	Organizing Principle	Secondary Organizing Principles
BodyBeing	Thru 8 ½	Rightful place	Boundary creation, strength
FeelingBeing	8 ½ - 13	Trust	Reciprocal cooperation
IdealBeing	13 - 17½	Autonomy	Personal power, free-dom, responsibility
ReasonableBeing	17½ - 23	Interconnectedness, Humor, Humility	Systems creation, humor, humility

Realization of the organizing principle leads to many questions.
Most important, how do we nurture each organizing principle in the
moment of its developmental supremacy? To answer this requires that we

know the nature of the stage. Thankfully, this brings us full circle. We have the work of the developmentalists and educators, and our field-work, to help us.

Other questions include: How do we apply this approach to family dynamics, to pedagogy, and to healing wounds? What are the implications for awakening self-growth for parents and professionals? The scope of these questions is breathtaking. They place each of us in the heart of our most precious concerns—optimal well-being, social competence, mutually supportive family relationships, spiritual awakening, meaningful and successful education, healing wounds, and the ability to work with problems and conflicts without turning into the parenting police.

Wisdom

The organizing principle is a psychological faculty inherent in every human. It has a locus, a purpose, and the means to accomplish that purpose. The locus, or space, that it occupies is similar to that for all psychological faculties. Memory, for example, does not have a form in the same sense as a concrete pillar, yet no one denies that memory exists and occupies a psychological space. That space is known by its function; to recall something from the past is to use one's memory; to organize reality, one uses the organizing principle. Recall is the means memory uses. A purpose of memory is continuity. The purpose of the organizing principle is optimal well-being, which means actualization of the physical, emotional, cognitive, and spiritual capacities of the developmental moment.

This is not intended to indicate a one-to-one analogy between memory and the organizing principle, but rather to point out that the organizing principle is a natural psychological faculty and is known in the same way as other psychological faculties. Other examples include perception, abstraction, and concentration.

The organizing principle organizes reality to maximize well-being. Wisdom is the medium in which well-being resides. It is not the source of well-being, for that remains a mystery. The organizing principle reaches into wisdom to know well-being and then applies it in the child's life.

As with the organizing principle, educators, psychologists, and secular and spiritual philosophers have anticipated inherent wisdom. The list is really quite long and includes such people as Thomas Merton, who spoke of a "hidden wholeness" in children; Alfred Adler, who named the child's unbending draw to greatness; Joseph Chilton Pearce, who spoke of stage-specific wisdom; Paul Tillich, who coined the term *ultimacy*; and

Ken Wilber, who made it the subject of *The Atman Project*, his extensive and erudite survey of child development.

Wisdom draws each human through the organizing principle of the developmental stage. Wisdom is a creative fount replete with all the child needs to fully actualize the potential in each developmental stage. Full actualization means more than can be said, but some facets include nonalienation, which means no illusion of separation; satisfying expression of individual talents and proclivities; competence in social as well as intellectual endeavors; and the ability to access the resources, within developmental guidelines, that further well-being.

Wisdom contains all the possibilities for the child in an infinite array.[17] This should not be surprising to anyone. Molecular biology also reveals an infinite array of genetic possibilities. Every human, for instance, has unique DNA. There are many humans on this planet and many more arriving every day, yet there is a unique DNA configuration for each person.

Moreover, every human system has a staggering array of possibilities. Consider, for example, the central nervous system and its captain, the brain. We are only beginning to realize how little we know of it, how complex it is in design, and how malleable it is as it responds to its environment. With more connections than all the stars in all the known galaxies, the human brain certainly provides infinite possibilities while expressing itself uniquely in each of the many humans on this planet.

Wisdom is of the same nature, though radically different in design, manifestation, and function. While investigating wisdom presents a different set of challenges than investigating the brain, the project is neither more daunting nor less important. As with the brain, wisdom has been the subject of intense inquiry for all of human history. This is not the moment to recount the history of that inquiry, though a natural history of wisdom would be a fascinating study. My aim is to establish wisdom as real and present, as natural to all humans. First we must answer the most common objection to the existence of wisdom—it cannot be touched, located, or measured.

We have already seen that psychological faculties cannot be located. Memory, that most important faculty for data storage, retention, and retrieval, has no known location in the brain.[18] Yet no one denies that it exists, because the effects of memory can be measured; indeed, it is the way all students are graded.

Can the effects of wisdom be seen? Unquestionably. Ethics, aesthetics, meaning, love, trust, insight—none of these are explainable by an epistemology that does not include wisdom. Each of us has experienced one or more of these. What would life be like without them? Empty. Unrecognizable. Life, *as we know it*, would not exist.

The difficulty many people have in considering wisdom is that even its effects are not measurable. That assessment is accurate. No one can measure love, ethics, aesthetics, trust, meaning, or insight. They cannot be touched, located, or measured. My answer is the same one Einstein had posted is his laboratory: "Not everything that counts can be counted and not everything that can be counted, counts."

Unfortunately, most people find it difficult to acknowledge the existence of wisdom. This is ironic. The very gift by which we know is the very aspect of ourselves that we most doubt.

Aristotle, a great naturalist, coined the term *entelechy* to describe how wisdom expresses itself in humans. Distilled to its essence, entelechy means the essential informing principle of a living thing. In religion, entelechy meant the soul. For instance, in Goethe's version, it is his entelechy that Faust trades with the devil. Soul, however, means too many different things for our purposes. Also, Natural Learning Rhythms eschews religious terms and any sectarian bias. Wisdom is natural; humans are born with it. Our interest lies with its value and use in life for each of us. To tie it to soul, age, or religious concepts obfuscates the fact that wisdom lives in children—and that parents, guardians, teachers, and other professionals can create environments that support wisdom and can live in wisdom-based relationships.

The list of "entellectuals" is long and distinguished. Gottfried Leibniz, a founder of calculus and originator of the notion of the perennial philosophy, used entelechy extensively to describe an organism's self-sufficiency and as the source of their "internal activities." Adler used the term to help describe the child's inexorable movement towards greatness. Froebel, and later Montessori, referred to entelechy to help describe the vital nature of the child and then developed pedagogies designed to maximize this vitality. Carl Jung, Gregory Bateson, Thomas Merton, and many others have used entelechy as a springboard to deepen appreciation of the source of knowledge, awareness, and the ability to self-reflect.

Wisdom is not something we put into a child—it is already there. In his book *The Farther Reaches of Human Nature*, Abraham Maslow asks, "What if the organism is seen as having 'biological wisdom'?" In every stage of life, there is wisdom that is present and available to the human. In every stage of childhood, wisdom is present and available in the child. We are born with it. The wisdom we are referring to is the same as that which Gregory Bateson called "systemic wisdom." In his book *Steps to an*

Ecology of Mind, Bateson defined wisdom as an awareness of the inter-locking circuits that connect the elements of the natural world. He said, "I use 'wisdom' as a word for recognition of and guidance by a knowl-edge of the total systemic creature."

In Natural Learning Rhythms, we refer to wisdom that is in the moment—the simultaneous knowledge/action that optimizes the well-being of the organism. This, we believe, is exactly what Bateson means when he states that wisdom is "recognition of and guidance by a knowl-edge of the total systemic creature." In a state of optimal well-being, a person can experience that which is most meaningful, beautiful, and true for their developmental stage and their moment of life.

Those who come to know wisdom throughout childhood know the best responses to life. In sequence throughout the twenty-three years of childhood, they come to know their place and their boundaries, to trust themselves and others, to govern themselves, and to appreciate their con-nection with life and the universe. This knowledge allows wise people to meet life's challenges reasonably and with great courage, strength, and perseverance. It allows them to be with their families and with children in ways that include firm boundaries, mutual respect, and generous sup-port for the wisdom in each person. It allows deep intuitive satisfaction that is beyond concepts, societal pressures, techniques and tricks, parent-ing as you were parented, and teaching as you were taught. It allows con-nection in the moment and mutual engagement. It allows families to solve problems without becoming adversarial. It allows enjoyment, care, curiosity, and novel approaches to seemingly intractable conundrums. It allows humor and humility with no loss of dignity and integrity.

Wisdom is inherent. It is not gained or taught. It is not achieved. If it is not denied, it is present and active. If it is denied, then it lives in the shadow—active yet unseen, limited in expression by the surrounding environment, and always ready to emerge full blown, unlimited.

Wisdom is infinitely creative. Therefore, nothing final or complete can be said to describe the child who lives with her organizing principle and wisdom matrix properly nourished. This way of living is wisdom-based emergent self-discovery. It is the joy of living. Wisdom-based rela-tionships are possible for whole families. This is what Natural Learning Rhythms is all about—this deep spirituality that lives in families and their relationships.

Relationship

The word *relationship* derives its meaning from the context in which it is used. Everyone is familiar with defining a relationship by the interactions between people. I respect you and so therefore listen closely to what you have to say. You do the same and we then have a respectful relationship. In a myriad of verbal and nonverbal ways—language, intonation, posture, facial expressions, what has been left unsaid, the process and structure of the conversation, subjective and shared feelings—we have signified to one another what we accept as "listening" and "respectful." Likewise, we could decide that we have a disrespectful relationship, or a kind one, or an adversarial one, and so on.

Part of this type of relationship is the status each person brings to it. For example, most parents have deeply ingrained expectations about the relationships with their children. These expectations vary greatly, of course, and are influenced by the dynamic matrix of their biographical history, ethnicity, wealth, and cultural fabric. The child enters the world with the parents' expectations intact and ready to be expressed. These expectations are then modified in the interactions with the child so that often, when asked, parents will answer with a description of the way the child meets those expectations. I have heard a parent say, "He's very loving but also incredibly stubborn." And, "She's so cute and smart, too. Come here, Rachel, and tell us how to spell *elephant*."

Contrast this context of relationship with the following:

I consider a tree.

I can look on it as a picture, stiff column in a shock of light, or splash of green shot with the delicate blue and silver of the background.

I can perceive it as movement: flowing veins on clinging, pressing pith, suck of the roots, breathing of the leaves, ceaseless commerce with the earth and air—and the obscure growth itself.

I can classify it in a species and study it as a type in its structure and mode of life.

I can subdue its actual presence and form so sternly that I recognize it only as an expression of [physical] laws...

I can dissipate it in number, in pure numerical relation.

In all this the tree remains my object, occupies space and time, and has its nature and constitution.

It can, however, also come about, if I have both will and grace, that in considering the tree I become bound up in relation to it. The tree is no longer an It...

To effect this it is not necessary for me to give up any of the ways in which I consider the tree. There is nothing from which

I would turn my eyes away in order to see, and no knowledge that I would have to forget. Rather it is everything, picture and movement, species and type, law and number, indivisibly united in this event.

Everything belonging to the tree is in this...all present as a single whole.

The tree is no impression, no play of my imagination, no value depending on my mood; but it is bodied over against me and has to do with me, as I with it—only in a different way.

Let no attempt be made to sap the strength from the meaning of the relation: relation is mutual.

This quote, from the book *I and Thou* by philosopher and humanitarian Martin Buber, offers a context free of expectation. He realizes that he enters the relationship with categorizations such as species, or perceptions such as the way nutrients move through the leaves of the tree, and so he has no pretense of mystical or supernatural insight. But by refusing to live by those labels—to make the tree into an "It"—he affirms that existence is mutual, interwoven, prior, and indestructible.

How does he apply this to human relationships?

If I face a human being as my Thou, and say the primary word I-Thou to him, he is not a thing among things, and does not consist of things.

Thus human being is not He or She, bounded from every other He and She, a specific point in space and time within the net of the world, nor is he a nature able to be experienced and described, a loose bundle of named qualities...

And just as prayer is not in time but time in prayer, sacrifice not in space but space in sacrifice, and to reverse the relations is to abolish the reality, so with the [person] to whom I say Thou. I do not meet with him [or her] at some time and place or other. I can set him [or her] in a particular time and place; I must continually do it, but I set only a He or a She, that is an It, no longer my Thou.

Even if the man to whom I say Thou is not aware of it in the midst of his experience, yet relations may exist. For Thou is more than It realizes.

Again, there is no denial. It is often necessary to relate to one another in time and space, in the context of experience and behavior in external interactions. But that, in itself, does not allow genuine relationship. It puts the relationship in time rather than time in the relationship. I-Thou relationship is the context—the frame by which time and all other variables take on their meaning. In that context, all the human attributes exist; nothing is denied. Meeting occurs—spontaneous, creative, alive. It is the meeting in which wisdom breathes as human beings.

I-Thou is not a regression to a fused state in which a person is one with another. They are two, but they exist in the unity of relationship that is an inherent spiritual capacity in each of them. As two people living in the context of I-Thou, they come to know one another and to know themselves. This is not a denial of our humanness; it is an affirmation of our beingness.

Many of the entellectuals who have turned their attention to relationships in families and with children have their own way of offering the same essential message.

Jiddhu Krishnamurti was discovered as a young boy by Theosophist luminaries at the end of the nineteenth century. By far the largest spiritual movement outside of organized religion—and still boasting millions of members in most countries in the world—Theosophy emphasizes occult and mystical experience and contact with hidden masters who appear to the initiated. Krishnamurti was to be the new avatar, and The Order of the Star was established for his followers as part of the Theosophical network. Adopted by the leader Annie Besant and educated in England, Krishnamurti was to announce his ascendancy during his twenty-ninth year at a huge convocation in India. With his world listening, Krishnamurti renounced the entire movement as a farce, claiming that "Truth is a pathless land." He steered people toward self-knowledge and away from gurus, hidden masters, slavish devotion to unrealized fantasies, and mass movements. You could say he walked away from the throne. He spent the rest of his life speaking with people, and he offered many profound insights into the conditioned mind and its imprisoning characteristics; and the nature of knowledge, freedom, relationship, and education. He started several schools in Europe and India and influenced many others.

In 1953, Krishnamurti wrote *Education and the Significance of Life*, detailing aspects of the well-being and greatness available when teachers relate appropriately to students. Concerning how to dissolve conditioning, he said:

The right kind of educator, seeing the inward nature of free-dom, helps each individual student to observe and understand his own self-projected values and impositions; he helps him to become aware of the conditioning influences about him, and of his own desires, both of which limit his mind and breed fear...[19]

How important is relationship? It is nothing less than the way of freedom.

Freedom comes into being only through self-knowledge in one's daily occupations, that is, in one's relationship with peo-ple, with things, with ideas and with nature.[20]

And what is relationship? It is nothing short of existence itself.

Existence is relationship; whether we belong to an organ-ized religion or not, whether we are worldly or caught up in ideals, our suffering can only be resolved by the understanding of ourselves in relationship.[21]

Humanistic psychology gave us two brilliant mentors in the latter half of the twentieth century: Carl Rogers and Abraham Maslow. Others certainly contributed—notably George Leonard and Michael Murphy in education—but Rogers and Maslow laid down the tracks for an approach to psychology that emphasized actualizing the human potential.

Maslow held that relationship ought to be "resacralized"; that is, people should see one another as "under the aspect of eternity."[22] He hated the medical model, and believed it disastrous to view therapy clients as sick. Maslow found a way of relating he called rhapsodic com-munication, in which a shared experience that includes parallel feelings allows for an intimacy in which trust and health are nurtured.[23]

Firmly committed to education and the progenitor of client-cen-tered therapy, Carl Rogers focused on relationships that brought forth the "fully functioning" person. In these relationships, people hold one another with "unconditional positive regard." This was not a lightweight talking, but a man who helped many play in the field of self-actualiza-tion, valued hard-core empirical evidence, and challenged the educa-tional hierarchy of his time. Unconditional positive regard does not mean that you ignore the constraints a person has, but that you approach him or her with trust and support for developing their highest potential. In *Freedom to Learn*, he wrote of the difficulty in describing the attitude that he had both experienced and seen others employ.

> It is hard to know what term to put to it so I shall use several. I think of prizing the learner, prizing her feelings, her opinions, her person. It is a caring for the learner, but a nonpossessive caring. It is an acceptance of this other individual as a separate person, having worth in her own right. It is a basic trust—a belief that this other person is somehow fundamentally trustworthy. Whether we call it prizing, acceptance, trust, or by some other term [Rogers uses "realness" in other places]...the facilitator who has a considerable degree of this attitude can be fully acceptant of the fear and hesitation of the student...as well as acceptance of the pupil's satisfaction in achievement.[24]

The appreciation of relationship as sacred, as necessary for self-knowledge, as critical for freedom, as the cornerstone of optimal well-being, is everywhere. Krishnamurti links it directly to wisdom.

> Wisdom is not marketable, it is not merchandise that can be bought with the price of learning or discipline. Wisdom cannot be found in books (not even this one!); it cannot be accumulated, memorized or stored up...Wisdom does not come through fear and oppression, but through the observation and understanding of everyday incidents in human relationship.[25]

Gregory Bateson also links relationship and wisdom. Bateson's "systemic wisdom" extends through all systems. He called it the "pattern that connects" because it is always fully operative within any system and between systems. A genuine Renaissance man, his inquiries extended into culture, communication, education, family dynamics, and ecology. Incisively, he arrived at the insight that mind and nature formed a single system, "a necessary unity," and the feedback between the two determined the reality of each.[26]

Systemic wisdom also provides a nonsectarian appreciation of spirituality. The sacred is inherent in the relationship between mind and nature and is realized by "being responsive to the pattern that connects." In this moment of responsiveness, of what Buber would call I-Thou, one finds the aesthetics of beauty, truth, and goodness. By participating in the pattern, you transcend the pattern: You see it everywhere and so participate in a greater whole— in a more complex reality—in which aesthetic is a natural quality.

Now we come to an essential point. There have to be two entities for being, for existence. If there were just one, Bateson points out, "it would be not different from being and not different from non-being, unknowable, the sound of one hand clapping." Two entities come into existence together in relationship. And the context that they create, the meaning given, depends upon their "double description." It is *never* one or the other. Moreover, the feedback between systems ensures that this double description dynamically evolves and can never be static.

The essence of existence—of being—is relationship. It is the way we know, the reality we live, the pattern that connects. And the sacred is immanent within those relationships.

Bateson playfully posits a God called Eco. Eco is not personal and instantly offers aesthetic feedback into the environment—into mind/nature. In other words, when there is no responsiveness to the pattern that connects—when the contexts and hierarchies are ignored and meaning is imposed upon rather than derived from their relationship— pollution immediately arises. Truth, beauty, and goodness are obfuscated. Pollution can be in the system of mind, the system of nature, the mind-nature system, the system of family, the family-community system, education, forests, governments, and so on. Mind/nature is a necessary unity, and the feedback among its systems is instantaneous and impersonal.

Spirituality

We now have the holy three: organizing principle, wisdom, and relationship. Nurturing their ongoing, dynamic exchanges are all that is necessary for the child to actualize her spiritual capacity.

I am not saying what spirituality *is*. I cannot, nor can anyone. Actually, there is no need to define it. Knowledge is familiar, intimate, and in the bones. Spiritual realization is known the moment it occurs.

Natural Learning Rhythms does not deny that there are unseen forces or bodies that play in the child's psyche. Great educators and sages, notably Rudolf Steiner in the West, Sri Aurobindo in the East, and Hazarat Inayat Khan in the "middle," have described some of these unseen forces and detailed how and when they arise in childhood. Ken Wilber, in *The Atman Project* and subsequent books, has attempted to trace the spiritual development of the child from the perspective of transpersonal psychology. In different ways, these works talk about forces like the etheric, astral, and causal bodies; about vital and psychic centers;

and about uroboric and centaur realms. These works add an important dimension to the discussion of the spiritual capacity of the child, and I shall compare them with Natural Learning Rhythms later.

Now, though, I must explicitly state that there is no absolutely no need for any parent or educator to concern themselves with these unseen forces. The child's spiritual potential can be fully realized by meeting the needs of the organizing principle, wisdom, and relationship. It can be done in families without any reference to a religion and without any special spiritual disciplines or practices. At the same time, it does not interfere with any cultural or religious predisposition a family might have unless the customs of that predisposition interfere with optimal well-being in the holy three.

These three form a dynamic system, with each feeding back into the other and constantly navigating toward health, holiness, and wholeness. It is dialectical, with new syntheses continually emerging. This system operates in the context of the developmental stage of the child. Therefore, it appears differently in each stage and requires the unique nurturing of the given stage. Any attempt to facilitate the child's spiritual capacity only has meaning as the capacities and limitations of that developmental stage allow.

As Bateson says, it is an egregious epistemological mistake to ignore or misjudge the context in which a system lives. So often, spiritually caring people make this mistake. Perhaps the most common example is the idea that the child is not spiritually aware because they lack the adult's more mature expression of spirituality. The child is seen as separate, damaged, confused, embedded in original sin and bad karma, and unable—due to immaturity—to redeem himself. Adults who see children this way have simply taken their concept of spiritual awareness and imposed it on the child. The same criticism applies to those who see children as closer to God because they have "just arrived from the disembodied realms." This simply has nothing to do with the child as we know her. Imposition of adult contexts and suppositions of heavenly realms are agendas that cloud, not elucidate, the relationship with the child.

Bateson's Eco is present here, for when contexts are not cared for then pollution immediately arises. This pollution will infect the child, the family, and the community, for these systems interact intimately. The pollution will have psychological and physical manifestations. Spiritual capacities will not be realized. Natural Learning Rhythms' response to this type of pollution is the subject of chapter 10.

Nourishing the Organizing Principle

It may sound simple, but the doorway to optimal well-being is just this: Nourish the organizing principle and optimal well-being, including spiritual development, follows. Relationship and the organizing principle are hand-in-hand. Only the parent or teacher in relationship to the organizing principle can understand it and nourish it. Health and vibrancy in the organizing principle guarantee access to wisdom, which is so important for spiritual awareness.

Once it is understood, nurturing the organizing principle can be done by most families with confidence. As Bateson says, nature, life, and Eco cannot be mocked. The potential for optimal well-being—for spiritual awareness—would not be granted unless there was a natural way to actualize it.

Here's how to do it.

Two caveats must be kept in mind throughout.

First, every child is unique. Appreciation of Natural Learning Rhythms does not lead to thinking about children as a mass, as stamped-out cookies in large batches. Just the opposite. When you see how your child actualizes rightful place, trust, autonomy, or interconnectedness, you will see their unique qualities and talents. No two children will do it the same way. Natural Learning Rhythms does not ask you to relate to children as *It*, but as *Thou*. The whole being that your child is will be more, not less, available when the organizing principle is nourished.

Second, each developmental stage has a unique set of nourishment requirements. All children are unique in the blend of nourishments they require and the way they process, or digest, them. It is the parent's responsibility to provide an appropriate blend of nourishments for their child.

Working with nourishments supports appreciation of the individual child and of diversity in our society. Just as each child needs vitamins, protein, and all the other proper nutrients, so in each stage there are developmental nourishments that the child requires. Just as each child has unique combinations of foods that they can digest well, and so it is with the developmental nourishments. Therefore, each child must be seen for who they are, or the blend will be incorrect. There is no right or wrong, and each culture—each family—can and must find its own way of preparing and offering the nourishments. No particular culture has more or less capability to provide the nourishments than another.

The following table summarizes the organizing principles, secondary organizing principles, and nourishments for each developmental stage.

Table 5-2 Developmental Table with Nourishments

Characteristics of Each Stage	BodyBeing	FeelingBeing	IdealBeing	ReasonableBeing
Primary Nourishment	Loving touch	Feeling mentors	Sensitive respect	Mature recognition, recognition of: commitment, equality, achievement, recognition
Secondary Nourishment	Security, warmth, textured sensory environments, flexibility	Fairness, justice, caring, concern, honesty, adventure, adaptability	Challenges, adventure, peer sensitivity, personal space, opportunity to explore ideals	Comparison, exploration, experimentation, discernment, recapitulation
Primary Organizing Principle	Rightful place	Trust	Autonomy, self-governance	Interconnectedness, humor, humility
Secondary Organizing Principle(s)	Boundaries, strength	Reciprocal cooperation	Identity construction, personal power, freedom	Systems creation, intentionality, incisiveness

Nourishing BodyBeing

Development begins at conception. Sensation is the mode of ingesting the world and selecting the needed nourishment from the environment. The touch centers of the brain are among the first specialized areas to become active and are more complete than any other at birth.[27] We naturally and universally envelop the newborn with touch. Breastfeeding demands it. We intuitively know that surrounding the baby with warmth, gentleness, and caresses creates the safe milieu for bonding and health. Loving touch, in its widest meaning of both physical and psychological sensations, is the most important nourishment for the BodyBeing child.

Many of us can easily comprehend the overarching importance of loving touch through the toddler years, but frequently we find it a stretch to see the same value through the age of eight. The need for loving touch, and the other nourishments, remains constant. However, its form must be modified continually as the child's perceptions and abilities change during the stage.

Loving touch establishes rightful place. It is the mutually recognized way to support the child's innate capacity to set boundaries. The child then accesses his ability to interact from strength and security and yearns to move out and explore the world. Without strength and security, the development of play and social interactions will be impaired.

Loving touch is key, but not sufficient by itself. The child's psychological balance requires other kinds of nourishments as well: security, warmth, textured sensory environments, and flexibility. As with physical diet, each child requires a unique blend of these nourishments for psycho-emotional health.

Security refers to both physical and psychological safety. For BodyBeing children, security often translates to knowing when and how they are to be cared for. Many children of this age need some regular routine. However, too much security can smother. It is critical to remember that boundaries can be explored only at the edge, where they exist. Throughout all developmental stages, there are greater opportunities for learning if we accompany children to their edge and provide unobtrusive safety nets rather than hold them to our notions of security. Therefore, security must be carefully balanced with the nourishment of flexibility, described below.

Warmth is the nourishing sensation of intimacy and tenderness; it is of the heart. BodyBeing children look for warmth everywhere and will even transfer it to objects such as stuffed animals.

Textured sensory environments refers to people, environments, and objects that support and invite sensation exploration. A good example is sensation-based learning tools that are inviting, interesting, creative, and pleasurable. Maria Montessori is among the educators who have long recognized the importance of the sensory environment. She says it best in *The Absorbent Mind.*

> The developing child not only acquires the faculties of man: strength, intelligence, language; but, at the same time, he adapts the being he is constructing to the conditions of the

world about him. And this it is that gives virtue to his particular form of psychology, which is so different from ours. Adults admire their environment; they can remember it and think about it; but the child absorbs it.[28]

Flexibility means that we nourish the child by offering sufficient time and patience to allow him to experience the world through sensation exploration. It is the ability on the part of the adult to yield, to engage in give and take, to be pliable, and to be open to modifying schedules. Flexibility leads to self-empowerment—which can occur only within a secure context. An unsafe environment is not flexible. Again, Montessori stated, "Therefore, it happens that if a child is prevented from using his powers of movement as soon as they are ready, this child's mental development is obstructed."[29]

Nourishing FeelingBeing

Who to trust? How to tell? Shaky in trust of themselves, due to the awareness of personal mortality and the novelty of the complexity of feelings, the child naturally turns to feeling mentors for guidance. FeelingBeing children seek the company of adults, older children, and, to a lesser extent, peers who feel trustworthy. It is not what is said, but how one *feels*, that is known.

We often describe the child's experience by a simple visualization. Imagine that each of your feelings has a color. The color scheme is your own creation. Now imagine that each of your feelings pulses that color and that the child can see the entire image in each instant. The colors do not blend. So, if we are happy to hear from our spouse and angry at the message, both colors pulse simultaneously. Analogously, the child "sees" the colors of the feelings of others. All the feelings of the moment are felt and absorbed, whether spoken or not. In the words of Frances Wickes, a colleague of Carl Jung's and perhaps the first transpersonal psychologist to focus exclusively on children, this direct reception of the feeling stage of adults by children is "a pitiless truth." Wickes traced the great majority of childhood dysfunctions back to the unconscious unresolved issues of their parents.[30] We cannot hide from our children; their perceptual capabilities are keenly attuned to knowing us for who we are. Their health, their survival, and their spiritual greatness depend upon it.

The difficult news is that there is no escape; the liberating news is that there is no need for escape, because there is no need for perfection. The notion of perfection, in this context, is oppressive. We all make mistakes. Nature factors our imperfections in as part of the process. It is the denial of our mistakes that hurts children. When one sees one's mistake and takes corrective action, the child is nourished. This is the nourishment of adaptation and allows the child the breath to explore the complexity of feelings without having to get it right or to always be good. Adaptation engenders reciprocal cooperation as it confirms that everyone is learning together.

Adaptation also nourishes the FeelingBeing child's connection with the natural world. All living things adapt. Mistakes and renewal are evident in all natural processes. The FeelingBeing child feels the rhythms of life while simultaneously feeling the greater balance inclusive of predator and prey, death and revival, and the suffering of individual creatures. This is not a logical contradiction to them, but simply the feelings experienced in the moment. They are not trying to reason with the processes of life, they simply feel them.

Often, the child recognizes a mentor by the mentor's willingness to share their feelings honestly, without an ulterior motive and using language in a developmentally appropriate way. Children of this age love to hear life stories, for they allow them to see how feelings developed. It creates trust and intimacy.

Community nourishes the child in several important ways. Community means access to people with a wide variety of feelings and ways of expressing those feelings, which provides a fertile playground for varied emotional explorations. Community means that the rules and regulations of society, so important to developing relationships in any culture, can be ingested and investigated safely, and that trustworthy people will provide feedback on the child's feeling state. Community provides a focus for friendship and relationship.

The child thrives on fairness and will bring attention to that which they believe to be unfair. Acting fairly and providing an environment where children are treated with fairness does not mean satisfying all their desires. In our experience, fairness for children often depends upon us listening to them and, if possible, implementing their suggestions. One listens not only to their complaint, but also to the perspective that lies behind the complaint. When a child says, for instance, that it is unfair that a sibling or a friend received a present and they did not, there is often a feeling of being passed over or uncared for that is at the root of the complaint. Non-adversarial conversation often reveals the deeper issue.

FeelingBeing children are developing their capacity for justice. Fairness is an aspect of justice that has to do with their own world, but justice is a unique capacity that has to do with the social and natural world. FeelingBeing children search the environment to discern whether people are emotionally engaging with others appropriately and whether they are engaging with situations appropriately. Justice has nothing to do with complicated situations such as war on terrorism or whether abortion is good for American society. Their capacities for that kind of analysis are not yet developed. Adults provide justice by living an ethically and ecologically sane life, not by superimposing moral standards based on abstract principles.

FeelingBeing children have an innate capacity for ethics and ecology. This does not refer to ecology as a political or social concern, but simply in its dictionary definition of "an organism's relationship to its environment." In fact, trumpeting ecology to FeelingBeing children displays a lack of trust in their innate capabilities. Children at this age need to develop and practice their natural ethical capacities, not to have ethics imposed from the outside. Likewise, instruction in a formal system of ethics—religious or otherwise—robs them of an inner locus of control by

- A Judicious Judge -

Mona, a superior court judge, attended a Family Retreat with her two FeelingBeing boys. As a busy single mom, she felt challenged by the need to supply adventure and justice to her children. Then, she hit on a novel idea. Why not bring the children to court for some interesting cases? It would be exciting and she would have a wealth of experiences in which to talk about justice.

Other parents in the retreat were interested. Mona told them they could bring their children to any court.

Two months later I spoke with Mona. She said that at first the children didn't understand what has happening and became bored. She asked her nephew, twenty-three, to accompany them and quietly explain the proceedings. The boredom disappeared; the children became enthralled.

Mona couldn't stop raving about the results. The conversation about relationships and justice reached into every aspect of their lives. The children also liked learning about their mother's workplace, a valuable side effect.

Mona had contacted some of the other parents from the retreat. They had mixed results. Some, however, had taken the children to their workplaces and that seemed to be positive nourishment in itself.

making them dependent on others to define their moral relationship to their world.

Elders act justly, and thus simultaneously provide the nourishment of justice, when they trust their children's innate capacity for ethics and ecology and then provide opportunities where the children can learn to fully maximize these capacities. There are many ways to do this, and each family and community can find their own expression. Some avenues to actualize justice are: non-moralistic storytelling, nonjudgmental yet facilitated exposure to other communities, sensitive explorations of varied natural settings, guidance in interpersonal affairs, and activities that allow children to express their feelings without being told what is right or wrong.

Adventure takes on a greater value for FeelingBeing children, as it calls forth that thrilling edge between life and death. For instance, FeelingBeing children are often daredevils and almost all of them, regardless of gender, play some sort of game where they are killed and come back to life, usually in the next breath. Adventure allows elder and child to go to this edge together. The need for adventure must be satisfied, as it nourishes trust in something greater, something beyond, something that cannot be named but can be felt. Adventure calls forth feelings they never experienced before. The children can then experience new appreciation of feelings such as courage, awe, humility, nobleness, danger, and so on.

Children this age seek inspiration through drama, myth, teaching stories, adventure, and nature. The child's emotional literacy expands to feel the meaning in any text. Innuendoes become apparent, and her understanding of character and plot expand tremendously. She vicariously travels to new worlds, feeling the characters and trying on their personas while expanding her horizons in relationship to what inspires her.

Nourishing IdealBeing

Under the aegis of autonomy and freedom, IdealBeing children project ideals and construct identities. This is at once an imperative and fragile process.

Sensitive respect is the key nourishment for IdealBeing. Sensitive respect tells the IdealBeing child that it is both safe and intelligent to explore identities. Nourished by sensitive respect, the child accepts the process of her own development with a minimum of self-consciousness and the absence of guilt. Ideal creation and the attendant identity explorations are accepted as valid ways to find one's core nature. When given the same latitude to identity explorations as for the infant learning to walk or for the FeelingBeing child learning to decipher interpersonal relationships, the IdealBeing child has the freedom to discern the value of each identity

Offering sensitive respect acknowledges the IdealBeing child's autonomy and their exploration of freedom. If the explorations seem too extreme, then the respectful response is to co-create the boundaries with the child. This co-creation is not a battle of the wills, but rather a mutually agreed upon plan that takes the needs of each person into account. Often, the parent's reluctance to state their own needs inhibits co-creation. Rather than state their fears about children wanting to stay out late or to associate with a new set of peers, parents often impose a rule, such as a curfew, and then cite an "objective" fact in an attempt to validate the rule. For instance, they might say that fifteen-year-old children should not be out past eleven o'clock. IdealBeing children realize the rule is a cover-up. They know the parent has fears. To hinge the discussion on the rule is disrespectful and often leads to arguments. When the fears are exposed, most children, especially if they are well nourished, see their validity. They also appreciate the honesty; they are being respected. Most will respect the parent in return. The parent and child can then seek solutions that satisfy each of their needs. A case history is offered in the sidebar to illustrate co-creation, and the subject is explored in further detail in the section "Creating and Maintaining Healthy Boundaries" in chapter 10.

- Co-Creating with IdealBeing -

Josh, fifteen, did not read social signals well, and many children ridiculed him.

At one of our family programs, Josh's father, Barry, spoke during a parent circle: "Josh is a very social guy. But his behaviors don't get him what he wants. He should have enough signals by now to know what to do. But he does not seem to be able to learn that and really take it in. Also, he doesn't want to listen to me. I want to know how to help him."

Later, Josette accompanied Barry when he went to talk with Josh about the day's activities. Josh was sullen and unresponsive. He blamed Barry for treating him like a kid and wanted to leave. Barry started to react by laying down the law: Josh wasn't going anywhere. Josh stomped off. Josette followed, waving at Barry to follow her.

Josh, of course, did not want to speak with her. She tried twice, and then told him that staff had told her that he had a hard time and it had something to do with cursing. Josh turned on her.

"Other kids curse all the time. How come when I do it everyone hates me?"

"I don't know," Josette answered truthfully, "but I know it must be painful for you. Do you want to try to figure it out?"

"You just said you don't know. What good is that?"

"I don't and you don't. Maybe we do together. Let's start with what happened."

Josh described an incident in which he clearly cursed loudly and at an inappropriate time.

"I would have been offended too," Josette said. "It sounds like you were trying too hard to be noticed or something like that, and you just blurted your curse for attention. I know what that's like," she continued softly. "It's embarrassing."

"Well, yeah, it is. I get going and I don't know how to stop. I want to stop, but I just can't. It's like a train going and I just can't stop it."

Josette had two choices. She could have started by trying to co-create strategies for better interpersonal interactions, or she could have let him know that his objectionable behavior was a boundary that could not be transgressed. She chose the latter because it is important in co-creating boundaries that the needs and values of both elder and teen be transparent.

"I get it," Josette said, "and I would like to see if we can come up with other responses. But before we do I have to let you know that it is not okay with me if you curse just to gain attention. That hurts you and it hurts everyone else, so that cannot be an option. Okay?"

Without enthusiasm, but without much resistance either, Josh agreed.

"Okay," Josette said, "now what to do we do?"

"But I don't know. That's the problem."

"What would you like to see happen?"

Here, Josette elicited his ideals. Josh went roundabout, but it boiled down to acceptance. Josette inquired into Josh's understanding of acceptance. See the next sidebar for a detailed description of inquiry. When they had a common agreement on acceptance, Josette once again asked Josh for his solution. Josh now had several ideas. The one he liked the best was to confide in a peer whom he trusted and ask him to surreptitiously signal him when he was acting poorly. It was not the solution Josette would have chosen, and she worried that Josh might suffer. Yet, her boundary respected, she supported it, asking only for permission to check in with Josh to monitor his progress. Josh agreed.

"So I guess you'll be staying in camp?" Josette asked.

"Never really an issue," Josh said, grinning.

Two nourishments, challenges in the realm of success and dynamic activities, serve the actualization of personal power. Challenges that lie beyond the child's capabilities undermine the new, fragile sense of self. Challenges successfully met, however, bring forth confidence and the acceptance of responsibility. Dynamic activities, especially when combined with adventure, allow the child to engage nature and peers. They leave the child feeling vigorous, alive, and powerful.

IdealBeing children thrive on the ability to explore and express their ideals. I take every chance I get—casual conversation, videos, politics, music, literature, personal and social situations, current events, family history, cultural history, food, fashion, sports—to inquire into their ideals. Then, where possible, I help create situations where they can directly experience these things. Several years ago, for instance, a nuclear power plant in Sacramento was going to be closed. People both for and against the closing were demonstrating. We escorted a carload of children with some for each side. Similarly, we encourage IdealBeing children to get involved in any issue that concerns them. We do not worry if their interest is short-lived, for that is the duration of the value of the identity for them. It is not the issue but the freedom to explore the identity and the resultant understanding of self that has meaning.

The final two nourishments are closely linked. Peer contact and the right to personal space guarantee that the developing self can indeed be self-referential. Personal space belongs to the child. If it is at all possible, even just by placing a sheet down the middle of a room, some type of personal space should be available to the IdealBeing child. Inside that space, the child is free to self-govern. Contact with peers is also an opportunity to explore freedom and to create relationships based on merits that the child, not the family, believes are important. Unless there is the threat of harm, neither personal space nor the right to peer contact should be violated.

Inquiry is the language of IdealBeing. Inquiry by the elder is simply a request for information, based on a desire to understand what the child means by their words or actions. Inquiry is rooted in the search for truth, information, or knowledge. With a little bit of forethought, compassion, and conscious intent, inquiry can bridge gaps previously uncrossed, shed light on motivations yet unknown, and reveal information critical to a deeper understanding of one another.

It is essential that the elder bring humility to the inquiry. One cannot believe one has all the answers. To ask the right question is far more important than providing an answer. The solution to a situation lies in understanding the situation itself. Inquiry is the key here—asking into the heart of the matter. The answer is not outside a problem; it is contained within it. One cannot look at the problem very clearly if one is concerned with what the answer should be or has an agenda for the solution.

Inquiry must be used with energy, care, and focus. It requires vitality, passion, and intensity to look directly into a situation. Once a situation is deeply engaged, responses appear. Simple, unprejudiced inquiry deepens insight and refines reasoning ability. Perhaps best of all, inquiry makes lecturing obsolete.

Once teens come to appreciate inquiry, they often eagerly use it themselves for both self-exploration and as a way to communicate with peers and family. It fits easily into their repertoire, for it allows the freedom to understand themselves and others without blame or shame. Inquiry allows parents and children to engage self-knowledge together. It is an exquisite dance step to do with teenagers and yields mutual respect.

One word of caution: Your first attempts at inquiry may well be a bit stilted. Some teens will find this offensive—as if you are trying to "technique" them. If this happens, explain what you are doing and why. Ask for their patience. Most teens will appreciate that you want to learn how to communicate with them without judgment. In a short time, using inquiry becomes intuitive. It is so useful that the self-consciousness soon drops away. The sidebar presents a detailed description of the inquiry process.

- The Form for an Effective Inquiry -

A few pointers for setting the stage for potent and stimulating inquiry follow. These basics develop into easy-to-use skills.

Face one another. Stop all other activity and conduct the inquiry with full attention and concentration. Honor the other person with your full presence.

It is helpful to establish contact—by physical touch, eye contact, or short and simple contact statements—to create safety, trust, and a connection with your partner.

Maintain the contact in an unobtrusive manner. You're trying to create a safe space where the attitude is, "I want you to receive me and I wish to be received by you." Meet the person in the present moment.

Inquire into what the other person is saying for the purpose of understanding them completely. Be sure to inquire by using their words and not yours. This means listening carefully to the words your partner uses and then asking about them, even if you think you know what they mean. Be careful not to project your meaning onto their words.

When you get responses to your question(s), make sure you understand completely what your partner has told you. Repeat what you heard and give them time to adjust or change their wording.

Paraphrase. After you have inquired into what your partner is saying and received several responses, paraphrase what you have heard. This time, you can use your own words to convey what you understand. You can begin the paraphrase with the statement, "What I understand you to be saying is..."

Give your partner space to change or correct your paraphrase.

Keep in mind that the form of the inquiry influences its efficacy. The little things—such as interruptions, seating arrangements, gestures, and postures—matter. There are always movements, inflections, and changes in facial expressions that indicate meaning. These can be inquired into as well.

There is an Aikido term *irimi*, which means "entering." When *irimi* is called for, and often it is when we enter heated moments of inquiry, we train ourselves to move directly into the heart of the situation. This entering movement is non-aggressive. It is done in order to blend with the problem and not oppose or strike back. So move toward the incoming energy in order to experience its vitality, and from there work with it gently and resourcefully.

Time and place can mean everything to the outcome of an inquiry. It can also set the tone for the conversation.

Allow your question to be fully received before you jump in with more comments.

Tone of voice mirrors your intention. Avoid any effort to stridently convince the other of your position. Your voice should not suggest any coercion. In heated conversations, whether around inquiry or not, coercion often generates negative reactions.

Word your questions simply without blame or assumptions.

State what truly is and was. Be honest as well as accepting.

Speak in the first person. Talk about yourself instead of your conception of what your partner may be feeling or thinking.

Avoid blanket statements, assumptions about the other's motivations, and generalizations.

Make every attempt to come to a mutual understanding.

Don't be afraid of the truth. Our fear of the truth is usually far worse than the actual fact of it.

Through this co-exploration, you acknowledge one another, define and re-define situations, mutually explore and compare data, continue inquiring, choose a course, and set up experiments for the future.

Inquiry demands practice, commitment, patience, humility, and humor. But, more than any of these, it takes a deep love of life.

Nourishing ReasonableBeing

Who I am? How is the universe ordered? What is my place in it? What values are truly enduring? These questions are a sign of maturity—of realizing how little one knows and how important it is to try to know. Elders cannot answer these questions for children. They can, however, recognize the child's maturity and pledge to support their search for the answers. This nourishes interconnectedness. The child knows that their elders honor their investigation into meaning by supporting them for who they are, as they are. Mature recognition, the name given to the key nourishment for ReasonableBeing, unequivocally proclaims that the child is the sun at the center of their solar system. Their investigation is recognized as important and valid. The child needs support for that investigation, not direction, unless it naturally arises in dialogue.

Mature recognition has four aspects. Providing them ensures the complex nourishment necessary for the subtle, interweaving qualities of ReasonableBeing.

In achievement recognition, the adult honors the values and intent of the child's life. Achievement recognition can center on a particular accomplishment, such as mastery of an instrument, or on the qualities of personhood, such as a developed sense of justice. With achievement recognition, the child can move forward to greater explorations with confidence.

Recognition of equality is the acknowledgement that the mystery of life cannot be grasped or defined by anyone. Therefore, any reasonable inquiry is seen as valid and is honored to the fullest extent possible. Elder and child are co-explorers into the meaning of life.

The ReasonableBeing child thrives on the recognition of commitment. Throughout the stage, the child develops increasing capacities for greater commitment to what is meaningful to her. Personal commitment means to give oneself in trust with the intention of persevering through time. The capacity to commit deepens tremendously when eternal values—such as love, truth, and beauty—are touched. Recognition of this capacity nourishes the child and creates fertile ground for its growth. Falling in love is to commit to another while honoring their autonomy and freedom. Surrendering to love with commitment opens one to the timeless.

Finally, the crowning nourishment for ReasonableBeing children is the recognition of the child's ability to recognize. This is the ability to step back, consider, and *intend*. ReasonableBeing children can now recognize enduring values. They can know meaning or create the conditions that might lead to meaning. They now have the ability to self-observe and

- Recognition of the Capacity to Recognize -

In her last two years of college, Jill rented a house with five of her classmates. They were a tight group of friends, and their graduation night was a party to remember. Jill believed that they were friends for life.

Jill continued on to graduate school in philosophy. Adventuresome and bright, she visited spiritual teachers and philosophers as part of her studies. About eighteen months later, she attended a reunion with her housemates. She returned home deeply disillusioned. Her mother, Rachel, immediately spotted it.

"I cannot believe how much they have changed. I mean Mary was always into organic farming but now all she wants to do is get married and grow vegetables. We were so close. And Quentin—all he wants to do is fix cars. The three of us were so close but they have totally quit on the deeper issues in life."

Rachel is a wise lady and knows a bit about dialogue. She threw down the gauntlet in one swift move.

"Did they?"

The question at first perplexed Jill, and she gazed at her mother in thoughtful silence. Almost to herself she mused, "Didn't they?" And then the light went on. "Are you suggesting that I heard it when it wasn't there?"

"I don't know what was or wasn't there."

"But how did I hear it?" Jill pondered.

"Like you needed to at the time?"

"Like I wanted the camaraderie more than I wanted to know what they really meant."

"So who changed?"

Jill smiled. "Maybe now I can really be their friend."

to reasonably investigate the world. The child recognizes that humans are the meaning givers. They see that there is a direct relationship between perception and perceiver, between the observation and the observed, between the meaning and the meaning giver.

The recognition of the capacity to recognize fortifies the ReasonableBeing child to engage one of the most perilous and potentially valuable investigations any human will ever undertake: finding the meaning, purpose, and substantive value of oneself and one's world. The sidebar illustrates a case history of recognition of the capacity to recognize.

There are secondary nourishments for ReasonableBeing children. These create opportunities for ReasonableBeing children to exercise reasonableness—specifically, to step back and appreciate values, to create and compare systems, and to make considered decisions. Dialogue, the most important mode of this activity, is discussed in a sidebar a bit later in this chapter. The ReasonableBeing child also needs the opportunity to work in diverse subjects and on multifaceted data sets. This work gives them the chance to exercise their capacities for investigation, experimentation, recapitulation, and discernment.

Nourishing Parents, Teachers, and Caregivers

Natural Learning Rhythms is fully aware of the challenges in parenting, and especially parenting in Western society in our times. Children seem to take over the parent's life. Most parents find their way of living radically altered by a child's presence. Parents give much to their children. The last thing they want to hear, or should be subjected to hearing, is that they do not do enough. I've said it before and I will say it again and again: Natural Learning Rhythms saves time, reduces stress, and supports family and children as a source of knowledge and rejuvenation.

Providing the nourishments places the parent in relationship with their child. They live "under the aspect of eternity." They have met the needs of the moment, and they can breathe freely, intimate with their child and engaging life as it arises. As we shall see in a moment, relationship endures and is deepened though participation in the wisdom of each developmental stage.

If this were all, it would be enough, but it is only half the story. Providing the nourishments is central to the dance—to actualization of the parent's capacity for relationship and wisdom. This is so important that it merits its own chapter in this book. In a constant, dynamic synergy, everyone's needs—from the physical to the spiritual—are met.

There is a *but*, and it has to do with the parent's honesty and integrity. When there is a problem in the family, the parents have to look at themselves as integral to the system. Wendy, for instance, became upset when her twelve-year-old boy, Mark, stated that he no longer liked his friends and didn't want to play with them anymore. Wendy immediately began to worry that Mark was somehow damaged in his social development. She did not look at her own interactions with friends and the importance she attached to interpersonal relationships. Nor did Sam, her husband and Mark's father, consider his rugged individualism and what impact that might have on the family system and how that influenced Mark's behavior. In other words, to the parents Mark was an *It* despite their best intentions. The barrier to I-Thou was easy to cross. All they had to do was examine and include their own attitudes in responding to the situation. That action supplied the nourishment of feeling mentorship. It took a couple of weeks to sort out and required a renewed commitment to family time, but Mark soon found friends and was well liked by his classmates.

Recognizing Wisdom

Wisdom cannot be nourished, though nourishing the organizing principles allows its profound, radiant expression. The effects of wisdom, however, can be recognized. Ethics, aesthetics, meaning, love, trust, and insight are some examples of wisdom's expression. In this section I consider recognition of these effects, and by inference wisdom itself, by first, elucidating the values of each developmental stage; and second, by describing eruptions of wisdom that allow each child to know the meaning of their developmental moment. I will leave love for a later chapter where it can get the necessary consideration.

Values

Relationship, as always, requires that we prize the child as she is, not as we want her to be or hope she will become. Therefore, as you read of the values in each stage, it is imperative that you do not assess them by the standards of your current life stage. Try to see through the child's eyes and feel through the child's heart. Their values are as meaningful and inclusive of their world as your values are for your world. And neither child nor parent is a finished product. Being is not closed, not entropic. The values of your current stage may not be the values of your later stages. The only question is whether the values of the stage allow optimal well-being, allow actualization of the wholeness of the organizing principle, and allow relationship and wisdom.

For the BodyBeing child, the sensory world is full of delight, mystery, surprises, and ever-new learning. Every sensory input results in like or dislike, in attraction or repulsion. Sophisticated maps are created with the boundaries of like and dislike clearly marked. When rightful place is nurtured, the world is a delight; when it is violated, the world is a claustrophobic prison. As might be expected with sensory-based values, that which is liked is possessed, is mine; that which is disliked is cast away, is not mine. Those who support rightful place are accepted and integrated—they are me and mine—while those who do not are rejected. Egocentricity rules the stage.

This is as it should and must be. This little child has to make this complex body work in this complex world. Sensory values are a great way to do it. They are immediate. They provide vivid contrasts and differ-ences so that information can be easily assimilated. They use the body and so call forth physical health. They connect to everything, for every-thing has a sensory aspect, especially the attitudes and dispositions of the people in the child's life.

BodyBeing children frequently experience the sensations of others vicariously. It is a sensation relationship through which the body con-nects to the outside world. This BodyBeing capacity is often mistaken for empathy. The BodyBeing child is egoistic, the center of the world. Sensation is the principal medium of communication. They learn to become aware of the effects of their physical sensations on others and of others' physical sensations in them as an unmediated sensation experi-ence.

BodyBeing children do not yet have the capacity for empathetically feeling another's feelings. Newly born babies often cry when they sense others in the nursery crying. It is not within their developmental capabil-ity to identify with or understand the feelings of the other babies. Six-year-old children will gather around a child who is injured on the playground, but once the pain dissipates the children disappear. They rarely have further interest in helping the child with tasks and show little concern with the long-term effects of the injury. Many BodyBeing chil-dren have to be cajoled or coerced to share and then usually do so to avoid the unpleasant sensation of the disapproval of their guardians.

BodyBeing children scrutinize their parents and observe others with considerable interest. In many ways, they know their elders better than the elders know themselves. For instance, our daughter, at age six, could assess my disposition by the way I closed the door. She could tell if I was playing a practical joke by a slight twitching in my lip. These sensation signals were part of her topographical map.

The refinement of boundaries depends on vicarious learning. By their capacity to hone in on sensations, BodyBeing children use their experience of the sensations of others to empower rightful place. Gradually the child learns to anticipate—a vicarious learning capacity that is enhanced by memory and an ever more refined competence at sensory-based evaluations. This anticipation is a type of judgment that engenders the formation of healthy boundaries. Anticipation leads to proficiency in navigating the world as long as the environment is suffi-ciently flexible to allow for trial and error.

Vicarious learning allows all feelings to be experienced, but the BodyBeing child has only the limited ability to categorize them into mad, sad, bad, and glad. Grief, jealousy, sentiment, gratitude, and a host of other emotions do have different sensation textures for the BodyBeing child. The sensation of sadness in grief is qualitatively different from the sensation of sadness when a friend leaves for the day. The simplicity of emotional categories is sufficient to define the boundaries for textured topographical maps. This efficiently serves rightful place.

As venerable as the sensory mode is, it is demonstrably incomplete for ensuring survival in this complex world. The child is absolutely dependent upon others for help. Of course we melt into our infants, but we also smile at our five- and six-year-olds—their egocentricity is wild, their bodily competence is high, surely they can do anything. They still need us, and most parents are honored to be so integral to another being's life. In this larger context, there is nothing incomplete in BodyBeing's incompleteness for it is an irresistible invitation to cherished relationship.

Parents have a reliable and accessible form of communication with BodyBeing children—touch plus the sensory environment they create. In the early years, this sensory communication gives them time to become acquainted with their child without pressure. It also gives both parent and child time to develop a spoken vocabulary without having to depend on it.

BodyBeing children play with words. Their truest expression is their body language. By observing the child, the parent can learn how their child maps the world, what natural talents they embody, and how their child best assimilates the nourishments of loving touch, flexibility, warmth, security, and textured sensory environments. In this way they know one another.

In optimal well-being, BodyBeing children establish rightful place in their own bodies and in their body's relationship to the environment. Rightful place is dynamic, not static. It is an opening, not an end. It is accepting *me* as the center of my life, as a willing and active being. Vibrant, strong, vivacious, explorative, curious, and unrestrained by social conventions, BodyBeing children roam their world, playing with boundaries, learning language, and establishing their place based on the elegant simplicity of sensory input.

FeelingBeing children value relationships. Every interaction, and especially human interpersonal interactions, yields vital information about navigating the natural and social worlds, about deciphering personal feelings and the feelings of others. Community becomes very important, and the mores of kin, clan, and community have tremendous impact. As the sensory environment is to the BodyBeing child, so the feelings and the interpersonal and moral environments are to the FeelingBeing child.

Vulnerable in their new birth—in their new way of organizing the world—FeelingBeing children begin by trusting their world. It is a tentative and naive trust, easily shattered by hypocrisy and prejudice. They need our guidance, our mentorship. Their development depends upon it.

Wisdom is impersonal. If conditions supporting optimal well-being exist, then FeelingBeing wisdom brings the integration of honesty, fairness, and justice with family and community. The child's innate ability to feel all the feelings in their world maximizes. Their natural ethical capacity develops in a way it never can when the child is subjected to hypocrisy and prejudice, is preached to, or is made to feel guilt and shame for their feelings and their expression of them. If conditions do not support optimal well-being, all wisdom can do is protect and defend. This defense can take many forms. Common ones include cliques, overly competitive play, inability to relate to people of varying ages, obsessive desire to be a teenager, and unwillingness to explore the ethics of a situation.

The development of conscience makes the point perfectly.

For four years, I facilitated a group of FeelingBeing children in a class named "Children in Nature, Nature in Children." It became so popular that some children would skip school, with their parents consent, to attend. Other participants were homeschoolers. The class met one day a week for eight hours. The format was to go to into a natural setting and play cooperative games and activities. I would also tell a story, and often we would put on a little drama about it. Interpersonal interactions were always a focus, and often we would stop the game or the drama to talk about them. When I told a story, I would often stop and engage the children in conversation about what "should" happen to a character. Sometimes these conversations would occupy whole afternoons.

Several of the children stayed with the class for all four years. Trust blossomed. New students, feeling the feelings of their friends and nourished in their organizing principle, also trusted. Contrary to what most parents supposed, the class had frequent interpersonal conflicts. Participating in these conflicts gave the children the chance to voice their feelings, many of which were unpopular in the group and in their home.

Jealousy is a good example. All children feel jealous at times. Rather than prohibit the feeling, or call it bad or wrong, the class provided the children the opportunity to express it and examine it.

At first, the jealousy of a character in the story provided the medium. A simple connecting question, such as "Have you ever felt that way?" usually started the conversation. Some of the children's surprising insights included: jealousy arises when there is a feeling of lack or deficiency; jealousy is sometimes an important motivator to get what you need; jealousy often hurts both parties; people sometimes invite jealousy from others so they can feel better about themselves; the feeling of jealousy should be treated as a warning that something needs to be rectified and it is often best to fulfill the need another way.

They felt the feeling, and the feelings inside the feelings, without judgment or prejudice. This process brought forth their knowledge of right and wrong. They did not need to be taught right and wrong. They needed to feel their feelings, to be mentored and nourished, and to be trusted to be fair and just with their community.

This is conscience. It is feeling the feelings without prejudice. This results in a balanced, responsive appreciation of justice. Here's Carl Rogers writing about conscience:

> It appears that the person who emerges from a theoretically optimal experience of personal growth, whether through client-centered therapy or some other experience of learning and development, is then a fully functioning person. He is able to live life fully and with each and all of his feelings and reactions. He is making use of all his organic equipment to sense, as accurately as possible, the existential situation [living in the moment] within and without.
>
> He is able to permit his total organism to function in all of its complexity in selecting, from the multitude of possibilities, that behavior which in this moment of time will be most generally and genuinely satisfying. He is able to trust his organism in this functioning, not because it is infallible, but because he can be fully open to the consequences of each of his actions and correct them if they prove to be less than satisfying.
>
> He is able to experience all of his feelings, and is afraid of none of his feelings; he is his own sifter of evidence, but is open to evidence from all sources; he is completely engaged in the process of being and becoming himself, and thus discovers that he is soundly and realistically social; he lives completely in this moment, but learns that this is the soundest living for all times. He is a fully functioning organism, and because of the aware-

ness of himself, which flows freely in and through his experience, he is a fully functioning person.

George Gurdjieff, the influential Sufi teacher who brought to the
West the spiritual path known as The Fourth Way, says it this way:
"Conscience is a state in which a person feels 'all at once' everything that
she in general feels, or can feel."[31]

The development of conscience depends on the ability to experience all feelings without fear of the feelings themselves. Every feeling has
a value in helping the child to learn the nature of relationship and to
ascertain which relationships are healthy for them. With conscience the
child assesses those feelings. When the child stays conscious of all of
their feelings, their innate ethical capacity organizes those feelings
toward trust and reciprocal cooperation. Children learn to trust themselves, not because they believe themselves infallible, but because they
can be open to the consequences of their actions and correct them without shame, guilt, or blame. If, on the other hand, conscience develops
under external direction of right and wrong, then shame and guilt will
be the way children distinguish right from wrong. If the field of psychology is correct, humans repress the feelings that cause them shame, and
this repression will show up in furtive behaviors such as
domination/submission activities, pornography, and prejudice of all
stripes.

Can we trust conscience, or do we need to fill it with our judg-
ments? Can we mentor its development, or are we compelled to control
it? What about the institutions our children inhabit? How do they relate
to conscience? What is their view of relationship?

I cannot emphasize how important a moment this is in the child's
life. The child is keen on meeting with her elders. Optimal well-being in
conscience leads to a child who is centered in their ethical capacities and
is able to respond to any situation without prejudice.

IdealBeing children prize their ideals and they prize freedom. The
combination of the two yields a surprise: IdealBeing children value the
shadow.

As was discussed previously, the shadow is a psychological term
introduced by the late Swiss psychiatrist Dr. Carl G. Jung, who is considered by many to be the father of transpersonal psychology. The shadow is
everything in us that is unconscious, repressed, undeveloped, and
denied. Everyone has a shadow.

IdealBeing children organize all the events of their lives to support, investigate, and extend autonomy, freedom, and personal power.

As with BodyBeing children, boundaries are there to be explored. Unlike BodyBeing children, who explore boundaries for their sensation value, IdealBeing children explore to learn the limits of freedom and personal power. Exploring is the action of autonomy.

As the ideal of freedom is often limitless, there are few, if any, boundaries that are sacrosanct to the IdealBeing child. Often it is the very values of their parents and society that must be explored first. We know of environmentalists from a rural lifestyle who have been severely chastised by their children for eschewing the benefits of the city. When confronted with their parent's ideology, the young teens merely said it was not their own. The same scenario is played out in the homes of many teens, albeit about different values.

In their highly energetic explorations, teens inevitably hit those values and personalities that the parents do not want to look at. When that happens and the parent responds with tension, the teen is drawn to examine the situation more closely. Tensions build as the parent resists. The teen is often labeled as difficult. The teen believes the parent to be controlling and hypocritical.

The teen's exploration of the shadow is not personally directed at the elder. It is a way of learning boundaries that is prompted by the idealistic exploration of freedom. The tension of the parent suggests that there are places that are closed to that exploration. The teen must find out why.

Yet the investigation is certainly presented by the teen in a personal way, and it challenges the elder's personally held values and identities. Inquiry helps to avoid this confusion. Boundaries can be co-created that serve each person's needs.

The intense strength of their sexual urges, thoughts, and feelings surprise the teen. True to IdealBeing dynamics, they project ideals and then develop identities to come to grips with sexual energy. This process translates to ideals about sexual freedom, the right to govern their own bodies, the way others should respond to them, and the attitudes of church and government. These ideals can lead to seemingly bizarre perceptions. Our daughter, for instance, insisted on wearing exceedingly skimpy clothes while declaring that others should not think lascivious thoughts around her.

The demand for freedom leads teens to examine the sexual mores of those around them, including their parents. They will sense those areas where there is dissatisfaction or repression. Often, their best clues come from the reactions of parents. The child dresses in an alluring way and the parent overreacts. Or the child identifies with the lyrics to a song with an explicit sexual message, and the parent clamps down with an arbitrary rule. The teen is probing the shadow. Jung and many others hold that confrontation with the shadow is essential for self-awareness.[32] If the shadow is not consciously reintegrated by adulthood, it usually expresses itself by the adult trying to suppress others.

Therefore, if the parent had to repress experimenting with sexual identities and has not integrated sexual freedom into his life, it will probably be a source of great conflict in the family. The parent will rebel against the child's probe and the child, fascinated by the rebellion, will likely probe more stridently.

We hasten to add that experimenting with sexual identities has nothing to do with promiscuousness or other extreme sexual actions. In fact, fieldwork strongly suggests that most IdealBeing children are quite chaste in their actions, whatever their thoughts or speech may indicate. This is the other classical aspect of IdealBeing dynamics. There is an undertow of insecurity behind every assertion. Sexuality is an extraordinarily powerful and complex energy. The insecurity asks them to pause. Our fourteen-year-old friend Jennifer, an ardent fan of rap music, simply shifted her eyes and briefly blushed in the direction of fellow student, Mikey, when we asked her if there were any boys in her life.

Elders know if their sex life is healthy. No standard is being suggested. If the elder has a healthy sex life, then the probing by the teen can lead to valuable inquiry into the many issues sexuality raises. The learning will be mutual.

Society also has a shadow, and teens reflect it continually. When asked why tattoos and garishly dyed hair are popular, a group of teens agreed that it was a ridiculous question given the degradation of the environment. In America, there is the claim to equal opportunity, but the shadow is prejudice and disadvantage for the poor. At the same time, a large amount of resources are poured into "protecting the peace" while violence permeates every walk of life. Gangs take root in these aspects of America's shadow. They know that power can be had through violence. They provide loyalty and protection that has the appearance of providing the opportunity for freedom and advancement. They give voice to the outrages of ideals ignored and freedom arbitrarily suppressed.

IdealBeing children value choice, and the choices they make reflect their ideals of the moment. Peers are important to validate their choices, to mitigate insecurity, and to provide new perspectives.

IdealBeing children value loyalty. I have had the delightful experience of teens "ringing the circle"—protecting me from further intrusion—at the end of a long family camp day so that I could rest. And, of course, they value adults who co-create with them. One of my earliest experiences was with a group of sixteen teens from diverse backgrounds. There were preppies, skaters, goths, slackers, nerds, and jocks, and about five different ethnic heritages were represented. Discontent was in the air, and so I asked if each person, in turn, would state their major grievance. At the time, I was surprised by the response, but it has happened so often that I now expect it. There were only two complaints: too much freedom or too little.

Reasonableness is a state of being. It is a dynamic whole that connects to the universe and the psyche. It can use induction to create viable systems that never existed before. It can use deduction to verify the value of those systems. Reasonableness has the confidence of a self that can question itself. Doubt is a call to action. The mystery of the first cause of life—of the meaning of existence—is there to be investigated, experimented upon, and dialogued about. Exercising reasonableness allows deeper and deeper penetration of these issues. Reasonableness is its own reward.

Throughout this investigation, reasonable people laugh. The notion of a terrestrial biped with only one hundred thousand years of practice using the most complex structure in the universe, the brain, to attempt to answer mysteries and find meaning is mostly preposterous. The universe, which is very big, is expanding. The brain has more dendrite connections than there are stars in all the known galaxies. According to our most revered scientists, the essence of matter is completely indeterminable. Earth, beautiful and alive, sits in the suburbs of a galaxy that has hundreds of millions of stars and is one of hundreds of millions of galaxies. We know little about death. Certainly, no one has come back to give a firsthand account. Yet we attempt to be reasonable in the face of our inability to answer life's greatest mysteries.

And then there are the questions: How long is a long time? The time it took to give birth? The moment of rapture during the deep peace of a sunset? The time spent in gridlock? The moment we fell in love? The time it would take to travel to the center of the Milky Way? The last second of life? Are physicists correct when they say there is no time at the speed of light? What can "no time" possibly mean? Is there existence beyond time?

Humans know so little and have such high aspirations. The questions are deeply embedded in our nature. Most of us gladly pay for Hubble telescopes, particle accelerators, and other exploration tools and ventures that can shed light on our ignorance. We feel the incredible beauty of nature, we see its exquisite balance, and we sense its omnipotent power. It fills us with humility. How can we understand? Where do we fit in? What is our meaning, our purpose, our potential?

The ReasonableBeing child's expanded perspective of time and the universe is fused with an expanded perspective of values. The projected identities of IdealBeing need to be greatly modified or dropped. They do not match the reasonable world. Identification with a type of music or clothing style, or a simplistic notion of the relationship between freedom and responsibility, do not speak to the complexities of committed interpersonal relationships, determining a course of study and career, or newly encountered values derived from expanded social contacts. What is really important and why? How are values, ethics, mores, and politics to be understood? These questions ring across scale and are asked of nature; of global, national, and community cultures; of school and workplace; and of family and self.

Children in ReasonableBeing perceive these awesome dimensions of time and of values, consider the questions, and take a step back. How can these questions be approached? Who am I at this moment of life? How can I actualize my capacities to find meaning?

Similar questions arise about human societies and about personal history. Why do people treat each other as they do? What is the purpose of a society? How can it be organized to allow recognition of meaning? And, what was my life like such that I turned out this way? Why was my past organized the way it was? What does it say about my future? What can I do about it?

For the first time in the child's life, she can recapitulate the past to discover more about herself in the present. With the former organizing principles in residence, she can draw on their information to understand:

- Her sense of rightful place, of physical centeredness, of her ability to recognize and create boundaries.
- Her feelings of trust and of her ability to be trustworthy and to cooperate with others.
- Her ability to be autonomous, to feel powerful, and to understand that freedom is coupled with responsibility.

This ability to receive information about personal history and reflect upon it with discrimination is crucially important for optimal well-being. It allows the ReasonableBeing child the opportunity to deliberately engage those actions that will heal past wounds. In this last stage of childhood, nature actually provides two ways to ensure that the child leaves childhood healthy and whole. First, there is the way that it is similar to the other stages. Receiving the nourishments allows the greater complexity of the new stage to rebalance that which was not actualized in the former stages. Second, ReasonableBeing has the extraordinary additional capacity to reflect on the nature of each stage and to assess what worked and what didn't. It can fairly be said that the child will need the entirety of the stage to learn how to do this well. Throughout, it will be cause of much consideration and many experiments.

The capacity to assess the health of the previous life stages serves three vital aspects of well-being. First, old wounds are healed, or at least strategies are engaged to attempt the healing. Second, the child recapitulates her life and thus becomes current with her own history. Hopefully, friends and family will aid in this process by supplying unprejudiced information to the child as to what decisions were made during her childhood that affected her and why. This recapitulation yields the third and perhaps most important result: The child claims her own life. Therefore, when the ReasonableBeing child finally steps into adulthood, there are no deliberately hidden secrets, no aspect of self or history that is unavailable for scrutiny. The child may not like what she finds, but the information is hers.

This process in the ReasonableBeing stage contradicts what I believe is a great lie that has been accepted by many psychologists and eagerly lapped up by many educators: that the personality of the child is determined in early childhood. Some advocates of this view claim this determination is fixed in the birth canal, in the first three months, in the first six months, in the first year, in the first three years, or in the first six years of life. They see humans as closed systems and often fail to account for relationship as a locus of development. Throughout this book we have maintained the opposite. Humans are dynamic, nonlinear beings. When in open communication with their environment and properly nourished, they naturally self-organize to greater levels of complexity. Past wounds can literally be redefined to allow optimal well-being.

In ReasonableBeing, this process can become conscious and deliberate. Healing is in the child's hands when their developmental needs are met. This is a tremendous growth in complexity. To be able to reflect on her own development and engage the steps to further it places the child's future in her own hands. It is a reasonable expression of the union of freedom and responsibility. Accepting the responsibility to attend to one's history yields the freedom to create the future. This freedom takes place now, moment to moment. For the ReasonableBeing child, past and future are present.

Unlike IdealBeing, ReasonableBeing children are able to enter into another person's perspective without feeling threatened by the loss of their sense of self. They can hold their perspective while entering into another's and then returning to their own. They can easily do this several times during a discussion. They are not moving from one identification to another. They are stepping back, allowing the influence of others, and absorbing that which helps in the search for substantive values. Then decisions are reasonable.

The value of change is known to the ReasonableBeing child. Change endures. Change allows for a timeless openness. The notion of a final state of perfection dissolves. Change teaches tolerance. It allows us to let go of holding others, and ourselves, as rigid and immovable. To move with change is vibrant and alive; it is the key to more complex self-organization. Thus, the recognition of the value and necessity of change sets the stage for the realization of the substantive values of love, beauty, and truth. Change itself is seen to have substantive value.

Dialogue brings connection to substantive values. The following is Bohm speaking of the dialogue between the artist and his work:

> There are many possible contingencies—ways of putting his materials here or there and with different techniques. It's open. That is the field in which he can work. And then from some perception—by some sense of internal necessity, some creative perception of necessity—he must begin to develop how this is done. Otherwise it won't hold together, it won't have value or any meaning. In other words, freed is the creative perception of a new order of necessity.33

It is by fully understanding meaning that one knows the appropriate action of the moment and has the freedom to actualize it. Again and again, the ReasonableBeing child values what endures and makes life profoundly worthwhile: truth, love, meaning, and beauty.

Eruptions of Wisdom: Meaning-Making Moments

Values are the bedrock of spiritual awareness and are sufficient testimony to spirituality. In the abundance of nature, however, there is much more.

Humans do not arrive at meaning in a linear fashion. There is no faculty that adds up bits of data and then says, "Aha, that is the meaning!" Even rationality, which depends on comparison, is not sufficient.

- Dialogue -

The language of ReasonableBeing is dialogue. *Dia* means to cut into and *logos* means the word, and specifically, the meaning of the word. To engage in dialogue means to cut through until meaning is found. The holistic scientist and philosopher David Bohm held dialogue to be of great importance. Bohm states that there are three qualities of meaning: significance, purpose, and value. All three are interrelated and when realized yield a powerful synergy. This synergy, this genuine meaning, allows one to live in necessity rather than contingency.[34] Contingency implies that there are many ways something can be done. It suggests choice. Necessity is deeper. Necessity calls for a response that prioritizes meaning and thus furthers well-being.

It is by fully understanding meaning that one knows the appropriate action of the moment and has the freedom to actualize it. It all begins with the desire for meaning. Once there is the desire for deeper understanding about a particular event, Bohm believed it "makes dialogue necessary...We have to start from seeing the meaning. And the perception of the meaning can get deeper and deeper as well."[35]

Dialogue can be done with oneself or with a group. Both are important and each adds to the value of the other. Culture, Bohm believed, developed around "shared meanings." Dialogue brings mutual understanding of those shared meanings. It provides a medium in which mutual understanding and respect arise.

Inquiry, the communication tolls of IdealBeing, calls for a disciplined structure in which respect is gained and meaning is broached. As one might expect, dialogue is more open and free-flowing. The boundary is the dedication to meaning itself. Dialogue assumes respect for one another, recognition of the maturity of each person, and commitment to the topic being considered. The purpose of the dialogue and the perception of meaning can change many times during dialogue. Therefore, its form must evolve throughout. Dialogue is a field of play in the search for meaning.

We may revel in the Sherlock Holmes myth of piecing the facts together, smoothly stepping back and with disdain for weaker minds, intoning, "elementary, my dear Watson," but it doesn't happen that way except in limited circumstances. It didn't happen that way for Einstein or for Archimedes. The knowledge gained from linear thinking is not knowledge at all, but only data that becomes useful when it is integrated into the whole of our being.

Meaning erupts into consciousness for children as well as for adults. If you believe that meaning is reserved for adults, you won't understand. For nourished children, their meaning is as conscious for them as ours is for us. They are aware of it and they express it in the language of their stage. Meaning making is the firstborn of the child's wisdom.

The meaning-making moment of a developmental stage starts with the eruption of meaning and ends with its firm implantation in the child's psyche. It does not include the years of practice, trial and error, and attaining competence that follow. It is not confined to a single event, but it rarely lasts more than a month. It occurs during the transition between two phases within the developmental stage, a topic covered in the next chapter.

The meaning-making moment for BodyBeing children centers on language. Infant babble is universal. As the child speaks a syllable of the mother tongue, the family reacts with highly pleasurable sensations. Gradually, through imitation and play, syllables turn into words. Between one and two years of age, it is not uncommon for children to sit in their parent's lap and watch their mouths as they form words. Then the great game of naming objects arrives. "Chair?" the child asks, pointing to the chair. "Chair," is the reply. "Chair?" "Chair." Over and over, again and again, with the chair, the dog, and object after object. In this way, the child connects the object with their sensorial experience. The child does not make generalizations: A different chair might stimulate the questions anew.

Now, somewhere close to two and a half years of age, a complex reordering of language occurs. In addition to representing objects, words now also represent categories of objects. At the same time, the child begins to form sentences and in a relatively short period of time begins to speak in simple paragraphs. Most amazingly, she begins to use language for abstraction. The child knows that words are not fixed to the objects they represent, but can be played with creatively. She can turn a piece of wood into a boat, name specific needs and desires, and make sense of other people's conversations. She will spend the next five or six years using language as a primary tool to establish her rightful place. Children can enter the conversation about boundaries and express their strength through words. The world comes alive with meaning.

This natural moment occurs effortlessly for the two-and-a-half-year-old child. To the adult, language development seems close to a miracle and is among the most researched topics in human development. Many believe that sophistication with language has led to humans becoming the dominant life form on the planet.

While almost everyone notices the language explosion, no one, to our knowledge, has appreciated the implications of meaning making. Some cognitive psychologists, for example, often point to this moment as a time of separation and loss.[36] They believe that frustration engulfs the child because the words do not match the richness and texture of the sensorial experience they represent. Moreover, children are just beginning the lifelong journey of the use of abstraction and language and are not yet good at it. This supposedly adds to their frustration.

This perspective makes sense if you are investigating the question of how children create mental maps. Clearly a rich new tool for mapmaking is present. Naturally there will be much trial and error before it is mastered, and there will certainly be frustration during the learning curve. The separatist perspective also makes sense if you are attempting to ascertain how neurosis and pathology form. If the meaning-making moment is not met with developmental sensitivity, then the child is wounded and will see himself as isolated and confused.

From the Natural Learning Rhythms perspective, this is a moment of greatness—of a new order of connection with self and the world. Words are new toys and BodyBeing children love to play. Learning mastery is enjoyable; the struggle is simply the game of life. Struggle is a way to maximize learning, for it brings the child to her edge, or boundary; it is one locus of boundary maturation. It is not suffering. The child struggled to learn to walk and will struggle at other times throughout the developmental process. For the child living optimal well-being, struggle assumes its natural function as an important operating mode of growth and development.

Brain research and many studies about memory indicate that it is around this time that humans can place themselves in the center of their memories; this process is called autonoetic memory by neuropsychobiologists.[37]. The event didn't just happen; it happened to "me." "Me" was there and my memory includes my place in the event.

This is an excellent example of the fact that development happens as a dynamic whole. This is systemic wisdom—wisdom that is recognition of and guidance by a knowledge of the total systemic creature. The child places herself in the center of the event at the same time that the capacity for language abstraction unfolds. The combination yields a "me" who can order the world with language. Simultaneously, the child is in the center of the topographical map she continually re-creates. Boundaries become pliable as words can be used to modify them. Vicarious sensory information can be checked for predictability and thus deepen the capacity to anticipate. Rightful place can be accessed from the new perspective of *me* with the new tool of language. This new perspective preserves the well-being of the child.

The child is now embedded in a richer, more textured world. A key has been discovered to a realm heretofore unimagined. What human would surrender the ability to use words as signs, representations, and abstractions? Emergence out of the plodding mind that needed a complete sensory profile for every event is a gift that opens us to greater opportunity. What artist plays "connect the dots" if they know how to paint with oils?

The case history of Heidi told in the chapter on play serves as a good example of the meaning-making moment in BodyBeing.

In my long history of leading programs, I have found that appreciating the meaning-making moment for the FeelingBeing child is very difficult for adults. Is this due to the corruption of conscience? Is it due to the lack of understanding of the importance of feelings? Is it due to society's aversion to death? There is so little understanding of FeelingBeing and the challenges the child faces in this stage.

How can the child make meaning out of all the feelings he experiences? How can he find meaning when he knows that he will die? Do we need to imagine worlds of life after death that we have no direct evidence of? Do we need to intellectually deduce that some aspect of ourselves persists or intellectually challenge ourselves to live without notions of an afterlife? Should we just deny the fact of our mortality and pretend that it doesn't matter? Have our natural capacities for relationship with death been exhausted by our awareness of its inevitability? Is that where a ten-and-a-half-year-old child is to be left?

By the age of ten and a half, the FeelingBeing child has spent approximately two years registering the spectrum of personal and interpersonal feelings. At this point, with the same natural ease as the BodyBeing child, the FeelingBeing child experiences a synergistic explosion of emotional capacity. The feeling landscape manifests as a textured, varied, and colorful whole. It is as miraculous as the development of language, and perhaps more so given the greater complexity of the stage. As the matrix of the rich complexity of human relationships, it is as fundamental and important to human greatness as any other capacity.

No one can predict the development of grammar, sentences, paragraphs, abstraction, autobiographical memory, and symbol manipulation from the mere behavior of pointing at an object and naming it. The meaning-making moment in FeelingBeing has a surprise of similar magnitude.

Integration with the feeling world awakens the capacity to feel transcendence— to feel the greatness of Nature. The child can access intimate awareness that all creatures die and yet can feel all creatures as connected in the greater whole. This is the meaning-making moment. It makes sense of the dance of predator and prey in nature and reveals how adults can live with the certain and nonnegotiable knowledge of their personal mortality. It does not explain suffering, but it can help the child accept it—for life makes it possible to feel the essence of life, the hidden wholeness, and the unexplainable and indescribable mystery. That feeling makes life endurable and, in fact, worthwhile.

In Natural Learning Rhythms terminology, this moment has three different names: the mystery window, the inspiration window, and the transcendence window. We give it these names because, like a fine jewel, it is beyond comparison and while words can never do it justice, many words can point to its exquisiteness.

Trust in relationship is crucial to the full actualization of transcendence. It is another step deeper into the wholeness of being human. It is awesome—simultaneously inspirational and frightening. As with all new learning, the child goes to the edge, points and questions, and looks for support. Knowledge of the depth and breadth of feelings when the transcendence window opens is directly related to the quality of the inspirational relationships in the child's life.

Evidence of the mystery window abounds for the skilled observer. First, though, it might be helpful to take a moment and recall your life at eleven years of age. Was there a moment when you felt the inherent worth and beauty of life? Was there a feeling that fairness abides, that every creature has a place and matters, that somehow the universe works beautifully well? Was there an instant when the light was different, when wind and birdsong and scents blended into a perfect harmony? It might have occurred in a religious setting or while you were alone in nature. It might have been in relationship with friends or family. Theater, skillfully crafted movies, music, and art can also stimulate feelings of inspiration, especially when they are experienced in the company of a trusted community.

Have you noticed that many FeelingBeing children are attracted to religious instruction? We enjoyed the company of Choegon Rinpoche from Tibet at our home recently and asked about his education. He told us that he was free to do as he liked until nine years of age; from that point on he was given intense religious instruction. Likewise, FeelingBeing children will often ask to attend Sunday school to learn about the culture—the myth and stories—behind the religion.

Most religious services are designed to engender inspiration. Some of the artifacts used for this purpose in religious institutions are incense, stained glass windows, choirs, community involvement, icons, and using uncommon languages to communicate with an unseen God—all mediated by a clergy who is the designated, educated interpreter and is seen as knowledgeable of death and mortality. The attendant feelings of allegiance often last a lifetime, even when the adult's lifestyle is obviously contrary to the institution's teachings and scripture.

Religious institutions tend to lose their effectiveness, however, when they resort to didactic moral teaching.[38] This is not experienced as inspiring and does not lead to trust and reciprocal cooperation. There is not an eleven-year-old in the world who truly understands what it means to covet a neighbor's wife. How could they if they do not have the attendant sexual urges? The developing innate capacity for ethical assessments atrophies. Conscience becomes vulnerable to imposed notions of right and wrong.

Yet, despite the fact that so much religious teaching is didactic, children remain attracted to it. There are two cogent explanations for this. First, the community and the religious authority take precedence, as they must, for the child knows he needs their love and support. Maintaining those relationships is the more fundamental need. If that occurs in church, then most children will at least investigate the church carefully. Second, as we will eat almost anything when we are hungry, so we will seek inspiration when the mystery window opens. If didactic religious teaching is all that is available, then the child will turn to it. This reflects the strength of the child's need to feel something that at least resembles inspiration.

The next most common community-based opportunity to feel transcendence in our society is sports. Fans can be fanatics and so feel free to let loose all their emotions. There are rules to the game that all understand and engage, and the child can add his feelings to the community mix and help the team along. In addition, there are palpable shifts in momentum that everyone in the stadium feels together. Bigger-than-life heroes dominate. Hope springs eternal, for there is always the next game or the next year. The recent history of the Boston Red Sox is a case in point. Fans brought memorabilia from the team's success to graves of their deceased relatives who never witnessed a Red Sox championship.

Both organized religion and sports call forth allegiance, not inspiration. Other allegiance-building social events include adherence to the belief that one's clan is better than another or that one's political agenda makes one superior to another. Each of these cases engenders false distinctions of superiority, competition, and inevitably envy, fear, and prejudice. Eliciting these feelings is a form of abuse in the sense that the child's innocence has been co-opted in the name of allegiance to cultural values. It demands that the child define trust according to the shifting sands of cultural mores, not according to their innate capacity to feel devotion and inspiration and to become open to the mysteries of life and death without fear. It places the child in terrible peril. Society changes rapidly, and a child without their internal ethical capacity fully awakened can easily get lost in harmful activities such as drug abuse, sexual promiscuity, and the many pits marking our social landscape.

FeelingBeing children often express meaning making in their love of poetry and music. After Josette's mother died, Sam, a ten-year-old boy who hadn't seen her in several months, wrote this to her:

When I heard that your mom died,
My stomach started to cramp,
I know how it feels,
It's like a part of your heart is missing.
I felt like that when my dog died,
I still haven't gotten over it, he was my best friend.
But LIFE goes on with death and birth.
My new dog Buffy opens a new part in my heart and comforts me.
This is a little poem for you:
Have sun in your heart,
If it is stormy or if it snows,
If the sky is full of clouds,
The earth full of sorrow,
Trust in God.
Do not lose your courage, spirit, heart, and strength.
Have sun in your heart and everything will be fine.
From your friend, Sam

Transcendence and mystery have the qualities of openness, awe, and wonder. They connect the child to a greater whole—one that is beyond definition yet draws her to optimal well-being. The yearning for transcendence is a direct response to acceptance of the fact of death. It reflects the knowing that both life and death are somehow interconnected, somehow parts of something that is beyond either of them. Fairness and justice, for instance, take on new meaning. Life includes the possibility of the direct feeling experience of transcendence. It is therefore worth living. Every human, and all life, should have the right to experience transcendence.

In other words, the internal capacity for ethics and morals comes to life for the child who experiences transcendence. Situations may be unfair, but life is fair, for in life lives transcendence—lives a feeling connection with Nature and Spirit.

If children have direct experience of their innate ability to feel transcendence, then they will trust themselves and nature, and trust that they are included in the greatest mysteries of life, and that they and others inhere in goodness. Relationships will be organized around reciprocal cooperation in an attempt to serve this goodness. Prejudice will seem equaled in absurdity only by wanton pollution. If the child feels himself to be both part *and* the whole, then unnatural destruction and hurt have no value or meaning.

There are many ways to provide inspiration during this meaning-making moment. EnCompass' Inspirational Journey program for FeelingBeing children embodies several of these. Some of the venues for this four-day excursion include attending the services at several different religious institutions and then having a private audience with the leader on the subject of death, backpacking into the wilderness and catching sunrise from the top of the mountain, and doing community service projects in different ethnic communities. In each case, there is ongoing conversation about relationship, nature, fairness, and death.

As always, each family and community can, and in my opinion must, find its way to provide inspiration. The form chosen comes from one's own meaning structures, intimate knowledge of the child and family, and recognition of how to nourish optimal well-being. Of course, this is a dance. By engaging the mystery and finding meaning together with the children, elders reinvigorate their own ability to inspire and be inspired.

In IdealBeing, by approximately fifteen and a half years of age, the properly nourished child has survived most of the insecurity—indeed has transformed it to support autonomy, freedom, and personal power. This is a great achievement. It brings clarity to ideals and provides the courage to take a further step toward full autonomy. The child feels the empowerment. They believe they have the strength to choose and to manifest those choices. They sense the potential of greatness in themselves. They count, they matter, and their sense of self has sufficient substance to project an exciting future. This is the meaning-making moment for IdealBeing children.

It's almost as if they can sense their core nature reverberating throughout their being. Their experimentation with identities becomes vectored toward their core nature and is longer lasting. Often, these values include their understanding of service toward the greater good of society. For many, there is also a thirst for challenges that acutely sharpen their sense of self. What are the limits of the self? What is the genuine nature of the psyche? Just how extraordinary are the capacities of a human? The IdealBeing child wants to fill out the picture. They want to bring it home, to their very own selves. It is a superb time for a coming-of-age rite of passage, as indigenous cultures have recognized for time beyond memory.

As always, development is neutral. What passes before the open window is what is learned. Ridicule at this moment can bring disaster. Co-creation of boundaries must be maintained, or the power of the age can become inflated and believe itself omnipotent and immortal.

One of the reasons that intelligent teens drop out of high school is that high school rarely provides an opportunity to make meaning. A useful reform would be for the teachers and coaches to be aware of this moment and to guide the children who excel in their subjects and sports so that, without fierce competition or proving their skill through winning, the children are acknowledged for their interest, excitement, and potential. It must be remembered that in an IdealBeing child, a statement of potential excellence and autonomy will be idealistically projected. Sensitive respect is critical. *Acknowledgement* means "with knowledge,"—with intimacy and familiarity that is known in the bones.

Chris's parents divorced just when he entered IdealBeing. His school grades suffered, and his engagement with life—already impacted by the developmental shifts of the early teen years—atrophied. Other members of his community with whom Chris had developed trust during his FeelingBeing years reached out to him. For two years, Chris lived at half-speed. When he reached fifteen, he decided to drop out of high school. His parents did not know how to respond, but Ben, one of the men Chris had turned to, couldn't bear to see the boy's potential wasted. He challenged Chris to keep learning and spent hours co-creating a plan with him. Ben worked with the apathy by appealing to Chris's potential. He answered Chris's endless objections by his willingness to facilitate the logistics, to mentor the academics, and by promising to do all he could to prevent failure. It was Ben's work as well as Chris's. Their plan included classes at the local junior college, apprenticeship on some weekends with outdoor education instructors, a part-time job at a coffeehouse, and lots of leisure, some of which would be spent reading books that Chris chose.

Three years later, Ben had the pleasure of taking Chris, brimming with enthusiasm, to his first day at an elite liberal arts college. Well-being had been restored.

At approximately nineteen years of age, the child recognizes that an awesome and humbling mystery underlies all life. The complexity of life and the exquisitely balanced systems it entails on ever-descending and - ascending scales literally takes the breath away. Everything is interconnected; everything matters; everything influences everything else. Every human is important, perhaps especially important because of reasonableness itself. Meaning is everywhere, and each relationship provides new meaning. The child opens to a self that is interconnected with the flux and beauty of the universe. Life has new meaning; it is not the feeling of transcendence, but its profound recognition.

The well-nourished ReasonableBeing child cognitively connects to the deep great mystery. They realize that just as ReasonableBeing is more complex than IdealBeing, and IdealBeing is more complex than FeelingBeing, that there may well be organizing principles that are more complex than ReasonableBeing itself. This realization is warmly welcomed. What allows deeper penetration of the mystery is what is valuable. The field of life is open, dynamic, and replete with meaning, purpose, and value.

If the meaning-making moment is not met with proper nourishment, the child has only past conditioning to rely on. Conditioning selects from predispositions, former beliefs, or past memories. Reinforcement of the past is not reasonable and does not allow for the discovery of substantive values.

In this meaning-making moment, ReasonableBeing children see life as a system and as transcending all systems. The whole is more than the sum of the parts. Feedback from the multitude of life's systems constantly changes every system. The whole is dynamic, moving. Knowledge is in the flow of this movement and is not bounded data.

Commitment comes when substantive values are touched—love, beauty, and truth. Committing to these values brings commitment to the people who share these values. For the first time in the child's life, he can commit to loving another person over a long time.

ReasonableBeing children peer into a sacred universe of ever more complex hierarchies while knowing their rightful place, knowing that they can trust and be trusted, knowing that they can self-govern, and finally knowing that they are interconnected. Humbled by that vastness, the child develops a pure, unbending interest in meaning and values.

Whatever did she do to deserve such insight? What is the right relationship to this sacredness? How can I deepen connection to it?

At this moment, nourished ReasonableBeing children begin to contemplate deeper modes of knowing and more complex relationships to the universe. They are aware of the spiritual values of body, feeling, and core nature, and they are able to organize time and systems. They can then explore various lifestyles for their value in providing greater access to life and the universe. It is a moment of awesome freedom and can only be undertaken with a sacred knowledge of responsibility. Nevertheless, there it is, built into natural development.

Joanna, a brilliant nineteen-year-old writer and university student, attended a Natural Learning Rhythms seminar. Afterwards, she approached Josette and spoke of her search for meaning in life and the roadblocks she was encountering. They dialogued. Joanna decided to take a trip for self-discovery. She designed it, presented it to Josette for review, made some alterations, organized the logistics, and spent her summer vacation doing it.

Joanna hypothesized that meaning comprised outward and inward components. Consequently, she first spent several weeks visiting people whose life she assumed to be meaningful. These included a psychotherapist who had spent years investigating healing with a South American shaman, a successful businesswoman, a family-run organic farm, a woman committed to mothering three children, a man who studies dolphins in the wild, and a ballet dancer. She stayed at their homes, watched them at work, and asked as many questions as she could. Then, in late June she went on another two-week journey, this time by herself into the Badlands wilderness. There, in addition to many other insights, a whole new set of questions for the people she visited dawned on her. It wasn't until August that she could arrange another two-week journey, in which she revisited the people and had her questions answered. The last entries in her journal eloquently describe meaning making for ReasonableBeing children. With her permission, I have excerpted a few relevant sections.

> When I started these journeys I had no idea what was happening to me. Everything turned in on itself, like some giant constrictor coiling in on its prey. Often, I myself was that prey, but I had no idea what constituted the constrictor. I was freaked out. Not even my pen brought relief.
>
> My first trip was so intimidating. I couldn't believe how competent they all were. Then I went to the Badlands and it

just blew me away. Vast, stark, endless—why would anyone call that desolate place sacred? I went into overload. All my early fears were right. I was being squeezed to death. There was no place for me. In haunting dreams I felt myself alone time and again. Abandoned and bereft—something dead. The first two nights I awoke inundated by the most awful stench, only to awaken to nothing but pristine wilderness surroundings. I was so disoriented I cried for an hour.

I don't know why it all changed. There was no flash of light, no mind-bending realization. Everyone I had visited had told me of flashes that had lit their way. I was actually depending on them. Every time a fear had come up I had answered it with: OK, just hold on. A flash will show up at just the right moment. Too much Hollywood. Never again. Henri [the psychotherapist] makes his living on Aha! moments. Marjorie [the mother] knew she should get pregnant, knew when she conceived and had a hallelujah epiphany during delivery.

But I just woke up on the fifth day and I could breathe. There was so much space, so much time, so much room. And the clarity. Everywhere I looked I felt my gaze could penetrate into the very essence of things.

I thought about how I had not asked the right questions at all when I was with "my people." My confusion had left me in awe of them and I had missed so many things. Like how Henri had been curt with his kid on the phone, or Marjorie seemed never to be able talk about anything but her children, or how Toni [the businesswoman] didn't care about the ethics of the companies she invested in. Like how I had not really gotten into my fears with them. Like a gawking student instead of a real person with real needs and tough questions. I knew beyond question that I had to go back...

Though they all had expressed affection for me, only Marjorie and the Johnstons [the farmers] seemed particularly anxious to see me again. But I pushed and they agreed. This time I went straight. They couldn't believe it, and neither could I. Henri actually ended up showing me some shaman rituals that were only for apprentices. Marjorie broke down in my arms and told me how lonely she was. I broke down in hers and told her how connected I finally was. We laughed through our tears. Even great mothers need other sources of love.

Table 5-3 Developmental Table with Values and Meaning Making Moments

	BodyBeing	FeelingBeing	IdealBeing	ReasonableBeing
Primary Nourishment	Loving touch	Feeling mentors	Sensitive respect	Mature recognition, recognition of: commitment, equality, achievement, recognition
Secondary Nourishments	Security, warmth, textured sensory environments, flexibility	Fairness, justice, caring, concern, honesty, adventure, adaptability	Challenges, adventure, peer sensitivity, personal space, opportunity to explore ideals	Comparison, exploration, experimentation, discernment, recapitulation
Modality of Communication	Sensory exploration	Feeling engagement	Inquiry into ideals	Dialogue
Primary Organizing Principle	Rightful place	Trust	Autonomy, self-governance	Interconnectedness, humor, humility
Secondary Organizing Principle(s)	Boundaries, strength	Reciprocal cooperation	Identity construction, personal power and freedom	Systems creation, intentionality, incisiveness
Meaning Making	Symbolic use of language	Feeling transcendence	Belief in personal greatness	Recognition of the mystery; realization of open-ended modes of knowing
Values	Sensory-based vicarious learning, anticipation, exploration of boundaries, toys (including words)	Interpersonal dynamics, cycles of nature, conscience, conversation/ stories	Projection, shadow, loyalty, co-creation, inquiry, cultural purity	Substantive (enduring) values such as beauty, love, and truth; commitment; time (past and future); dialogue

The journal goes through Joanna's experiences with "her people." She concludes with an insight that is ReasonableBeing at its best:

> It isn't enough to say that I had been changed during my journeys. It is the nature of that change that must be known. It's hard to describe. I could encompass more, could allow myself to think about how it all worked together. It's impossible to say that my thoughts about my past were more (or less) important than my dreams in the Badlands or playing with little Sherri Johnston or confronting Toni. I could just allow it all to be there and then it all started to fit together. And I saw that I was in the middle of it. And it was open and connected and creative.

Wisdom-Based Relationships

Parents who nourish the organizing principles live in wisdom-based relationships with their children. The have created the conditions in which all family members, themselves included, can participate in self-knowledge. Relationship, not separation or alienation, flourishes. Wisdom, which is not an *It*, expresses itself as the relationships that family members live and as the extraordinary awakening of human development, of human beingness. It is natural and sane—it is hidden yet gives a consistent invitation to allow creative responses to family life and education. This is the essential spirituality of Natural Learning Rhythms.

Wisdom-based relationships form the basis of the dance; they seal the case that development is the key to awakening consciousness in humans. The dance is the subject of chapter 9.

Summary

The table on the previous page summarizes our understanding thus far.

Chapter Six

TRANSITIONS

At first you are trying out ideas for size. You are playing in the field of ideas. You are learning more and more about what you like and what you don't like. You may fall in love with a certain idea for three or four days and then find by the end of the week that you are completely bored with it. You may think little of an idea at first and then find that it grows on you and you eventually like it.

—Robert Fritz, Composer, Mathematician,
Creativity Seminar Leader

Transition dynamics are intense. The way the child was disappears; the way the child will be begins to peek out; the way the child is, is either one or the other with no clue as to when she is which. Parents are surprised, nonplussed, and often shocked. Whatever happened to the child they knew? Is this really my Johnny? Perplexed children experience new thoughts, feelings, and behaviors that seem at once alien and yet appropriate. Their parents' response can seem cramped, yet their need for relationship is great. There are so many painful, confused interactions. Parent and child grow impatient. Why doesn't he or she see? Why don't they get it together?

In carefully scrutinizing the lives of children, each developmental discourse—behavioral, cognitive, social, and spiritual—has provided excellent observations about children. Embedded in these observations are facts that help to decipher transitions. The Gessel Institute details a composite of the behavior of American children in each year of their life. Piaget specifies the relative complexity of mental constructions based on laboratory experiments and observations. Rudolf Steiner, Ken Wilber, and Sri Aurobindo take on the difficult task of explicating spiritual development. Steiner concentrates on the unseen metaphysical "bodies" that activate the child's maturation; Wilber is more concerned with the psychological dynamics. Of course, each discourse has many other practitioners who have made important contributions.

However, to our knowledge, none of them have investigated the dynamics of transitions or their effects on family dynamics. Perhaps only the perspective that focuses on the being of the child can do this, for it is inclusive of relationship with self, family, and community. Perhaps only the perspective vitally focused on optimal well-being has the courage to enter the intense dynamics of transition and see the fabulous learning opportunities for child and parent. Perhaps only the perspective simultaneously softened and tempered by years of experiential learning with whole families can know how imperative it is to enable families—to help them let go of the angst and pathologizing of transition behaviors and see their natural value. Perhaps only a combination of all three perspectives, such as ontological epistemology, is sufficient.

It is work that must be done.

Two simultaneously emerging and interweaving trajectories, the relationship between child and nurturing elders and the unfolding of the innate capacities of the child, dictate the quality of the transition. Both factors are thrown into high relief due to seemingly chaotic bouncing from one stage to the other and back again, so transitions are often a challenge to navigate.

Each stage of development features a new way of organizing the world. The dramatic events in the transitions between these stages are the subject of the first part of this chapter. There are also three phases within each stage—receptivity, trial and error, and competency—that have critical transition dynamics. Their description and the surprising insights they contain compose the rest of the chapter. However, a brief summary of the phases is necessary background in order to understand the life stage transitions.

The entry into each life stage is a new birth, and the child perceives the world in a brand-new way. This is both awesome and compelling. The child in the receptivity phase is wide open, vulnerable, and absorbing, absorbing, absorbing. A moment comes, however, where the rudiments have been received and it is time to fully engage experimentation. It is as if the structure and the basic "laws" of the stage have become known and their synergy results in a creative explosion. Applications appear everywhere as the child tries it all; error teaches successful usage. Trial and error results in the extraordinary empowerment of using the knowledge in endlessly creative ways to explore and reshape the world.

And then, competency arrives as the fulfillment of what has been successfully learned during trial and error. It is the phase of stabilizing the learning of the stage.

To begin at the beginning, let's turn to a transition that we are all familiar with: from conception to birth.

Conception to BodyBeing

As the physiology of the transition from conception to the birth of the physical body has been extensively researched, it provides a good basis for understanding transition dynamics.

The relationship between fetus and mother is the nexus of health for each of them. This, at least, seems obvious. Mothers are routinely cautioned not to smoke, not to drink excessively, to eat well, and to get lots of exercise. What may be less obvious is how profoundly interconnected mother and fetus are. All transitions animate physiological changes for parent and child. Unique to this transition, these changes have been carefully researched. Their relationship can be traced physiologically. By taking just one example from each trimester, the inspiring intimacy that is the fact of their lives can be made apparent.

Of the three hundred million sperm that enter the upper part of the vagina on the road to fertilization, only one percent (or thirty million) enter the uterus, and, of those, but one penetrates the zona pellucida (the strong membrane around the female's egg) and joins with the egg to create the zygote (the fertilized egg). At this moment, and throughout the amazing life of the human embryo and fetus, there is a relationship that is reflected in the continuity of the morphology, physiology, and endocrinology of the gestating child and the mother. In addition, there are places and sequences—interfaces—where it seems impossible to distinguish between the two.

As the blastocyst (the embryo as one thin layer of cells) implants at approximately a week after fertilization, the trophoblast (the outer layer of cells on the uterine wall) transforms into the chorion (the membrane enveloping the embryo).39 The process could easily be described as the mother receiving the blastocyst by surrendering part of her lining in response to a welcoming signal. The ovary continues to produce progesterone, while HCG (human chorionic gonadotropin) is released through the trophoblast. These hormones cause enlargement of the endometrial gland and the site swells with new capillaries. This is the rudimentary beginning of the circulation system of the embryo. In the meantime, estradiol is there to counterbalance progesterone and to ensure proper maintenance of blood flow. As embryologists Moody and Guidice put it,

"Successful implantation requires precise synchronization between blastocyst development and endometrial maturation."[40]

In other words, it is a single system. While mother and fetus each contribute specific endocrine production and physiological functions, they operate as a whole. There is a constant dynamic interplay that both defines each entity's present state and determines their future. If, for instance, one malfunctions it completely changes the other. Development is a synergistic "macroplay" of all systems taken as whole in the present moment.

As an example of just how connected they are, the interpersonal relationships in the mother's life influence the fetus. Consider the psychology of people when they learn that they are pregnant. There are statistical studies about this,[41] but they are, in a sense, ridiculous. We already know. Lifestyle is reevaluated. Attitudes are reevaluated. Are we in this together? Do we have sufficient funds? How will the home be reorganized? Do you love me? Can we make it through labor? Is the baby healthy? If the answers support the new relationships, every family member—including the one in the embryonic stage of development— is nourished. If they do not, the anxiety and stress limit optimal well-being.

High levels of stress deplete the system. Mother and child suffer. According to a study from the University of California at Irvine, excessive stress actually changes the delivery timetable and increases the chances of preterm arrival. Certainly, as a UCLA study confirms, it changes the hormone balance and hormones run the chemical theater. To put it in strictly scientific terms, if you mess with the hormone mix everything goes kerblooie![42]

In the second trimester, the placenta exemplifies the nature of the mother-fetus relationship. It matures to its full weight and thickness and becomes the source of the signals for the best timing for the growth of the fetus. The placenta "function[s] in many ways like, the mature hypothalamic-pituitary-end organ endocrine system." In other words, by mediating the chemical interface between fetus and mother, it feeds back into each what is necessary for homeostasis—the right rhythm of emergence—for each of them. In the words of Mooney and Guidice, they function as "one unit." Yet, most amazingly, the placenta stands, in a sense, outside of each of them. And, of course, it is expelled soon after delivery. Yet it still has value, and mothers in many traditional nations eat the placenta and find it a rich source of nourishment for rejuvenation after birthing.

The function of the placenta is to transfer materials. In the process, it regulates metabolism, confers a high degree of immunization, and nourishes. It never gives more importance to either the mother or the child. The placenta makes sure that the transfer of materials is not a struggle and expects merely normal health and development from mother and child to perform its function.

The interchange of hormones is fundamental to the way the placenta accomplishes its purposes. By the early part of the second trimester, the placenta has completely taken over progesterone production. During this second trimester, it is believed to be the principal agent of immunization. The placenta relies on material from both fetal and maternal adrenal glands to produce estrogens. Estrogens seem primarily concerned with the regulation of the all-important blood flow.

The relationship between mother and fetus maintains perfection at parturition. Prostaglandins become plentiful in the mother's blood and in the amniotic fluid. They both induce labor and help with clotting if blood vessels are damaged. The pituitary-generated hormone oxytocin is stimulated in the mother when the fetus moves into the birth canal. It then finds many receptor sites in the myometrium, the smooth-muscled wall of the uterus which contracts and provides critical impetus for the safe passage of the fetus. Oxytocin also stimulates lactation to ensure the fetus has a good meal waiting after its exhausting journey. Last, oxytocin has been called the "love hormone" because it seems to stimulate emotions of care and acceptance. And at this time, a "placental opioid-enhancing factor" is released that helps with the pain of birth. Mothers often get "high," and parturition can be a blissful experience. It's not as if there is no pain, but rather that there is the support to transcend the pain and enjoy relationship through the birthing process.

According to Mooney and Guidice, the "fetal-amniotic fluid-fetal membrane complex" triggers labor.[43] Komisaruk[44] is eloquent on the topic: "Parturition in mammals occurs in the context of sensory, neurochemical, and endocrinological factors that are orchestrated and timed so that maternal behavior and the object of the behavior, the neonate, 'emerge' almost simultaneously."

Thus life emerges in the matrix of relationship.

The second trajectory, the unfolding of the fetus's innate capacities, is every bit as miraculous as the first. Early in the first trimester, the embryoblast develops three germ layers—the ectoderm, mesoderm, and endoderm. The ectoderm will form the nervous system as well as the nose, mouth, anus, and skin. The ectoderm sprouts the notochord, and by the end of the second week a neural plate emerges with a groove in the middle. This neural groove is two millimeters long. It closes the amniotic sac, and the embryo changes shape from looking like a pointed egg to the more easily recognized C. By the end of the fourth week, thirty-eight pairs of somites can be seen along the edges of the neural groove. They will develop into the different parts of the central nervous system. In the sixth week, the skeleton begins to harden. The first brain waves, as discerned by current technology, appear.

Unlike the first and third trimesters, growth in the second trimester does not overly emphasize the brain and nervous system. There is a recognizable human body, and each of its systems matures rapidly. In the nervous system, neurons proliferate and the characteristic folds in the brain develop. While fully functioning myelination (surrounding of the nerve fiber by the myelin sheath) must wait until the third trimester, the nerve fibers do develop a "whitish" look. These are early myelin deposits. The spinal cord thickens, supported by increased muscular and skeletal strength. The forebrain enlarges. The midbrain is covered by the cerebral cortex. Facial expressions can be seen, and the fetus can hear.

By early in the third trimester, brain convolutions are prominent. The fetus sleeps and most likely dreams. By week thirty, the brain is growing so rapidly that the skull is literally pushed out. Myelination, spurred by the maturing and proliferating Schwann cells, spreads rapidly. The brain folds, and folds again, increasing its surface area dramatically in proportion to its volume. These convolutions create the space for a seemingly infinite amount of neuronal connections. In this trimester, a large proportion of the blood flow is primarily to the brain in order, no doubt, to nourish this increased growth and complexity. By the end of this trimester, the child will have the full complement of neurons for life. The future holds only more myelination, pruning of unused neurons, and, most important, increased dendrite connections.

And with this huge head, the senses, directly wired to the brain, come alive. The eyes are completed, except for tear ducts and postpartum growth. The optic stalk develops into the optic nerve, which, of course, is part of the brain itself. However, myelination of the optic nerve needs some ten days of light stimulation after birth for completion.[45] The eyelids are now open for the first time since the tenth week. It seems fair to guess that the new light and images coming into the brain stimulate its development as well.

The ear is quite complex. It is only now that its various parts migrate to their final positions on the head. The mucous plug that has filled the tympanic cavity dissolves and the tympanic membrane sets the proper acoustical environment for hearing. The tympanic cavity can now host the mastoid antrum, a hollow tube communicating sound between the middle and inner ear. Amazingly, no mastoid cells are present until two years of age, and the entire development of the middle ear is said to take until puberty. We have to marvel at the complex interconnectedness as the senses develop and feed the brain and the brain develops to accommodate the senses. The whole is emergent and transcendent of any of its parts.

As term approaches, the importance of the lungs accelerates. If the baby doesn't breathe, it doesn't live. If the brain does not have a large and continuous supply of oxygen, there is severe injury and, in a relatively short time, death. Thus, by the twenty-sixth week, capillaries appear that feed the thin airway passage cells and sacs.[46] More oxygen is delivered to the lungs. More oxygen increases the lungs' manufacturing capacities. In lock-step coordination, autonomic nerves myelinate. The central nervous system message relay system is now intact. The brain can tell the lungs of its requirements. The lungs rapidly develop to meet these needs. The capillary network gets denser and richer. The alveolar walls are intact, and almost all the "dead air" space is taken up with the honeycomb cells. All systems are ready for life outside the womb.

The skin is the largest organ of the body and the external locus of touch. It is the best developed of the sense organs at birth. In this trimester, the skin usually loses the last of its soft, downy coat, which may well increase its sensitivity. As Ashley Montagu, an internationally recognized anthropologist, points out in *Touching: The Human Significance of the Skin*, the parts of the brain that receive and transmit the sensations of touch are the most "hardwired" of any of the brain's sensory transmitting and receiving stations at the time of birth. This suggests that the touch in the birth canal sends crucial signals to the birthing child.[47]

And so the child is born. Transition completed. In this new stage of life, most people simply want to hold the baby, sneak a finger in her little fist, press him to the breast, smile in her presence, speak softly, with a moment of eye contact if possible, think thoughts for a great life, and feel feelings of love. Loving touch, the most important nourishment for BodyBeing children, is naturally present.

Welcome.

From BodyBeing to FeelingBeing

Cognitive psychologists suggest four aspects of death—irreversibility, finality, causality, and inevitability—that once known, demonstrate full understanding by the child. Irreversibility, also called irrevocability, is the understanding that once a living thing has died, its physical body cannot live again. Finality, also called cessation of function, is the understanding that all life-defining bodily functions—including metabolism, feeling, movement, and thought—cease at death. Inevitability is the understanding that all living things must eventually die. Causality is the understanding of the physical-biological factors that result in death.[48]

There is universal agreement that these aspects are first truly understood by children around the age of six to seven. This is when children are most fully competent in their bodies and in their mastery of the sensory world. Their egotism is at its strongest. Witness the abundance of Superman, Power Ranger, and princess costumes for children of this age. It is at this moment of confidence and competence in their bodies that the ultimate physical boundary, death, appears. Without the confidence and the underlying strength developed over the BodyBeing years, the reality of death might be debilitating. The lesson, though, has to be learned. The entire sensory world ends. All things die and there is no going back.[49]

Thus, the limits of the stage are built into the stage itself. The search for boundaries and place in the physical world leads directly to the boundary of all physical forms themselves.

I recall a conversation I had many years ago with the director of a well-established and highly respected private school. I asked how she and her colleagues dealt with the question of death with the children. "For the children around six," she said, "there is a great fascination when a school pet, like a gerbil, dies. The children want to touch it. They poke it and confirm to one another that it is 'deaded.' Then they want to go out and play. It is slightly different if someone loses a relative—they acknowledge that the relative is not coming back and that the affected child will probably be sad. It is a topic of short-term interest, but we do make sure to bring it to the children's attention.

"Around nine things change. All the children seem to engage in some play that 'kills' them and from which they can spring back to life. When we see this in their play together, it is time to create a forum with the topic of death included."

This evaluation matches the results of our fieldwork and the fieldwork of many others.[50] Maria Nagy had noted this in 1948.[51] Gesell Institute researchers note that six-year-old children are more aware of death in their surroundings and begin to show concern that a parent will die, but most still believe that death is a reversible process.[52] By seven, they know of death but firmly adhere to the life-after-death beliefs of their family.[53] At eight, children are actively interested in death as a subject and seem to accept its inevitability.[54] And as I noted in my first book, in her work with dying children, Elisabeth Kubler-Ross found that children below nine are concerned whether they will have the same malformed body after they die. At nine years of age they open to the mystery: Where will I go when I die? What really continues on?

Dr. David A Gershaw, a psychologist at Arizona Western College, states the case most succinctly. Speaking of the ages five to nine, he says:

> During this period, the concept of death is becoming more factual and accurate. Children recognize the finality of death, and they also start to fear death. Early in this period, most children accept death as an eventuality. However, death happens only to other people—not to them. They may worry that their parents may die and leave them. Excluding accidents, murders, and serious illnesses, they have some understanding that death is more likely with older people.
>
> Later in this period, children suspect that they too may die but many still deny the fact. By nine, most children accept the fact that they will die, but this death is seen in the distant future. They may have preoccupations with hospitals, funerals or burial. In contrast, they could also be less willing to talk about death, hiding their feelings about highly emotional situations.

The nationally accredited Wild Iris Medical Education offers continuing education for nurses. In addition to noting that awareness of personal mortality occurs around nine years of age, they emphasize that children of this age experience greater death anxiety than children at any other age.[55]

At seven, the child knows the nature of death. But it is usually not until nine that the child knows that she herself dies. At that point, the sensory mode loses supremacy. The world has a definite limit. No egotism can resist the certain knowledge of personal mortality. The old stage transforms as a new stage is born. A different mode of knowing is called forth.

The years from seven to nine, then, mark the transition from BodyBeing to FeelingBeing. Tracing the child's perception of death doesn't, however, inform us of the child's experience during this important time. It is there that we now turn our attention.

The child switches back and forth between BodyBeing and FeelingBeing during transition. He is always in one stage or the other. Switches can happen quite frequently and in a short amount of time. The same dynamics hold for all transitions, including from FeelingBeing to IdealBeing and from IdealBeing to ReasonableBeing.

At the beginning of transition, there are many more BodyBeing moments than FeelingBeing moments. At the end, it is almost entirely FeelingBeing. If we picture BodyBeing as dots of red and FeelingBeing as dots of yellow, then behavior at seven years of age would have approximately 90 percent red dots and 10 percent yellow dots. The reverse would be true for the eight-and-a-half-year-old. There are no orange dots. The child is always one or the other. By nine, with sure and certain knowledge of personal mortality, it is all FeelingBeing. A new birth has occurred. The same surprise and wonder that the newborn baby has when she opens her eyes to the world, the nine-year-old has when she opens to the depth of her own feelings and the feelings of others.

Going from a sensory-based mode of knowing to a feeling-based mode of knowing can come as a shock to children. They have spent all of their lives assuming their bodies would always be there and be dependable.

Joyce had no children and came to a Natural Learning Rhythms seminar to understand her own childhood. Before we were even settled in our chairs, she spoke up: "I need help to understand one moment in my life." We stopped the opening exercises and listened as Joyce went on. "When I was a child, we had a game set up in our backyard. There was a small trampoline in front of a low wall. We placed mattresses and pads behind the wall and we would run, jump, do acrobatics in the air, and soft land on the other side. I loved to do it and often did daring and exciting flips. Then one day, I just could not do it. For the first time, I felt a fear in my belly as I prepared to run. Three steps into it, my legs were wobbly, and by the time I reached the wall, I was at a complete stop. Tears welled up which I tried to push away. I willed myself to start over but knew something was different. Finally I just walked away. I was morose for days. And I am still puzzled. What happened?"

The switch often mystifies parents as well. We used to joke that if we simply offered consultations for parents of eight-year-old children, it would occupy all our time. But there is sadness in this joke, too. Many transition behaviors are the result of the natural extension into a new mode of knowing, a new way of organizing the world. Parents often interpret these behaviors as pathological and seek counseling or medical help to "fix the problem" and "make the child normal again."

That might well have happened to Maria had she not attended a Natural Learning Rhythms seminar. The mother of an eight-year-old boy and six-year-old girl, Maria found the seminar useful and enrolled in the more advanced seminar. During introductions, she surprised everyone by holding a stained T-shirt with several large holes aloft. "You may notice," she said laughingly, "that this T-shirt is ironed. I did not believe what was said in the last workshop about the transition between BodyBeing and FeelingBeing. I believe it now. I would have ignored my son's demand to iron this T-shirt before the workshop and knowing him, he probably would have erupted. Instead, I simply treated it as an ordinary event. He quietly thanked me. It was only later that night that I noticed that our day together was so smooth. We even disagreed about when he should do his homework but we worked it out just fine."

These two stories are representative of transition behaviors as the child moves from BodyBeing to FeelingBeing. Children, however, being unique and creative people, come up with many variations. One child insists that her parents park between the lines in the shopping center. Another becomes upset that Grandma will be insulted if they are five minutes late for an afternoon visit. An eight-year-old boy decides on the spur of the moment to serve all twelve guests their soup at his grandfather's birthday celebration. A nine-year-old girl ingenuously and with quiet joy tells Josette that she "never knew there were so many kinds of love." An eight-year-old boy becomes angry with his mother when she is effusively friendly with her cousin soon after he heard her excoriating the cousin to his father.

These are the less disturbing transition behaviors, yet they usually cause great concern. What is my child doing? He was always a rough-and-ready boy and now he spends forty-five minutes combing his hair...She loves the wilderness and camping and now she won't go out in the dark...She didn't like that uncle who lived far away and whom she rarely saw and now she is crying inconsolably because he had a heart attack...He used to love school and now he won't go and complains that his teacher is unfair...She used to enjoy the humor of changing the rules of the board game and now we must follow them exactly...He used to have no concern for manners and now his friend tells him it is disgusting to chew with his mouth open and he stops immediately.

Other transition behaviors can be even more disconcerting to parents and teachers. Regressive behaviors like nightmares and bedwetting are not uncommon. Some children become daredevils and take frightening risks.[56] Others revert to baby talk or wish to play only with much younger children. Superstition can take hold. Unwarranted premonitions, such as fear of turning a corner, stepping on cracks in a sidewalk, or of saying goodbye to a parent in the morning, might appear. The self-consciousness natural to the moment might turn into zealous perfectionism. Some children feel that if they are perfect in everything, then they are good, right, and protected.

- An Exercise in Feelings -

Here's a thought experiment that many seminar participants have found useful. Do not consign it to some wastebasket by labeling it "touchy-feely." On the contrary, to recall emotions from childhood and re-experience them as adults allows history to be changed and new perspectives to dawn, and can bring greater empathy for children. Treat it seriously and take your time.

Close your eyes and get comfortable. Now drift back to the time you were seven or eight years of age. It may help to call up the image of a room, a pet, or a sibling from that time in order to activate the memory. Take some time with each suggestion that follows. [Pause.] See yourself at the dinner table or at a family gathering. [Pause.] See yourself at school, in the classroom, and on the playground. Can you see any embarrassing moments? What are you feeling? [Pause.] Can you see any examples of the described behaviors or something similar? [Pause.] Can you see any difference between your experience as a six-year-old and as an eight-year-old? Was there a death or a divorce in your family or in a family with whom you were close? Can you recall your own feelings? Did you have an older or younger sibling or cousin? Can you recall their reactions? Were there any differences between their perception of the event and yours?

I have seen all of the above and more. It certainly is perplexing—yet that is only half of the picture, for these newly arising FeelingBeing behaviors are part of a transition from BodyBeing. Therefore, many BodyBeing behaviors are still present. In an instant, the child can move from one stage to the next and back again.

Transition usually begins at around seven years of age.57 BodyBeing is at its highest competency. Egotistically driven imagination soars through the child. Many BodyBeing children can "fall in love" with an older person of the opposite sex whom they are sure will "wait" for them. We know of one six-and-a-half-year-old boy who slept at the foot of the bed of a twenty-two-year-old friend of the family. Joyce's expectations were also typical egotistical BodyBeing. She had been reveling in the adulation of her physical feats.

The contrast between the two types of behavior is startling. Joyce freezes, feeling self conscious and exposed. What if she fails? How will people feel about her? The boy realizes that his romantic intentions will fail and is inconsolable.

The FeelingBeing behaviors are tentative exploration of the nature of relationship. They seek to find the context in which feelings can be explored. The child is vulnerable, tender, and naive. She is trying to appreciate the rules of the social game. Never having done it before, her attempts are crude, abrupt, unexpectedly silken, ridiculously contradictory, and alternatively fearless and fearful. The BodyBeing behaviors fully express all the sensory-based egotistical learning. They are the behaviors to which parents and child have grown accustomed for the past eight years. Even excessive exhibitionism, once considered cute, might be tolerated if the behavior is strongly endorsed by family members, as happened with Joyce on her trampoline.

The child transitioning from BodyBeing to FeelingBeing does not yet have reflective cognizance. She is concerned neither with the "why" of the behavior, nor with where it might be leading. It is simply there. This sensitive, vulnerable child depends on feedback from family and friends to integrate her experiences. Optimal well-being can flourish if there is developmentally sensitive acceptance and nurturing during this time. Shame and excessive fear can take hold if the new behaviors lead to rejection or humiliation.

Parental understanding is the most important nourishment during this transition. First, which stage is running the show, BodyBeing or FeelingBeing? Parents find it easier to respond to BodyBeing, since they have been doing it for eight years. They also tend to see BodyBeing when FeelingBeing is there.

I've made the mistake myself. At a family camp, an eight-year-old girl came to the dinner line late. She saw the length of the line and groaned. Treating her like a BodyBeing, I took her to the front. Her anger flared. She only wanted to be on line with her parents, where she would have been had she not gone on an errand for my staff. It wasn't fair for her to be penalized when she followed the rules. Her unhappiness had nothing to do with BodyBeing egotism.

Parental understanding has many dimensions, especially when the new stage peeks through. Stacey attended a Natural Learning Rhythms workshop at a homeschooling conference. Excited, she went home that evening extolling its virtues to her husband, Ron. He, suspicious, was about to challenge Stacey when Toni, their eight-year-old daughter, came into their bedroom rubbing her eyes, frightened from a nightmare. This was the fourth time Toni had done this in the last week. Ron saw his chance and threw down the gauntlet.

"Let's see what Natural Learning Rhythms has to say about this," he said. "It's no good if we can't use it."

They found an essay in the workshop material that described the concerns with mortality of this age child. Ron, impressed but still skeptical, decided to talk with Toni about death. At first, she was confused as he asked her a direct question about her "perception" of death. But she did not push him away. She asked if he was talking about the way their cat died. Ron alertly switched the topic, and from the cat they went to their feelings about each other, including two siblings who were fast asleep, to their feelings about themselves. Ron, Stacey, and Toni lay on the bed, talking by candlelight, for over an hour. In the dreamy softness, Toni told her parents that she worried about their death. They asked her about her own. She said that sometimes she felt so alone and empty and it scared her. Two months later at family camp, Ron told me he had not felt that intimate with his child since her birth.

Look at the several ways in which Stacey and Ron understood. First, they understood the salient facts about development. Next, they understood that their response contributed mightily to the shape and definition of the moment. Toni's reality and their response were not separate. Third, they understood that they had to be welcoming and patient. Stacey told me at family camp that everything in her wanted to tell Toni that she was a big girl now and had outgrown coming to their bed four years earlier. She did not act on those thoughts. Instead, she found herself mesmerized by the conversation and appreciating Ron's delicacy, tact, and obvious care for his daughter.

Watch for the signs that awareness of death is taking hold in your child. Toni had nightmares, a common indicator. Kelsey became very upset when an aunt died, even though they were not close. Other children react intensely during a tragic story or movie. James suffered bouts of melancholy. Typically, he was obsessed with his parents' death. Soon his fears about his own death surfaced. The melancholy disappeared when his parents connected with him.

As the child is transitioning and still connected to BodyBeing, the body often reveals the deeper emotions. If the anxiety is strong and there is no outlet, the child's body may become tense, almost rigid, around the jaw line and shoulders. Physiological symptoms might appear, such as stomachaches, nail-biting, and sleeplessness.

And it is in these moments that I have seen parents make the terrible mistake of pathologizing the behavior and turning to therapy and antidepressants to fix the child. All that is needed is understanding and connection. The symptoms arise from the natural need for relationship during this dawn of the awareness of personal mortality. The family can and must respond. Therapy and drugs stigmatize the child, cost the family time and money, and bury death in the shadow. They worsen the situation in every way.

When parents understand and children are nourished, the transitions are often humorous. Marie laughed when her son asked to have his T-shirt ironed. All the children in the nature class gave me a stern lecture for changing a rule in a game without informing them. Eight-year-old Karen wore a dress to a social gathering but brought jeans along "just in case." She changed within five minutes. Ken cried for ten minutes when the young hero in the movie *Simon Birch* died, and then he suggested a trip to the ice cream store.

Children in transition often need protection. While the transition from FeelingBeing to IdealBeing is well recognized, this transition is not. James Moffett, a brilliant educator and mentor to the New York City school system for thirty years, asked me once if I knew why third-grade teachers had difficulty with their classes. His question was not surprising, as we had been asked similar questions by teachers for more than twenty years. Few people understand this transition. They are confused by the dramatic changes in behavior and perception. Children are expected to act grown up, which means with BodyBeing competency, and their new vulnerability is neither expected nor welcomed. Confusion and dissonance frequently follow.

At this moment, protection can save the day. Validate the child's feelings if teachers or classmates have been insensitive. Inform family and close friends about transitions so they will be kind during the shifts and changes. Don't let anyone belittle the child for her naive attempts to implement social rules and mores. Acknowledge the challenges in growth and change. Express your love and your long-term commitment to the relationship.

Understanding, talking about death, and offering protection are the essence of feeling mentoring during the FeelingBeing to BodyBeing transition. Just as loving touch, the primary nourishment for BodyBeing, was naturally called for at the birth of the physical, so feeling mentoring, the primary nourishment of FeelingBeing, is naturally called for at the birth of the emotions.

From FeelingBeing to IdealBeing

Transitions, as we are seeing, are tricky and often difficult for all involved. They startle with their complete newness. In the transition from BodyBeing to FeelingBeing, the belief in the body is completely undermined by the unfolding realization of personal mortality. It is not that the body is no longer perceived as a mediator of pleasure and direction. Rather, the child's relationship to their body no longer determines the meaning of an event—it no longer is the ultimate realm in which the organization of experience and action takes place. That Mary is a fast swimmer who explores and enjoys all sorts of water activities is no longer a significant aspect of Mary's definition of self. Those around her who insist on continuing to bestow social status on her for her water skills lose credibility to her.

While the transition from BodyBeing to FeelingBeing suffers from relative anonymity, the exact opposite is true for the transition from FeelingBeing to IdealBeing. It is the most celebrated transition in all of childhood. Unfortunately in the West, this celebration is often of its steep challenges rather than of its inherent health and greatness. As one parent humorously stated when asked her reason for joining a seminar, "It's because my child is about to turn into a t-t-t-t-teenager." Because of the inherent difficulties and subsequent confusion about all transitions, and especially that from FeelingBeing to IdealBeing, it seems well worth our time to take a moment to consider the underlying dynamics of all transitions. To do this, we must turn to the discipline of complexity theory.

Dynamics

Complexity theory attempts to describe the dynamics of change for whole systems. It arose in part because previous scientific attempts to understand the nature of time had failed. If you cannot describe time accurately, then it is impossible to describe change accurately. Newton had to pose an "objective" world of space and one of time in order to posit his classical theory. In Newtonian dynamics, if one knows the coordinates of any event in space and in time, one can determine both the history and the future of that event. There is no "arrow of time." Though it was somehow unnoticed for two hundred years, Newtonian physics fails to account for what is common sense to all of us. A broken glass does not reassemble itself, milk mixed into coffee cannot be separated, and children do not return to previous developmental stages, no matter how much parents may wish they did! There is an arrow of time. I can know the coordinates, but I cannot re-create the pouring of that milk. It no longer exists. It is in my coffee and both it and the coffee are changed forever.

The study of the dynamics of large systems begins with an understanding of thermodynamics, and thermodynamics began with the study of the steam engine. In the latter part of the eighteenth century, James Joule discovered that there is always equivalence between heat, work, and energy. This finding led to the formulation of the first law of thermodynamics, which states that energy will always be conserved in physical processes. Work plus heat equals energy produced. Experimentation soon showed that work cannot account for all the energy in a process—some must be lost as heat. And heat always flows from hotter to cooler. This finding led to the second law of thermodynamics, which states that there is an inexorable loss of heat in all work. This heat loss has come to be known as *entropy*, and it strongly suggests an arrow to time. Heat that is lost cannot be recaptured, and therefore a process cannot be reversed.

While very useful in the development of the machines that ran the Industrial Revolution, the concept of entropy also led to all sorts of mistaken notions. Most prevalent, and perhaps most pernicious, was that the universe was moving to some sort of steady-state cold death. In science, this state is called equilibrium and is defined as that state from which no further exchange of work, heat, and energy can take place. In other words, no change, no heat, and no life occur at equilibrium.

The problem was that thermodynamics was originally conceived by studying closed systems such as steam engines. All the variables are known and controlled in closed systems. Thus, linear equations can describe the relationships of work, heat, and energy in a closed system, because each variable can be precisely measured.

But life does not work that way—only certain kinds of human inventions. In life, not all the variables are known and controlled. Complexity has clearly shown for more than fifty years that molecules, rivers, the weather, hearts, humans, and all natural processes are open systems. Natural processes are in continual communication with the elements of the system and with their environments.

Open systems are said to be far from equilibrium. Emergence—which shows that highly complex, unpredictable and seemingly counterintuitive objects and patterns can emerge from relatively simple contexts—is one of the most important characteristics of systems far from equilibrium. Proof of emergence and the vitality of open systems started with the study of molecules. Ilya Prigogine and his colleagues at the Brussels Free University, in the 1960s, showed that molecules, when treated as open systems, self-organize to greater levels of complexity. This finding leads to the extraordinary conclusion that the molecules were somehow communicating with one another to allow this greater whole to manifest. And the new whole could not have been predicted from the parts that composed it. It emerged due to the dynamics of the system itself.

Differential equations can be used to describe systems that are far from equilibrium—that are open. They describe "the instantaneous change of properties with time."[58] In other words, in the series of equations used to describe a process, the results of the first equation become a variable in the second. With the aid of computers, the many changes that happen throughout a process can be modeled by these equations. Countless studies ranging in subject matter from cities, to ants, to weather, to computer games conclusively demonstrate that any change can have disproportionate effects on the system, depending on the condition of the system when the change was initiated. The results have set science reeling, changing the way humans conceive of evolution, epidemics, the weather, heart attacks, boiling water, geometry, and just about everything in between.

Conditions at the moment when a perturbation occurs are called the initial conditions. Most important for our inquiry into transitions in human development, chaos theory has shown the overarching importance of initial conditions. Under certain initial conditions, an arrhythmic heartbeat might go unnoticed; under others, it might mean a heart attack. Tsunamis, tornadoes, the course of rivers, and chemical reactions are among the many events where the initial conditions when a perturbation occurs are critical to its future.[59] Complexity theory is addressed again in chapter 10, "Reunification," for it has much to offer for helping us understand how to heal family dysfunction.

This theory underscores the importance of the transitions between developmental stages. We have slowly come to realize this in relation to the birth of the body. Home births, birthing rooms, the presence of fathers at parturition, and increased sensitivity among many parents reflect a commonsense appreciation of the value of the way we welcome the newborn.

We now need to extend this sensitivity to the birth of the other developmental stages as well. A vulnerability similar to that of the newborn is characteristic of the receptive phases of the other developmental stages as well. At this moment children and their families have heightened vulnerability and instability. The familiarity and confidence developed over the years of living with the former stage are gone. The dawn of each developmental stage is a new birth—a new way of understanding—of relationship and of meaning. The initial conditions present when a child enters a stage play a critical role in the child's ability to organize their life for optimal well-being.

Thus the dynamics of open systems, such as a child, are described by the synergy between initial conditions and the ongoing quality of communication with the environment. If a child's natural needs are met, then he remains far from equilibrium, in a dynamic flux that allows the greatest possibilities for complex self-organization. Clearly, support for our children as they enter a developmental stage is a gift we can all offer. Likewise, we can create high-quality communication opportunities for their whole being—psychological, physical, cognitive, emotional, social, and spiritual—by responding to their developmental needs throughout the stage.

As complexity and the attendant emergence suggest, this synergy will have completely unexpected results. Each stage has a rich, unique complexity that cannot be comprehensively predicted from the data from the previous stage. Understanding change and attuning ourselves to its rhythms nourishes optimal well-being.

There is one more important implication of complexity theory to consider before we turn to the specifics of the FeelingBeing-IdealBeing transition. Concern arises in most seminars when parents realize the problems they now face with their children may well have their roots in inadequate nourishment during previous developmental stages. They now wonder how to approach the child. Should they "go back" and try to supply what was missed? Or should they meet the needs of the current stage?

The answer is clear: You cannot go back and neither can they. There is change and there is an arrow to time. There will never again be those same initial conditions, nor can the child organize their world now as they did then, even if they want to.

Some people see this constraint as a condemnation to a suboptimal life; others, of similar persuasion, believe it is proof that early childhood experiences determine the course of a person's life. It is, in fact, a key to liberation and indicates the way to overcome early childhood deficits. Each developmental stage is a new birth—a fresh moment with new initial conditions. Each new organizing principle changes the child's, parents', and family's perspective radically and thus demands new forms of thinking, feeling, and communicating. New stages insist on new perspectives and new perceptions. Humans could not be closed systems even if they tried, which unfortunately many do, to everyone's detriment.

Therefore, go through the open window. Relate to the child according to the developmental imperatives of the moment. Help the child actualize optimal well-being at the current level of complexity. As parent, child, and family come to live in optimal well-being, they come to know it ever more deeply and to consciously participate in bringing it to the fore. Wisdom-based relationships emerge.

Initial Conditions for IdealBeing

First and foremost, parents must give up wishing for the FeelingBeing child to remain. To resist the changes is to treat the child as a closed system. FeelingBeing, with its care for relationships, devotion to the community, sensitivity to morality, and feel for transcendence is passing. But those attached to the values of FeelingBeing tend to have a hard time opening to the learning of the new stage. For many parents, it seems the competent FeelingBeing child is the one they hoped to parent—the one closest to fulfilling their desire for a certain kind of child. The behavioral developmentalist Arnold Gesell called twelve years of age "the golden age of childhood." This, combined with the anxiety implicit in the cultural prejudice against teens, sometimes leads to grasping for who the child was and thus prevents appreciation of who the child is.

The other initial condition that serves optimal well-being is to understand all that we can about the coming stage. Its actual arrival will be a surprise, no doubt. Consider the first time you held a newborn child. For most of us, all the books, stories from others, and experiences with other children fell away. Who was this child? How did this miracle occur? In the same way, the arrival of IdealBeing will be a surprise. If we understand its inherent health and greatness, we can greet it with the same delighted anticipation that we did the newborn.

The Transition

At the end of FeelingBeing, the child has maximized their ability to trust and to reciprocally cooperate. She can decipher her own feelings and the feelings of others. She values her connection to the family and community. In the best of situations, her world view has expanded to include personal mortality with some direct experience of inspiration, transcendence, and metaphysical mystery. Aesthetics count and the beauty of nature and feelings in music are alive.

In the transition from FeelingBeing to IdealBeing, the certainty of trust in feelings, friends, and community is shaken. The child becomes conscious of the need to self-govern, which includes taking control of her relationships. Ideals begin to form and to be projected as a way of expressing this movement toward autonomy. This process is often exasperating for elders. Here is this child with little experience of the world claiming that they know how it should be run. Many children do this quietly, either by word or deed. They often highlight what they believe is not right and how it should be remedied in home, school, and the world. The naive projection of ideals has arrived.

As the child alternates between FeelingBeing and IdealBeing, wildly disparate behaviors often manifest. I have seen children of this age cuddle in the parent's lap one moment and two minutes later leave with their peers without saying goodbye. Some early teens disavow interest in the sports teams or religion that once bonded them to their friends and family. Others simply redefine their relationship to these institutions. They no longer turn to the adult as the authority on whether a relief pitcher should be called or what Jesus meant when he said, "Turn the other cheek."

I have been with children while they went to see both animated fairy tales and horror movies in the same day. One exquisite example of the wide swing of behavior that can happen in a short time involved Mandi, a young friend of ours. She abruptly left the Saving Nature Club that she had helped found, declaring allegiance to it "nerdy." A few hours later, she became angry with her beloved grandfather for tossing a candy wrapper on the ground. She dismissed him and his actions with a sneer and putdown of his disregard for the environment. That evening, she was inexpertly trying on cosmetics. When reminded that some of them were tested on animals, she rationalized her actions by saying that "some things are okay if kids learn from them."

Mandi's discomfort when she was confronted about the cosmetics was obvious, yet she did not let reason sway her. This might infuriate some, but to me it is natural and humorous. IdealBeing children are not motivated by reason. It is as absurd to use it with them as it is with BodyBeing children. They are searching for an autonomous sense of self and they have never done it before. It is a scary moment for them. They are asserting and insecure in the same moment, and they know it. Yet they are compelled to do so. It seems compassionate to give them the latitude of their experimentation. Elders do not ridicule children while they learn to talk. Hopefully, they will not ridicule eight-year-old children while they learn to relate socially. Now, the child is going to experiment with identities and ideals while they fulfill the human imperative of developing their sense of self. Can we accept them in their struggle?

The rapids engulf IdealBeing children. Though the onset of the stage is not identical with the onset of puberty, the urges that puberty brings are present in the transition. Sex is scary and alluring, peers are necessary yet intimidating, parents are great yet embarrassing, and the opposite sex is, well, there. Yearning for freedom pulses through the child along with a crude appreciation of the responsibility it entails. Fear of failure often follows hard on the heels of the persistent desire for challenges. Lassitude can alternate with bursts of frenetic energy. And in the midst of these rapids—in the midst of these changes—the moorings of emotional attachment to family and community often loosen. Without proper nourishment, they may well break free.

Part of a massive study, the National Longitudinal Study of Adolescent Health, initiated on a grant by the National Institute of Child Health and Human Development,[60] mirrors this well. The sample cut across economic and cultural lines. Eighty-five percent of the teens said that family relationships were extremely important to them. Eighty-five percent also said that "It's up to me to get what I want out of life." Only 34 percent viewed upholding traditions and time-honored customs as important.

Get ready. Traditions and customs will be challenged and sometimes disingenuously discarded. Do not take it personally. The BodyBeing child was weaned and moved on to a more complex diet. He did not leave the dinner table. The IdealBeing child gives up attachment to some traditions. He is not leaving the family system.

Stay connected—that is the natural state of relationship. The child may become moody and distant and desire alone time. That can be healthy, as she has much to integrate in these rapidly changing moments. However, do not lose connection. The alone time should not lead to excessive isolation. It should not cut you out of the child's life. At the most basic place of human beingness, you are profoundly and uninterruptedly connected. If that is forgotten, if that is lost, then the initial conditions support the illusion of separation. It may be years before the natural state of interconnectedness is regained. The cited study found that emotional distress, suicide thoughts and attempts, violence, early sexual activity, cigarette use, alcohol use, marijuana use, and pregnancies were significantly reduced when parents had four contacts a day with their teens. Connecting at breakfast, after school, at dinner, and at bedtime are so important that the study named it the most important factor in teen health. Never is it more important than in the tumultuousness of transition.

The simplest way to stay connected is to offer sensitive respect, the primary nourishment for IdealBeing children. That respect naturally emerges within the context of recognizing that parent and child are navigating the rapids together, though each faces her own challenges.

From IdealBeing to ReasonableBeing

In the transition from IdealBeing to ReasonableBeing, doubt cracks the IdealBeing assertions. Ultimately, ideals are brittle things, and they shatter with the tensions of data and experiences that cannot be incorporated into their romantic and quixotic structures. The complexity of life itself brings the irrevocable awareness that imposing one's will and beliefs will never be sufficient for organizing a life worth living. Early teen romance evaporates. A boy has to register for the draft and reevaluate his relationship to war and nation. The periodic table of elements suggests infinite chemical combinations. The human brain has countless connections. The observable galaxies just expanded exponentially when the Hubble telescope revealed a universe five hundred million light years larger than previously had been seen. These facts humiliate, which means "to bring back to earth," overblown ideals.

It is a moment of cognitive dissonance. The child becomes aware of the contradictions between ideals and reality. With guidance, the cognitive dissonance can be met with inquiry, dialogue, and support, and confusion can be avoided. Ideals can only exist in limited, simplistic conditions. As consciousness expands once again, the view becomes wider, broader, and more textured and nuanced. What is known in one context, becomes unstable when the context changes. Doubt is the healthy beginning of reasonableness.

The child's values serve identity formation in IdealBeing. As the transition to ReasonableBeing dawns, deeper questioning of the value themselves arises. Are there substantive values—values that last through all time and are not subject to shattering?

One night I was visiting Corey, our seventeen-year-old neighbor. He was sitting on the counter in the kitchen while Elaine, his mother, was making a pot of tea. He seemed despondent. When asked about his mood, he just shook his head as if clearing cobwebs. Corey is an accomplished student and a skilled carpenter, and he has many friends. His mood was unusual, and Elaine gently persisted.

"Nothing makes much sense," he said. "I just don't know what to think."

"What's the problem, son? You know we can work together to solve it."

Corey thought for a full two minutes. "There is no problem; that's the problem. I mean there's nothing specific." He paused, quite still, gazing out the window. "I think it's that I don't how to think about my thoughts." Elaine and I listened respectfully while he puzzled his way through, but I must admit I was inwardly smiling. Meanwhile, Corey was wandering in his contemplations. "I just don't trust my own thinking process anymore. How do I know I am approaching anything in the right way?"

At that moment, he doesn't know and parents who insist that he does will only turn doubt into confusion.

Elaine took several minutes before responding. "Is there something wrong with not knowing?" Elaine asked. "Are you supposed to be sure of the way to proceed?"

Corey turned to face her. He seemed focused and intent when he answered her. "It's really hard. How do you take on a relationship with anyone? How do you decide what's worth studying? How do I decide how to answer you?"

Elaine pondered his reply. She held Corey's eyes with her own soft gaze. Slowly a big smile spread across her face.

"What?" Corey said.

"It's just that, well, your answer a minute ago was pretty definite. You seemed very sure that it is difficult and how the difficulties play out."

Corey stared at his mother. "I don't get it."

"Start over. Are you supposed to know how to proceed? Is there a problem with not knowing?"

"Yes, it is hard. I said that before."

"Okay, how do you know? I thought you didn't trust your own thinking processes anymore. Yet you trust them when you say how hard it is."

"You're making it worse." Corey was getting peeved. "I've got to start somewhere."

"Oh."

"Is that what you're saying? That I've got to work with what I have?"

"You're already started. You're alive. It seems that in life there are times of doubt. Why did you believe it would be otherwise?"

Elaine did not try to save her son from his doubt. Actually, her reasonableness—her ability to relate with love and discrimination—increased the complexity of the moment for Corey. In this growth of complexity, Corey has the opportunity to gain new perspective on his ideals.

It is so important for the parents to simply stay connected with the child. As Elaine demonstrated, it is not about trying to save or protect the child—not to end the doubt but rather to provide companionship so the child can safely explore it. The child may express a generalized doubt, as Corey did about his thinking, or it may be specific to her ideals, such as no longer believing that skateboarding is important. In either case, the response is the same. Do not argue. Let go of the desire for the doubt to be gone. Ask questions. Stay connected. If possible, extol the value of doubt and remind the child that values that endure can be actualized. How can that happen, the child might ask. Now there's an interesting question. How can it happen for you, I might answer.

There is danger in this transition. In a type of self-betrayal, the value of values themselves can be doubted. Cynicism, despondency, depression, hedonism, or amorality can occur. The child needs connection and guidance to accept doubt as a reasonable way to engage the world. In doubting former values, the child creates the space for substantive values to emerge. It will take the years of ReasonableBeing for the child to integrate those values that last beyond time.

Doubt arises as the enormous dimensions of the universe become apparent and identity constructs fall apart. There is a need to find one's meaning in life and one's place in it. Perception of time expands to include past, present, and future. Children are now able to see that their past experiences in large measure determined their present moment and that the way they live in the present critically affects the life they will live in the future. As always in transition, the new field of play is at once enormous and compelling.

Surprisingly, most parents do not welcome the end of IdealBeing. The contrariness, the insistence on ideals, the assertive explorations into seemingly excessive realms, and the parade of identities have, for many parents, been a trying ordeal. Yet, by IdealBeing competency, most par-

- A School Sensitive to the IdealBeing to ReasonableBeing Transition -

David Marshak visited the Aurobindo Ashram in India and observed their comprehensive Centre of Education. Their college-level program is called "Knowledge." When the students enter the program, teachers ask them to revisit their notion of freedom. What does it mean to be free? How is freedom reflected in action? What do they wish to do; how do they hope to do it; and, most important, why do it? As Head of Knowledge Mr. Mukherji explained to Marshak, "What is the exact nature of the movement that is occupying my field of consciousness at this moment? Next, the how of the movement, for its genesis, how it rises to crescendo, how it goes down and disappears. The third question is the delicate question to answer, which requires great insight and honesty. Why? Why, at this particular moment, you felt like that, your react like that, you decided on this."

In other words, instead of rushing students to choose a career or a field of study, or even which class to take, the school insists on pausing and considering who one is and how choice is made. The student must step back and reasonably assess himself and the world. Only then can a free choice be made; only then can the student and the world benefit from education.[61]

ents have found a way to relate to the children. They have been through the rapids together and in that struggle found important bonding. They may, for instance, have had glimpses of the child's core nature and seen her potential greatness. Some find ways to not take the child's probing of the shadow personally and so experience a richer understanding of themselves, their parents, and their child. Others have found themselves protected by the IdealBeing's loyalty, even if at other times the child has distanced himself from them.

The IdealBeing child might well be self-satisfied and also reluctant to have the stage end. They have learned to self-govern in an ever-widening variety of social venues. They have attained some personal power and some measure of freedom. For many, their investment in their beliefs has paid off in significant achievements in areas of their interests, such as academics, hobbies, athletics, or social interactions. Friendships have formed, and the trials of the age have been engaged. They have found a sense of themselves as autonomous, and there is little desire to abandon it.

And so neither parent nor child is prepared for the collapse of these well-constructed identities. It is stunning for the child of eighteen to doubt what he has so stridently invested in. When the belief in the identity shatters, the child in the IdealBeing to ReasonableBeing transition may destabilize. Some want to radically change plans that have been carefully prepared, such as deciding to not go to college or to pursue a special interest. Many simply want to talk. The conversation can go over the same ground time and again as the children try to come to grips with the doubt that seems to permeate their being. Some children become emotionally volatile, surprised themselves by the range of feelings a seemingly insignificant event can engender. Many children suffer their biggest doubt in the very arena in which they formerly identified. Lots of college students drop out at this point, for instance, castigating academic learning as irrelevant.

On the other hand, many IdealBeing children concretize into the identity in which they have had success or deeply believe in. Some get married; others commit to a career or to the military, based on their idealistic projections. They short-circuit the process and hope to find comfort and certainty in their niche. If the people around them reinforce their beliefs, then Reasonableness will atrophy and meaning will never expand to interconnectedness. Their loyalties have become allegiances and it is almost certain that belief in separation—and in the superiority of those who hold that allegiance—will follow.

Exceptional is the elder who can allow everything to be questioned, who can easily forfeit their investment in the child's identity. Some parents feel double-crossed; others distance themselves from a perceived problem and wish for the child to "work it out on his own." It can be difficult to accept the child coming back for nurturing and acceptance when they have spent much of the previous five years concerned primarily with their own self-governance. Moreover, after eighteen years of parenting, it is disconcerting to hear the child proclaim they have little idea of who they are and of what values are important.

Most developmental paradigms group IdealBeing and ReasonableBeing together as one stage. Even less attention has been paid to this transition than to that between BodyBeing and FeelingBeing. It's as if everyone believes the child is grown up, fully matured, or at least should be left to "make their own decisions," as so many parents have said to me. It's this inattention that hinders development of the gift of reasonableness. The initial conditions are compromised. Parents, society, and even child development experts have missed this precious moment.

Therefore, with society's ignorance and the inherent destabilization, this transition can rapidly spiral downward into extreme confusion. I am not saying that ignorance of the transition is responsible, but suicide is the second leading cause of death in college students. I am saying that nourishing the transition will increase the chances of well-being. Children need to be welcomed; the pace of life needs to be slowed down. Everyone needs to pause, breathe, and reaffirm their relationship. Both parent and child have to be sure that everyone is ready for the new stage. The birth of ReasonableBeing is an enormous departure from the way the world was previously organized. The stakes are high because self-knowledge in ReasonableBeing is very complex and brings connection on scales heretofore unimaginable. The child is about to inhabit the universe.

Hesitancies

Joyce prepares to run, jump on the trampoline, and flip over the wall, but cannot move—she hesitates. Mandi zigzags between saving nature and using environmentally destructive cosmetics. She seems like she is going nowhere fast. Corey can't get off the kitchen counter. These moments of holding back, of doubt and indecision, are hesitancies.

Hesitancies are natural rhythms of growth. They are natural rhythms of growth. Repeating the sentence is not a misprint. I have seen parents confuse hesitancies for illness many, many times, and in a significant number of cases they resort to intense therapies and antidepressants in response. It scares me. Not only has the mutual growth opportunity of the hesitancy been missed, but the child has been stigmatized for simply living her life.

Hesitancies are often accompanied by seemingly regressive behaviors. Children in the BodyBeing-FeelingBeing crossover may have periods when they become afraid of the dark or want to play only with younger children. Those transitioning from FeelingBeing to IdealBeing may want to be cuddled as if they were toddlers or deny their ability to stay home alone. We have seen what can happen during the passage from IdealBeing to ReasonableBeing. Corey forgot that he was thinking as he wondered whether he could think!

During hesitancies, parents often feel like knocking on the door and asking if anyone is home. Can the growth that the child had so clearly achieved just vanish? Is she faking it? Should I remind her that she already has been alone in the dark many times, or that she used to jump over the wall as easily as a bird flies?

To exacerbate matters, nightmares and poor health often come with the hesitancy. Last, and perhaps most difficult of all to comprehend, children in hesitancies often refuse to engage in their favorite activities. It might be a type of food, or a preferred entertainment, or a visit with friends, but in my experience, somewhere during hesitancy something that was previously desired is shunned.

What is a parent to do? In addition to the above remarks on the specifics of the transitions between stages, there are some general understandings to keep in mind. Hesitancies are a gift to the parents and to other family members. They always signal that a major change is about to occur. Their message is: Check all systems and prepare for an important new development in the child and in the family. They ask everyone to pause and to reaffirm their connection. The best move may well be to do very little—to welcome the child in their regression and assure them that they have your support.

Hesitancies occur just before and just after the birth of the life stages, and just before and after the arrival of the phases, of receptivity, trial and error, and competency. As initial conditions are so important, the response to the hesitancy greatly affects the rest of the stage or phase. There is a hidden opportunity here, for well-being can be reestablished in these gaps between both stages and phases. As always, optimal well-being depends on understanding the rhythms of development and providing the proper nourishment. I will incorporate descriptions of the hesitancies as we explore the dynamics of the phase transitions.

From Receptivity to Trial and Error

Each meaning-making moment marks the end of the transition from the phase of receptivity to the phase of trial and error. The child enters the transition, hesitates, makes meaning of what has been received, and then can deliberately experiment according to the capacities of that stage of development. Thus this phase transition is bookended. In the front is the hesitancy; at the end is the meaning-making moment. The hesitancy signals the change that is about to occur. The meaning-making moment signals that the new phase of trial and error has arrived. The interval between these two events is usually two to eight weeks; if it lasts longer, then a remedy as described in chapter 10 may be called for.

Cognitive psychologist Margaret Mahler studied this hesitancy carefully. She coined the term *rapprochement* to describe the way the child re-approaches the parents for support and nurturing. Of great interest, Mahler showed a strong correlation between this moment of rapprochement and the early teen years. If the child is welcomed, there are far

- A Classic Hesitancy -

Two-and-a-half-year-old Jonah loved to cook with his mother, Jeannie. He would pull over his stool, put on his apron, and mix. He loved to mix. Jeannie and Jonah would sing while they cooked, often for a couple of hours.

Seemingly overnight Jonah quit. He also rebelled against his bath and wanted nothing to do with his six-year-old brother's friends when they visited. His sleeping habits became erratic and he fussed when tired. Jeannie informed Larry, her husband. As they had been playing with NLR for four years, they were ready.

They did not force any issue, save the bath, which they insisted on gently and firmly. Using simple, concrete terms, they spoke with their older son. "Jonah needs time to do more quiet things," they said. Then, using photographs, they reminded him about when he was two and some of the special attention he had needed. Most important, they welcomed Jonah as he was and rechecked his nourishments of loving touch, flexibility, warmth, security, and the texture of his sensory environment. They did not coddle.

Four weeks later, Jonah exploded into sentences and paragraphs. Simply naming objects completely disappeared. His grammar was good and rapidly improved. The fussiness disappeared. He enjoyed his bath and his brother's friends more than ever. While he still enjoyed cooking at times, he did not return to it with the same enthusiasm. Sleep patterns became consistent once again.

fewer difficulties for the teen and between the teen and her parents. If the child is rejected, then trouble in the early teen years is predictable.[62]

Some behavioral descriptors that often apply to children in this hesitancy include obtuse, difficult, demanding, testing, autocratic, and fussy. Many want to be treated like an infant once again. If they are not nourished, the "terrible twos" follow. If they are nourished, it is more likely to be the "terrific twos." Some children may withdraw a bit, but most will draw repetitive attention to their needs.

The transition from receptivity to trial and error in FeelingBeing begins with a hesitancy that is often manifested as sudden fears, moping, obsessing over perceived insults, lying, nightmares, and rejection of familiar and previously welcomed social engagements. Much younger children may be preferred, and the ensuing play is reflective of the younger person's interests. Children hesitating here may give curt and sometimes dismissive answers to adults who ask about the reasons for their choices. Some children cling; others avoid.

The meaning-making moment is the opening of the mystery window—the first taste of the feeling of transcendence. Spotting this moment can be very difficult. It may be stimulated by music, theater, movie, art, or literature. The arts, after all, do aim for catharsis and the child is primed for emotional epiphany. While the aftermath will probably linger for several days, the crucial moment itself will very likely last a few hours or less. The mystery window will remain open for the whole of trial and error, but the end of transition is marked by the first experiences of feeling transcendence.

The Western zeitgeist presents additional problems. FeelingBeing itself is rarely recognized. The mystery window has no place in the behavioral-cognitivist paradigms that dominate the information markets about parenting and education. And yet in seminars, parent after parent has told me of experiences they have had between ten and eleven years of age that they now realize were meaning-making moments. Many are relieved to finally have a way to talk about these experiences that doesn't leave them feeling crazy or vulnerable to rejection by peers and family. Also, I have seen children go through the mystery window in EnCompass's Inspirational Journey program and family camps and family retreats. I am faithfully reporting my experiences and those of some parents who emphasize optimal well-being. The mystery window exists.

Joseph Chilton Pearce, the author of the 1970s best sellers *The Crack in the Cosmic Egg* and *Magical Child*, helped me clarify my observations about the meaning-making moment in IdealBeing. An octogenarian, Pearce still maintains a busy schedule as a conference presenter and advisor to academicians. While we were co-presenting several years ago in California, we were comparing his notion of biologically based stage-specific wisdom with NLR's ontological descriptions. He asked me about fifteen-year-old children. I related several anecdotes. He kept smiling and nodding. "I've seen this belief in their greatness and their possible future, too." Everything fell into place.

The hesitancy that marks the beginning of this phase transition often includes exaggeration of the challenges not yet successfully met in the receptivity phase. Shyness can appear as fear of the opposite gender. Insecurity may lead to blindly following peer direction. Rejection of responsibility can turn into fixating on FeelingBeing memories. The child may become confused and cynical if he is intimidated by the imperative to self-govern.

As hesitancies last only from two to eight weeks, it is important to observe the child carefully and make sure they come out on the other end into their meaning-making moment. If cynicism, continual capitula-

---

- Case History: From Receptivity to Trial and Error in IdealBeing -

Cranky Chris, as his friends called him, is an excellent soccer player. Dedicated to the game, Chris hopes it will be his ticket to college. During his first few years in IdealBeing, Chris was a perfectionist. When a teammate made a mistake or he disagreed with a referee's decision, Chris complained, sulked, and sometimes played selfishly. Of course, he was hardest on himself, and his mistakes left him withdrawn and belligerent.

Just after his fifteenth birthday, his bad pass cost his team an important game. In the bus on the way home, Chris silently berated himself while glaring at his teammates when they approached him. His coach, Don, sat down next to him, trapping him in the window seat. For the entire two hours of the ride home, Don talked. He told Chris that truly great people are not defined by the game they play but by the life they lead. He used examples, pro and con, of famous athletes and of those he personally knew. In skillful inquiry, he found out that Chris believed greatness was becoming the hero on the field. Don respectfully disagreed. Chris held his ground. Don elaborated, speaking quietly and from his heart. He told Chris that he respected and admired him but that his mistaken notion of greatness stood in the way of Chris becoming truly great. Chris softened. Don never asked for Chris to capitulate, but he did not stop speaking until they returned home.

Cranky Chris disappeared.

tion to peers, or fears of the other gender or ethnic groups persists, then remedies are called for as described in chapter 10.

The child usually refuses to take part in favorite activities during hesitancies. Josette and I were facilitating a seminar in Marin County, California. During the dialogue about IdealBeing, Joan, single mother of fifteen-year-old Jacques, related that her son had worked two jobs to fund skiing, one of his preeminent interests. This was the weekend of trials for an important race, and Jacques was leaving within the hour. Joan said that she was glad to have the weekend free. At that precise moment, Jacques burst into the room and insistently asked his mother to step outside. Of course, this attracted everyone's attention, and when Joan returned all eyes turned to her. "He's not going," she rued. "Did he say why?" someone asked. "He said he doesn't know why. It's just that he knows he can't go. He hoped I wouldn't be mad."

By ReasonableBeing, the child is able to deliberately consider and evaluate their actions. "Why do I act as I do and what does it mean?" often occupies the child's thoughts. This is reflective cognizance, a human trait that seems to be both a blessing and a curse. Reflective cognizance, when based in optimal well-being, allows great latitude in choosing one's response to a situation. It is the foundation for system creation. We not only can evaluate many of the variables in most situations, but we also can include ourselves—our actions, thoughts, feelings, and capacities. We know that who we are determines the quality of our lives.

It's a scary realization. Reflective cognizance changes responsibility into commitment. Maturity implies that when I say something, I mean it; it accords with my values, capabilities, and intent and suggests the future that I will live. This realization takes hold during receptivity. The reaction to it defines the hesitancy between receptivity and trial and error.

Second-guessing marks this hesitancy. The questioning doesn't stop. All the choices that have been made and are being made are questioned, questioned, questioned. Answers lead to more questions. Children plunge into experiences just to have the experiences; they are tired of the endless evaluations. Without support, the child can be debilitated. Substance abuse and compromised or promiscuous sex is often used to turn off the questioner. Children change course by leaving college, or resigning themselves to a mediocre job, or choosing partners and peers that indulge frivolity.

Then interconnectedness hits. The reason that questions about some things lead to questions about most things is that the universe is a continual weave in which some things lead to all things. The meaning-making moment dawns; systems creation matures. The questions lead to the underlying interconnectedness. Humility may come in the form of powerful and meaningful romance or in appreciation of how dialogue opens into insight. Humor often follows. The universe is vast, interconnected, mysterious, and approachable. Reflective cognizance is a gift. Life is sacred.

From Trial and Error to Competency

Rudolf Steiner believed that changes in the physicality of the child marked the transition between life stages. He summed up his description of the child in the first stage as "one big sense organ."[63] The child in the second stage develops the ability to love and is feeling-centered. Transition between the two, Steiner ardently insisted, begins with the change of teeth, between six and seven years old.

Jean Piaget believed that the last stage of cognitive development began at eleven or twelve with formal operational thought. Assimilation equals accommodation and adaptation inevitably results. Thought has reached its pinnacle.

In Natural Learning Rhythms, the second stage births at about nine years of age with the awareness of personal mortality. The transition to that stage begins at approximately six and a half. The third stage births at approximately thirteen years of age, with the transition beginning at eleven and a half.

The implication is that Steiner and Piaget are looking at the first evidence of the stage and calling that its birth. The importance of recognizing the conception of each life stage cannot be overestimated. But the stage has not birthed yet. It needs to gestate, and the time of that gestation is the transition. Steiner and Piaget have noticed important changes. Natural Learning Rhythms sees those changes as indicating the phase transition from trial and error and to competency.

Interestingly, Steiner believed that a "smaller cycle" begins at nine years old, principally characterized by an "awakening to the difference between self and the surrounding world."[64] Steiner asserts that, at nine, breath and pulse synchronize. Only then can the child receive and appreciate fine music. Only then is there the capacity for a deep love of nature. Steiner noted that nine-year-olds can be moody, withdrawn, and irritable. We have already seen that Wild Iris's research shows that children of this age have significantly more anxiety about death than those at other ages. If Steiner had just added the realization of personal mortality, he might have seen the stage birthing here, at nine. But he did not have the benefit of the many excellent advances in psychology in the last eighty years, nor did he spend hours in fieldwork. His work derived from his spiritual experiences and his love of children.

It seems to me that the contrary imperatives of the two stages, the one conceiving and the one expressing competency, may well be the dynamics underlying hesitancies. In the BodyBeing, during the transition between trial and error and competency, the self-perception of "I am the Center of the World and the World is an extension of My Body" is slowly but inexorably undermined by the certainty of physical death. In the FeelingBeing trial and error and transition to competency, the relational perspective of "I and Other" rubs against the growing realization of the necessity to self-govern. In the IdealBeing trial and error to competency transition, the self-referring perspective of "I must learn to do things for myself" meets the irresistible validity of interconnectedness. And in that last phase transition of childhood, between trial and error and competency in ReasonableBeing, the inclusive perspective of the vastness of the universe and the complexity of its inherent systems encounters the insistence of the freedom and responsibility of choice. "Knowing what I know, what will I do with my life?"

No wonder the child hesitates. The call for the family to reaffirm connection, take a breath together, and prepare for the next iteration of the growth of the child is a natural response to the chaos of the contrary imperatives. It is a time to let go of expectations and to simply say that being together validates our existence and is proof of the sacredness in life.

Competency will dominate for the next couple of years. The specifics of how receptivity, trial and error, and competency manifest in each stage will be described in the next chapter.

Now we will turn to some behavioral characteristics of the hesitancies between trial and error and competency so that they can be easily recognized and responded to with support—not pathologically. All ages are approximate. All behavioral descriptions describe trends I have personally seen, that have been reported by a cross section of parents and teachers, or that have been discovered in trusted research. Every child is unique, and the following is intended to stimulate and invite observation, not to define.

Six and a half can see the return of tantrums or their escalation if they haven't been dealt with properly yet. The child can show violent tendencies toward objects, which may be as benign as pulling leaves off of plants or, or more dramatically, toward animals and other children. The child may become easily upset by altered routines or broken promises. Some children prefer to play mostly with toddlers and talk baby talk.

At eleven and a half, FeelingBeing children can become overly sensitive about interpersonal slights and perceived insults. Some regress to bedwetting. The child might exaggerate bossiness or timidity, or alternate between the two. Moods such as loneliness and despair may grip the child, who then will probably become possessive of her familial relationships. The child may obsess about justice in the world.

Sixteen and a half can find the IdealBeing child self-critical about her current identity: "I'll never be good enough to really excel" or "I can never influence this world to change for the better." An undertone of violence towards self and others often accompanies the self-judgment. The opposite also occurs. Some children invest so completely in their ideals that they become oblivious to other aspects of their lives. They may suddenly fear strangers, fixate on the faults of others, or cling to friends and family.

At twenty and a half, the existential dilemma of the cold emptiness of being alone in such a vast universe can gnaw at the ReasonableBeing child. He can become genuinely despondent and somewhat overwhelmed by the notion of meaning. Awkwardness often ensues as the child cannot find the right response in social interactions. Life may seem absurd and wasteful, and the child can react with anger and/or apathy.

As the zeitgeist of our times clings to progress, hesitancies are seldom recognized and are rarely nourished. Therefore, as an aid to parents and teachers—who can in large measure determine whether the hesitancy will be a mutual learning moment or riddled with confusion—I will end this chapter with some reminders. Hesitancies last two to eight weeks; if they persist longer, there is a malfunction. Refer to chapter 10 for possible responses.

Children will usually refuse to participate in a favorite event or activity, especially in the hesitancies between stages.

- Hesitancies are marked by seemingly regressive behavior.
- Hesitancies signal that a new growth spurt is on the rapidly approaching horizon.
- Hesitancies call for reaffirmation of connection and familial support. Elders need this reaffirmation as much as the child. The new phase or stage will have many challenges for them as well as for the child.

And some last reminders about transitions:

As children bounce back and forth between the departing and arriving stage or phase, elders often cannot discern which child they are facing.

It is best to choose correctly and supply the developmental nourishments for the stage the child is facing. However, when in doubt, which will happen, respond to the arriving stage. It is less of an insult to the child.

Don't pathologize transition behaviors. Go slowly. It is often helpful to dialogue with partners or conscientious friends in order to decipher transition behaviors.

Transitions provide the field in which the initial conditions for new learning occur. If the child is nourished, previous wounds can be healed and optimal well-being can be restored. The child and the family can reactivate relationship if it has been lost. If the child's needs are neglected, the bifurcation leads towards conflict and separation.

Above all, don't worry! There will be an intimate, vital opportunity for relationship in the new phase and stage. Transitions call for restructuring towards ever-greater complexity and intimacy.

And if the transition has been neglected and a malfunction appears, there are Natural Learning Rhythms responses (see chapter 10).

Chapter Seven   # BEING QUALITIES

Break the pattern that connects the items of learning and you necessarily destroy all quality.

—Gregory Bateson

Natural Learning Rhythms is an
ontological epistemology of children. It elucidates how knowledge
emerges within the matrix of relationship. It depicts the being of the
child.

We have examined play and spirituality, two qualities of beingness,
to appreciate this ontological approach to child development. I mean
appreciate in all the senses of the word: to recognize with gratitude, to be
fully aware of, to prize and hold dearly, and to acknowledge. Of course,
play and spirituality are not the only two being qualities worth appreciating, and in this chapter we turn our attention to others.

A word first on what is meant by *being qualities*. The word *quality*,
which originated with the Greeks, meant "of what sort." It is a question
in a word. Of what sort of thing or person are we talking about? What is
her quality?

Therefore, the quality of something is its distinguishing attribute.
Being qualities are those distinguishing attributes by which we know the
essential nature of a person.

Play and spirituality are excellent examples. They are natural,
unalienable, and omnipresent. Children know through play, and play
extends beyond the customary notion to include interpersonal dynamics, identity construction, and systems creation. Spirituality unfolds in
consort with the stage's organizing principle and awakens in the matrix

of wisdom and relationship. Our close look at spirituality and play clearly names the field Natural Learning Rhythms plays in.

All of this is, to quote a teenage friend, "very cool." We must keep in mind, however, that we have looked at being only through the lens of optimal well-being and must wait until chapter 10 to see what happens when the child is malnourished and how to respond to it.

The great challenge that must be overcome in order to give a comprehensive description of human beingness is that being emerges—it is fluid, changing, and ever creative. Therefore, describing the qualities of being cannot be static or didactic. Active open minded participating is required for complete appreciation of the description of being qualities. I can only hope that your mind is questioning and creatively extrapolating as you read. Even more, I hope that you play with the insights of Natural Learning Rhythms, as that is when they truly come alive.

Often those who dialogue in being are not great writers but live in a powerful understanding. That may well be the case with the book you are reading. The task lies beyond words, yet words are the available tools. Any carefully detailed model that helps in appreciating being is worthwhile.

It may be that an ontological epistemology of children has not been tried because of the difficulty in describing being. It saddens me to think this may be so. That which composes the essence of our existence has been left out of our description of children. It is, to my eye, a gross oversight.[65]

In this chapter, I am going to describe the qualities of beingness from a Natural Learning Rhythms perspective—remembering that the qualities are not the thing, that the thing is not a thing, and that the synergy that is the realm of being can only be known as emergent, as real to those participating. And since it is not a thing it will not have a shape onto itself, but its shape, its density, its color, its feel, and its expression will be unique to the participants. To know your child's being, you have to participate in it. Being is mysterious, emergent, and yet accessible to all.

In addition to play and spirituality, the qualities of being include love, time, space, identity, respect, community, sex, death, and aesthetic. Their developmental expressions are summarized in the tables on the following pages.

The Terms of the Table

Together these qualities yield a reasonable view of being a human being. While each being quality may be considered separately it is the multi-dimensional net of their relationships that creates the synergy that is the being of the child. Please open the table for reference while reading this section.

Every being—plants, orangutans, and six-year-old children—orders time. This ordering reflects their capacities and determines the resources and relationships that they access. *Time* originally derived from "da," which meant to cut up or divide. Time is the way we cut up eternity. Later, *time* also came to mean "continuous, unbroken duration." No matter how often you cut it up, it still keeps on coming. Time lasts. These are the two senses of time that we live with, and each stage has its relationship to both. In the table, *scope* (extent) refers to time as endless and *duration* (to make hard) to how the endlessness is divided.

The ordering of space is twin to the ordering of time. There is both boundless and bounded space. *Breadth*, which refers to the width of something, states the child's perspective of boundless space; *boundary* states the limits.

Respect means to look at something twice—to spend time with it. Respect is that to which we pay attention, both abidingly (scope) and in the moment (duration). Community is space made social; it is our alliance with others. Breadth points to the field in which alliances can be made; boundary names the limits of the alliances.

Identity derives from *identidem*, which means "over and over" and points to the sameness in the way we view ourselves. Life stage dynamics reveal the process by which identity forms. The capacities of the given stage act as filters the child uses when he selects from the environment. In a rudimentary and often clumsy fashion, the child in receptivity plays with the new organizing principle and expresses herself and her capacities in the ordering of time and space. In trial and error, the ordering becomes more refined, and identities spring from the sameness of repetition. By competency, they are in lock-step with one another. One cannot name the identity without naming the ordering of time and space. In receptivity, identity tendencies can be discerned; in trial and error, identity forms can be seen; and in competency, the child fully inhabits identity. The cycle is then repeated in the next stage.

There is a capacity for love in each stage of development. In and of itself, love is real and complete for the child. In the dance chapter, we will see that the parent needs relationship to that love in order to actualize their own capacity to love and to be loved.

So universal and unquestioned is the being quality of love that the word appears in remarkably similar forms in all the Indo-European languages. Its meanings range over all that we commonly mean when we

	BodyBeing		
Primary Organizing Principle	Rightful Place		
Secondary Organizing Principle(s)	Boundaries Strength		
Primary Nourishment	Loving Touch		
Secondary Nourishment	Security, Warmth, Textured sensory environments, Flexibility		
Modality of Communication	Sensory Exploration		
Being Quality	Receptivity	Trial and Error	Competency
Time	*Scope*: Eternal now punctuated with sensations; little or no filtering. *Duration*: Impact of sensation event	*Scope*: Interest in sensory moment. *Duration*: Long for pleasant, short for unpleasant sensations	*Scope*: Navigating physical and social terrains according to sensory value. *Duration*: As long as it takes to actualize sensory value
Space	*Breadth*: Flux; beginning distinctions within topographical maps. *Boundary*: Unpleasant sensations	*Breadth*: Using words to define place; expanding social and physical territories with home base the secure center. *Boundary*: Remembered and immediate unpleasant sensations	*Breadth*: Ever expanding physical and social terrains; memory of home sustains longer explorations. *Boundary*: Beyond the borders of pleasant if memory suggests pleasant might follow unpleasant
Identity	Merged with sensory world	Egotism arises with autonoetic memory	Boundless body egotism; willing to engage new tasks

Respect	Scope: Momentary sensation Duration: Interest in the texture of the sensation	Scope: Pleasurable; textured; firm without threat Duration: Until sensation thoroughly digested	Scope: Sensory positive and textured events which allow for egotism and for exploration Duration: Long for pleasant, short for unpleasant
Community	Breadth: Family; all those who are not sensory repulsive Boundary: Minimum memory, new to most things, needs constant repetition	Breadth: Family; familiar people and objects Boundary: Retributive sense of justice, limits ability to share in common; threats; limited appreciation of social contexts and the words which describe them	Breadth: Ever widening; memory allows greater complexity but assessment still sensory based Boundary: Egotism
Love	Incarnate; limitless acceptance; embedded and secure	The exciting play of sensory exploration	The joy and strength of experiencing the body as connected to the environment
Sex	The sensual exploration of the world, including touching his/her own body. Interest in other children's bodies prevalent as competency begins and many children play games which allow contact with genitals.		
Death	Total annihilation: "no more"; may project magical fantasies about death; often wonders if body mutilation persists after death; reacts to sensations of others, and perhaps of the deal body if in the presence, when death occurs. Aware of death as finality by competency but still projecting about life after death.		
Aesthetic	Pure sensory, sensual, textured; that which invites sensory exploration; pleasing to egotism, creation of topographical sensory maps; perfect pitch at five.		
Play	Words, objects and events engaged freely within the restraints of their sensory qualities in the service of establishing place and exploring frontiers of both the physical and imaginary worlds.		
Meaning Making	Symbolic use of language		
Values	Sensory based vicarious learning; Anticipation; Exploration of boundaries; Toys (including words)		

	FeelingBeing		
Primary Organizing Principle	Trust		
Secondary Organizing Principle(s)	Reciprocal Cooperation		
Primary Nourishment	Feeling Mentors		
Secondary Nourishment	Fairness, Justice, Caring, Concern, Honesty, Adventure, Adaptability, Inspiration		
Modality of Communication	Feeling Engagement		
Being Quality	Receptivity	Trial and Error	Competency
Time	*Scope:* Opening to the vastness of nature and to the depth of feelings *Duration:* Absorption of the given feeling	*Scope:* Relationships, both interpersonally and in nature *Duration:* Selection of relationships which are either trustworthy or inspirational	*Scope:* Cycles of nature, cycles of relationships *Duration:* Rhythms in cycles, able to endure short periods of untrustworthy relationships in the name of community
Space	*Breadth:* Vast in nature and in interpersonal interactions *Boundary:* Primarily, feelings of family, than community and peers	*Breadth:* The sweep of nature and the ability to feel it as it is, including creation, destruction and Great Nature *Boundary:* Availability of inspirational opportunities, family and community mores	*Breadth:* Unending interplay of organisms and their world *Boundary:* Myths community lives by
Identity	Vulnerable; attached to significant elders; concerned with appearances	Able to enter mystery window; clannish; concerned with fairness	Just and caring; feeling interconnected with community and life

Respect	Scope: The feelings on self, family, extended family and community; rules and conventions Duration: In the moment; some linger but there are soon new ones to digest	Scope: Those who care for the family and community; those who can inspire Duration: As long as it takes to appreciate the relationships	Scope: Trustworthy relationships Duration: To the extent that there is trust
Community	Breadth: Those who feel just, honest, fair and caring Boundary: Unfamiliarly	Breadth: Those who share similar values of friendship; animals Boundary: Family and community mores; lack of perspective of long term results of relationship	Breadth: Life; respected elders and friends Boundary: Lack of awareness of past and future; cannot discern true commitment
Love	Awareness of personal mortality and the powerful longing to end separation	Reverential feeling of transcendence; those who can be trusted	The feeling emerging from the synergy of respect and community; Admiration and care for members of family and community
Sex	The need to have an intimate feeling connection with others, especially those who are trusted. Children may attempt to "practice" romance with trusted elder, particularly family member, as competency begins. This may include clumsy sexual embraces.		
Death	Awareness of personal mortality marks the psychological birth of the stage. Sets the imperative for relationship and interpersonal learning. Leads to awareness of cycles of life and death, of creation and destruction, which stimulates fascination with nature. By trial and error the yearning arises to know what lies beyond death. Mystery window opens. Searches for inspirational experiences to yield transcendent feelings. Vulnerable to community myth and religion.		
Aesthetic	Awakening to beauty in nature and the feelings of Life, of Great Nature; artistic expressions according to talent; appreciation of music especially, but of all the arts; sensitivity to feelings as a quality of life		
Play	Myth, drama and life stories, as well as interpersonal relationships engaged freely within the constraints of their feeling qualities in the service of establishing trust and exploring frontiers of the feelings of self and others. Rules of the game are critical for safe play and for deciphering reciprocal cooperation.		
Meaning Making	Feeling transcendence		
Values	Interpersonal dynamics; Cycles of nature; Conscience; Conversation/stories		

IdealBeing			
Primary Organizing Principle	Autonomy Self-governance		
Secondary Organizing Principle(s)	Identity Construction Personal Power Freedom		
Primary Nourishment	Sensitive Respect		
Secondary Nourishment	Challenges, Adventure, Peer Sensitivity, Personal Space, Opportunity to explore and express Ideals		
Modality of Communication	Inquiry into Ideals		
Being Quality	Receptivity	Trial and Error	Competency
Time	*Scope:* Future dawning; projections serve shifting ideals; conceptual abstraction. *Duration:* As long as event matches ideals	*Scope:* Appraising the future; believing in ability to meet it. *Duration:* Insistent; based on growing confidence in self	*Scope:* As far as the asserted personality can see. *Duration:* As long as the ideal demands
Space	*Breadth:* Selected according to ideals; all possibilities but little awareness of probabilities. *Boundary:* Underlying insecurity; unrefined selection process	*Breadth:* Pushing towards freedom; working on matching ideals to actual possibilities. *Boundary:* Inability to non-selfishly interpret events; residue insecurity	*Breadth:* All possibilities in the realm of personal power. *Boundary:* Social restrictions; lack of awareness of relevance of persona history
Identity	Asserting, projecting, yet insecure; Sexual urge; glimmers of the Shadow	Self conscious; interested yet modest about sexuality; ideals very strong	An I has been forged and is well worth defending, for it is autonomous and mostly free

Respect	Scope: Self primarily; peers and sensitive elders Duration: Until see for its value for self and for personal power	Scope: Ideals, assertions, projections including shadow; peers for support; those who accept identity exploration and confirm the child's ability to meet the future Duration: Until it is known if the identity is part of core nature	Scope: Self as a unified concept; the condition of the world Duration: Wedded to the defined self
Community	Breadth: Those who support identity exploration Boundary: Insecurity; lack of experience of standing outside of family	Breadth: Self, peers, respected and respectful elders Boundary: Inability to admit self imperfections; belief the world will bend to the ideals	Breadth: Peers, family and elders who meet the needs for autonomy Boundary: Self centeredness; inability to assess personal history
Love	Acceptance of responsibility for self fulfillment	Purity of ideals; confidence in self ability; Loyalty	Intense idealistic affection; willingness to be free and autonomous and to wish that for others; loyalty
Sex	Biology kicks in and Receptivity is often a wild ride between idealism/purity and prurient fantasies. Freedom and personal power can get tied to sexual expression. Aware of sexual shadows in family and society. Complex motivations for each child behind sexual choices. By competency many children have intercourse though sexual activity will usually change considerably in ReasonableBeing.		
Death	Accepted as a fascinating fact. How does it fit with freedom, with personal power? Are there noble ways to day, ways which demonstrate idealistic loyalty? Is Death a way out from the frustrations and insecurities which seem never to end? Is Death the ultimate shadow which then must be glimpsed in order to truly have control? By competency death is integrated into the ideal which many are willing to die for.		
Aesthetic	Choice itself; the right to choose; peer influenced; reflective of ideals and prominently displayed; reflects sexual identity; non-negotiable; able to practice diligently by competency		
Play	Tries on identities to explore ideals in search of core identity; self created challenges implicit in ideal accepted as a matter of honor; shadow is a toy, the arts are a serious toy, can engage complexification in competency		
Meaning Making	Belief in personal greatness, in the fact that they matter and will have a significant future		
Values	Projection; Shadow; Loyalty; Co-creation; Inquiry; Cultural purity		

	ReasonableBeing		
Primary Organizing Principle	Interconnectedness Humor Humility		
Secondary Organizing Principle(s)	Systems Creation Intentionality Incisiveness		
Primary Nourishment	Mature Recognition Recognition of: Commitment, Equality, Achievement, Recognition		
Secondary Nourishment	Comparison, exploration, experimentation, discernment, recapitulation		
Modality of Communication	Dialogue		
Being Quality	Receptivity	Trial and Error	Competency
Time	*Scope*: Dimension *Duration*: Determined by comparison; relativity dawns and time is a variable	*Scope*: Past, present and future; instantaneous and infinite *Duration*: Analysis of the event; ability to delay and study in order to determine meaning and value	*Scope*: Relative and absolute; immanent and transcendent *Duration*: Inherent in the event, with self included as part of the event.
Space	*Breadth*: Dimension, infinity, personal relationships past and present *Boundary*: The meaning value for the sense of self	*Breadth*: Wherever investigation leads *Boundary*: Relative to the event under scrutiny; access to data; myths the culture lives by	*Breadth*: Interpenetrating events of various dimension without beginning or end, in both "objective" and "subjective" worlds *Boundary*: Arbitrary, yet consistent with nature of the event and investigation of a given inquiry

Identity	Dawning of systems and their value in the world and their meaning for self	Focused arena's on inquiry; certain knowledge that there are modes of knowing beyond reason; playing with systems and generalizations about the self and world	Inference; induction and deduction; able to move from particular to system to Universal and back again; able to investigate modes of knowing beyond reasonableness
Respect	*Scope:* All events and data, especially those that fit nascent sense of meaning *Duration:* Determined by quality of data, interest and availability	*Scope:* Data that meets interest and meaning; non-prejudiced perspectives that open to the whole of the Universe, seen and unseen, known and unknown *Duration:* Until the meaning of the event becomes clear	*Scope:* Systems, generalizations and the ability to move freely between the two to discover more about each *Duration:* As long as it takes to conceive integrated whole that account for all data and events
Community	*Breadth:* Whoever has a piece of the child's puzzle *Boundary:* Condescension; available resources	*Breadth:* Those who share interest in child's investigations and meaning; those who can support the child's pursuits *Boundary:* Dogmatism; past allegiances and identities	*Breadth:* Abstractly—everyone and everything; Practically—those who agree or support child's reasonable perspective *Boundary:* Cause and effect; comparison and dualism
Love	Intensive investigation, comparison and analysis of life	The ability to see the whole in a part; to give meaning to past, present and future; to appreciate the elegance and precision of the Universe; to engage in committed romance	Interpersonal love; recognition of knowing beyond reasonableness; love for all the developmental Organizing Principles; appreciation of the Universe and all its parts

	ReasonableBeing, continued
Sex	Full adult sexuality with all the passion, emotional involvement and complexity that entails. As the child seeks enduring, substantive values—those that last beyond time—the natural inclination towards commitment arises. The awe and wonder of romance speaks to a world beyond reasonableness. Sexuality is one facet of the inquiry into self that is so important at this age.
Death	An awesome mystery. What is death's meaning? How does it affect choices in life? What does religion/spirituality/philosophy have to say? Is it valid? How does fully facing death influence values and ethics? What is Love's relationship to death? Any dialogue that ignores death is not reasonable.
Aesthetic	Mind itself; the meaning implicit in the expression; able to switch perception when meaning becomes clear if initially repulsed; as varied a humanity; willing to see every act for its aesthetic value; Beauty is Truth and Truth is Beauty and that extends to all events and objects, including oneself
Play	Hypothetical perspective; accepts play format to settle the most serious concerns such as law, philosophy and science; Healthy skepticism and humor add to commitment and seriousness but do not detract from playfulness
Meaning Making	Recognition of the Mystery; realization of open-ended modes of knowing
Values	Substantive (enduring) values such as beauty, love and truth; the unalterable fact of change; Commitment; Time (past and future); dialogue

speak of love: affection, friendliness, desire, pleasing, dearness, and care. All of these meanings count. Affection points to a forceful attraction. It specifically insists that this attraction is beyond the ties of blood and family. *Friend* originally meant love not bound by romance or sex, but enduring—a substantive value. Desire and passion fuel love. Of course, this has nothing to do with sexuality but rather with our fondest wish for our family's optimal well-being. As one mother recently said to me, "Before I had a child I had no idea that I would willingly give up life itself for another human being." Pleasing one another is so gratifying that we often do it at the expense of well-being, as when we give the child one more sweet because of the delight in his face and the bond that we feel. We hold our children dearly and so they are naturally inclined to hold us in the same way. Finally, without care, none of it makes sense. That is why nourishing the organizing principle is the key to optimal well-being in children and families. It is the sanest form of care.

Phases are shown for the top six in order to elucidate phase changes and give you specific details of their subtleties and nuances. The next four being qualities are sufficiently described by their stages alone. The careful observer will be able to see their phase expressions in their direct contact with children.

This table has meaningful implications in every interaction with every child. It is most helpful when it is studied and digested so that it is retained. This takes practice and study. I often go back to this table when I'm pondering an interaction with a child.

There is no directive as to how to implement the table; how to implement it is unique to each situation—to each child, family, and context. Natural Learning Rhythms is not a technique. It is an ontological epistemology, a way of understanding and relating to being. Optimal well-being is nourished in each moment, and approaching it with a set methodology limits options for responding.

One excellent way to study this table is to use it. The rest of this chapter will be devoted to examining the development of freedom and responsibility in children from the ontological perspective.

Freedom and Responsibility

Reasonable people know that freedom and responsibility are intertwined: There is no freedom without responsibility and no responsible action that doesn't serve freedom. Since this statement is a broad generalization, I will take a minute to clarify my meaning. I think you will find it to be common sense.

Jake, my fifteen-year-old neighbor, stormed over to my house, fuming over an argument he'd had with his parents. After he calmed down a bit, he told me about it. Jake had decided that he hated household chores and would do them no more. He thought that his parents used them for punishment and that he was forced to do a disproportionate amount. They thwacked him with a litany of all that they do for him, citing their work hours, carting him to tennis practice, and helping with his homework. He told them that if children were so much trouble, then they shouldn't have had any. They called him ungrateful. He called them hypocrites. They called him...he called them...they...he...

You get the idea.

I asked Jake if he was looking forward to getting his driver's license.

"Yeah. Definitely. It will give me some freedom to do what I want."

"And are you going to go drinking to celebrate that first night behind the wheel?"

"Are you crazy? Of course not. You know that's a stupid question."

"So you want the freedom to drive and you recognize the responsibility that goes along with it."

"Okay," Jake said slowly, "and this has what to do with my parents?"

"Think about it."

The Oxford English Dictionary tells us that *responsibility* means to be morally accountable for one's actions and *freedom* is the state of being able to act without hindrance or restraint. Can anyone act without hindrance if they are not morally accountable for their actions? Put another way, if you have guilt and shame, is there freedom in action? And if you have acted in a way you believe is right, who can hinder you?

Here's how deep it goes. James Gilligan, the former director of clinical services for the criminally insane in Massachusetts, has written a compassionate and insightful book, *Violence*. With violence in his own family background and his close contact with some of the most violent perpetrators, Gilligan allows his readers a perspective that goes right into the heart of violence. Unequivocally, he makes the same point over and over (bolds are his):

> The first lesson that tragedy teaches (and that morality plays miss) **is that all violence is an attempt to achieve justice,** or what the violent person perceives as just, for himself or for whomever it is on whose behalf he is being violent, so as to receive whatever retribution or compensation the violent person feel is "due" him or "owed" to him, or to those on whose behalf he is acting, whatever he or they are "entitled" to or have

a "right" to; or so as to prevent those whom one loves or identifies with from being subjected to injustice. **Thus, the attempt to achieve and maintain justice, or to undo or prevent injustice, is the one and only universal cause of violence.**[66]

Gilligan is teaching us that the perpetrators of the most heinous crimes believed they were acting responsibly. Without that belief, they could not have taken the freedom to act as they did.

There is always moral justification for an act. When the clergy turn against a war, for instance, as many did in the Vietnam era, the end of the war is near. If democracy is not "better" than totalitarianism, then why has anyone died in Iraq? War is always a crusade.

Gilligan's firsthand research has led him to the same conclusion as that of psychoanalyst Alice Miller, who wrote such classics as *For Your Own Good* and *The Drama of the Gifted Child*. I mentioned Miller and her concept of the "poisonous pedagogy" in chapter 5, "Spirituality." If we have been oppressed, Miller holds, than we will oppress others.[67] Oppression is violent, whether subtle or overt. Gilligan states the case plainly: The roots of violence are in the family and specifically in the way the child is treated. Neither researcher pulls punches.

Deprivation of the necessary nourishments to fulfill developmental imperatives is oppression. It creates a distorted sense of justice, a feeling of being unloved, and confused expressions of freedom/responsibility.

The first step in the development of freedom/responsibility is for parents and elders to accept this truth. Turning away is deliberately ignoring the child, is not being held morally accountable, and is not an act of freedom. No amount of external justification, whether appeals to social norms or to religious epistles, can mitigate the violence of oppression experienced by the child. The corollary to this holds and also is impervious to external justifications: The violence in families, whether subtle or overt, is a consequence of developmental deprivation. Another corollary also holds: Mind/body calming techniques can never dissolve violence. Exercising for peace, breathing for peace, demonstrating for peace, thinking for peace, and wishing for peace can never address the root of violence. These activities are palliative at best, exquisite forms of repression at worst.

Capacities are innate; development occurs in relationship. As we use the table, we must keep in mind that the relationships in the child's world create the conditions for optimal well-being in freedom/responsibility. The inevitable conclusion is that if we intend for our children to have a healthy understanding and expression of freedom/responsibility, we have to live it. We do not live it by imposing our beliefs, but rather by nourishing developmental needs and cultivating the child's capacity for freedom/responsibility. When we do these things, optimal well-being results. Children are strong and self-reliant within the capacities of their life stage. The possibilities of gratuitous violence diminish.

Perhaps we can never be completely beyond the reach of the social norms and religious strictures, but at this moment we can get pretty close. It is just parent and child. The focus is optimal well-being. The knowledge is that external impositions oppress. The realization is that by providing for optimal well-being, the parent offers an accessible model for the child to actualize freedom/responsibility.

Jake thought for a while. "Are you asking me to look at how my parents help give me freedom?"

"Yes, but not to trick you out of your feelings of unfairness. I trust that you perceive something is out of balance. I only want to see the whole picture."

Jake, like every teen I have ever encountered, had a fairly accurate representation of his parents' support. And like other teens, he did not emphasize the same things as his parents. Instead of his parents driving him places or giving him an allowance, Jake spoke of their willingness to help him explore life and to "be himself."

"What are the responsibilities that go with that freedom?"

Jake knew the question was coming. With rueful resignation and some humor, he said the magic word: *Respect.* And then, being oh so IdealBeing, he added, "But they are not respecting me when they order me around."

"From what you have told me that sounds accurate. They may not be respecting you in that moment. Are you saying that means that you shouldn't respect them? How can that lead to freedom?"

"Okay, it can't. But what should I do?"

"I don't know," I answered honestly. "Can you trace how you lost sight of your goal of freedom? Maybe you can pick it up with your parents from there."

"That's easy. Impatience and anger. It is so frustrating to hear that I am ungrateful. It hurts like hell."

"Do your parents know that?"

"I don't know. They should. They're the parents."

I smiled. "I don't think they do. It would mean they were deliberately trying to hurt you. Doesn't seem like they would if they have been supporting you to be yourself. Sounds like you should ask them."

"You mean talk about the hurt? What if they just pile it on?"

"What if they do?"

This is Jake's moment. He has acknowledged the risk of living in freedom/responsibility, and now he must make a choice. No one can do it for him. I had done all I could. I offered sensitive respect, the primary nourishment for IdealBeing. I helped him look at the identity he presented to his parents. I reminded him of freedom and its marriage to responsibility. He now has the opportunity to self-govern. He is facing a choice every one of us faces every day. Will he take the risk that freedom/responsibility often entails, or will he let his hurt and the resultant smoke screens of anger and impatience imprison him?

A Walk through the Table

What is freedom/responsibility to a BodyBeing child? What is their capacity and how can we support it?

There is not much moral accountability in a child who sees himself as the center of the world and the world as an extension of his body, who is seeking pleasant sensations and treats much of the world, including words, as toys. The will to act without hindrance is unfettered—edges are there to be explored—and must not be destroyed through threats or violence. Patience is needed, as BodyBeing often needs many repetitions to gain mastery. The best support for these qualities of BodyBeing children is to create loving sensory-based boundaries so that they are safe, secure, and have many textured sensory environments to explore.

Much can be done, however, with a child who absorbs sensory information vicariously. Consider a child who gets hurt on a school playground. Many BodyBeing children in the immediate vicinity will actually feel the sensation in their bodies. Different children will register it more or less dramatically. Some of the children will gather round. They want to make sure that the hurt knee can be fixed. Vicariously, that knee is their knee.

The children will also immediately register the sensory characteristics of the adult's reactions. If they are punitive, harried, fearful, flustered, or overly solicitous, then the vicarious learning is that the hurt child is bad and the other children become sad. The belief that the hurt child is bad stems from their observation that the adult is displeased. The sadness the BodyBeing children experience does not arise from their caring for the hurt child, but from a sense of hopelessness in the situation. The adult's contracted sensations register as threat and call forth anxious defensiveness. None of this supports freedom/responsibility.

If, on the other hand, the parent is aware that her words and feelings are being instantly absorbed by the children and she provides the

BodyBeing nourishments, then the children are glad that there is freedom to explore and that reliable help arrives if trouble occurs.

No moral judgment should accompany the making of a boundary if
one is needed to ensure safety. The hurt child should not be used as a
justification. "See what happened to Bobby? So don't stand on the
swings anymore," reinforces the sensation of badness. Getting down on
the children's level, reassuring them that are physically well, and firmly
prohibiting standing on the swings reinforces gladness. Bobby is taken
care of, and the elder will hold the boundary. It's safe; let's play.

Awareness of personal mortality brings a more complex appreciation of freedom/responsibility. FeelingBeing children feel morality

- BodyBeing and Genital Exploration -

Competent BodyBeing children often explore genitals—their own and
others'. While there is pleasure in this at varying times throughout the
stage, the competency phase often allows boldness in interaction with others.

Therefore, parents face a dilemma. The social norms generally exclude
this exploration, and there is the real danger of sexual molestation. Parents
can use the BodyBeing child's natural yearning for boundaries to teach
them about the boundaries concerning their bodies. They can gently but
persistently help children become aware of the effect of their touch on others. They can ask simple questions of the child when he is touched so that
the child can make sensory discernments as to what is safe and acceptable.

The media present an additional problem. BodyBeing children
exposed to sexual images may well try to imitate them. I have come across
children putting their mouths on the genitals of others and exhorting their
partner to moan and groan. I know of children who have stuck objects into
one another's orifices. This, I believe, is not in the natural course of events.

Yet the exploration—when innocent, simple, and short-lived—is natural and might even be useful to a healthy sexual life and to healthy free-
dom/responsibility. Also, shame and guilt, while strong negative sensations
that do create barriers for children, do not serve well-being. The BodyBeing
child just feels bad. He has disappointed his parents, and the extremely
unpleasant sensations may lead to repression or rebellion.

It's a dilemma of our times and I know no pat response. Certainly,
helping the child become aware of the effects of their touch and of being
touched helps. BodyBeing children also should not be exposed to sexually
explicit images. Yet the reality of our world demands precautions. Sexual
hurt can be difficult to heal. Sex is a precious being quality.

keenly. If the BodyBeing child is somewhat impervious and approachable only through vicarious experiences, the FeelingBeing child is ultrasensitive and vulnerable to moral suasion. If they are mentored in a way that evokes their own ethics and morality, then they eventually gain the prized freedom of being self-referential about what is right and what is wrong. Conscience remains the locus where feelings are felt without judgment. Emotional knowledge emerges in the context of their life and their current environment. They are not hindered by attempts to fit didactic abstractions to a given situation. If there is an implied "thou shalt not," it is to the parents: "Thou shalt not clutter the child's heart and mind with 'thou shalt nots.'" To teach a FeelingBeing child by a litany of "thou shalt nots" is to treat her like an It and not a Thou.

There are many opportunities for the FeelingBeing child to engage freedom/responsibility. Their aesthetic includes nature, whose balance is based on the continual cycles of life and death, of creation and destruction. Listening to a life story is a participatory experience as they explore the feelings of each person. Their love of drama and myth put them in the center of human feelings with the struggles and the risks entailed in finding what is right and doing it.

Freedom/responsibility sparkles when the mystery window is nourished. Experiencing the feeling knowledge of Nature, the underlying justice hidden in the patterns of natural relationships, and the perpetuity of life frees the child from believing the world is unfair. They then can take the responsibility of acknowledging and attempting to correct situations that are unfair, for they are not hindered or burdened with the task of altering the universe or depressed with the idea that there is no fairness in life.

The future is not in the present for FeelingBeing children. Notions of freedom/responsibility that depend on delayed gratification or consideration of long-term implications burden the child. Tied to this, the community of FeelingBeing is the family and the other people with whom the child has contact. Morality and the freedom to act are in the moment and with the immediate community. National and world politics are both far away and assume a history and a future that is only rudimentarily present for the FeelingBeing child. Teaching these things does not foster freedom/responsibility but only forces the child to pretend that facts are knowledge in order to be accepted by the community. The tacit message to the child is a demand to pledge allegiance based on the taught facts. After some time, the pretension forms a shell around knowledge.

How, then, do we nourish optimal well-being in FeelingBeing children when the news is broadcast to our homes regularly? One way, obviously, is to minimize subjecting them to multiple newscasts. A second way is to deal with the feelings of an event, rather than the politics of it. I was asked to address the people of my local community at the time of the first Gulf war. I suggested that they minimize media input and speak with the children about anger—their own and their children's. What do they do with it? Does it ever boil into violence? Do they know the dynamics of how hurt turns to anger, how anger turns to violence, and how violence is the cry of the disempowered for a shred of justice? Spoken conversationally, laced with life stories and backed up with books and age-appropriate videos that shed light on these concerns, our guidance can help the children empathize with the struggles of the conflicting sides. Though my audience resisted my advice, I stand by it and I have had the pleasure of watching numerous well-nourished FeelingBeing children grow into discriminating observers and players in the political realm.

- Companions -

BodyBeing children have buddies with whom they share pleasurable sensations. By the competency phase, the ties can be quite strong, but if the friendship doesn't cross over into FeelingBeing, it is soon only a distant, albeit pleasant memory. IdealBeing children connect to peers—to those who somehow serve their identity exploration. But FeelingBeing makes friends. It is not at all unusual for FeelingBeing children to simply walk up to each other and say "let's be friends." Also, in social situations, such as with extended family or in blended family visits, many FeelingBeing children will engage in friendship quickly and for the duration of the event.

FeelingBeing friendship is based on the feelings in the moment and is fueled by the developmental imperative to learn about interpersonal relationships and dynamics—to decipher personal and social feelings. It has significant emotional power, and memories of the friendships often endure. Children also have "best friends" in whom they vest overflowing goodwill and confidence.

The word friend originally meant "to love, to favor" and is closely related etymologically to free. To have a friend is to share love, to share freedom in the relationship, to support one another's freedom, and to offer no hindrance to their happiness. A friend is I-Thou, and although FeelingBeing cannot comprehend the complexity that Buber intends, they can participate in the feeling and play with pure friendship. The ethics and mores entailed in this play are known to each participant. They are the rules of their relationship. Breaking a rule is a serious offense.

Children need both latitude to explore friendships and guidance while engaging them. This guidance is best done unobtrusively. Joining children in social activities and taking an interest in their projects allows the opportunity to observe, to converse, and to gently provide direction when it is needed.

As the spelling suggests, a fiend is the opposite of a friend; the word originally meant "a foe" and is derived from the Old English word for "to hate." It soon came to mean a diabolical person, which, given the religious atmosphere of the Dark Ages, meant a person literally connected to Satan. If you lived then, you wouldn't want to be known as a fiend, and definitions to this day include words like wicked, grisly, and execration. In Natural Learning Rhythms terms, we might say that a fiend is a friend stripped of freedom/responsibility.

FeelingBeing children, especially but not exclusively those in the receptivity phase, feel interpersonal relationships along the continuum from friend to fiend. Prejudice, for example, makes the targets into demons to the FeelingBeing child. This is the time when clan, tribal, and ethnic hatred takes root.

The most difficult divorce I ever worked on involved a betrayed FeelingBeing boy. His father had proclaimed his love for his family time and again, swearing his undying fealty. At the same time, he was in the throes of a passionate affair and soon decided to get a divorce. He went from friend to fiend in his son's eyes. His mother, hurt and angry, reinforced the perception. The damage wasn't repaired in FeelingBeing, it became an ideal in IdealBeing, and the hatred lasted for years.

Freedom/responsibility is essential to IdealBeing. Holding an ideal, in and of itself, is an act of moral accountability—a statement of the worthiness of a perspective. The IdealBeing child has taken the responsibility to say "I am here and this is what I hold as valuable." Having taken the responsibility, they then expect the freedom.

Hold on, for this is a wild ride. The IdealBeing child has it right: I accept the responsibility and expect the freedom. In receptivity, however, the worthiness and appropriateness of the ideal itself does not often match the world the child lives in. The freedom/responsibility lies in naming the ideal itself, not in its content. If he is ridiculed for content, the child loses personal power to self-govern. The ridicule then has had an effect opposite to that the parent intended. Instead of leading to more responsible choices, it leads to the child's loss of faith in the value of taking responsibility. She may do as the parent wishes, or she may rebel. Either way, she is beginning to lose her tenuous grip on freedom.

Two important aspects of freedom, a secondary organizing principle for IdealBeing, have been explored in previous chapters. One is the necessity for co-creation; the other is fascination with the shadow. It remains only to clarify the moral accountability in each to see their importance in the development of freedom/responsibility.

The first, co-creation, is less controversial. The question that parents and teens need to answer is: "As we make this decision, who should do what in order for everyone affected by a particular decision to be treated well?" Inquiry helps clarify the answer. The question implies an important boundary. It states that whatever we co-create will include the well-being of all affected. It doesn't say how this will be accomplished; that is to be co-created.

As the teen matures, this question naturally entails more complex concerns. This leads to a steady increase in the complexity of moral accountability and insists that the teen modify their projections about freedom. They can then shape their ideal and the resultant identities to more closely approximate their core nature. Any IdealBeing child who integrates clear perceptions about her core nature has optimized freedom/responsibility for this life stage.

The shadow can be approached with moral accountability only when co-creation exists in the fabric of the family. Especially important is the co-creation of boundaries.

Margaret Mahler, as was mentioned in chapter 6, "Transitions," established many important correlations between the way children learned boundaries at two to four years of age and the way they behaved in the early teen years. Therefore, boundary creation, a secondary organizing principle for BodyBeing, comes into play during IdealBeing. It was critical for actualizing rightful place—for safety and the freedom to explore—in BodyBeing, and during IdealBeing, it is critical for freedom/responsibility. Learning about boundaries in BodyBeing is the starting place for boundary co-creation in IdealBeing. And in both instances, boundaries are created in everyday interactions, by determining what is allowed as well as what is prohibited. Boundaries define the shape of the family landscape.

The creation of prevention boundaries, which is a conflict resolution technique for dealing with crises, is most often needed when optimal well-being is missing. Prevention boundaries are a subject of chapter 10 in this book.

Shadow play often strikes close to the bone. Nothing is off limits, and sex is generally the hottest topic. Most people maintain privacy and even a cloak of secrecy about their sexual proclivities and experiences. For the media, on the other hand, sex is currency. In education, sex can barely be spoken of in schools. In society at large, pornography is everywhere, and soft-core porn can be found in many television shows, commercials, and movies. And, as our table says, the child is playing, with his sexual identities. In the midst of contradictory messages and compelling urges, how can there be moral accountability?

- Allowance, IdealBeing, and Freedom/Responsibility -

I personally have found the following to be very successful in helping teens understand the connections between money and freedom/responsibility, a topic of abiding interest for many of them.

When Josette and I were sure that our daughter was done making the transition and was firmly planted in IdealBeing receptivity, we gave her the details of how and where we spent money for her needs each month—leaving out food, housing, and medical expenses. We then presented her with that sum and told her that if she wanted help budgeting, we would be glad to provide it. She could expect the same amount at the beginning of each month.

In the first month, she ran out of money by the tenth. When she asked us for more money, we repeated our offer to show her how to budget. She complained that she was going to have to skip dance class. We empathized but did not rescue her. When she was short the second month, she again asked for help. By the fifth month, she allocated the money in accordance with her goals, which had changed appreciably and more accurately reflected her ideals rather than our values.

An interesting insight came when we did this with a teen who was temporarily living with us. He held out for four months. When he did enter inquiry with us, he revealed that it made him feel important to be the "guy with the money." When he was out of funds at the end of the previous month, his peers seemed less attracted to him. This precipitated a discussion with them in which he asked if they were avoiding him because he was broke. They insisted that they were just busy, it had nothing to do with his money, and they were insulted that he had suggested it did. He knew differently. We talked for hours about friendship. When he asked why they wouldn't admit the truth, we explored shadows together—his peers', his own, and ours.

Co-creation depends on a combination of the parent's willingness to explore their own shadow, the discrimination of when and how to expose it, and the sensitivity and respect for the risks involved by all participants. Much of the responsibility lies with the parent. The teen is exploring the shadow, but they do not have the reflective cognizance to fully understand what they are doing. They are responding to a developmental imperative more than making a conscious choice, though there is some choice in it. The parent can truly choose to meet the shadow directly.

The next two parts of moral accountability in dealing with the shadow—discrimination and respect—have to be learned in relationship with the teen. Every child, parent, and family has their own meaning structures and values; the timing and territory of discrimination certainly belong to each and every family. Co-creation can never be imposed from without.

Based on my experience as a dad as well as a professional, I can offer some hints to promote the healthy development of discrimination and respect in dealing with shadow issues. It is often best to name a tender issue as tender when it arises. This alerts you and the child that you are in delicate territory. Then go slowly. Ask questions to make sure the child understands you. She doesn't have to agree with you, but without mutual understanding, the topic should be abandoned. Don't take it personally. You are in new, sensitive territory, and it is going to be an ongoing exploration. When there is no understanding, state that this is as far as you can go right now. Invite the child to take the conversation in a new direction. You may be surprised at their loyalty and tenacity in relating to you.

This is a most precise and sensitive dance. Imposition and control have no place; questions are more important than answers; there is no escape from the deep feelings brought forth; and the learning goes right to each person's core nature. Issues get more complex, and the relationship grows to meet the challenges. Genuine autonomy—the right and freedom to self-govern—emerges.

Actualizing the capacity for freedom/responsibility in Reasonable-Being demands precision because the payoffs are extraordinary: substantive values; recognition that ReasonableBeing may not be the ultimate mode of knowledge; systems creation; committed romantic love; ability to meaningfully intend a future; and, perhaps most important because it makes these payoffs possible, reflective cognizance.

ReasonableBeing children are reflective in that they can stand outside of their actions and evaluate them, and so look at life and decide which aspects are valuable and which are not. They can then skillfully direct their lives toward the greatest meaning.

Reflective cognizance, when based in optimal well-being, allows great latitude in choosing one's response to a situation. It is the foundation for system creation. The child can not only evaluate many of the variables in most situations, but can include himself—his actions, thoughts, feelings, and capacities. Reflective cognizance is what allows such things as ontological epistemologies. It is the medium in which we are meeting in this book.

By the trial and error phase, ReasonableBeing children realize they are the meaning givers and that all of their actions in the world are expressions of themselves. If their dialogues and actions with others, the universe, and themselves include moral accountability, then they will have the freedom to create the systems they need to find meaning, express meaning, and engage modes of knowing beyond reasonableness (which are discussed in Appendix A). They will be able to organize their

- The Effect of Imposed Responsibility on ReasonableBeing -

Fifteen women of Mills College sat in a circle. Most didn't know one another, and only two had met Josette. She asked them to write down what they would change in their college experience, listing the most important change first. She expected a variety of answers and wondered if any of them would include her premonition. She was floored when everyone had the same first point, which was exactly what she had been thinking.

They would make it possible to attend college without going into debt.

And every one of them, without being asked, also wrote their reason: Debt prejudiced the courses they chose. Time and again, they told stories of taking classes that they believed would improve their chances in the marketplace at the expense of classes that were more in line with their talents, skills, and interests. They had little moral accountability in these courses, often regurgitating data to get a high grade that would be included on their transcript.

The rest of their lists had a variety of responses and in general they approved of their college experience. The scent of resentment and missed opportunity remained in the air, however. They all had the feeling that their expression had been diminished. Many believed that society suffers when a person's talent is subjugated to commercial interests that are not chosen.

bodies, emotions, and ideas to know; they know that knowledge emerges, that change is, and that to accept change helps attune oneself to emergence. By the competency phase, they will have the experience of being in relationship with themselves—with their own Thou and interconnected in a universe of Thous. The following quatrain by William Blake captures this well:

> Love seeketh not Itself to please,
> Nor for Itself hath any care.
> But for another gives its ease
> And builds a heaven in hell's despair.

Summary—Homage to Play

In play, children order their world. They define a time and space. The play activity is their aesthetic. Play is freely chosen and responsibly is engaged within developmental parameters. Play is the medium of contact with successively more complex organizing principles. Through play, they come to know rightful place, trust, autonomy, and interconnectedness. In play, humans effortlessly express and explore all being qualities—time, space, identity, respect, community, love, sex, death, and aesthetic. Play is truly the medium of learning for children.

Chapter Eight

INTELLIGENCE
AND ACADEMICS

The possibility of a straightforward psychological achievement of this idea [simple stages of human development applied to pedagogy] depends on the recognition of the difference between the method of unfolding man's fundamental capacities, which follow certain unchangeable laws, and the methods adopted in teaching special branches of [intelligence] and special dexterities in which those powers are applied.

—Johann Pestalozzi

"How can I support my child in achieving academic excellence?"

As the saying goes, if I had a dime for every time I have been asked that question, I would not have a mortgage. Implied in the question is another question: "What is the nature of my child's intellect and how can it be nourished?"

This chapter provides insight into the two domains where the answers reside: the nature and education of intelligence and the application of ontological epistemological child development to academic excellence. In other words, in the theory of multiple intelligences articulated by Howard Gardner and his colleagues at Project Zero, and in Natural Learning Rhythms. Project Zero sums up and extends the best of cognitive psychology; Natural Learning Rhythms includes the work of the great "entellectuals" in the history of education. Each offers unique and penetrating observations of education and suggests valuable ways to respond for optimal well-being. In some places, they converge, the domains overlap, and one substantiates the other. In other places, they diverge and seem to force a choice of one or the other. Near the end of the chapter there is a section that suggests a combination of the two that I have found successful, at least from the parents' point of view, for achieving academic excellence.

The team at Project Zero has taken on a very difficult task and one that I feel deserves our gratitude. To appreciate just how far they have reached and the profound ramifications for all children if their work was to mature and be embraced by educators, a bit of a history lesson is needed.

A Brief History of Education in America

As Diane Ravitch notes in her excellent history of school reform since the late 1880s, *Left Back*,[68] there has always been extreme restlessness in the minds of professional educators in the public sector as to how to educate children and to what end. What are schools for? And, of course, education does not exist in a vacuum. It has always been influenced by the latest psychological theories, such as intelligence tests in the early 1900s; by scientific discoveries, such as Sputnik in the 1950s; and by socio-political concerns, such as the waves of immigrants in the years around the turn of the twentieth century. Controversial goals and volatile social and political issues have dominated the course of education in America, and schools of thought have represented all factions. While there has always been a government-supported education agenda, it has, as we shall see, been influenced and significantly modified by nontraditional approaches many times.

From the moment there were public schools, there were private schools. Many private schools, such as prep schools, stress more advanced intellectual standards than the public schools. Most religions practiced by Americans have their own schools for the young. Beginning with the utopian community led by Robert Owen in New Hope, Indiana, in the 1830s, continuing through the free schools of the 1960s, and to present-day charter schools, there have been schools that specifically emphasize values such as emotional and interpersonal skills, vocational training, and multicultural education. One can even see the most far-reaching reform effort in the history of public education, progressive education in the early 1900s, as a movement away from the then-current values of the traditional academic curriculum and toward a public education that offered something for everyone.

The world of post-secondary education is even more diverse. Harvard was founded in 1632 as a theological institution, and like its predecessors in England and its contemporaries over the next one hundred years in America, was dedicated to developing learned ministers. Now the range of past-secondary education is immense. It includes colleges and universities that teach only certain subjects, such as computer science, to institutions with tens of thousands of students that offer courses in almost every endeavor in which humans engage.

Almost all forms of education, public and private, contend that they serve the democratic ideals of America. Educators who held to this rationale include Benjamin Rush, one of the leaders of the American Revolution; John Dewey, who insisted that the classroom be the crucible in which democratic values are learned; and Dr. Ron Miller, who argued against the federal government's Goals 2000.[69] Actually, one can go back even further, for the Puritan's insistence that their child learn to read and write had as much to do with learning the law as it did with learning religion.[70]

Education has always been a field where competing ideologies vie for dominance. The dominant trend in education is almost always reflective of the dominant cultural paradigm. This has led to heinous acts, such as forcing Native American children to go to missionary schools, to be cut off from their families, and to be prohibited from speaking their native tongue. It has led to what Jonathan Kozol has called "savage inequalities" for women, children of color, and most immigrants when they first come to America.[71] It has also led to progressive education, social efficiency education, allegiance to testing as a way to assess learning, the most extensive secondary and post-secondary education system in the world, and the rise of powerful teacher unions. Good schools make good citizens. Good citizens are those who support the goals and values of the political powers. Noted historian of American public education Joel Spring[72] titles the first three chapters for his book, *American Education*, now in its eighth edition, on the current state of affairs "The Political Purpose of Schooling," "The Social Purpose of Schooling," and "The Economic Purpose of Schooling."

What, then, are schools for? This debate has raged since the Puritans landed, and it still goes on today.

Early Times

The Puritans were the revolutionaries of their time. They held fast to the notion of religious freedom, explored the New World, and had attempted to overthrow the monarchy of England and take power through the Parliament. They understood the importance of literacy and used it to further their goals.

The church was the center of town and of all civic, as well as religious, activities. Everything social had to be in line with church doctrine. Therefore, one had to read the Bible in order to be a good citizen. To not know the Bible was a sin. Drama and religious music were the work of the devil.

Puritans sent children who were too young for formal school to dame schools, where they were introduced to the fundamentals of reading. Dame schools were run by a village woman and seem to have been a precursor to our modern day care.

In order to prepare future leaders, Puritans created the Latin grammar school. As one reads the following description of the Latin grammar school by Tonjia Miller, one cannot help but conclude that they were developed with the same justifications that have accompanied school policy throughout the history of America.

> The first Latin Grammar School was established in Boston in 1635. These schools were originally designed for only sons of certain social classes who were destined for leadership positions in church, state or courts. The study of Latin and Greek and their literatures was blended with the religious denominationalism coming from the heritage of the Protestant Reformation. The only pupils who were even considered for these schools were the male students who belonged to a certain class bracket. Girls were not considered for these schools because all of the world leaders and important "persons" were males from the upper class brackets.[73]

Thus, the purpose of the school was to develop men who would control the dominant political establishment—in this case, the church. It would not be until the 1850s that women would be admitted to post-secondary schools. And even when Oberlin did break the gender barrier, women were consistently given a second-class education.

Religion and the law were the glue of society, and those who had knowledge of them were the uncontested leaders. By the mid-1600s, laws were being passed that made providing education the obligation of the citizens. The Massachusetts Law of 1642 stated that parents had to teach their children to read and write and that masters of a trade had to make sure their apprentices were able to demonstrate the academic skills needed for their work. This law formalized the education of children and named it a social responsibility. The Massachusetts Law of 1647 required towns of more than fifty families to hire a schoolmaster and towns of more than one hundred families to have a grammar master who could prepare children for the recently chartered Harvard College. In each of these commitments, the Puritans reiterated their goal of social harmony through religion and education.

Revolutionary Times

Thomas Jefferson graduated from the College of William & Mary and was a founder of the University of Virginia. Benjamin Franklin, always an innovator, pushed, unsuccessfully, for schools that would teach English rather than Latin and would emphasize science. Noah Webster influenced all of education by creating the first American dictionary, recognized by Congress as the national standard in 1831.

But it was a lesser known American Revolutionary figure who may well have had the most telling long-term impact on American education. Benjamin Rush, a graduate of Princeton (then the College of New Jersey), wrote and spoke often about the need for education to serve the new American republic. His famous essay, "Thoughts Upon the Mode of Education Proper in a Republic," made the point several times over that children should be educated to serve the republic. Dr. Ron Miller, perhaps the foremost historian of holistic education of our times, believed that Rush represented the conservative view in American education. He quotes Rush as stating that "Man is naturally an ungovernable animal." Furthermore, the individual "does not belong to himself, but...he is public property." For Rush, schools are for indoctrinating children into republican political ideals. Miller shows how far Rush was willing to go:

> I consider it as possible to convert men into republican machines. This must be done if we expect them to perform their part properly in the great machine of the government of the state.[74]

Rush advocated that education take place in the United States and not abroad, that Latin and Greek be eliminated from the course of study, and that women be educated in the principles of democracy and how to manage their homes and then should be the educators of young children.

This left important questions unanswered. How can education be so selective and indoctrinating and still adhere to the principles of freedom and equality? Is it possible to hold the belief that "man is ungovernable" and needs to be made into a "machine" along with the belief that humans have unalienable rights of "life, liberty and the pursuit of happiness"?

Nevertheless, the promotion of nationalism and patriotism were added to religion and the law as legitimate goals of American education. The minds of the young, as always, were seen as the place where the cultural future lay. They were therefore to be molded according to the values of the times.

Pedagogically, the academic curriculum of Latin, Greek, the classics, and Protestant religious training dominated formal schooling. Learning was by rote, by memorization, and by recitation. The teacher was also to aid in the development of character. Corporal punishment, including whipping, was at the teacher's disposal to guarantee the children's obedience. For most children, apprenticeships into a trade occurred during their teen years. Except for the very few elite who attended the growing, but still small, number of colleges, this was the extent of their education.

From the Revolution to the Civil War

With the consolidation of common schools into a system designed to offer the same education for free to every child and the arising of normal schools for formal teacher training, the movement toward national standards and curricula took a solid step forward. Standard school texts began with the enormously popular McGuffey readers. The first laws making education compulsory were enacted in 1852 in Massachusetts. Waves of immigrants arrived, and states had to decide whether they were to be part of the labor force, trained to enter the labor force, or educated for academic excellence. Schools were divided into grades, and by the 1850s a school principal was an accepted and expected part of the education landscape. Latin grammar schools turned into publicly funded high schools, and the debate over the purpose, function, and curricula for secondary education assumed widespread national importance.

Without doubt, the most influential person in education of the era was Horace Mann. First, he took the disorganized, charity-run common schools and turned them into publicly funded schools providing elementary education for everyone. This action reflected Mann's ideal of education as the "ladder of democracy." Perhaps stimulated by the poverty of his own childhood and the status he gained from attending Brown

College, Mann repeatedly strove to create quality education for the citizenry. Unfortunately, this meant white Christian males. He did hold, however, that a strong academic education for as many as possible was necessary for a morally and economically strong nation.

Though there was no official national education policy, there was a growing *de facto* agreement in that direction. As Diane Ravitch says,

> At [the nineteenth] century's end there was no American educational "system." There were thousands of district schools, hundreds of colleges and universities, and scores of normal schools that trained teachers...Education was very much a local matter, controlled by lay school boards made up of businessmen, civic leaders and parents...
>
> Despite local control, the American public school was remarkably similar across regions. Everywhere the goals were few and simple: Children learned not only the basics of reading, 'riting, and 'rithmetic, but also the basis of good behavior. Principals and teachers considered character and intelligence to be of equal value, and neither was possible without "disciplining the will," which required prompt, unquestioning obedience to the teacher and the school rules.[75]

This remarkable coherence without federal control is directly attributable to Mann's innovations. As superintendent of schools in Massachusetts, he not only brought about publicly funded common and normal schools, but he also led the way to legislated compulsory education, meaningfully applied the law that resulted in the spread of high schools, and helped pave the way for the establishment of kindergartens.[76]

Pedagogically, Mann was not an innovator. The attitudes toward moral development remained as they had been since the Puritans: Corporal punishment was necessary and expected in response to certain behaviors; what needed to be learned were the three 'R's, religion, and the principles of democracy; these things needed to be taught through rote, memorization, and moralistic texts; and the teacher had unquestioned authority. As this approach spread from Massachusetts, it can be inferred that it was the natural extension of the Puritan education ethic to a developing, vigorous country with a rapidly increasing population. Of course, this would play right into the coming Spenserian age, when the socially fittest would be those who could master the basics of education.

Consistent with the growth and incipient centralization of education, colleges and universities slowly but surely expanded in number, size, courses offered, and political power. The Northwest Ordinance of 1787 provided that land be set aside for universities in each of the territories and states. A section said:

Religion, morality and knowledge being necessary to good government and the happiness of mankind, school and the means of education shall forever be encouraged.[77]

Of course, this not only spurred the development of higher education, it also showed America's complete commitment to the education of the young. Religion and morality were still considered the province of education.

Even though the influential Yale Report of 1828 reinforced the narrow academic curriculum as the only right one, by 1850 Yale was offering courses in German, French, mineralogy, chemistry, math, and political economy in addition to the classics in Greek and Latin and divinity training. The Supreme Court's decision in the Dartmouth College case helped solidify institutional autonomy and political clout for post-secondary schools. By opining that Dartmouth was private by virtue of its charter rather than public because it accepted state funds, the Supreme Court laid the basis for private institutions to access large amounts of public money and yet not answer to public standards.

There always seem to be educators who believe that children are good, that they have inherent capacities for knowing right from wrong, and that they can be reached through kindness and the stimulation of their curiosity rather than through overbearing rewards and punishments. These educators provide an undercurrent to the publicly accepted and funded view that schools were to teach morals in traditional Christian ways and impart knowledge according to the traditional curriculum. During the period between the Revolution and the Civil War, this view was represented by the Transcendentalists and led to experiments in social living, with attendant schools such as Brooke Farm and New Harmony. Championed by people like William Ellery Channing, Ralph Waldo Emerson, Henry David Thoreau, Louisa May Alcott, and Robert Owen, the repeated theme of transcendental education was the attempt to honor human nature and nurture its potential. For instance, consider this quote by Channing:

All our inquiries into morals, religion and politics must begin with human nature...No book can be written wisely, no plan wisely formed for the improvement of mankind, which has not its origin in just reverence for the power of the human spirit.[78]

This sounded the countervailing note to education as solely for vocational and academic purposes. Unsurprisingly, every educator mentioned had detailed justifications as to why their approach was the most democratic and best reflected American ideals.

While relatively few students attended schools such as Alcott's or Thoreau's, they represent a trend in American education that has been highly influential at different moments in its history. By the early 1900s, child-centered education and its stepchild, progressive education, were using many of the ideas of the transcendentalists and would become a dominant force in public schools. The values that informed the free schools of the 1960s and today's homeschooling are direct descendants of it.

From the Civil War to World War II

In many ways, the period between the Civil War and World War II serves as the benchmark for American education. Free public education was the norm. High schools began to flourish. By the end of this era, the greater majority of Americans would attend and graduate free public high school. The traditional academic curriculum of Latin, Greek, and the classics would be updated to include what reform educator William Harris called "the three moderns"—modern science, modern literature, and modern history.[79] This was the beginning of what we still know today as the liberal arts curriculum. It emphasized academic disciplines but continually extended to include all fields of human knowledge.

By the 1880s, a continual stream of immigrants was coming to America. By 1900 the stream became a river; by 1910 the river became a flood. These immigrants created a great challenge to society and especially for education. How were all these new people to be educated? How was one to deal with the fact that few of them spoke English? Which of the rights and privileges of society were to be extended to them, and which were to be denied? Moreover, a question that was always at the center of American education had to be addressed in a new way: How were these people to be taught the principles of democracy?

One of the answers to these dilemmas was the idea of vocational training, which was often coupled, by the 1890s, with the social efficiency movement. Based on the idea that immigrants were to take their place as the laborers in society, it was deemed a waste of time and money to provide to them—and, by extension, to anyone not destined for a ruling, managerial, or supervisory station in life—an academic education. Thus the poor, women, and African-Americans were thrown into the pool. Business leaders flocked to the ideal of vocational schools and supported them vigorously with funds and political lobbying. This support was a direct blow to Mann's promotion of education as the ladder of democracy.

The notion of education for social efficiency fit in well with the zeitgeist of the times. Herbert Spencer, attempting a social extrapolation of Darwin's ideas, came up with the term "survival of the fittest." Simply put, this meant that society stayed strong and vigorous by not offering too much help to the needy and the "weak." If a person or ethnic group could not succeed at the rules of the game, it was better if they fell by the wayside. Their continuance would only drag the rest of society down. And, of course, nothing could be worse than to educate these people to social leadership positions, for then the weak would be leading the strong.

At the same time, America, recovering from the Civil War, was robust. Westward expansion seemed to promise unlimited opportunity. Technology—in the form of the steam engine, telegraph, and machine and farm tools—opened the land, and the minds of people, to notions of previously unfathomable wealth. Internationally, America became a holder of colonies for the first time in its history. Robber barons amassed great wealth. The competitive, aggressive nature of capitalism suggested that anyone might do the same. The growing middle class, already more wealthy than most of the people in the world, seemed a partial fulfillment of this promise.

While vocational schools were designed to give a minimal education to those perceived as inferior, the manual training movement sought to combine the best of intellectual and manual skills. Attributed to the influence of Pestalozzi, manual training schools attempted to help students "realize at an early age the connection between knowing and doing."[80]

They were eventually swallowed up by the vocational schools.

Intelligence testing came at the end of this era, and it was to change American education forever. It began in 1905, when Alfred Binet first started administering questions that were supposed to test intelligence to French children, but it became popular as a way to evaluate personnel for officer training in World War I.[81] Before long, men like Edward

Thorndike and Lewis Terman would invent scales like the "intelligence quotient" and refine tests to measure where a person fit. But this is ahead of the story, for it would be possible for an administrative innovation such as testing to take over only when there was a recognized hierarchy of teachers' colleges and an educational bureaucracy to administer it. It is noteworthy that as soon as this hierarchy came into being, it was but a short time until its policies dominated American education.

How does one blend the philosophy of the transcendentalists, Spencer's social Darwinism, the study of psychology in the 1880s, the need to further the teachings of democracy, the blending of waves of immigrants, and a deep caring for children? These seem like contradictory ideas, forces, and needs, yet, in a remarkable way, they were blended into a single approach to education by the founder of the child-centered movement, G. Stanley Hall. The first person to receive a Ph.D. in psychology from Harvard (thus showing the expansion of studies available there), Hall believed that parents and educators had to concentrate on the child's health and well-being. As Diane Ravitch notes,

> Hall encouraged legions of volunteers in the child study movement to collect data about children's development; he counseled them that education should be based on a child's own nature and needs, not on subjects that existed outside the child's immediate experience. Teachers were wrong, he warned, to believe that their primary responsibility was "perfecting the art of imparting knowledge" when they should be learning from the child: "Too often the ideal of knowledge for its own sake is held up. This is narrow and selfish, and antagonistic to evolution, for it places the interest of the individual before those of the race." Scientifically trained educators, he held, exhibited "a willingness to fit the school to the child, rather than the child to the school."[82]

Here we see the basis of what became the progressive movement. Children have innate values and they should be scientifically studied so that their values could be understood. Education should then attempt to meet these values. Only then can a successful society ensue. These themes would be greatly elaborated by Hall's most famous student, John Dewey.

Hall's child-study movement gained instant and wide popularity. Both Spencer and William James of Harvard endorsed it, and child-study groups formed both nationally and internationally. Many rallied to the idea of different curricula for different children as a way to make education more relevant to the individual talents of the child. Many were thrilled to see Latin, Greek, and religious moralizing marginalized.

For the forty years following the Civil War, the educational bureaucracy grew rapidly. The population expanded, and high schools became a common reality. Institutions of higher education, and especially teachers' colleges, became the accepted authorities in the field of education. The roles of principal and school superintendent were clearly defined. Local school boards may have had control in most communities as to what their schools taught, but almost all had the same bureaucratic infrastructure.

The National Education Association (NEA) had been formed in the 1850s. Like many new organizations, it had relatively few members for a number of years. However, with the changes noted above, the NEA grew steadily in size. As the pressures for a national approach to education became evident, the social and economic institutions necessary to support it flourished.

By 1910, the question of how and what high schools should teach became critical. The NEA took the lead and decided to form a blue ribbon panel to research and recommend the appropriate curriculum for high schools. This was revolutionary in a number of ways. First, it was to be the first national panel of leading professionals—university presidents, superintendents, high school principals—in the field of education to make such recommendations and so revealed how powerful the education hierarchy and bureaucracy had become. Second, though the United States was vast and consisted of forty-six states with widely different histories, a *national* policy was sought. It wasn't each state for itself, but one policy for America. Third, it showed how confused and chaotic the situation had become. No one had any idea how to educate the flood of immigrants. No one had any idea of the best way to prepare a child for post-secondary education. Fundamental questions, such as how many students should be in a classroom and how students should be grouped, were unanswered. Perhaps most fundamental of all, the question of which was the best approach—to train the mind through academics, which might have a salubrious effect on all subsequent endeavors, or to teach a skill directly, using the vocational curriculum. Fourth, it was the first significant movement to standardize college admissions. By 1890 it was obvious to many that a college education led to social and economic advancement, yet there was no uniformity in college admittance standards. Though many educators denigrated the classics, for instance, long translations of Latin and Greek might still be on admissions tests.

Called the Committee of Ten, the panel was chaired by Harvard president Charles Eliot. It called for a uniform academic curriculum taught in the same way in all high schools. While eschewing religious moralism, rote learning, and the study of the dead languages, it espoused what we now call a liberal arts academic education. In short, all high school children should study language arts, math, some foreign language, history, government, and some science. In true American fashion, it was immediately attacked by traditionalists who wanted the old ways retained, and by progressives who believed that one curriculum for all children was a heresy.[83]

The dominant trend of the era was the rise of the progressive movement. When one considers the pressures and needs of the times, the ascendancy of the progressive position seems inevitable. There was the need to make sure all the new students learned about democracy. There was the need to include curricula that extended beyond academics. There was the need to articulate an educational philosophy that met America's perception of itself as renewed, powerful, and able to meet the challenges of the rapidly changing times. Education had to provide a labor force to run the expanding industrial economy, to maintain belief in the democratic ideal, and to train future leaders. The stage was set for the man who many believe was the most influential American educator of all times, John Dewey.

The progressive agenda began to gain power surely and steadily. Its beginnings can found in transcendentalism and in the child-study movement. Progressives came to prominence and maturity during Dewey's long life as a philosopher of education and a prolific writer. By the late 1890s, Dewey's work had attracted enough attention that, at the University of Chicago, he, with his wife, Alice, was able to start his famous laboratory school. Along with work that Montessori was doing at approximately the same time in Italy, this was perhaps the most noted reform of education in the world.

Dewey deeply believed in the value of experience and constructed his pedagogy around it. It was relevant experience and the meaning derived from it that constituted genuine learning. Dr. Ron Miller points out that Dewey saw experience as "whole, organic and unsundered."[84] Thus school should be a place where the child has enjoyable and meaningful experiences and thus embraces learning. For example, the curriculum of the Lab school, as it came to be called, centered on issues such as food production and shelter. Through field trips, historical study, and hands-on "occupations," children worked through the attendant social and economic issues.

At the time, experiments in psychology, which today seem horribly flawed but were canon then because they were arrived at via the scientific method, "proved" that mental discipline had no value.[85] Study for study's sake did not make smart people—the mind was not a muscle to be exercised. For Dewey, a staunch believer in the scientific method, these conclusions fueled his belief that knowledge could be gained only through experience. To be more precise, he saw knowledge as being created during experience. The factors in this creation were the meaning the child came with, the experience itself, and the meaning the child derived from it. At the same time, he saw spiritual pursuits as mostly worthless, for they saw knowledge as fixed and something to be gained rather than knowledge as something to be created anew in each experience. For teaching to be effective, therefore, the teacher had to be aware of the meaning structures the child came with and the way the child derived meaning from the experience.[86] In this, Dewey helped define a trend that would come to dominance eighty years later in the multicultural movement.[87]

It wasn't that Dewy was anti-academic, but rather that he approached knowledge in a different way. As experience was the key to knowledge, the properly chosen experiences would allow children to learn academics and whatever else was relevant to their lives. Most important, they would learn social skills, and they would be become intelligent citizens in a democracy. It cannot be overemphasized how strongly Dewey believed that progressive education would develop the best possible citizens for a democratic society.[88]

The progressive pedagogy opened the door for any subject matter to be an acceptable part of a curriculum. When William Kilpatrick—a student of Dewey's at Columbia's Teachers College—developed the "project method," it was hailed as "the quintessential statement of the child-centered school movement." The Rockefeller and Carnegie Foundations gave money to progressive educators to fund their experiments. Mostly influential in small private schools at first, their ideas and innovations started making large impacts in the public schools by the 1920s. Teachers were taught by experts to develop curricula that attempted to speak to the child's needs. The progressive agenda seemed to be carrying the day.

The child-study movement had turned into the child-centered movement, which had turned into progressive education. Progressives like Charles Bobbitt believed that curriculum development was a science and had to be handled by expert "curriculum engineers." Of course, the curriculum was to be child-centered and promote social awareness.

Progressives also employed "scientific" intelligence testing for assessing children.

With scientific justification, a well-articulated priority of social democracy and the pedagogy to teach it, and a vibrant response to what was for many the dreary and seemingly meaningless rote relationship to facts-as-education, progressivism appealed to many. With the immigrants, the growing suffrage movement, the end of slavery, the colonization of the West, the growing complexity of government, and the beginning realization of the abundant wealth of America, an educational approach dedicated to social intelligence had much appeal.

Many argue that it is a mistake to identify Dewey with the child-centered movement.[89] Clearly, Dewey was a philosopher first and was attempting to show that knowledge is socially constructed within the context of social institutions. Therefore, the schools had to take responsibility for themselves as such institutions and exemplify social democratic values. This could be done only through experiential education and a specifically designed curriculum that was relevant to the child. This does not mean that the child is *the* decision maker or that the child understands social needs and mores and is thus able to influence a curriculum.

There is also some controversy as to how much influence progressive programs had on the public schools. Joel Spring suggests that due to the power of teachers' unions, most public school education is teacher-centered rather than child-centered. He suggests that the complexity of Dewey's thought is lost on most people and that political and economic pressures determine the nature of education.[90] Modern reformers such as John Taylor Gatto would certainly agree.[91] Ravitch disagrees and points to long-lasting changes such as project-based learning, the whole language movement, insistence on greater teacher sensitivity to student needs, and the many diverse curricula that have been implemented.[92] It seems to me that both are right. The progressive changes gained much momentum in the 1930s amid the social unrest of the Depression and loss of faith in capitalism. They gained even more power amid the social unrest of the 1960s.[93] However, teachers and administrators still seem to rule the classroom. Most are trained in the traditional curriculum and tend to teach what they know.

Other than the traditional academic curriculum, which through WW II held sway in the public schools, the only other option at the time was the social efficiency movement. The rationale for social efficiency was a rehash of the argument that children should be educated for the work and station in life that they were likely to fulfill. Education is not a ladder; it is a chute to one's predetermined place in society. Perhaps the best of social efficiency is the notion of vocational training, which can have value for some people and has a place in American education today. But there is the insidious issue of who determines the placement of the child, and on what basis. Hindsight strongly suggests that the immigrants, poor, females, African-Americans, and other disenfranchised people were to be routed to the lower-paying and thus less-powerful jobs. The social efficiency movement would have placed these people in separate schools, not just in different curricula.

There were strong voices, especially from businessmen, in the camp of vocational education. There had been a growing controversy as to when children should be shuffled out of the universal academic curriculum and into vocational training. There was an outcry against spending public funds on academic training for children who were destined to non-leadership positions. Many wanted the grade at which children were classified to be lowered. Junior high school was the accepted compromise. It was believed that by using intelligence tests from as early as fourth grade educators could anticipate a child's future by the time they were twelve (which was similar to the age children started apprenticeships in colonial America). Junior high schools could then offer several curricula, including the vocational one.

African-Americans suffered. The post–Civil War South was not kind to them, and the *Plessy* Supreme Court decision cemented *de jure* segregation. Booker T. Washington did start the Tuskegee Institute and other educational institutions for African-American youth. Though his obsequious attitude infuriated many and would lead to W.E.B. DuBois' scathing criticism, Washington at least paved the way for people to believe that educating African-American people was in the best interest of everyone. Of course, DuBois, founder of the NAACP, and other great African-American leaders and their successors would fight for the next seventy-five years to establish equality in education for African-Americans. With the *Brown v. the Board of Education* court decision overthrowing the "separate but equal" law and with the legislation following the civil rights movement of the 1950s and 1960s, African-Americans finally had the law on their side for equal opportunity in education. However, no one believed that prejudice disappeared because the law forbade it. Thus, there are continual attempts to "level the playing field" with programs such as affirmative action, Black history, and incentives for teachers to work in underprivileged communities.

Females also suffered. Myra and David Sadker, in their comprehensive study of education and females, *Failing at Fairness: How Our Schools*

Cheat Girls, point out that through the 1970s, vocational training for girls was almost entirely centered on nursing, secretarial skills, teaching, or "home economics." At the elementary school level, gender bias was rampant and is still much in evidence. Boys were called on more often, given better instruction, praised for innovation, and excused their excesses. At the post-secondary level, scholarships for women were virtually unthinkable. The Sadkers' chronicle how both Harvard and Johns Hopkins had to be bribed to open their doors to women.

Underlying both the progressive approach and the social efficiency approach, and rapidly becoming highly influential in the public schools, was the new "scientific" phenomenon of intelligence testing. Endorsed by just about everyone, intelligence testing was seen as the answer to how to group children, how to assess their ability to do post-secondary work, and how to decide what kind of curriculum suited them. Led by Thorndike of the ever-influential Teachers College at Columbia, intelligence testing soon set the standards of what should be known by the child. According to Nicholas Lemann, Thorndike and Terman of Stanford, who gave us the term *IQ*, believed that these tests could actually measure the "innate capacity of the brain." It is easy to see that endorsed in this way, testing was seen as the gift from the gods to educators.

As Lemann points out, America is still dominated by the testing mentality. We certainly saw this in the presidential campaign of 2004, when each candidate vied with the other over who would do the most testing of students and teachers if elected. (Of course, this begs the question of who would test the testers or who would test the testers' testers.) In recent years, the gender and cultural bias in the SAT has become well known. Yet it is still used as the principal benchmark for college admission. In a way this might be expected. A test that the president of Harvard in the 1930s believed would scientifically allow the "natural aristocracy" to rule the United States will probably not die easily.

Post–World War II to the Present

On the surface, it would seem like society has become so complex and the corresponding changes in education so dynamic, that the history of education has been writ anew in the last sixty years. Below the surface, however, a different story exists. The same issues have motivated recent changes as have motivated those of the more distant past. How can education best serve democracy? How can education develop citizens who can maintain America's position in the world power structures? How can education accommodate diversity without losing the "American" identity? Who holds the power in education—teachers, students, administrators, politicians, families, or communities? Perhaps the last question is better asked, how is power shared among the above-named constituencies? As we have seen throughout, the curriculum that will be offered will reflect the current way that power is shared. And scientific testing will be used ubiquitously to justify the educational choices of the moment.

Another trend prevalent throughout is the importance of the private school. . Many often forget that at its inception, Catholic school education was a break from the established educational hierarchy. From the Transcendentalists to the Dewey Lab school, American education has been influenced time and again by educational philosophies from the private sector. In fact, it is fair to suggest that by 1950, much of the progressive agenda had found significant expression in the public schools. The influence from the private sector increases as American education is forced to become more and more responsive to its diverse populations.

Yet at the same time, teachers' unions continue to grow in strength and numbers. School administrators increase in numbers and influence. Universities have turned into mega-institutions with huge endowments and government funding. Their scope extends far beyond teaching young adults and now includes corporate and government research, adult education, extension classes that often offer courses in nontraditional subjects, social science research, and great social importance for their athletic teams. In other words, the incipient growth of these institutions seen in the eighteenth and nineteenth centuries has exploded into a dominant force in determining the direction of American education.

Vocational education has also expanded in a number of ways. Every occupation in America, from truck driving to English as a second language to computer programming to restaurant management, has its own type of school and is the subject for extensive course work at Universities.

The debate about the school's role in building character remains robust and, at times, contentious. While corporal punishment is more or less eliminated in public schools, therapy and drugs have moved in. Learning disabilities has become a popular diagnosis. In other words, the child's character is judged and controlled as much as it has ever been. Now, however, the "humanitarian" response is to find pathology and medicate it when the child does not conform to the educational and social goals of the school.

Thus, below the surface, one might accurately say that in terms of American education, *plus ça change, plus c'est la même chose* (the more things change, the more they stay the same). Trends and concerns remain the same, but restlessness pervades American education as it continually seeks to find a form, or forms, that truly express the needs of the contemporary constituencies.

Despite the many revisions, reforms, and outright attacks upon it, the traditional academic curriculum is the central focus of American education, perhaps now more than ever. Goals 2000 and No Child Left Behind have solidified the traditional curriculum's power base by tying desperately needed federal funding to testing results in language, math, and science.

Throughout, the academic curriculum has been seen as the breeding ground for the leaders of society. Supported by intelligence testing and manifold social science studies, and accepted as the principle criteria for admission to higher education, reinforcement for the value of the academic curriculum is embedded in America's conception of education. It is one area where the ever more powerful teachers' unions, politicians, and the ever-burgeoning school administration bureaucracy agree. Most telling, it is the educational response whenever the citizenry feel threatened by outside sources, such as the launching of Sputnik or the economic power of China as the *A Nation at Risk* report, Goals 2000 and No Child Left Behind attest.

It may well be that many of the reforms have had more to do with how the traditional curriculum is taught, then whether it is the correct approach. For instance, as I know from my personal involvement, the charter schools of California have willingly agreed to have their students tested by the state, although these schools originally began as a movement against traditional education. This is *de facto* agreement that all children should have academic competency as the state education bureaucracy defines it.

This is not the experiential education that Dewey and the progressives had sought. It is not education that serves transcendental values. It is education as it has always been—data retained, reformulated, and repeated at the request of an authority.

Multiple Intelligences

In a brilliant stroke reminiscent of Alexander's sundering of the Gordian knot, Howard Gardner and his team sliced through the political power struggles encasing education and intellectual learning by redefining intelligence. Rather than look at education as a way to reinforce cultural values, they attempt to describe intelligence *per se*, as it lives in each and every human. In so doing, they have brought into question almost every value that traditional education holds dear. Some of their conclusions are that testing reveals little about a child's intelligence and may actually inhibit learning; obsessive emphasis on verbal-linguistic and logical-mathematical intelligences inhibits the development of other, equally important intelligences; and that each intelligence has a developmental trajectory that suggests when it can optimally nurtured.

Implied in their work is that each child has a blend of intelligences and that learning is optimized when the curriculum matches that blend. Furthermore, it is a type of cultural genocide when education neglects any of the intelligences, for society never actualizes the full value and meaning of that intelligence. Generations of neglect can lead to an unbalanced society, decaying from within.

Backed by the status and resources of Harvard, Gardner and his team seem to have the wherewithal to be a significant force in American education. They stand on the throne of cognitive psychology, the most influential school of psychology in education today. They use the new queen of psychological science, brain research, as a principal justification for their theory. Careful application of anthropological and sociological research validates their claim to multicultural relevance. By demonstrating that tests which address only one or two intelligences are biased and reinforce intellectual aristocracies, they have undermined the principal assessment tool of the traditional curriculum.

The idea of multiple intelligences is child-centered in that it examines and respects the intelligence blend of each child; it is teacher-centered in that the teacher's expertise is used in evaluating the intelligence of the students and in creating and implementing the curriculum. By focusing on intelligence and not on cultural preferences, multiple intelligences reframes the tired tensions of race and gender bias and of vocational versus intellectual education. They simply do not matter. The issue, and the only issue, is the nature of intelligence. Everyone's got it, each in their unique way. Optimizing it is the goal of education. Multiple intelligences seems a genuinely democratic theory.

Intelligence, according to Gardner, has the following components:

- Cultural usefulness—in all cultures, not just America or the West.
- Can be isolated by locating brain damage—and is therefore mediated by specific brain locale and function.

- Can be seen in exceptional individuals—for example, Mozart in music.
- Has an identifiable core set of operations—music operates differently than verbal-linguistic.
- Has a distinctive developmental trajectory—for example, it is said that the best work in logical-mathematical must be done before forty.
- Has an expert end state—each culture may define this differently but each will have their revered expert in that intelligence.
- Can be supported by experimental psychological tasks—which defines the intelligence according to international scientific standards.
- Can be measured—though the calibrating device will be different for each intelligence.
- Can be encoded into a specific symbol system—numbers, letters, etc.
- Is broader than highly specific computational systems and narrower than most general capacities like analyses, synthesis, or sense of self.

In Gardner's *Frames of Mind: The Theory of Multiple Intelligences*, published in 1983, the seven named intelligences are:

- *Verbal-linguistic*—awareness of the sounds, rhythms, inflections, meaning, order, and functions of words.
- *Logical-mathematical*—creating and operating on strings of symbols that represent "reality."
- Musical—the controlled movement of sound in time.
- Bodily-kinesthetic—mastery over motion of the body and the ability to successfully manipulate objects.
- Spatial—the capacity to accurately perceive, transform, modify, and re-create aspects of the visual world.
- Interpersonal—the ability to notice and make distinctions among others, and oneself in relationship to others.
- Intrapersonal—access to one's own feeling life, range of affect (emotions), discriminate among feelings, and ability to enmesh them in symbolic codes.

In *Intelligence Reframed*, published in 1999, Gardner added naturalistic intelligence—the ability to distinguish among, classify, and use features of the environment. He also considered existential intelligence, a concern with "ultimate issues" and states that it "scores reasonably well on the criteria." However, he believes empirical evidence is sparse—and although a ninth intelligence might be attractive, Gardner is not disposed to add it to the list. "I find the phenomenon perplexing enough and the distance from the other intelligences vast enough to dictate prudence—at least for now."[94]

The theory of multiple intelligences shifts the focus from educating children to fit American cultural expectations to educating to maximize intellectual capacities. It breaks the deification of verbal-linguistic and logical-mathematical intelligences. It implies—and Natural Learning Rhythms confirms—that optimal education nurtures the child's blend of intelligences. All intelligences are important; the competent expression of each has the best possible consequences for society. This idea is a long way from Benjamin Rush. Learning the Bible and the Constitution are not the goals of education. Improving society and creating jobs are not the goals of education. No child left behind leaves part of everyone behind. Having children do well on IQ tests and meeting government standards are not the goals of education. The bringing forth of intelligence, in all its forms, is. The care and nurturing of the intellect is.

Gardner seems to be suggesting that the synergy of everyone actualizing their blend of intelligences will provide the intellectual basis for a reasonable world. The true calling of education is the recognition and development of our natural blend of intellectual gifts.

This, to me, is the essential excellence of the theory of multiple intelligences.

Gaps in the Theory of Multiple Intelligences

For Gardner,

"Natural development" is a fiction; social and cultural factors intervene from the first and become increasingly powerful well before any formal matriculations at school. The fiction seems a useful one to maintain in the preschool years, however. For one thing, most children do not receive any kind of formal instruction at that time; for another, the regularities continue to be quite impressive. Once the child reaches the age of six or seven, however, the influence of the culture—whether or not it is manifest in a school setting—has become so pervasive that one has difficulty envisioning what development could be in the absence of such cultural supports and constraints.[95]

Gardner's model for natural development is the work of Piaget, who he dismisses as "describing the developmental habits of thought and mind gained in school...[According to] many investigators...Piaget-style formal operational questions simply make little sense when posed in a completely nonscholastic setting."

Chapters 3 and 4 of this book have, hopefully, shown that Piaget's genetic epistemology is but a shadow of natural development. There, I pointed out Piaget's egregious error of deliberately excluding social and cultural factors from his considerations.

It is not what Gardner says but what he leaves out that leads to the gaps in his theory. As with all cognitive scientists, thought rules, and only the development of thought and symbol creation is being traced, not the whole child. The being qualities are not considered, or they are relegated to a particular intelligence that does them scant honor. Is identity, for example, the perception grown from intrapersonal intelligence? Is it a combination of interpersonal and intrapersonal intelligence? Or is it a combination of those two plus the actualization of the rest of that child's blend? If so, is the whole greater than the sum of the parts? Is the synergy of a different complexity, a different order of knowing, than the isolated intelligences?

Flawed appreciation of the dynamics of culture in the development of the child results, in my opinion, from attempting to view the child as an isolated phenomenon. Gardner and Piaget are cognitive scientists. They live in the logical positivist paradigm. The only truth is that which can be empirically observed, and verified. Metaphysics, from Plato to Moses to Kant, is worthless. It is not surprising that Gardner can find only "scant evidence" of existential intelligence. Analyses of empirical data are all that counts. Though science does use hypotheses as part of its method, it still insists that only hypotheses that can be analytically verified are given credence.

As the world is a messy weave of many interrelating events, logical positivists seek to reduce the world to its constituent verifiable parts. As we have seen so often, separation is built into the mind-set. The child is examined unto himself, eliminating everything that cannot be empirically verified. Empirical verification means measurement, which is one of Gardner's criteria for intelligence. If it cannot be measured and experimentally verified, it does not qualify. Thus culture, which is not measurable, does not fit (and therefore "intrudes"). Piaget deliberately ignores it; Gardner suggests that we pretend it's not there for a while and then abandon notions of development because of it.

This seems to be a contradiction. If culture perverts the sequence of development, then why is the developmental trajectory a critical criterion for the existence of an intelligence? Is Gardner's argument only with Piaget's genetic epistemology? And if so, is that sufficient to make the claim that there is no natural development?

Holding to the logical positivist paradigm has notable consequences. Consider Gardner's endorsement of the Suzuki method of teaching the violin. Virtually from birth, the child is regularly exposed to the twenty short songs that will compose her curriculum once she starts to use the violin. At two, the child attends group lessons. She will not yet use her instrument, but will listen to other children and join group games and exercises. Her mother is always present and always encouraging. At home, her mother plays each day on a small violin similar to the one her daughter will eventually use. Soon the mother lets the child touch the instrument, and when interest is "sufficiently aroused," the child is allowed to begin to play. Mother and child take lessons together. If the child loses interest, the mother is blamed and counseled on techniques to restore the child's interest. Soon the child plays alone. Over the next years, the child spends many hours each week following a highly structured curriculum that includes direction and encouragement from mother, group lessons, oft-repeated listening to recordings of preselected songs, and highly regimented practice sessions in which "a single note can be repeated up to a thousand times." Children soon perform very well and adults marvel at the capability and proficiency of these five- to ten-year-old children.[96]

All the BodyBeing attributes are exploited in the name of advancing the musical intelligence. The mother-child relationship, crucial to rightful place, is employed to spur the child's motivation. BodyBeing's exquisite sensitivity to sound is channeled to the violin. The child is given a steady diet of imitation and repetition, a preferred BodyBeing mode of learning. Rewards, such as the right to touch the violin and then to play with the group, are plentiful. The sensory environment is safe and textured, unless the child loses interest. Then, mother's distress and her subsequent use of prescribed techniques, probably sensed as punishment, bring the child back to the fold.

According to Gardner, Suzuki's aim is to develop "strong, positive, and attractive character—a means that could be achieved by any artistic experience." Gardner obviously approves. But where is the evidence that learning violin by rote between birth and six leads to strong, positive, and attentive character? Are Suzuki musicians leading the way to social justice? Are they more successful at avoiding pitfalls of substance abuse, divorce, or intolerance? Is there less sibling rivalry? Does the child have a healthier, lifelong relationship with his mother due to this experience? Are family members able to meet life's challenges together, or do they default to adversarial positioning?

Gardner's endorsement seems especially puzzling. How does anyone know the child's blend of intelligences or whether this very rich diet of musical training serves the individual child?

By adolescence, most Suzuki students give up their instrument. They do not comprise a disproportionately high percentage of professional musicians. They do poorly at reading music later in life. So concentrated has their experience been with the prescribed curriculum—Western baroque and romantic—that they have trouble with music from other genres. Nor do they attempt to express the music individually. There is one right way, which they have heard and practiced countless times, and that is the only way they play it. Few go into composing. Is this evidence of strong, positive, and attentive character?

Amazingly, Gardner notes all of these problems and then concludes: "These deficits are perhaps minor in comparison with the pleasures of skilled playing that the Suzuki method has given to many individuals." He then says that the method is "probably apt, since an individual can advance in the intellectual domain [of music] without needing much general knowledge about the world." He believes the method needs some tweaking, but the principle and technique should be applied to the cultivation of other intelligences.

Completely forgotten, by the way, is the effect of culture. Does the Suzuki method impart cultural preferences to preschoolers? Obviously. Which "regularities" are inherent in it that invite us to participate in the "fiction"? That BodyBeing children mediate the world through sensation? Then why not look at the mediating faculties of other developmental stages? Why default to the thinking structures of Piaget?

And the child? If it was so pleasurable, how come so few continue with the method into adolescence? Why are rewards and punishments needed to hold the child's attention? What has the child missed by spending so many hours with the violin? What has the mother missed? What has been the effect on their relationship?

To me, the only difference between this and *Brave New World* is that in the book, they start playing the recordings during gestation and that the goal of a social caste system is less politically correct than a rote rendition of Mozart. The adults have imposed an agenda and subverted the capacities of BodyBeing to actualize it. Suzuki is for the adults, not the child. It calls for a performance in the same way as coercing the two-year-old to "tell the man your name and how old you are" in order to demonstrate the child's intelligence.

Judging children by their performance, which can be measured and compared, places the emphasis on what a child does rather than who a child is. And yet the theory of multiple intelligences takes umbrage with IQ tests and railroading children into culturally specified intellectual endeavors. To its credit, the theory has taken the giant step of pointing to the blend of intelligences inherent in our species and uniquely expressed in each person. In the end, unfortunately, it still evaluates children based on their performance. It is concerned with the "what" and "how" of intelligence, but not the "why" and the "who." And while it correctly places the "where" of intelligence as innate capacities in the child, it completely misses the "where" of development, which is in relationship and not in the individual.

Gardner then makes an egregious oversight that seems to be pandemic to our age. He acknowledges the importance of emotions in learning, than basically ignores them. He states that even if "cognitive mechanisms are in order, educational progress will not necessarily result...such factors as proper motivation, an affective state conducive to learning, a supporting cultural context and...the proper motivation" are necessary for successful education.[97]

Every one of these factors depends on emotional well-being. None of them are cared for in Gardner's theory. The statement itself lacks emotional insight. For instance, how can "cognitive mechanisms" be "in order" without "a supporting cultural context"? Humans live in relationship; it is the air we breathe. There's only disorder without healthy relationships. Moreover, though Gardner rarely speaks of the relationship between teacher and student, it is, if the educators such as Montessori, Steiner, and Dewey are to be trusted, perhaps the most important factor in creating "an affective state conducive to learning." Love, sadly, is mentioned nowhere, and Goethe's imperative that we learn only from those we love has no traction.

In describing intrapersonal intelligence, Gardner shows great respect for feelings, pointing out that they underlie and guide behavior. I agree. They motivate. What, other than love, do we all seek? What, other than feelings of connection and devotion, can make life worth living? What, other than feelings, connects us with the rest of the sentient world?

Gardner, however, comes to the same conclusion about emotions as Piaget. They belong under the auspices of the will. Proper development of emotions is to label them and enmesh them in symbolic codes and then to draw upon them as a means of understanding and guiding behavior.[98]

There is a leap that must be made. Optimal well-being requires healthy feelings. Feelings need to be known as feelings, not as chemical transactions in the brain or by the name they are called. The word (symbol) *jealousy* has nothing to do with the jealousy I feel. The word may mean envy of another's success, it may be the etymological sibling of *zealous* and refer to being "thin-skinned," and it may allow some empathy from others when I use to word to describe the feeling. But the feeling I feel is a feeling, not a word, and has a unique value to me based on my history, my psychological moment, the object, which I covet, and the society in which I live. The symbol is not the feeling. The chemical messaging is not the feeling. If I never used the word jealousy or considered synaptic neurotransmitters, I could still experience jealousy exactly as it is. It is not symbol dependent, and the cognitive mapping of symbols does not dial me into the meaning and value of the feeling.

Feelings are feelings, and until they are treated as such, there will always be gaps and confusion in the understanding of children and learning. They are central—not peripheral. They are at the basis of every decision. Is abortion right or wrong? Should prisoner torture be condoned with terrorists lurking about? Should the state have dominion over euthanasia? Is the environment a resource to be exploited or the nurturing matrix of life? Is a certain race or gender superior? Every one of our responses to these and similar questions resolves to feelings. Until we know and respect feelings-as-being, we can never adequately appreciate the human mind.

Awareness of feelings cannot be confined to one intelligence. Nor can they simply be a factor in other intelligences. Full expression of the musical intelligence, for example, is impossible without healthy feelings. It is not just that feelings are supportive of musical awareness; it is that genuine musical talent is impossible without awareness of feelings. This may explain why the Suzuki method does not necessarily produce a lifelong love for an instrument.

Feelings give meaning to life. They are not an adjunct; they are at the core. At one point, Gardner, who obviously loves music, cannot think of the reason for musical intelligence since it does nothing to aid survival. This is not marginalization of feelings; this is blindness. Music awakens the cornucopia of feelings: It reminds us of love, respect, care, and devotion. It reminds us of rage, sadness, confusion, and conflict. We are humans. Without meaning, we die. Without meaningful feelings, the world would be black and white and not worth living in.

Of course Gardner cannot think of a reason for music. Feelings are feelings, not thoughts. Can he feel the reasonableness of music? As his magnificent contribution to education in America, multiple intelligences, shows, he certainly can. He just needs to shed the cognitive positivist cloak and connect to the trust of FeelingBeing. Then he will enjoy the reciprocal cooperation of feeling connected to all life. Culture will come alive as innate and intrinsic to development and mutual growth and happiness. Children will not be isolated, and the illusion of separation that supports logical positivism will dissolve. To quote the muse: "There'll be dancing in the streets."

Natural Learning Rhythms bridges the gaps in multiple intelligences. Together, as the next section shows, they form a coherent approach to academic excellence.

Natural Learning Rhythms' Pyramid of Academic Excellence

Knowledge of the Academic Capacities in Each Stage of Development

Knowledge of the Academic Strengths and Weaknesses of Our Children

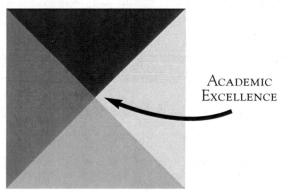

Academic Excellence

Implementing Developmentally Appropriate Curriculum

Proper Home Support

The four cornerstones of the pyramid of academic excellence are an interconnected system. Erosion in any one of them yields a tottering edifice that will soon crumble. Erosion in two, and the edifice falls down. Also, minor erosion in one inhibits optimal well-being in the others. Lack of proper home support, for example, undermines the child's ability to engage the curriculum, no matter how developmentally sensitive it is. A chain reaction ensues, spiraling down to academic mediocrity. But in this system, the reverse is also true. Injecting well-being into any of the four cornerstones has a salubrious effect on the others.

- Cognizance of the academic capacities in each stage of development
- Cognizance of the academic strengths and weaknesses of the child
- Implementing developmentally appropriate curricula
- Proper home support

Gardner's work is for teachers and only peripherally includes parents. Natural Learning Rhythms is primarily for families, though it has

- Parent/Teacher Relationship -

Teachers have large groups of students, multiple pressures from administrators, job security concerns, and the diverse values of the students' families to coordinate. They have learned some classroom management skills. Most of these specify how to use rewards and punishments and modes of constraint based on the power hierarchy of the school, such as being sent to the principal's office or expulsion. Most hold that parents should manage their children so that homework gets done.

Parents have one or a couple of children with whom they share an abiding intimacy; they want their children to be seen as individuals and taught so that they will succeed; they have greater interest in social and emotional intelligence; and they believe the teacher should be responsive to their concerns. Not all support homework and many do so reluctantly. Parents have the difficult task of balancing work and home, and many want their home time to be devoted to warmth, enjoyment, and connection.

It is not a good match. Parents do not as a rule communicate well with teachers. Some are intimidated, as they fear reprisals the teacher may take on their child, or they defer to the teacher's "expertise." Others try to control the teacher, reluctant to give up authority or simply defending what they hold as their child's best interest. Teachers, feeling overworked and not necessarily skilled in interpersonal dynamics, give in to the frustrations from their many pressures. Often they have to explain and defend administrative policies they don't agree with but have to implement.

And yet everyone, from the PTA to teachers' unions to administrators, agrees that without meaningful parental involvement, academic excellence is difficult to attain.

Into this breach I offer this pyramid of academic excellence. After I explicate each of the four cornerstones, I feel certain you will see why and how it can heal this rupture.

much to offer teachers. In addition to leading many seminars for parents and for teachers, I have facilitated courses with both teachers and parents present, worked with many teachers who are parents, and mediated dialogues between parent organizations and committees of teachers. While both parents and teachers might desire academic excellence, they do not necessarily agree on what that means or how it should be attained. This book serves both constituencies and includes suggestions as to how they can serve one another.

Proper home support refers to nourishing the organizing principle, which was described in chapter 2, "Spirituality," and has been discussed throughout this book. Enough said.

Consideration of children's academic capacities and of their academic strengths and weaknesses, the first and second cornerstones, leads directly to the theory of multiple intelligences. To recognize a child's strengths and weaknesses means to have an accurate profile of his blend; to recognize their capacities means to combine this accurate profile with an accurate assessment of their developmental moment. Excellent academic achievement is the fulfillment of their blend of the intelligences in each moment of their education.

Developmentally appropriate curriculum, the fourth cornerstone, is the natural outcome of multiple intelligences and Natural Learning Rhythms. The following table describes a cross-correlation between Natural Learning Rhythms and multiple intelligences. I wrote "a correlation" and not "the correlation" because all of the charts are intended to stimulate your own creative thinking. Every family has unique educational values and goals and so can modify the table accordingly. Also, the chart is comprehensive, not exhaustive. Nothing in this book is intended to be slotted into a static data bundle. Knowledge is emergent, and new insights and applications will arise in the learning moment.

The naturalistic and existential intelligences are omitted. If you have decided that they should be included, it would be an excellent exercise to detail the curriculum expressions yourself.

The Cornerstone of Academic Capacity

Academic capacity can be traced through the life stages by the way children classify. Successful classification requires a synthesis of the available intellectual capabilities for it calls upon an accurate rendering of an object, process, or event as well as the relationships they engender. As children grow classification becomes increasingly complex. If academics

- Parent/Teacher Relationship #2 -

Using the pyramid, parents and teachers can communicate clearly and efficiently about the children. Obviously, proper home support is the province of the parents and developmentally appropriate curriculum belongs to the teacher. Yet noninvasive snapshots of these can be shared, even as emails. Parents and teachers can easily educate themselves about the developmental capacities of children, the first cornerstone, and then compare perceptions of the developmental moment of the child. Together they can then deduce the child's academic strengths and weaknesses. They now have a common vocabulary that is respectful of their concerns and of the child's needs.

Consider the academic benefits: Teacher and parent in alignment. Curriculum supportive of the child's blend of intelligences. The child bathed in developmental nourishments and intelligible communications. Relevance. Sharp consistency. And that most reasonable of values, accommodation of change and growth.

This is not an unattainable utopia. In fact, you have taken a significant step in this direction by simply reading this book.

are too far beyond their abilities, or too simplistic, then learning, and the self esteem which supports it, suffers.

BodyBeing children classify according to color, temperature, shape, and similar qualities. The context for their classifications is the sensory attributes of the objects. Even words are known by their sensory qualities. This is easy to see for children younger than five, but as many reading comprehension tests and surveys show, children between five and eight understand the words for their concrete meaning, isolated from the nuance of their overall context.[99] Second-graders, for example, believed it is as easy to read a list of random words as it is to read the same words presented as a coherent text. These same second-graders also decided that the purpose of reading was to sound out words, not to understand the meaning of the text. Barbara Laster, an associate professor of reading, special education, and instructional technology at Towson University in Baltimore County, Maryland, sums up the situation nicely:

> Grade Three is critical as the time when you hope the majority of kids can learn to be fluent readers. The tender years are vitally important but *learning to read at age two doesn't mean better readers at age six.* Parents need to talk to kids and engage them in

BodyBeing
0-8 years

Involve the body in learning! Be flexible in attitude, expectations and use of teaching tools; include tools and environments which allow safe exploration of boundaries.

Most Important: Textured exploration opportunities.

No Threats; minimum confinement; low need for formal education, especially before age four.

Verbal Linguistic Awareness of the sounds, rhythms, inflections, meaning, order and functions of words	Textured letters, i.e., from dough, sandpaper, wood, etc.; singing together; opportunity to link objects and names; clear communication with elders; gentle humor; tongue twisters; looking through the pages of books; listening to stories; Montessori teaching tools
Logical-Mathematical Creating and operating on strings of symbols which represent "reality"	Cooking; building; balance scale; gardening; beginning Cuisinaire rods; measuring growth of living things, i.e., height of plant, weight of gain of baby animals, own height and weight; manipulatives for shapes, i.e., pattern blocks; Montessori teaching tools; games which use the child's body to make numbers, letters, etc.
Musical The controlled movement of sound in time	Many opportunities to listen, touch and dance; use rhythm sticks with numbers and multiplication; playful instruction with contact with skilled musicians; non-coercive lessons on simple instruments

Intelligence	Description
Bodily-Kinesthetic Mastery over motion of the body and the ability to successfully manipulate objects	Continuous support to explore handwork, dancing uninhibited running, swimming, jumping, etc.; minimize instruction; rough and tumble; free time in nature, parks and home; games which encourage full body participation; kites; much texture and climbing opportunities in the environment
Spatial The capacity to accurately perceive, transform, modify and recreate aspects of the visual world	Lots of colors, i.e., in room, outdoors, plants, learning tools, games which place shapes into holes; people games with lots of movement; activities in wide open spaces and in close spaces; climbing; coordination games; clay sculpting; rough and tumble; gentle verbal and sensory based reminders of physical boundaries
Interpersonal The ability to make distinctions among others, and oneself in relationship to others	Opportunities to express oneself in modest public performances and daily life; cooperative games with peers which emphasize the body; interest in the child's interests, including conversation; no put-downs; minimize excessive praise or disapproval; minimize social expectations; make constructive suggestions for improvement
Intrapersonal The ability to know oneself	Enter child's imaginary world through playing together while following the child's lead; humor; chance to touch both live and dead creatures; acknowledgment of feelings; some control over own life, i.e., letting child direct play for a half hour

FeelingBeing

9-12 years

Feeling Mentors who will relate to feelings, justice, and the spectrum of feelings. This relationship is in being, not in doing or speaking. Involve the child in the fairness of curriculum choices. **Most Important:** Opportunities to safely explore their own feelings and the feelings of others in the community.
No Hypocrisy

Verbal Linguistic Awareness of the sounds, rhythms, inflections, meaning, order and functions of words	Reading and listening to books and stories, particularly inspirational ones; acting and all performing arts; opportunity to classify things; writing without constraint, i.e., poetry; dialogue with friends and close elders; Eurhythmy; foreign language
Logical-Mathematical Creating and operating on strings of symbols which represent "reality"	Continuation and expansion of manipulatives, i.e., Mortinsen math; continuation of home based math in cooking, building, etc.; cooperative learning, i.e., rhythm games; beginning abstractions; simple word problems; lots of music, i.e., beginning relationship to scale, chords and notes as well as sophisticated listening to compositions
Musical The controlled movement of sound in time	All the music the child's willing to engage; lessons where appropriate but minimum pressure to perform; dance; singing; music inclusive of all time periods and cultures; some reading and notation

Category	Description
Bodily-Kinesthetic Mastery over motion of the body and the ability to successfully manipulate objects	Cooperative play; increased skill training; some team sports, but minimize winning and losing; rhythmic exercises, especially dance; nature/wilderness exploration, i.e., canoeing, drama; Eurythmy; lots of free time
Spatial The capacity to accurately perceive, transform, modify and recreate aspects of the visual world	Painting; drawing; building; sewing; opportunity to explore rhythms of seasons; plant and animal life from cell to whale; beginning astronomy; model making; journeys to skyscrapers, caves and the ocean; varied movement modes, i.e., horseback, bicycle, motorboat, roller skates; advanced Cuisenaire rods; sophisticated use of patterns and shapes and blocks
Interpersonal The ability to make distinctions among others, and oneself in relationship to others	Acting and all performing arts; safe space to explore feelings with friends and close elders; cooperative activities which emphasize values; chance to exercise fairness, i.e., deciding chore responsibilities for all family members; full participation in class government; ecology; helping the less fortunate; conversations about death
Intrapersonal The ability to know oneself	Acting; myth; support to understand personal feelings through inquiry and humor; time with trusted teenager; conversations about death; non-lecturing exploration of elder's feelings; inspirational environments, i.e., cathedrals, mountain tops, etc.

IdealBeing
13-17 years

Social and academic challenges should allow them full engagement of their ideals. Honor the search for individuation. Involvement with freedom coupled with responsibility. **Most Important:** A wide range of social environments where identities can be explored allowing the child to discover their own core nature.
Never Ridicule

Verbal Linguistic Awareness of the sounds, rhythms, inflections, meaning, order and functions of words	Public speaking; grammar; creative and academic writing; reading in all subjects; foreign language; debate; world affairs; history; media review with guidance, inquiry
Logical-Mathematical Creating and operating on strings of symbols which represent "reality"	Computer skills; genuine abstraction, i.e., algebra and up; biographies of great mathematicians; hands-on surveying and engineering; beginning "hard" sciences; beginning logic; physiology; farming; practical calculation skills, nutrition
Musical The controlled movement of sound in time	Individual's preference - support for intensive skill development; beginning musical theory; dance; opportunity to listen and play and participate in all types of music

Intelligence	Definition	Activities
Bodily-Kinesthetic Mastery over motion of the body and the ability to successfully manipulate objects		Strong challenges in nature, both individually and in cooperating groups; wilderness skills; ropes course; support for intensive skill development in arena of preference, including crafts and fine handwork; disciplined movement, i.e.; ability to move silently, martial arts, miming, massage
Spatial The capacity to accurately perceive, transform, modify and recreate aspects of the visual world		Exotic experiences, i.e., spelunking, using high powered telescopes, space camp; computer modeling; travel, especially in varied landscapes; hands-on creations, i.e., carpentry, mechanics, pottery; drawing to scale; navigation; control over personal territory; introduction to computer geometry
Interpersonal The ability to make distinctions among others, and oneself in relationship to others		Forums for expressions of ideals, i.e., U.N. Simulation, activist marches; apprenticeships; peer contract; supervised challenging group activities; travel, especially to third world countries; projects that engage a cause; mutual setting of boundaries with family; caring for toddlers, the less fortunate and animals
Intrapersonal The ability to know oneself		Psychology; apprenticeships; introduction to philosophy and religion; Vision Quest; cultural and physical anthropology

ReasonableBeing

18-23 years

Recognize the each child's maturity! Respect their new ability to comprehend the fullness and expanse of space/time. Be willing to engage change and an inquiry into substantive values.
Most Important: Opportunities to absorb data and guidance in organizing that data into systems.
Eliminate Condescension

Verbal Linguistic Awareness of the sounds, rhythms, inflections, meaning, order and functions of words	Etymology; advanced debate and public speaking; study of original sources in all disciplines; history of language; all social sciences; research papers; general semantics; influence of language on culture; dialogue
Logical-Mathematical Creating and operating on strings of symbols which represent "reality"	Higher math; formal logic; advanced science; the history of math and time, the philosophy (including ethics) of math and science; computer science; business and economics; farming
Musical The controlled movement of sound in time	Musical theory; the math of music; the history of music; opportunity to specialize and practice intensively; public performance; cultural value of music; relationship of music to dance

Intelligence	Definition	Methods/Activities
Bodily-Kinesthetic Mastery over motion of the body and the ability to successfully manipulate objects		Opportunity to specialize and practice intensively in both gross and fine motor activities; fasting; challenges that test limits and require strength and coordination; sitting still and silent; linking breath to movement and concentration, i.e., modern dance, pranayama and yoga
Spatial The capacity to accurately perceive, transform, modify and recreate aspects of the visual world		Emphasize correlations, i.e., the music of architecture, the science of painting, the dance of logic, chaos theory as poetry; travel; extended journeys to exotic events, i.e., Himalayas, Amazon, pyramids, Tokyo sewer system; detailed scale drawing and model making; electron microscope to huge telescope; archeology to futuristic simulations; landscaping
Interpersonal The ability to make distinctions among others, and oneself in relationship to others		Simulations of all types of government; travel; intimacy; exchange student; special interest activism; interaction with peers and people of varied cultures; inquiry
Intrapersonal The ability to know oneself		Philosophy, contemplation; meditation; prayer; Vision Quest; all branches of psychology; use inquiry and dialogue

oral language in order for them to be good at written language. If kids are denied oral language development, they will have a problem reading text.

FeelingBeing begins at nine years old. In a landmark study of brain development[100] in nine-year-old children, the most surprising result for the researchers was an enormous burst of activity in the language areas. At just this time, reading comprehension leaps to include contextual understanding.

Contextualization relies upon understanding the relationships among plot and characters. In drama, children are now able to act in accordance with the subtleties of the character they are portraying. This is evidence that classification has changed from the sensory to the relational. Learning centers on the interactions between things, not only the physical things themselves. For instance, many children this age readily learn Carolus Linnaeus' classification scheme of natural flora and fauna based on the simple notion that a species is defined by those who can mate and produce fertile offspring.

Of great importance, relational skill building extends into the child's social and interpersonal world. The social worlds of all living things provide the material for classification. Proficiency in understanding relationships yields greater appreciation for the context of the written word and for the deep feelings of music. It was Steiner who insisted that only at nine are children able to truly appreciate music, a startling counterpoint to the Suzuki method.

- A Classic Mistake in Teaching Academics -

There is a high cost when abstract conceptualization and data retention and retrieval are overemphasized during the BodyBeing and FeelingBeing years. The basis for the full fruition of these skills erodes. After a recent talk, a parent asked for my advice. Her seventeen-year-old daughter was about to graduate from high school with a 4.0 grade point average. She had successfully reached the academic goals the family held dear. But the daughter had trouble making decisions. She couldn't decide on a college or a career. She couldn't decide on what clothes to wear or to buy. She couldn't choose a boyfriend. She could do math, science, and two languages. But without relational skills, she was isolated and lacked the ability to find a meaningful context for her skills.

Classifying in the first stage, BodyBeing, is based on the sensory qualities of the object; in the second stage, FeelingBeing, it is based on the interactive relationships between objects. Overemphasis on data retention and retrieval and abstract conceptualization that is not rooted in the sensory object or in the relationships between objects actually lessens academic competence. These important academic skills ripen in their own time.

The beginning of IdealBeing is the birth of the abstraction of a sense of self. This self is endowed with the ability to self govern. Therefore, abstraction is a natural capacity of the life stage. Classification according to abstraction increases in sophistication for all of IdealBeing and ReasonableBeing.

The importance of classification based on abstract properties cannot be overstated. The chemistry student, for example, uses the symbol C for carbon. That C calls forth many things, such as carbon's atomic structure. The student can then compare this with other atomic structures and speculate on the possible combinations of the atoms to form molecules. She can create a specialized notation for all atomic and molecular structures and use that notation to develop hypotheses. She can then carefully experiment and test her results. Most important, she can use the results of her experiments in other, novel applications. She may even produce a new product, such as a plastic, that has never before existed.

That skill is the pinnacle of academic achievement. I have given a scientific example, but the same approach applies to music, philosophy, and all other intellectual pursuits. Abstract conceptualization takes two full developmental stages, IdealBeing and ReasonableBeing, to come to fruition.

The IdealBeing child has the skill, but he is organizing his world to optimize autonomy. To do this, he tries on identities that meet his ideals. He then plays with these identities for the next five years. He is in search of his core nature, he operates under the imperative to learn to self-govern, and he uses idealistic identity exploration as the means to attain these goals. He has the ability to abstract his conceptualizations, categorize them, and operate on them, but he is interested only in doing so when it matches his ideals.

This reveals why many IdealBeing children find much of high school boring and irrelevant. Their ideals and identity exploration command their interest, not data or abstraction for their own sakes. And it reveals why many high school teachers get frustrated. They see that their students are capable and cannot understand why they don't apply themselves more diligently. They do not realize that the material will only be

---

- University Academy -

Josette and I have had the pleasure of working with the teachers at University Academy in Kansas City. Serving inner-city youth, the only admissions requirement for this charter school for grades six to twelve is the intention to attend college. They do not care if academic skills are underdeveloped. The standards are high, but the support is there to meet them. Teachers work long hours, offer additional tutoring, and are sensitive to diversity.

Toward the end of a seminar on the application of insights of IdealBeing to interpersonal and social development, a teacher of English reported that while many of his children responded well to his requirements, too many were failing. He had learned this morning, he said, that he had not accounted for the insecurity so prevalent in IdealBeing receptivity. He had also considered the developmental nourishments. One of them, challenges in the realm of success, was missing. He wondered if there were any other suggestions to help the struggling students.

Almost in unison, the other teachers hit upon the same answer: Tie the lesson plan to the ideals of the child and gear the writing assignments toward self-expression rather than "objective" composition.

It worked.

---

compelling if it matches the ideals/identity and is a fit with the IdealBeing child's blend of multiple intelligences.

From the perspective of the well-being of the child, this makes abundant sense. Classification based on abstract conceptualization is a highly sophisticated and powerful tool. It takes a lifetime to master. Learning has the most meaning and is most quickly and skillfully accomplished when it arises out of self-interest. The IdealBeing child becomes skillful at both abstract conceptualization and autonomy by engaging them through her own ideals.

Recently, a civics teacher in Sacramento asked me to help him with his eighth- and ninth-grade students. Most of them wanted academic success, but they were not able to understand how studying the works of the founding fathers helped. Led by a few alienated students, the children had become disrespectful and disruptive in the classroom.

My first response was to lead the children in a series of games and activities that allowed them to share their individual strengths and talents. After this, I led an inquiry into their ideals in both life and the classroom. This naturally led to a discussion of what was missing in the classroom for them.

Surprising to the teacher was the revelation that the students were crying out for an end to hypocrisy and for *relevancy*. Their notion of each was quite sophisticated. How could you talk about democracy and equality when the school itself was obviously an oligarchy? Paraphrasing and summarizing their comments, and hoping to catch the intensity with which they spoke, led to the following restatement of their comments: Curriculum was handed down, behavior codes were handed down, tests were handed down, and rewards and punishments were handed down. Disputes were summarily decided by those higher up. Parents had some say, but not much, and it was costly in terms of time and effort. How could this be the right environment to learn about democracy?

This inquiry took three hours over the course of two days. At its end, the civics teacher simply stood up and told the class that they would now have democratic control over the class. He told them that as the teacher, he would insist that their actions could be justified as democratic and not capricious. Two months later, he told me that the disruptive behavior had ceased and that the class had sorted itself out so that each member had a democratic function. Only some were doing the formal study of the principles of democracy, but they were teaching others in small groups at specified times. He couldn't be happier.

ReasonableBeing children organize their world to maximize interconnectedness. They seek to understand the meaning of events and interactions. They accept and engage change. Consequently, they discover, define, modify, and create systems in order to describe the interconnecting patterns in the world. Systems discovery, whether it relates to the person's psychology or the distant nebulae, indicates that abstract classification has been freed from idealistic identifications. Systems definition shows the wide range of data now available to the ReasonableBeing child. Systems modification and creation shows that data, abstraction, and categorization can now be used to change the world.

The Cornerstone of Assessing Academic Strengths and Weaknesses

Assessing a child's academic strengths and weaknesses requires skill and courage. I am going to describe the Natural Learning Rhythms approach in this section. Gardner and his associates at Project Zero have done superb research and experimentation with assessment. Josette and

I have synthesized this work into a formal essay, "Assessment, Not Evaluation." If you would like a copy of that essay, please visit *BaLuvmour.com*. Using it and the information that follows will provide a remarkably clear intellectual profile of your child or student.

The body tells the truth for BodyBeing children. They play with words, so their verbal feedback is not always reliable. But the sensations register in the body. The value of the sensation is in their face, their voice, their shoulders, and their jaw. A hint: It comes to their face first, though it may pass through quickly. Careful observation of the child's body opens the door to recognizing intellectual proclivities.

To be effective, observation must occur over time and in different settings, as many variables must be considered. As we saw in chapter 4, "Play," BodyBeing children register many aspects of the sensory environment. A threat to rightful place will take precedence over enjoyment in a given activity. Competing intriguing sensory opportunities can mask interest in the one(s) not chosen.

Consistency in the teacher is crucial, as BodyBeing children learn vicariously. If the teacher is scattered, the child will be scattered and all observations will become skewed. A task may be presented suboptimally relative to that child. Spatially intelligent children, for example, learn math differently than bodily-kinesthetic children. The correct transmission medium has to be found before a valid analysis can occur.

These challenges are hardly insurmountable. Patient, detailed observation in multiple learning situations overcomes all of them. Two observers are better than one, and three is excellent. A rich dialogue awaits parents and teachers when they compare observations of a BodyBeing child.

Montessori knew BodyBeing, and her method is brilliant. She notes that when children are absorbed, their bodies are relaxed and focused. Children tend to use only the muscles required for a task. They are tension-free and refreshed throughout.

Building on the work of Froebel, Montessori created textured sensory learning tools. Each tool is placed at it own station in a room. The children circulate among the stations as they choose which one to engage. Sometimes there is a morning circle during which children name the tool they are going to play with that day. Children of different ages learn together. A natural order ensues. The younger children are attracted to the older ones, who quite often teach them how to use the particular learning tool. But they teach much more. Vicariously, they impart how to behave and how to care for the learning tools.

The teacher observes and carefully catalogues the children's interests. The children may approach the teacher with a question or to demonstrate proficiency with a given tool. Due to the time he has to reflect and observe, it is expected that the teacher will be able to anticipate the children's learning in all of the intelligences. He may suggest a tool if he is convinced it is best for the child at that moment. In the event of conflict between the students, the teacher works with the offending parties quietly and personally. He embodies rightful place, the ground upon which the creative expressions flow. Knowledge is emergent, and the teacher participates without controlling. He is well aware that the sense impression the children receive from him is the compass by which they guide themselves.

Founded by a group of concerned parents after WW II in the rural foothills of Italy, Reggio Emilia has become perhaps the "hottest" approach to early childhood education in the last ten years. Reggio Emilia is the name of a district in Italy. There are about a dozen tightly knit preschools there, all practicing the same unique approach. It seems a BodyBeing paradise.

Louise Boyd Cadwell, an American teacher who studied and subsequently was influential in bringing Reggio Emilia to the United States, names eight fundamentals of the approach.

First, the child is seen as a protagonist. This means that they are strong and capable, and their curiosity and interest are critical to what is learned and how it is learned. Second, the child is a collaborator. Peers, adults, and community are integral to the learning process. Third, the child is a communicator, and opportunities to communicate abound. All artistic and verbal-linguistic media are available. A special space, call it the atelier (workshop), is set aside for creative expression. Fourth, the environment teaches. The design and use of space are carefully considered to allow children maximum flexibility and safety. Fifth, the teacher is a partner, nurturer, and guide. They emphasize listening, observation, and support, and, within limits, they modify activities so that children can test their creations. Sixth, the teacher is a researcher. This astounding innovation allows everyone to continually understand and modify their approach to both meet the child's needs and improve their teaching practice. Seventh, documentation is an important form of communication. The research the teachers do, as well as the work of the children, is taken to be the expression of the nature of the education. As such, it is deeply valued and scrutinized by parents, teachers, and community. Eighth, the parent is a partner. This is very different from the marginalized role that parents play in Waldorf Education, the international approach founded on the works of Rudolf Steiner, where they raise money and create pageants, or the non-role of parents (outside the home) in Montessori. Rather, parents in Reggio are encouraged to be part of the classroom—to bring ideas and skills and to be treated collegially by the teachers.[101]

As the FeelingBeing child operates from the matrix of relationship, we must look there for information about their blend of intelligences. Trust is so important. An untrustworthy teacher or unfair social climate prejudices the learning opportunities for the child. A child may excel at music, for example, and yet perform poorly in the midst of unsupportive people.

Words are now mostly reliable. Listen for the *fairness* word and try to respond to it if the child's request is not capricious. Remember that adaptability is an important developmental nourishment and so try many different modes to nurture each intelligence. Try combinations, such as math and music together or spelling by passing a ball back and forth or drumming together while chanting the words. Introduce learning in different social groupings. Many children learn better cooperatively and will only maximize their intelligence when supported by friends. Fewer, but a significant number, prefer to learn in solitude. Most prefer a combination.

Knowledge of a child's blend of intelligences is deepened by noticing how each intelligence manifests in diverse social situations. It is a mistake to assess a child's intelligence based on its expression only in school, or only in the company of friends, or alone, or with a tutor they may not like. Go slowly and keep the conversation alive with stories from your education experiences. Use examples of the diversity in nature and in social customs to help your child understand that they have a unique blend of talents and that childhood is a time of discovery. Listen carefully. Your child will give you many signs of their blend of intelligences.

Steiner offered many great clues for FeelingBeing education. The emphasis on music, poetry, and the visual arts speaks directly to the child's need to express the deep feelings that compose much of her everyday life. Generally, children will choose the artistic mode of expression most closely aligned with their strongest intelligence. Steiner also advocated the teaching of creation myths during the FeelingBeing years. This leads to feelings of tolerance and connects the child with cycles of creation and destruction.

Steiner's greatest contribution, in my opinion, is his recognition that the teacher is so important that, if possible, there should be only one for the entire life stage. The teacher can then become a feeling mentor and come to know the child so well that they can name her intelligence profile. One caveat: The Waldorf curriculum, designed for a 1920s cigarette factory, pays no heed to the importance of varied social learning milieus to decode or deepen the child's blend of intelligences.

True to IdealBeing nature, deciphering the intellectual composite of a child in this stage begins to twist and turn. Saturated with idealistic projections, early teens consistently fail at lucid self-evaluation. They either overestimate or undervalue an intelligence in order to forge the identity that allows them entry into the asserted ideal. A mathematically astute teen, for instance, may downplay his ability in order to be part of the skater peer group.

Parents and teachers see the young adult in the teen. They become concerned that the child has the skills to succeed as an adult, and they often pressure the child to achieve in the traditional curriculum, neglecting the child's unique blend of intelligences and the pull of his ideals. This leads to conflict in the home and disaffection toward academics in the teen. Hopefully, then, parents and teachers know the intellectual gifts of the child before he enters IdealBeing.

If not, there are clues still to be gleaned. The depth and quality of each intelligence becomes more apparent by the way the child expresses her ideals and identities. It is the expressive mode rather the ideal or identity itself that points to the intelligences. The rebel identity, for example, can be expressed in music, poetry, debate, or physical resistance. The child has the most confidence in their strongest intelligences and so will choose them to play out the desired identity.

Inquiry, as described in the sidebar in chapter 5, "Spirituality," acquaints the elder with the ideals and identities of the child. Academic projects can then be co-created. The child's performance will indicate their intellectual moment. The results of the project can be used for further inquiry. As long as parents and teachers remain flexible in project design and duration, the ongoing inquiry will lead to optimum use of the child's intellectual capabilities. Obviously, as the project becomes aligned with the child's ideals and identities, it will spark greater enthusiasm and commitment. Subtly, the inquiry itself develops verbal-linguistic, interpersonal, and intrapersonal intelligences.

ReasonableBeing children simply require opportunity and dialogue for accurate intellectual assessment. Opportunity provides access to data, teachers, research facilities, travel, apprenticeships, or whatever else is necessary to actualize interconnectedness and systems creation. Dialogue reveals the meaning of the endeavor so that the child can hone the blend of intelligences most suited to her intended future. Analysis belongs primarily to the child. If parents and teachers recognize the maturity of the ReasonableBeing child, and are neither controlling nor condescending, they will be included as respected advisors.

One last hint: Always work from the child's strengths. Parents and teachers often mistakenly believe that academics should focus on the weaker intelligences. They assume that the stronger intelligences need less help since they are competently manifested. This assumption undermines self-esteem. Everyone learns better when their talents and intelligences blossom and are valued by others. The safe, powerful place of intellectual competence provides the courage and willingness to explore the unknown territory of the weaker intelligences. Develop strengths, work from safe space to the unknown, and try to introduce learning in the weaker intelligences in combination with a stronger one. For example, sing math, play games that use the whole body to teach reading, draw stories to introduce interpersonal learning, or use poetry to draw forth the intrapersonal intelligence.

SECTION III   *The* *Family*

We've defined *integration* as the process that creates coherence in the mind. *Coherence* is the state of the system in which many layers of neural functioning become activated and "cohere" to each other over time. Complexity theory gives us some insight into why this linking process may occur: States of the system that maximize complexity achieve stability. In this way, integration defines the self. As the mind moves toward complexity, it recruits various layers of processes into a cohesive state of mind. *Cohesion* is thus a state in which subcomponents become linked together at a given moment in time. As the mind emerges across time, cohesive states become a part of a coherent flow. The linkages of subcomponents—whether in a given moment (cohesion) or across time (coherence)—are achieved by the process of integration. Integration recruits differentiated subcomponent circuits into a larger functional system through a fundamental reentry process. The co-regulating, mutually influencing state of reentrant connections is called "resonance." In other words, *integration utilizes the resonance of different subsystems to achieve cohesive states and a coherent flow of states across time. Such a process creates a more complex, functionally linked system, which itself can become a subcomponent of even larger and more complex systems.*

—Daniel Siegel, *The Developing Mind*

Chapter Nine

THE DANCE

At the most basic level, the brain can be considered as a living system that is open and dynamic. It is an integrated collection of component subsystems that interact together in a patterned and changing way to create an irreducible quality of the system as a whole. A living system must be open to the influences of the environment in order to survive, and the brain is no exception. The system of the brain becomes functionally linked to other systems, especially to other brains. The brain is also dynamic, meaning that it is forever in a state of change. An open, dynamic system is one that is in continual emergence with a changing environment and the changing state of its own activity.

—Daniel Siegel

Properly responding to the expressions of the organizing principle in young people precipitates a simultaneous development in adults. This relationship serves the deepest development of both children and adults. It is a dance of reciprocal growth toward self-knowledge. It is a vital example of opportunities naturally built into the developmental moment. Recognition of the dance can change chauvinism toward children, for the child's importance for the self-actualization of the adult is unmistakable.

As I wrote in chapter 5, "Spirituality," the essence of existence—of being—is relationship. It is the way we know, the reality we live, the pattern that connects. It is within relationships that the sacred comes to life. Up to now, the chapters in this book have shown their value for the child. It is now time to consider the adults in the child's life.

Welcome to the dance.

The dance is a unique Natural Learning Rhythms contribution to child development and family dynamics. Many have spoken of the family as a system. Natural Learning Rhythms, focusing on optimal well-being, specifies the possibilities inherent for the parent when they are nourishing the developmental needs of their children. While nature continually provides reciprocal value in all its relationships, it is nevertheless surprising and gratifying that the parents can heal wounds and grow in self-knowledge by participating in their child's development.

The dance can be best understood when seen as a whole. Accordingly, I am going to relate a series of case histories that touch upon aspects of each developmental stage. There are many variations on each dance step. Every family dances in their unique ways.

The Healing Dance—Dancing as Parents

Very few parents escape that overwhelming wish-it-would-never-end wave of love that accompanies the arrival of the newborn into their lives. Sharon and Robert had felt it when Michelle arrived, and so they thought they were prepared when Allen was born four years later. But they weren't. Robert summed up his experiences:

> With Catherine I just stood in awe and cried. The only thought I had was that I would give my life for this little girl. Then I started to laugh through my tears at how ridiculous it was that I just met her and there was nothing, *nothing* I wouldn't do for her. So the excitement built as Allen's birth drew near. But there were complications and at the last minute we had to have a Caesarean delivery. It was crazy-making to first hear of the problem and then have to make a quick decision to do something that we didn't want to. And then I was worried about the health of Sharon and the baby. I had been in the birthing room for Michelle, but this time I had to wait outside. My mother and Michelle were at the hospital with me. All I felt was relief when they told me that my wife and son were healthy. Michelle and I went into the room, and she went to snuggle in the bed with her mother and newly born brother. I just stood there and watched the three of them and to my utter amazement I was completely calm inside. There was a moment when the world was beautiful and right just as it was. I was so present, but there was no sense of time. I had no compulsion to move towards them or to say anything. Nor did they view my stillness as strange or call me over.

Sharon described birthing her two children as similar in that they "confirmed my sense of place in the world. I had been the agent of creating life, and it felt as a fulfillment and an ordering of my world. I also found courage, especially with Allen."

Healing Wounds from Sibling Rivalry

Sibling rivalry erupted in the Stanchion household when Randy was three and Carl was eighteen months old. Then Carl, firm on his feet and able to speak, repeatedly invaded his brother's territory to play with his toys. Randy appealed to his mother, but when the behavior continued he took matters into his BodyBeing hands and pushed Carl. These exchanges became a pattern, and one Saturday a fight erupted. John, the dad, set a sensation-based boundary. Within an hour the conflict returned. Both parents, John and Mary, responded, but the sibling rivalry only became more frequent over the next two weeks.

John and Mary became increasingly annoyed with the children. They believed they were reacting appropriately to the conflict. John, frustrated, thought that maybe some punishment or spanking would get their message across better. He knew that was how he had been disciplined and also knew that it led to bitterness. He remembered that BodyBeing children learn vicariously. He examined his own sensations when his children had conflict and realized that he had very little patience for it. Anger arose and his jaw tightened as he recalled how quickly his parents would punish him and his brother when they fought. John realized that when his children pushed one another, he added to the conflict with his own tension.

Mary and her siblings had been parented very differently. They had been left alone to "work it out." Consequently, though she did not prize her experience, she tended to leave Randy and Carl alone until the conflict led to chaos. Of course, this exacerbated John's impatience. When John intervened, Mary saw chaos looming. Peeved, she felt forced to respond. Neither liked this torque in their relationship.

John and Mary decided that the best remedy would be to provide high-quality developmental nourishments. John had little problem with loving touch, but, given his impatience, he struggled with flexibility. Nevertheless, he made his best attempt and called in Mary to help when his patience eroded. She reconsidered how she was supplying security. She knew that fear and anxiety had accompanied the fights with her siblings and realized it might be the same for her children.

Within a month, the worst of the rivalry disappeared. Significantly, each parent healed their childhood wounds. John had to learn to be patient with himself as he struggled to provide flexibility. He also found that he could be appropriately impatient—that there were times when some tension helped establish healthy boundaries. This newfound well-being showed up in his work, in his marriage, in his confidence and self-esteem, and with his own parents. Previously, he had rationalized their intolerance by telling himself "it was the best they could do." Now he was able to relate to them how much their behavior had hurt him and the problems it had caused him in his life. John was not confrontational; he just needed them to know his truth. Afterward, he reported that he had greater respect and better boundaries with them than at any time of his life.

Mary simply provided security for both of her children. She realized that the fight hurts the "winner" as well as the "loser." She placed her body between theirs as soon as a physical threat appeared. She held them and talked with them.

Later, with John, she cried. "It was so beautiful," she told him. "I felt so connected. It was as if I was taking care of myself, as I wished I had been when I was in the middle of it with my sibs."

The Stanchions are dancing, BodyBeing style. Of course, your family and my family will dance in our unique ways. It may not be physical punishment or abandonment during crises that precipitated our wounds. Our reactions probably won't be tense impatience or skewed evaluation of security. And the issues may show up during a different phase of the life stage.

The flashing neon sign that points to a need to heal is the difficulty or inability to provide the needed developmental nourishment. In my experience, if you didn't get it, it is arduous to give it. This is why most people, despite their avowed intentions, parent as their parents did. It is not only that they have been oppressed, but also that they failed to develop optimal well-being in that capacity and so are crippled in their ability to provide it.

It is the adult capacity for reflective cognizance—their reasonable-ness—which allows them to make meaning of the dance. Reflective cognizance, when based in optimal well-being, allows great latitude in choosing one's response to a situation. Aware of interconnectedness, we ask why and look at whole systems for answers. We can not only evaluate many of the variables in most situations, but we can also include our-selves—our actions, thoughts, feelings, and capacities.

At that moment, for their own health, it is imperative for the adults to make prodigious efforts to supply that nourishment. By giving, they receive. Well-being is built into the nature of relationship. It is reciprocal. And though it may be arduous to supply a nourishment, it is quicker and less expensive than therapy and certainly less onerous than suboptimal family relationships. I have seen scores of childhood wounds healed through the simple, natural act of providing developmental nourishments to children.

A Transition Dance

Transition dancing calls for special choreography. Connie went through the BodyBeing-FeelingBeing transition relatively smoothly. A few nightmares, seeming uncontrollable sobbing at the loss of a grandparent, and an attraction to games in which the players repeatedly die and come back to life alerted her parents, Emily and Howard Donley, that the moment had arrived. Gently, in everyday conversation, they talked about death. They read books in which the characters faced death. Connie settled into the family, secure in relationship.

It did not go as smoothly for her younger brother, Tim. Just as every family is unique and must find their own blend of the nourishments, so every child is unique in the way they receive and digest the nourishments. The analogy to food is apt. One child thrives on the protein in meat and cheese; another does well with beans and rice. Each will have a healthy body, which is the goal. This is why techniques work only episodically and why NLR eschews them. Each of us needs and deserves to be seen as we are.

The Donleys could not miss Tim's entry signs—nightmares, bedwetting, and refusing to listen to any story that had anything to do with loss or death. When the pet rabbit died, he wouldn't go near it, nor attend its burial. The Donleys chose the same tact they had with his sister. Tim did not respond. Clearly a terror had invaded and was sharpening all edges of the transition.

Emily considered therapy; Howard resisted. Howard considered therapy; Emily resisted. Finally, feeling desperate, they hit upon a novel response. This is NLR at its best—the family uses developmental guidelines and then assesses the situation according to their own needs and meaning structures.

Neither Emily nor Howard had a strong fear of death, but they certainly had strong fears. Emily loathed snakes, and Howard feared interactions in which he had a financial stake in the outcome, such as with businessmen who used his accounting services. The Donleys decided that they would deliberately engage these fears with Tim at their side. If, they reasoned, Tim felt their feelings directly, then he would feel their struggle and, whatever their reaction, see that they lived through it. This, they felt, was feeling mentoring.

At the zoo, Emily stood outside the reptile house breathing deeply. Tim held her hand, attentive and silent. Howard and Connie waited on a nearby bench. Emily looked down at Tim, gripped his hand tightly, and went up the steps. She did not know it, but the zoo, for dramatic effect, had a large glass cage with a reticulated python facing the front door. Emily opened the door and there it was: twenty-six feet of snake slithering along a branch. "I thought my heart stopped," she told Howard later, "I was so shocked. I didn't realize for a moment that I was crushing Tim's hand. I started to sweat and breathe heavily. Tim disentangled our hands and then gently held mine. He was watching me and watching the python. Slowly my breath came back. Tim, to my momentary chagrin, moved us deeper into the house. Dazed, I let him lead. We went directly to the turtle and amphibian pool. His love of turtles came bubbling up, and I had to smile as he identified different types and recited their habits. After a while, we took a brief, cursory tour of the other reptiles and left."

Emily felt radiant when she came out. According to Howard, she looked radiant as well. The family enjoyed a day of laughter and repose, the tensions of Tim's transition momentarily abated.

Howard's nervousness increased when he brought Carl along to a meeting with his clients. He had chosen an informal meeting with the two owners of a coffee roasting company who wanted to sell him a minor share in their business. He had previously explained that his son needed to attend the meeting for a school project. They thought it unusual but agreed.

Sweating and stiff, Howard walked two steps ahead of Tim and could barely look at him as they entered the office. He could feel the others examining his son and wished that he had not started this stupid experiment. *The boy will grow out of his problems anyway*, he thought.

The business negotiation began. Within two minutes, Howard was absorbed in the facts and the figures. Tim sensed the change of focus and relaxed, intently studying the men around him. After an hour, the men had all the "deal points" on the table and decided to take a short break. Howard took Tim to the restroom. Tim spoke the first words to pass between them since they had entered the building.

"The old man is very angry."

Nonplussed, Howard tried to make sense of his son's comment. The man had appeared to be very convivial and seemed to be the moderate voice in the room. He continually put forth compromises that Howard had agreed to. At the same time, aware of FeelingBeing's emotional perceptiveness, Howard did not summarily reject Tim's words.

The negotiations resumed, and Howard soon saw that Tim was right. Something was bothering the man. Howard decided to triple-check the accounting. The other side had cleverly cooked the books when they recorded the cost of merchandise.

In that moment, Howard realized that his social anxiety detracted from his business acuity during meetings. By responding to a need of his child, he came to a deeper understanding of himself.

When Tim's transition terrors reappeared, his parents did not try to talk about them, read books, or change his experience. They no longer felt anger or shame about his bedwetting. "We just stayed connected," Emily said. "We had a new feeling inside us that somehow included Tim. If I had to analyze it, I would say that we knew that we had survived our own fears because of courage rediscovered in our relationships. But that's just analyses. With Tim, we knew that we didn't have to do anything but to *be* with him."

Dance steps always start with well-being. The Donleys refused to pathologize Tim's transition, difficult though it was. Rather, they turned to the nourishment of feeling mentoring in order to deepen their knowledge of one another and of themselves.

There are dance steps in every moment of life with children. Obviously, I cannot include all the dance steps available in a life stage. These case histories relate situations with all the nuances and subtleties of life's circumstances. In general, dance steps can most easily be recognized by the characteristics of the life stage. The following table names some of the principal characteristics of BodyBeing and the accompanying dance steps. As we move through the stages, there will be a similar table for each stage.

An Inspirational Dance

During FeelingBeing, Michelle was very much Daddy's little girl. Alex enjoyed their easy and affectionate camaraderie. He attended her plays and soccer games, and they often "hung out" together. At times, Michelle pushed her mother away. At first, Hilary did not respond, as she valued the closeness between her daughter and husband.

Table 9-1–Dance Steps for BodyBeing

Child	Parent
Birth	Love, awe, connection to mystery, joy.
Loving touch	The acute sensitivity to just how important and powerful even our merest touch is. The reawakening of our ability to receive touch.
Nursing/weaning	Attachment/separation. We give all in our nurturing and become attached. But, due to this nurturing, growth occurs and we must separate. This separation allows for a new, more complex relationship.
Unbending curiosity	How knowledge takes root in the human psyche; the fundamental drives by which we learn. Acceptance of the inevitability of human inquisitiveness. Also, reconnection to learning without prejudice or inhibition; learning for learning's sake.
No threats	Our aggression and need to control is highlighted when we cannot threaten, for now we have to find a different way to relate. Also, insight into how we use threats to cover our feelings of frustration, impotence, etc.
Imitation	Mirror of the way we talk, walk, etc., as well as the values we hold shows us much of who we are.
Exaggerated egotism during competency	Humor. Chance to see how egotism forms and its appropriate role in life.
Body tells the truth of their moment	How to observe and appreciate nonverbal communication. How to develop a relationship to our own nonverbal communication.
Plays with words	Exploration of self as communicator via sensation rather than language. Humility when the facade of verbal superiority is dropped.
Plays roughly with animals and plants; self-centered, sensation-based relationships	Discrimination between a sensation and a feeling.

New developments accompanied Michelle's eleventh year. One night, she and her dad were reading while lying close to one another on the couch. Michelle continually rearranged their bodies so they "fit better," as she said, which finally meant stretched out face to face, and close. Alex could feel incipient sexuality. Without drama, he sat up, stating it was a more comfortable position for reading.

That night, he retold the incident to Hilary, including the sexual stirrings he sensed in himself as well as in his daughter. He was certain he would never act on them, but he realized that to deny their presence inhibited his options for a relational response. Hilary appreciated his honesty. She told him that Michelle's comments had become sharper and sharper when she disagreed with her. They concluded that Michelle was experiencing the first urges of her coming puberty. Naively but intelligently, she had "selected" Alex as the place to practice. There was an equally naive possessiveness attendant to these urges that came out in the rebukes directed at Hilary. It was, at best, a hypothesis, but one that seemed viable to them.

Both parents felt apprehension when they realized that a conversation was needed. They would have to be honest and just and could not allow even the whiff of guilt to creep in. Alex intuited that he might have to answer Michelle's questions about his own sexuality. While he was prepared to do that when she was in IdealBeing, he did not believe it was appropriate at this time. Also, they had to steer clear of any notion of personal affront. This could not be a battle of Michelle versus Hilary for Alex's affection.

How could they approach Michelle? This was a moment of empowerment for her—the beginning step to womanhood. Cultural platitudes or imposed sexual mores might temporarily hold her because of the reciprocal cooperation with her parents. But the long-term effects seemed troublesome. IdealBeing children question platitudes and mores. What sexual identities would Michelle have to play with in order it find out if these mores had value for her autonomy?

Inspiration. It was Hilary who said it—inspiration and the mystery window.

They carefully planned a trip. Starting out early one morning, they backpacked into the Five Lakes Wilderness area of the Sierra Nevada mountains. By afternoon, they reached base camp at Glacier Lake at the foot of the Sierra Buttes. Hilary cajoled her daughter and husband into swimming in the frigid pure water. They camped the night.

At four the next morning, they were on their way. Gear left at base camp, they climbed the north edge of the buttes to the lowest part of its long, jagged peaks. They then followed it to the southwest, navigating narrow ledges, snowdrifts, and a series of saddles as they ascended from one peak to the next. Mostly silent except to help one another and ensure safety, they reached the crest at five-thirty. The sun broke on the far eastern horizon, inundating the endless mountain range with a spectrum of suffused pastels. Stars highlighted the purple sky to the west. Glacier Lake, five hundred feet below, remained deep in shadow, a plum smudge of indeterminate depth. Hues of every color oozed from the snow, which somehow retained its pure whiteness.

Inspiration. Mystery. Trust reinforced by a journey successfully completed.

There, the three conversed. As they swore me to confidentiality, I cannot report what was said. I am sure that each family would have their own form of inspiration and their own conversation. I do know, however, that soon thereafter Alex and Hilary decided to live a more deliberately spiritual lifestyle. They directly attributed their decision to that morning on the mountaintop.

Dancing with Self

Sometimes the dance can be dramatic.

Ernest and Maria Huerta, concerned about the coming teen years, came to a Natural Learning Rhythms event when their son, Cesar, was twelve. Quick learners, they met the transition well and provided the nourishments for IdealBeing during the receptivity phase. Then the bottom seemed to drop out. Cesar, brilliant in science and president of the biology club, began skipping school. He was seen more often with "stoners." Ernest tried to inquire, but Cesar stalled him. One night, Cesar did not come home until two in the morning. This was an unacceptable breach of the curfew they had co-created.

Ernest, Maria, and Cesar sat together in their living room that night. Cesar expected his parents to be angry, but they knew that a family breathes as a system. They were not trying to attach blame but rather to understand what was out of balance.

"We have a problem," Maria began. Cesar, expecting to be reprimanded, said nothing. His curled body and sullen grimace, however, loudly proclaimed his isolation and anger. "I said 'we,' not 'you.' Are you upset with us? Have we somehow insulted you?"

Ernest approved of Maria's words in his mind, but his feelings screamed that the boy just needed to be forced into line. Wisely, he said

Table 9-2–Dance Steps for FeelingBeing

Child	Parent
Very vulnerable receptivity phase	Stimulates our ability to be tender and caring. Realization that a new stage brings new and different challenges.
Awareness of personal mortality	Opportunity to reexamine our own relationship to death and metaphysics, inclusive of our relationship (or non) to transcendence. Do we access deep inner feelings of love and connection in our own lives?
Feeling mentors	Valuable opportunities for us to stay conscious of our feelings and the effects of our actions on others. Challenges us in our notions of perfection or imposed standards on others or ourselves.
Developing sense of trust	Opportunity to reexamine your self-trust and ability to trust others. Are you trustworthy? Do you follow through on your word?
Seeks inspiration	Invites us to rediscover and express inspiration in our lives. Are we able to feel devotion?
Community-oriented	Invites us to reevaluate our community relationships and revitalize unhealthy, strained, or codependent ones.
Seeks social cohesion	Opportunity to reexamine the myths and rules we live by.
Feels the feelings of others	Insight into the importance of feeling for the evolution of society, and how feelings influence our sense of justice. Realization that our children feel our feelings as we feel them ourselves. There is nowhere to hide.
Developing relationship to conscience	Reminds us of the opportunity in every moment to openly experience all of our feelings.

nothing. But there is no fooling the IdealBeing child who is exploring the shadow.

"You may think it's we, mom, but he doesn't. He thinks it is me."

"No he doesn't. Do you, Ernest? Do you think Cesar is the problem?"

Ernest's struggle lasted but a second. Careful to articulate each word and looking directly at Cesar, he said, "I do not think that, but in truth, I sometimes feel it."

Cesar sprang out of his chair. "Well, why don't you do something about it?" he shouted, contemptuous, as he ran up to his room. The door slammed.

Ernest and Maria sat in the deepening gloom. Something had changed in Ernest when he had admitted his confusion to his son, but he was not sure what it was. Maria, appreciating Ernest's honesty, asked why he felt their son was the problem.

At first, classical shadow issues appeared. Ernest's father certainly had blamed him if he behaved in ways outside the family norms. But Ernest had already comprehended that information based on his NLR seminar. That was why he didn't think Cesar was to blame. It did not help with his emotions, however.

His son's words rang in his ears: "Why don't you do something about it?" What could he do? His parents were dead, and he wouldn't know what to say to his father if he were alive. "I do not know," he told Maria. "Do you?"

Maria did not. She suggested that they try to see the situation from Cesar's perspective. Together, they examined Cesar's developmental needs and motivations.

Something was blocking Cesar's ability to live in his strength and power. Transitioning from IdealBeing receptivity to trial-and-error meant that he was in the meaning-making moment. Was there a place in this world for his greatness? Could he self-govern and attain happiness and recognition in life? Can Cesar take his place in the world as a fully empowered person?

The Huertas' first reaction was to list Cesar's strengths—his excellent intellect, ease around people of all ages and backgrounds, and sense of humor. But he knew he had all of these and either wouldn't or couldn't draw upon them. Then they considered the questions from the perspective of the family dynamic. It was Ernest who asked the liberating questions.

"Was there a place in the world for my greatness? Was there a place in the world for your greatness, my darling wife? And when we were facing the immense future and our place in it, what kind of support did we receive?"

Emotions flooded each of them. They sat in silence, the sadness palpable. A tremor of disgust rippled through Ernest. "Why don't you do something about it?" Because he never thought that he could. It wasn't so much that he had accepted the path his father had insisted upon. He was a good surgeon and enjoyed his work. It was that the choice had been ripped away and that despite his accomplishments, he never felt himself a great man.

Maria suffered that night. She suffered for all girls who have been dumbed down in school and for all women who have been railroaded into constraining social roles and never had the chance to actualize their greatness. She suffered because she never had the chance to open to the possibility of her greatness. And a white hot anger came to life in her.

That night, or really that morning at four, Ernest and Maria Huerta made a pact. She would attend college and freely choose her studies. He would pursue his unfulfilled passion for painting.

They would mention their choices casually to Cesar but follow through assiduously. They now knew that he needed them to challenge and inquire into their own identities if they expected him to do the same. They would do something about it. That's what he called for. They were only too happy to oblige.

When the Huertas recounted their dance at a family camp, I had cascading insights about the shadow, about IdealBeing, and about my own life. The Huertas' development triggered my development. I realized, for example, that integrating the shadow required more than just naming the shadow issue; it had to be felt deeply so that a liberating response arose that was apropos to the moment, not to the past. The tensions they described reminded me of how challenging autonomy is—how we are inexorably drawn toward it and why it is such a sacred prize.

Their recounting threw me back to my fifteenth year. I tasted the alienation and disdain but also saw the beacon that lighted my way. My parents never let me believe that I could not realize my dreams. This was not a dance step for them. They did not change nor were they able to reach into my unhappy life. But if I ever suggested that I could not achieve my goals, they told me I was a fool and to quit the nonsense. So close is well-being to the surface, so consistently does it draw us to our greatness, that this simple concept provided sufficient ballast for me to live through that dark time.

The Huertas realized that they had to change and question their own identities so that their son could question his. Only then could he

Table 9-3—Dance Steps for IdealBeing

Child	Parent
Sensitive respect	Learning to stay centered and connected even when we disagree or are challenged. Acceptance of the insecurity in identity formation in our children and ourselves.
Sudden rapid changes	Nonattachment; keeps us alert and aware; reflects the amazing human capacity for change and growth.
Explores the shadow	Reflects our shadow and insists that we work on it. Allows insight into cultural and personal defensiveness. Calls forth honesty.
Idealistic assertions	Reawakens our own ideals. Forces us to question how we relate to ideals. Places ideals at the center of cultural evolution.
Engages freedom	Shows the limitations of community; stimulates empathy for the trials of individuation. Invites us to reexamine again and again the nature of freedom.
Insecure, yet assertive	Breaks down prejudice and judgment; teaches that you cannot tell a child by their behavior.
High-adventure challenges	We all need high-adventure challenges, but, in our society, rarely have the chance. Yet here it is, part of the natural course of parenting.
Looks profoundly, yet naively, at sexuality; may challenge our sexual expression.	Brings forth compassion as we recall our own struggles with sexuality. Draws us to reexamine who we are sexually.
Solidifies a self	Allows us to see how "self" solidifies, and how our "self" solidified, thus teaching us about evolution, psychology, and our strengths and weaknesses. Prepares the ground by which we can question our notion of self.
Ends in doubt	Teaches the limitations of assertion and "me-first" freedom. Provides a chance to reconnect to our children in a humble and vulnerable way.

see the identities' value for his core nature. Most parents have difficulty with this dance step. Some find it imposing. Why should they have to change? They are comfortable in their life and proud of their achievements. Others find it daunting. They fear that the dance may lead them to question their religion, sexual behavior, or issues of similar magnitude.

There are, of course, many excellent dance steps for parents and their IdealBeing children. In my experience, this one has the greatest value for everyone: Parents refine their connection to their core nature; children find the room to grow into the powerful realm of autonomy.

Dancing with Meaning

Josette and I met Arthur when he was finishing his undergraduate work as a music major at the University of California. A year later he graduated and asked if he could join the apprentice program that Josette and I offered to those who wanted to deepen their appreciation of Natural Learning Rhythms. Later that same year, Nancy, a physics major whom Josette had met at Mills College and who had also graduated, asked to join. We happily accepted both of them. At the time we, had no idea that they would fundamentally change the course of our lives and NLR.

At first, their influence was personal. Josette has little aptitude for arithmetic, so, at the time, I handled the finances in our household. I, however, have little aptitude for budgeting and bookkeeping. Tracking expenses bored me. Josette, on the hand, understood bookkeeping and budgeting very well. She just kept making mistakes with the math and feeling bad about it. Irritation beset us. This was not a dance, but a toe-stepping shin-kicking frustrated state of helplessness.

Nancy saw Josette's math skills and just laughed. "You don't need to worry about that anymore," she said. "The answer is right over there." She pointed to my computer. I had been introduced to computers in the 1960s when I was an undergraduate and started to use personal computers as soon as they appeared. However, as I avoided finances, I did not know how to use them for bookkeeping. Even though the programs were primitive compared to what is available today, they were sufficient to handle bookkeeping tasks and compensate for Josette's math weakness.

At first Josette resisted, which puzzled Nancy. Josette held that it would be too much trouble to learn all the complexities of the computer. Nancy patiently explained that there was a learning curve but that the time invested was soon rewarded with exponentially greater efficiency.

Josette still resisted. I reminded Josette of the ReasonableBeing nourishment of recognition of achievement. Also, I asked whether she dialogued with Nancy. What exactly had computers meant to Nancy in her life?

Josette asked that exact question. Nancy enthusiastically described how computers had allowed her to follow her passion of theoretical physics by helping her with complex calculations. Josette was incredulous. "You mean," Josette asked, "that you had poor math skills too?"

"Not really poor, but not good enough for some of the complex math that physics requires. I would have never gotten my degree without computers crunching numbers and formulas for me."

Nancy gave Josette lessons. Within an hour she was hooked. That night, brimming with confidence, she showed me how she would use the computer to do the math. She stated that the finances were hers. In truth, I was happy to be free of the obligation and relieved to live within the budget our means indicated. The tension dissolved—no more bruised toes or shins.

The confidence and skill that she actualized in her dance with Nancy continues to blossom. To achieve in graduate school, Josette has had to demonstrate competence in statistics. This would have scared her off before, but now she is making it through unscathed. Our finances have become more complex as we have aged, but she spends less time with them and is able to project financial scenarios quickly and accurately. Due to this, we have had considerable freedom in deciding which projects to engage. For instance, the time it took to write this book became available because of careful budgeting and subsequent reasonable agreements about the use of disposable income.

Arthur loved music and played the clarinet well. He had plentiful musical intelligence. I, on the other hand, believed that I had none. One night, I heard him playing the clarinet in the small cottage on the back of our land and went to listen. The sounds and the play of his fingers were mesmerizing. I found his ability to switch from jazz to baroque flabbergasting, and jealousy and confusion faintly stirred within me.

Arthur knew of my self-perception as a musical moron because I had joked about it as I explained Gardner's work in seminars. "So," he asked, surprised at my attendance at his third practice session, "how does it make you feel?"

"Huh?" Make me feel? I had not been paying attention to feelings. When he asked, though, I discovered that every piece had significant emotional impact. The feeling qualities determined the intensity of my affinity with the music. In my ignorance, I had been attending only to the sensory qualities of the melody and the sounds of the notes.

"Play another."

Arthur did, and the music came to life. By the end of the following week, I was feeling my way into the multitude of musical genres. I rediscovered spiritual music—from gospel to mantras—by disregarding the words or the spiritual intent. I felt like a kid in a candy shop.

"Now," Arthur told me, "you are ready for your education." Over the next months, I learned about the history of music, the skill evident in a virtuoso performance, the structure of chords and harmonics, and the relationship among the violins in a symphony. I learned much more than that. I learned to listen to music with all my capacities. I learned that I had been hurt as a child when my elementary school teachers humiliated me for singing off key. I learned that I heard the interweaving melodies best when I was still and that physical movement, such as dancing, distracted me from the music. I learned that musical intelligence found expression in listening. I listened to John Cage and learned to hear the silence in the music, the space between the notes, and the dynamics of the transitions.

Arthur's and Nancy's apprenticeship occurred during the first seven years of our work with NLR. I had always enjoyed contemplating the conclusions of physics and evolutionary theory but had yet to see their implications for NLR. One night, a lively dialogue about wisdom and the life stages led to an insight that changed NLR forever.

Josette had described wisdom as the source of creativity from which the child draws—according to their stage-specific capacities and blend of intelligences—what she needs for optimal well-being. In terms similar to the ones used in chapter 5, "Spirituality," Josette said that wisdom contains all the possibilities for the child in infinite array. Arthur pointed out that each stage cannot have an infinite array of possibilities because then it wouldn't be a stage. Nancy caught Arthur's intention. BodyBeing, for instance, had only the infinite array of what could be expressed through sensation and connected the child to rightful place. There might be infinite choices, but they would have to be accessible through the qualities and characteristics of BodyBeing. And the same held true for each life stage. That, I contributed, was stage-specific wisdom, a term coined by Joseph Chilton Pearce. But it referred to the way children know wisdom. Wisdom itself did not have boundaries.

"Then," Nancy said with great seriousness, "you are right in line with Bohm's implicate."

The rest of us burst out laughing. The incongruity of her comment, combined with the gravity of her tone, left us gasping for air. Nancy smiled and waited patiently for us to calm down. She then told us that she would write a short essay describing the connection so that we would have time to assimilate her idea and could intelligently debate its merits.

Here is the essay, reproduced as she wrote it so that you can see and feel the incisiveness of dancing with the ReasonableBeing child.

In *Wholeness and the Implicate Order*, David Bohm establishes a fundamental connection between matter and awareness. Bohm contends that all that we know as "real" arises from a deeper wholeness which he calls the implicate. By rigorously tracing quantum physics to its source, Bohm shows that matter exists in the implicate as an enfolded potential, waiting only for the right conditions to make itself explicate, to take physical existence.

Consciousness, which has its beginnings in the flux of the implicate, is the way we know that which is explicated. In Bohm's words: "each moment of consciousness has a certain explicit content, which is a foreground, and an implicit content, which is a corresponding background."

Bohm, a fierce wisdom warrior, does not back down from the difficult questions implied in his research. If matter and consciousness arise together from the same source, what about the mind and the body? "In the implicate order we have to say that mind enfolds matter in general and therefore the body in particular. Similarly, the body enfolds not only the mind but also in some sense the entire material universe. Mind and body are the outcome of related projections from a higher ground, i.e. the implicate."

Bohm's conclusion is that a human as a mind/body participates in all of nature and all of humanity by virtue of their interdependent arising from the same source, the implicate. "So it will be ultimately misleading and indeed wrong to suppose, for example, that each human being is an independent actuality who interacts with other human beings and with nature. Rather, all these [self, others, and nature] are projections of a single totality."

Thus, our wholeness includes one another and all of nature. That wholeness arises within consciousness, of which we partake in a human way. Consciousness arises from the implicate, an ever-changing flux of unlimited potential whose ultimate nature lies beyond our knowledge.

Nancy's essay became the subject of our dialogue for many weeks. We were drawn more deeply to consider the "sciences of wholes" which include quantum mechanics, chaos and complexity theory, and the theories of relativity. The first direct application emerged when we put together data from complexity theory about initial conditions and the dynamics of transition between the life stages. Confident that we'd found a gold mine, we looked for other usages.

Josette and I had been struggling to create a suitable way to describe dysfunction from the perspective of well-being. Natural Learning Rhythms shows that optimal well-being exists and describes its manifestation. What, then, blocked optimal well-being in children and families? According to NLR, the various forms of dysfunction were the result of certain blocks. The remedies, therefore, should act to restore well-being rather than to dissolve the symptoms. Our dialogues on the sciences of wholes gave us the lexicon and data to form a system that described this insight. As you will see in the next chapter, that system has evolved into a remedial approach to treating family dysfunction that any family can apply with confidence and at little cost.

And all the while we were dancing.

Recognizing the ReasonableBeing child's interest inevitably leads to a dance step. Eugene, twenty, traveled through Europe and North Africa, stopping at countries' waste disposal facilities. His parents, fascinated by his insights, uncovered many of their prejudices and unchallenged assumptions about these cultures.

Linda, twenty-two, has a passion for spelunking. Her parents assumed that she was attracted to the physical challenge and the exotic environment. After a Natural Learning Rhythms program, they asked her about the meaning of spelunking. Linda spoke of the absolute silence and the extraordinary reverence that enveloped her in a cave. Often she solved emotional problems while spelunking. Her comments sparked an interest in the nature of mind and consciousness for her father. Her mother, always active, asked if she could join her in the activity.

Dancing with Children with Special Needs

Gary has always wanted a son. A self-made multimillionaire with a wide range of interests—including artisan knives, Buddhism, and antiques—Gary believed that he could teach his son how to have a happy and successful life. He felt this act would be the perfect completion to a life well led.

Table 9-4–Dance Steps for ReasonableBeing

Child	Parent
Needs mature recognition	Their maturity calls forth ours. It also demands that we stay current with their interests, which keeps us in touch with our world. We also prepare for releasing them into interdependent adulthood.
Loves to explore	Keeps us fresh and alive. Shows us once again of the ever-opening nature of curiosity and the natural motivation to learn.
Expanded awareness of space/time	Inhibits concretization around a fixed notion of nature, of the universe, and of our own minds.
Understands that there are ways of knowing beyond reasoning	Stretches us to acknowledge our deepest potential as humans. Shows us both the greatness and the limitations of comparison.
Aware of the other organizing principles	Illuminates the precision of the developmental process, for there is one last powerful chance to heal before full maturity.
Falls in love	We let go of being their primary love, only to reorganize into new, more complex relationships with the child. We also appreciate the child's ability to commit and so reconnect to the value of commitment in life.
Begins in doubt	Teaches that doubt is a critical aspect of reason. We begin to value our doubt rather than fear it.
Creates systems	Allows us to look for connections; ends illusions of isolation We realize that systems exist everywhere and so appreciate the connections between events of any sort as highly relevant.
Need their life recapitulated as they step out fully on their own	By impartially recapitulating their life, we clear up misunderstandings and guilt. We are free to let them go and enjoy their maturity. We are free to take on new aspects of our life.
No condescension	Humility. It insists we find an open-hearted way to share our knowledge.

He did have a son, but the son, Lee, had special needs. Diagnosed with multiple learning disorders, Lee often wandered off the subject when she was speaking. Teachers and psychologists had labeled her as having "diminished social skills." Lee showed minimal physical or emotional affection toward anyone, including Gary and his mother.

Adding to Gary's woes, Lee walked on his toes all the time due to problems with his Achilles tendon. Gary had taken Lee to the best toe-walking doctors in America. Despite myriad therapies, the problem persisted. As a result, Lee had an ungainly walk that only accentuated his pudgy body type. Whatever Gary had hoped for in a son, Lee did not have. Lee was not the child of his dreams.

Many parents of special-needs children suffer disappointment. Though the gap between the child they desired and the one they received may not be as dramatic as it was for Gary, most of them hoped for someone singular, or at least normal. In addition, these parents fear that they will not be able to relate to the child, that they will not have the patience to meet the special needs, that there will be no remedy for the special need, and that their child will be shunned or treated as a pariah. It is a challenging experience to be at once disappointed and frightened.

The actuality can be as difficult as imagined. In my experience, doctors, psychologists, counselors, and school personnel are rarely sensitive when they discuss the child. Extended family can be supportive, but they often assume standards that are not applicable to the child. Conventional academic approaches have little to do with the blend of intelligences in special-needs children. Other children often treat them badly. Some siblings and spouses resent the attention given to the child. Testing and treatment can be costly. Family outings are circumscribed by the child's capacities. Development can be delayed, or the signs of development can be obscured, making it more difficult to anticipate their needs.

Gary and Lee first came on a family river trip just after he turned eight. Given the nourishments, he flourished. By the second day, Lee insisted that he could assume the front position in a two-person canoe with her father. Skeptical, he agreed, secure in the fact that the paddler in the rear controls the canoe. Lee impressed everyone but herself with his skill. He did not respond to compliments.

At the evening camp, Lee steered all conversations toward movies he had seen. At first, this behavior pushed everyone away. Then he mentioned a movie that Donna, a ten-year-old child from one of the other families, had seen. With great animation, Donna started to relate a part of the movie. Looking past Donna and not at her, Lee spoke the long dialogue verbatim with all the nuances and inflections of the original. He was very funny and people gathered. At first I thought Lee might be an idiot savant, with a prodigious memory for certain verbal-linguistic tracts. But I had not seen any other signs of it and supposed one of Lee's many doctors would have spotted it before. Also, as he finished to an audience of all forty campers, a wisp of a sly smile crossed his cheeks.

Someone asked if he had seen *Liar, Liar*, the popular Jim Carrey movie. Without answering, he did two long scenes. His rendition included all the parts and had the same timing as the movie. This time when he finished, he let out a squeal of delight. Everyone laughed. The smile moved to his eyes. But then he abruptly went to bed.

I asked Gary if this behavior was typical of Lee. "Abruptly walking off, sure. Able to render parts of a movie, sure. But I had no idea that she could manage so many parts and for so long a sequence."

"What do you make of it?"

"That's not what's blowing my mind. It was the squeal. Did you see that? Now that's completely off the charts."

The next day, Lee, without asking, assumed the rear paddler's position. Concerned, for there were tricky class three rapids to navigate, Gary wanted him to move to the front. "I can do it," he told him, looking off to the side. After discussing it with the river guides, Gary decided to risk it. He did insist that Lee communicate with him so that their paddling was coordinated.

Lee did very well. Gary kept looking back at her, not to comment on his ability, but out of sheer disbelief. By that evening, he realized that he hadn't known his son's capacities. Lee, of course, was on call and entertained the camp for forty-five minutes with scenes from yet another movie.

We stayed in camp the next day. Gary, puzzling over his experience, wondered how Lee could demonstrate such competence. Josette suggested that he ask him. Gary did.

"Because I can use my body in the boat and I don't have to walk on these stupid toes."

Humiliated, Gary felt like crawling into the earth. This simple answer had never occurred to him. Moreover, he had never thought to ask. He had been so preoccupied with Lee's special needs. Most of his time with him was an attempt to cure the problem, and he had neglected the obvious. In the canoe, Lee could let his strengths manifest. He had no impairment in his upper body or in his ability to read the river, which, many will say, is more difficult than reading a book.

Later that day, Gary asked Lee about his ability to re-create the movies. How did he have such concentration when he could not focus on schoolwork? Lee's answer devastated him once again.

"Because no one is there to bother me. It's quiet and I like to do it."

I will refrain from caustic comments on the testing, counseling, academic criteria, and rude blindness that led to the oppression of Lee. It is Gary's dance that concerns us.

Lee's challenges are real, and they must be addressed. As a result of participating in a program that nourished his son, Gary learned to recognize and activate Lee's strengths before he turned to the challenges.

For Gary, as for so many other parents of special-needs children, the dance is the realization of how vulnerable they are to society's definition of their child, how tightly they are locked into their expectations, and how narrowly they envision nature's greatness as it lives in each of us.

Lois, the mother of a child diagnosed with Aspberger's syndrome, had a similar breakthrough. After she cast off the blinders of worrying about what others might think of her, she responded in new ways to his social behaviors. When he ducked under the table in the presence of company, she went with him. She brought him along when she volunteered at the preschool and at the home for the elderly and infirm. He related well in both situations. Lois found her son had musical and athletic talents. For three years, she supervised and mentored him when he was with his peers. Finally, she rejoiced when he was selected to the little league all-star team.

The Dance of the Nontraditional Family

America is a land of diversity and perhaps the noblest social experiment in history. It is a country founded on the principle of human rights, not on ethnic homogeneity or religious persuasion. People, not institutions or customs, have unalienable rights. America can be a success only if the people have the freedom to live, the freedom to be. Nothing else can redeem the sacrifice of even one soldier.

The diversity extends to family structure and composition. Divorce has led to many single-parent families. Remarriage has led to many blended families. One parent may have stayed single and the other remarried, divorced, and remarried again. Children have two and sometimes three homes. They have two and sometimes three sets of siblings, grandparents, and aunts and uncles.

Marriage between people of different races and different ethnic and religious backgrounds is common. Though it remains controversial, there are also same-sex marriages, whether or not the state sanctions them. Many of these couples have children from a prior divorce, adoption, or artificial insemination. In a landmark study, The American Academy of Pediatrics found that same-sex parents are as competent as heterosexual parents and that their children are as psychologically and physically healthy.[102]

While nontraditional families face unique challenges, the dance steps remain the same: Provide the nourishments, meet the developmental imperatives, accept the responsibility of participating in the child's way of organizing their world, and enjoy the freedom attendant to self-knowledge. Every dancing parent in the case histories described above—Sharon, Robert, John, Mary, Howard, Emily, Ernest, Maria, Lois, Gary, Josette, and I—experienced new freedom in our relationships with our children and our work. We healed wounds and rediscovered long-forgotten aspects of ourselves. We came face to face with our humanness in the form of our well-nourished children. There is absolutely no difference in the dance dynamics for nontraditional families. The same possibilities of freedom and self-knowledge can be actualized through developmentally sensitive relationships.

At the end of her time in family camp, Kelly, one of the moms in a same-sex couple, asked what she could do to help others learn about Natural Learning Rhythms. Because many parents like to speak with someone who has experienced a family camp before they enroll, I asked if she would field some of their questions. She agreed. At the closing of the next camp, Jeanna, also a parent in a same-sex couple, publicly thanked Kelly for encouraging her to attend. She started to laugh. "I asked her if there was free time for dancing in the camp. I was looking for "time off." She said that after the second day, she did nothing but dance and that she never became tired. I asked what she meant. Kelly just laughed. Now I know what she meant."

The Transcendence Dance—Dancing as Elders

How can transcendence be described? No one finds this easy to do. The Kabbalah's Tree of Life describes several transcendent states, but, true to its Hebraic roots, will not even write or speak the name of God. Tibetan Buddhism has rich descriptions and uses thangkas, which are paintings of deities, as an integral part of its vocabulary of transcendence. As José and Miriam Arguelles show in their well-documented book, Mandala, many cultures, East and West, use mandalas to depict extraordinary modes of consciousness. The Fourth Way, an incisive and startling spiritual path from the venerable Sufi tradition, mathematically delineates vibratory frequencies of ordinary and transcendent modes of consciousness and then describes the capacities of each mode. The *Bhagavad-Gita* gives detailed phenomenological details of transcendent states and the disciplines necessary to access them. Patanjali's *Yoga Sutras* is the archetype of philosophical minimalism, with brief statements intended to show the nature of mind, the training needed to still the mind, and the resultant transcendent awareness. Christianity, like most religions, relies heavily on the life stories of its saints and sages. Apophasis, (described in detail in footnote 66) names transcendence, names the limitations of the name, names transcendence from a different angle, and then unnames that name, and so on, emphasizing that the nature of mystery lies in its inability to be definitively described.

Natural Learning Rhythms cannot readily apply any of these brilliant approaches. The dance can occur only in relationships that play in the field of optimal well-being. It comes to life in participation with children. That moment can be neither said nor unsaid. There is no supporting art or icon. There are life stories, as the case histories illustrate, but every family is unique and knowledge emerges apropos to the dancers. Case histories are helpful, especially when the Healing dance is being described, but they are not sufficient for the transcendent dance. Also, there is the danger that people will turn a case history about transcendence into a parable, a stricture prescribing 'shalts' and 'shalt nots.'

I will simply say what I know the transcendent dance to be. This dance is knowledge. It is not a theory, which refers to conceptions, mental schemes, and speculation. It is not about information. The qualities of this dance, such as devotion and service, should not be mistaken for data about devotion and service. This is not cognition of the transcendent quality, but knowing the quality itself, as it is in you. It is direct, alive, and unmistakable.

The transcendent dance occurs naturally when we nourish children and our childhood wounds no longer bind us—no longer glue us to the past. It cannot be grasped or taught. It is hidden when sought. It is the gift of undiluted freedom bestowed upon the adult when she/he participates in the responsibility of relationship with children.

It is a dance of the elders, for those who know how short life is and have actualized some substantive values—values that endure beyond time. The elder has realized meaning as ethics, aesthetics, love, trust, insight, or some combination of these. This dance is not known through reflective cognizance but as wisdom. The elder breathes relationship.

Dancing with the developmental needs of BodyBeing—loving touch, security, flexibility, and warmth—dissolves the false boundaries of separation. Rightful place expands to include all of humanity. At that point, we can begin to use the full command of the power of our bodies in service and compassionate action for others. Everyone is included. To serve rightful place is to invigorate the vitality and security of every human being. In this moment, the limitations of identification with survival of only the personal self are transcended. Without question or doubt, this relationship, this touch, is the right place—that place of great mystery that has no name.

Dancing with the developmental needs of FeelingBeing children—feeling mentors, honesty, justice, adaptability, fairness, and adventure—helps us access the deep potential of trust. Trust of self and the need to reciprocally cooperate with others naturally call forth our capacity for empathy. Trust, cooperation, and empathy are a rich medium from which an undiluted love frequently emerges. This love transcends the type of love that is dependent on an object. It is immanent and transcendent effortlessly. It is love that realizes the extraordinary sacredness inherent in life. Naturally and immediately, devotion arises. The elder wishes only to allow all life to actualize this sacred love. She sees the falsity of imposing projections of what the destiny of the child should be as she realizes that that all destinies find fulfillment in love. When she transcends personal love, the elder actualizes love beyond reason.

Dancing with the developmental needs of IdealBeing—sensitive respect, challenges within the realm of success, freedom connected with responsibility, wider social experiences, peer support, and the opportunity to express and act upon ideals—helps the elder access the deeper potential of autonomy. Any identity has worth only in that it allows the elder to experience and express her core nature. By staying open and questioning, she engages her innate capacity to become free from identifications that bind. The story of her personal biography and the associated conditioning are transformed. The elder becomes truly autonomous and free of reliance on tradition, ritual, or false notions of chivalry. The identities of nobility, hero, or victim dissolve. The transcendent potential to express one's core nature for the benefit of humanity comes to life. There is no need to refer to an ideal. The elder simply is the natural expression of her core nature. Having the full command of an autonomous self, the elder's personal power naturally expresses itself in the service of social goodness and human greatness

Dancing with the developmental needs of ReasonableBeing—recognition of achievement, recognition of equality, recognition of commitment, and recognition of the ability to recognize—awakens the deeper potential of interconnectedness, humor, and humility. Time, space, and thought itself are open to investigation. Thought itself is transcended, and with it all concepts of time and place. Love beyond reason, joy that can be known only by a free heart, and pure, unmitigated being connected to all beings become self-evident. Life itself becomes pure beauty— endlessly changing yet effortlessly perfect.

The End of Chauvinism

Chauvinism toward children is everywhere. It is institutionalized in schools that bully students into becoming "good citizens" and support only a narrow band of the intelligence spectrum; in government, where politicians continually use children for campaign promotions and then fail to provide the funds needed for education and family support; and in homes, where parents continue to rationalize the hurt from their own childhood and end up parenting like their parents parented.

Chauvinism is an ugly word. The dictionary defines it as "exaggerated patriotism of a bellicose sort; blind enthusiasm for national glory or military ascendancy," and says this it is akin to jingoism. Etymologically, it's a French word derived from a general who thought Napoleon and empire were the reasons for living. It is also etymologically twin to Calvinism, a movement started by the Protestant reformer famous for his belief in predestination—which held that "eternal life [is] ordained for some, eternal damnation for others."

In other words, a chauvinist believes that either you have it or you don't. And the "it" is whatever the chauvinist believes is superior based on some inner revelation or social custom. If you don't have it, then you are lesser and undeserving of life, liberty, and the pursuit of happiness. In many cases, you are so much less that you are undeserving of a good meal and a safe home. Or so much less that you are chattel.

Thus, for feminists, society traditionally has viewed males as superior. This chauvinism justifies treating women rudely and denying their franchise in personal and social spheres. We have noted this in education in chapter 8, "Intelligence and Academics."

Horrible as it was, and is, at least women were seen for having some value to society as mothers, teachers, nurses, and secretaries. While humiliated in their disenfranchisement, they at least had enough power to gain the right to property; the right to vote; and respect in business, academics, politics, and athletics.

The chauvinism toward African-Americans and people of color has been worse, if miserable treatments can be compared. Slavery is revolting and there is no economic, political, or social justification for it. It is a testament to human resiliency and greatness that African-American people have contributed so significantly in all American endeavors. I am grateful for the modeling.

The chauvinism directed toward children is unique. This chauvinism is not confined to one race or economic system. It is considered normal. Many adults actually believe that children are helpless vessels waiting to be filled with their direction and teaching. Control and imposition rule. Being is ignored. The tyranny of data retention and regurgitation, of information used as currency and power, and of judgment based on performance turns children into objects, into Its.

The chauvinism permeates the highest reaches of academia and of spiritual teachings. Progressive intellectual disciplines, such as complexity and emergence, study everything from ants to cities to computer games to just about everything but children. No one asks how their consciousness emerges. No one, until Natural Learning Rhythms, asked if there are "strange attractors," so central to chaos and complexity theory, in children's lives. Steven Johnson, in *Emergence*, marvels over the local communication between ants and the developmental stages of an ant colony but does not consider the local communication between children—or their developmental stages.

Gregory Bateson initiated a revolution in family therapy when he showed that the way parents communicate with children is a significant factor in childhood schizophrenia. This, and much research since, has shown the importance of the way parents communicate with children. But what about the importance of the way children relate to parents? How does that affect the parent's optimal well-being? Research has been confined to investigating whether parents have less stress when their home life is copasetic. That, obviously, is all about the parents. It is also pathologically driven, as it investigates stress and not well-being. Unsurprisingly, this investigation is well funded by business in the name of work-life balance. The goal is greater productivity. The child remains a sacrificial pawn in the game of sustaining the culture. Children are looked at as a necessary burden. There is no evolution without them, but why do they have to act like...children? It will be better when they grow up and don't have to be "brought up."

Perhaps you can already intuit the grand irony—that cultural health is best served by centering on optimal well-being in children, and yet time and again, they are passed over.

The Children's Institute of Portland, my hometown, takes a slightly more progressive approach. They are "proving" that caring for children younger than eight has economic advantages. They hope to take the proof to the legislature and get them to reallocate public money so that it used wisely. This project will take a number of years and might not succeed. But chauvinism is so strong that proving the economic benefit of caring for children may be the only way to change the societal norms.

Socially, children pay a great price for chauvinism. The gifts they bring to society, a subject for chapter 11, "Social Justice," go unseen. John Holt, an educator and father of the current homeschooling movement, once pointed out that adults would never be as rude with one another as they are with children. Despite the fact they are the decision makers of the future, they are the beneficiaries of only a small fraction of social resources. Can anyone seriously contend that acquiring more billion dollar fighter jets has more long-term social value than investing that money in children and families?

Spiritual leaders of all stripes are infected as well. Josette and I were asked to help families integrate into the main congregation of Ananda, a large international fellowship with strong roots in both Christianity and Vedanta. Founded on the monastic-householder model, which places meditation at the center of life, many of the congregant's children had grievances with the lifestyle. There were many instances of chauvinism in the church's relationship to children, but one stands out. At the front of the main auditorium, a huge sign proclaimed that "The Guest is God." At the same time, BodyBeing children were expected to sit quietly through long services, and FeelingBeing children were punished if they violated the ethical teachings of the church. The children were clearly not the guest. Fortunately, the family ministry, after several Natural Learning Rhythms programs, realized this and changed it, at least while we worked there.

We had a similar experience when working with a New Thought church of more than four thousand congregants. When we conversed with the leader, she acknowledged the validity of Natural Learning Rhythms but insisted that children be taught to follow the precepts of the Bible, since all religions agreed on them. She then chronicled the disaffection of the teens in the congregation and her problems with her "step-teen" at home. Her only concern was which behavior modification techniques we thought best to bring the teens "into line."

Nationally known Buddhists Myla and Jon Kabat-Zinn wrote a caring book on parenting, *Everyday Blessings: The Inner Work of Mindful Parenting*. The book contains many stories and anecdotes of the grace and beauty that result from the effort to see the world through the child's eyes. Their "Twelve Exercises for Mindful Parenting" include five reminders to participate in the child's perspective. Three of the exercises call for the parent to keep the greatness of the child in mind, and two have to do with meditation practices that can help when elders are relating to children. As well meaning and well written as the book is, it leaves out the child's contribution to the parents' development. As with all spiritual paths that I have examined, old and new, the parent brings the gift of spiritual awareness, achieved wholly or mostly in isolated spiritual practices, to the child, who then reaps the benefit. The child is not seen as critical to the parents' spiritual awakening. Their love does not count in the development of the parents' self-knowledge.

Ananda, the New Thought Church, the Kabat-Zinns, and many other spiritual leaders and institutions are intelligent and caring, with genuine interest in children. I chose them as examples for just this reason. If they do not see the chauvinism, who does?

Worst of all, perhaps, is that there is no public acknowledgement of the chauvinism. Alice Miller is correct: If we have been oppressed, we will oppress others unless we truly heal the wounds from that oppression. Frances Wickes, the psychologist who Jung turned to for understanding of children, wrote, at age ninety, in the new preface to *The Inner World of Children*, that she had never come across a child's malady that wasn't connected to the psychology of the parents. Jung was more explicit:

> The children are infected indirectly through the attitude they instinctively adopt towards their parents' state of mind: either they fight against it with unspoken protest (though occasionally the protest is vociferous) or else they succumb to a paralysing and compulsive imitation. In both cases they are obliged to do, to feel, and to live not as they want, but as their parents want. The more "impressive" the parents are, and the less they accept their own problems (mostly on the excuse of "sparing the child"), the longer the children will have to suffer from the unlived life of their parents and the more they will be forced into fulfilling all the things that parents have repressed and kept unconscious...The only thing that can save the child from unnatural injury is the efforts of the parents not to shirk the psychic difficulties of life by deceitful manoeuvres or by remaining artificially unconscious, but rather to accept them as tasks, to be as honest with themselves as possible, and to shed a beam of light into the darkest corners of their souls.[103]

If our natural learning rhythms have not been honored we have been oppressed. It is, in fact, a murder. In our paper for a conference to update the UN Charter and Universal Declaration of Human Rights to include children, Josette and I wrote:

> Murder is the unlawful killing of a being. It is certainly a human right to not be murdered.
>
> The destruction of any human capacity or well-being is murder. It leads the person to believe that he/she is separate, an isolated entity cut off from self, family, community, society, Earth, nature and Spirit. In this perceived isolation all abuse, violence and aggression (both passive and active) is rationalized as an act of justice. It is the vain attempt to reconcile the loss of wholeness, a wholeness that the organizing principle toward well-being makes effortlessly self-evident. The killing of any of these capacities for well-being is murder because it violates the natural law of human access to Being.
>
> All special interest groups, no matter how humane, are reactions to the murders. Indeed, the need for a council on Spirit and Human Rights could only be convened in the wake of a society torn by isolation and separation. As Meister Ekhart, the great Christian sage of the Middle Ages, said: "We only need all these churches because we have lost our relationship to God."
>
> Let us not equivocate on the term murder. When a human capacity for well-being is destroyed it is not as if a "part" of them is gone. Perhaps this ancient teaching story says it best. A sage came to a new land but noticed something was missing. After a while he realized there were no birds. When he asked why he was told that they all had left. Everyone said this was sad, but no one knew why it had happened. Then the sage came to the edge of town and saw the forest decimated through clear cutting. "This is why the birds have left," he announced to the villagers. "No way," they cried, "we had a special edict passed that no one could harm the birds. And not one person had to go to jail for harming a single bird."

Last, the argument can be made that all the other chauvinisms stem from the chauvinism toward children. We have already seen that racial and gender prejudice, for example, has its roots in malnourishment of FeelingBeing children. We shall see more examples in later chapters.

Enter the dance, the antidote to chauvinism. The dance shows that children have "it" in every way. They are not a burden to society but are integral to the health of every human on the planet. Their value is in their being, which, when honored, is nothing less than the locus for healing and for transcendence. Resources allocated to their well-being pay off a thousandfold in greater justice for both people and the environment and in greater freedom in self and civic government.

Hurt children become hurt adults who then make decisions in the midst of that hurt. Psychologically healthy children become healthy adults who then make decisions in the midst of well-being. This can only lead to a better life for each of us and to a better world. Adults are not "bringing up" children. Adults and children are in an evolving developmental spiral in which consciousness is either hindered or furthered.

Go dancing. End the chauvinism.

Chapter Ten

REUNIFICATION

Every family is its own culture.

—Josette Luvmour

It doesn't matter whether it was Hippocrates or Galen who first offered this sage advice: "As to diseases, make a habit of two things—to help, or at least to do no harm." Everything that you will read in this chapter has the potential to help with dysfunction in the child and the family. Nothing can hurt. Therefore, you can use the suggested remedies with impunity. At the very least, they will foster greater family intimacy. At the most, they will heal chronic dysfunction and help reunify the family.

Natural Learning Rhythms, due to its focus on optimal well-being, calls for a new etiology and a new lexicon to describe dysfunction in children and families. *Etiology* is the study of the cause of dysfunction. A *lexicon* is the chosen vocabulary for a task. According to Natural Learning Rhythms, the cause of dysfunction is a block to the flow of well-being. The symptom points to the block; its principle value is for diagnosis. The remedy does not attack the symptom. The remedy does not attack the block. The remedy reactivates well-being. Well-being dissolves the block.

The first step to reunification is to ensure that well-being is clearly understood—including its manifestations and its dynamics. Much of this work has already been accomplished in the previous chapters. However, the description of the dynamics of well-being must be as precise as possible in order to pinpoint where blocks occur. Accordingly, I will first review what has been established so far; then I will detail the dynamics of well-being and the dynamics of the descent into dysfunction.

The second step is to specifically apply this description to the development of the child. How can we understand the symptom—the behavior—in terms of the child's developmental moment? As development occurs only in relationship, the family must be included. What is the ambiance in the household? Is it contributing to the problem? Is the parent's shadow at play? How can it be recognized?

With these two steps, a diagnosis can be formulated.

A diagnosis carries the imperative to respond. Remedies are needed. Natural Learning Rhythms offers many suggestions for relieving and curing dysfunction. However, every family is unique. The family must be responsible for when and how to apply the remedies. Moreover, by going through the process of reunification, each family can devise its own remedies. Natural Learning Rhythms is not a passive approach. Remedies are not like taking a drug. They are active family-centered engagements that restore health through reunifying all members of the family. They are not therapy, though therapy may be chosen as a remedy during the overarching process of reunification.

Then, with a clear picture of the dynamics of well-being and dysfunction, where and how the block developed can be diagnosed and possible remedial responses can be considered. A viable reunification strategy can be created that speaks directly to the needs of the child and family. That is the goal of this chapter: to empower the reader to design their own strategy for family reunification that is based on well-being and specifically addresses the challenges in their lives.

A Brief Recapitulation of Optimal Well-Being

The heart of well-being is proper nourishment of the organizing principles of each life stage. This unequivocally must be the center of all relationships with children when well-being is the goal. The "Introduction" and chapter 3, "Ontological Epistemology," established the importance to well-being of both understanding how children organize their world and participating in the child's perspective. Those chapters indicated the necessary switch from a pathology-based view of children—founded in separatism and striving to become normal—to one based on optimal well-being.

An ontological epistemology explores, examines, and describes the essential nature of children. It elucidates how children know. It answers these questions: How do children organize their world? What are the innate capacities of children and why do they appear when they do, and to what purpose? What is the nature of optimal well-being in children? What kinds of environments allow well-being to thrive and what kinds cause it to shrivel? How and when do children make meaning from their world?

Natural Learning Rhythms offers operating instructions, not a blue-print, for finding those answers. Blueprints emerge when family members live in optimal well-being.

Chapter 4, "Play," explicated how play provides the perfect medium for a child's exploration of the organizing principles. It also showed that in play the child can connect to the profound qualities of the organizing principle. Participation in play is recursive in that the feedback from each instance of play is important to the quality of the next instance. Play that nurtures, furthers; play that furthers, nurtures.

This dynamic—that participation both nurtures and furthers—is a critical aspect of emergence. It will be an important factor in family reunification.

As the organizing principles were introduced, this claim was made: "Well-being optimizes each individual's opportunity for self-knowledge." Knowledge itself is emergent, not fixed, and lives intimately in each of us. Data is not the currency of knowledge. Knowledge emerges through participation. In play, children participate and the breadth and depth of the organizing principle emerges and is knowable.

Chapter 5, "Spirituality," revealed how the simple act of providing the nourishments could allow access to wisdom, a realm of great complexity. Both Gregory Bateson and Abraham Maslow pointed directly to a systemic wisdom that operates in humans. The nature of wisdom, while beyond description, can be appreciated through the values and the meaning-making moments evident in children. According to Krishnamurti, wisdom is realized only "through the observation and understanding of everyday incidents in human relationship."

Relationship, when viewed as I-Thou—when the child is seen as a being, as an essential unity—automatically includes nourishing the organizing principles. And with that nourishment, the dance springs to life. Once again, there is recursion and emergence. Biologists Humberto Maturana and Francisco Varela call this process autopoiesis and show how it is common to all living things. *Autopoiesis* means "self-making"; I prefer "self-creating." For Maturana and Varela, the essential unit of life is a network of processes that produce and continuously regenerate and realize the network that produced them.[104] Autopoiesis is the epitome of self-organization. The life form continually self-organizes to define a space in which to optimize well-being—to regenerate and realize itself.

Autopoiesis implies well-being. Here, Maturana applies his theory to social life:

> We as human beings exist in a network of social systems and move from one to another in our daily activities. Yet, not all human beings caught in the mesh of relations generated in this network of social systems participate in it as social beings. A human being deprived of autopoiesis—deprived of the relationships that support regeneration and self actualization—is being used by the social system but is not one of its members. If the human being cannot escape from this situation because his life is at stake, he is under social abuse.[105]

Without well-being, there is abuse; a human being is not a member of society, has no rightful place, trust, autonomy, or interconnectedness. Relationship is reduced to I-It. No one is nourished; no one dances. Self-organization is impaired and dysfunction seeps in.

Self-organization, as chapter 5, "Spirituality," shows, emerges to ever greater levels of complexity. From the humble beginnings of nourishing the organizing principle, there emerges the realization of values and of meaning, and of wisdom. In optimal well-being, fluid self-creating is the child and family norm.

The brief overview of education in America in chapter 8, "Intelligence and Academics," recounted how traditional education has not served well-being, for it prioritizes cultural values at the expense of being qualities. Nevertheless, there have always been "entellectual" educators who have attempted to marry education and well-being. Gardner's work is a step in that direction, but it falls short in that it treats intellectual intelligences—verbal-linguistic, logical-mathematical, spatial, musical, bodily-kinesthetic, interpersonal, and intrapersonal—as the point of reference. But the reference point should be the relationships in the child's life and the way they influence the expression of the intelligence. Intellectual components, by themselves, are impotent in regard to self-creation. Great musicians, as Mozart exemplified, do not necessarily self-organize to greater complexity as human beings.

The four cornerstones of academic excellence reintroduce well-being into the academic dialogue. Proper home support means nourishing the organizing principles, always the rock upon which well-being is built. Developmentally appropriate curricula match academic content with the organizing principles and so provide additional nourishment for them. Appreciation of the child's capacities, and of her academic strengths and weaknesses, deepens the relationship between child and parent, for it demands participation by the parent in the academic life of the child.

Participation

There is no standing outside well-being; there is no learning about it. Remedies, for this reason, must always embrace the whole family. Reunification emerges through family participation.

All histories of computers, cybernetics, and chaos and complexity theory must at some point refer to the British mathematician Alan Turing. Of his many contributions to these disciplines, his theory of indeterminacy, proved in the 1930s and so important for understanding emergence, trumpets the importance of participation. Turing simply showed that there will always be algorithms that behave unpredictably. An algorithm is simply a set of rules used to describe a process. All computers use algorithms to transform the keystroke into the appearance of the letters on the monitor, for example. No one, Turing showed, can know the outcome of an algorithm unless they run it.[106]

Medically, the word *algorithm* refers to a step-by-step procedure for reaching a clinical decision or diagnosis; it is often set out in the form of a flow chart, in which the answer to each question determines the next question to be asked. We will use this process when we choose remedies and create reunification strategies. And when we do, we will have to remember indeterminacy. We won't be able to know the value of the algorithm without running it.

Indeterminacy is writ large throughout child development. Who would expect that when FeelingBeing is nourished, the child would feel transcendence and the adult would deepen his devotion? Who would expect that playing with identities leads a teen to realize her core nature? A glance at the table of being qualities shows unpredicted emergences everywhere.

Emergence could not occur without indeterminacy. Ken Wilber summarizes their relationship concisely: "Emergence also means that *indeterminacy* is sewn into the very fabric of the universe, since *unprecedented* emergence means *undetermined* by the *past.*"[107]

Wilber, in his usual inclusion of research from all fields, concludes that "emergence is neither a rare nor an isolated phenomenon." And then, quoting Varela and his colleagues, he names lasers, genetics, chemical oscillations, evolution, ecology, and geophysics as some of the fields with emergent dynamics.

Emergence also means that co-evolution is, to use Wilber's phrase, sewn into the fabric of the universe. Here are the words of Mitchell Waldrop, who was chronicling complexity as it was seen by evolutionary biologists of the Santa Fe Institute: "Indeed, evolutionary biologists consider it so important that they've made up a special word for it: organisms in an ecosystem don't just evolve, they co-evolve. Organisms don't change by climbing uphill to the highest peak of some abstract fitness landscape...Real organism constantly circle and chase one another in an infinitely complex dance of co-evolutions." And he concludes, "co-evolution is a powerful force for emergence and self organization in *any* complex system."

Chapter 9, "The Dance," illustrates Natural Learning Rhythms' appreciation of co-evolution. I would like to add that the dance also takes place between siblings and with extended family. They are in the system too, and a comprehensive approach to family well-being will consider their relationships carefully. With siblings, the response is straightforward: Nourish them.

The dance improves relationships between parents and their parents. When parents dance with their children, they heal the wounds of their own childhood. They then see their own parents more clearly and relate to them with greater health and respect. Well-being flows in the system. If they are included, grandparents' communication with all family members improves. Children receive the mentoring of parents and grandparents dancing together, which is especially important during FeelingBeing. Generational dancing might well become embedded in the family.

Co-evolution means that no one part of the system can be isolated. The notion that the child is the problem denies the fact of co-evolution. For optimal well-being, reunification must include the whole family.

We now have the constituents of well-being. Through nourishing the organizing principle, we participate in emergence—in self-organization at greater levels of complexity. We relate; we co-evolve. That emergent co-evolution is indeterminate—we cannot definitively predict the form it will take, though we can say it will be in the realm of well-being.

Most parents grasp this point. They can see that their agendas often impose on the family well-being, especially when those agendas ignore the nourishments. At the same time, most parents have an extremely difficult time surrendering those agendas. I sympathize, empathize, and understand. I am a dad. I want the best for all the children in my life, and for all the children on the planet. It is out of respect for this difficulty that I am carefully building the case for well-being. I am hoping that the insights I present loosen the grips that agendas have on family existence. I hope that when parents appreciate that emergence is the underlying dynamic of child development, they will accede to indeterminacy. They will put their faith in well-being. They will trade in their agenda for participation.

Natural Learning Rhythms remedies, designed to dissolve the blocks to well-being, allow families to emerge as unities. Their path is then undetermined. They can continue to emerge, regenerate, and realize themselves as more complex unities. This dance need never end.

But how does emergence happen? What are its dynamics? The answers to these questions will light our way to the remedies and to family reunification. The scientific disciplines of chaos and complexity, along with insights from spiritual philosophy, provide the medium in which to explore these questions.

At the Edge of Chaos

In chapter 6, when discussing the transition from FeelingBeing to IdealBeing, we briefly considered complexity. Non-linear equations, which are used to model the dynamics of complexity, use the results of the first equation as a variable in the next. When run as a series, these equations show how simple processes repeated (iterated) many, many times, yield complex ones. James Gleick, in his best-selling book *Chaos*, describes the difference between linear and nonlinear. "Linear," he writes, "is easy to understand. *The more the merrier.* Linear equations are solvable...you can take them apart and put them together again—the pieces add up. Nonlinear systems generally cannot be solved and cannot be added together." Using the example of a puck sliding on ice, Gleick points out that friction cannot be exactly defined because it changes with speed. Speed, in turn, depends upon friction. "That twisted changeability makes nonlinearity hard to calculate, but it also creates rich kinds of behavior not found in linear systems...analyzing the behavior of a nonlinear equation...is like walking through a maze whose walls rearrange themselves with every step you take."[108]

In nonlinear systems, including children and families, a small change (a perturbation) in a system can, when iterated sufficiently, move that system to chaos—to a point where its present order no longer holds.

As the system approaches chaos, a bifurcation appears. *Bifurcate* means "two forks." The system, whether it is water evaporating or a population of waterfowl, oscillates between two states. The closer it gets to chaos, the more rapidly it oscillates between the states until finally all order breaks down. Just there, at the edge of chaos—the region where

- Self Similarity -

I was shocked the first time I saw bifurcation graphs. They depicted the organization of the lungs at different magnifications, from the entire lung to one bronchial tube. The graphs were close to identical. The patterns kept reappearing despite changes in scale. Chaosologists call this self-similarity. Self-similarity holds no matter how deeply one investigates. Magnify the leaf structure of a fern, and you will find exactly the same pattern as for the fern as a whole. Magnify the branches of the river and you will find branches within branches. Examples of self-similarity abound in nature:[109] The basic shape of a river is similar to that of a tree, which is similar to that of the lungs, which is similar to that of the circulatory system, which is similar to that of the nervous system. There seem to be certain patterns that, when iterated in open systems and therefore nonlinearly, repeat across scale and form.

Gleick says that "life blooms" and where the oscillations are the most rapid—the bifurcations are giving way to a new order: emergence.

Spiritual philosophers from every time and culture have been telling us about chaos and self-similarity. Many of them ascribe to what Neo-Platonist Plotinus called "the great chain of being." After describing the links in the great chains, he used an alchemical formula that was ancient even when he wrote it nineteen hundred years ago: "As above, so below," to show that the same structural dynamics that compose the great chain can be seen throughout all inorganic and organic manifestations in the universe.[110] Patterns repeat themselves endlessly on different scales, but within the same rhythms, formulas, and laws. Using the octave as a universal calibrator, Sufi teacher Gurdjieff described the same truth.[111] In a brilliant article, Daniel Godman shows that Meister Eckhart and Sri Ramana Maharshi, considered the greatest Hindu sage of the twentieth century, not only articulated a great chain of being, but that their versions were, for all practical purposes, identical.[112] Not surprisingly, when their chain of being is compared with that of Plotinus, the match is eerily similar. Without great effort, concurrence can be found in Hopi mandalas,[113] verse 42 of the *Tao-te Ching*, the poetry of Sufi mystic Rumi,[114] the Kabbalah,[115] and the Tibetan Buddhist prayers and instructions for the dying.[116] Ken Wilber takes the great chain of being as the starting place in his book *Integral Psychology*. He includes twenty pages of comprehensive charts showing corollaries throughout the spectrum of human cultures.[117]

When science and spiritual philosophy agree it seems fair to conclude that human development also goes from order to bifurcation, to the edge of chaos, to emergence/chaos/emergence, to order. This sequence is natural and the "walls will rearrange themselves," as is most obvious during transitions between stages and, self-similarly, between phases. That rearrangement is most often to a state of well-being, not dysfunction. It is the dynamics of emergence, of self-organization at a more complex level.

Emergence occurs because the new level of complexity acts as an attractor in the system. Chaos calls these *strange attractors*, and they have been shown to exist wherever there is emergence; that is, in every open, fluid system. Gleick likened them to magnets embedded in a rubber sheet. Paul Kordis and Dudley Lynch, who pioneered the application of chaos theory to business development, refer to them "as tethering rings around which pendulums subject to gravitational forces, swing."[118] Ken Wilber elaborates:

> The regime, canon, code, or deep structure of a [whole] acts as a magnet, an attractor, a miniature omega point, for the actualization of that [whole] in space and time. That is, the end point of the system tends to "pull" the [whole's] actualization (or development in that direction), whether the system is physical, biological or mental.[119]

Wilber believes that the attractor contains the entelechy of the system. The entelechy, as Aristotle and Leibniz defined it, means the essential informing principle of a living thing.

Spiritual philosophers, were they familiar with the term, would find nothing strange about strange attractors. Amazingly, across time and cultures, they have used the principles of strange attractors in their attempts to accomplish the difficult task of describing the full range of psyche and spirit. We have already come across several examples in this book: Thomas Merton's hidden wholeness, Marguerite Porete's God, Gregory Bateson's pattern that connects, Steiner's spiritual bodies, Lao-tzu's Tao, and Ken Wilber's Atman. In each case it is, in the words of verse twenty-one of the Tao-te-Ching, "elusive and intangible, yet within is image; it is elusive and intangible, yet within is form."

The great chain of being is a cosmology—a reasonable description of order in the universe. Why is the universe ordered according to the great

chain and not in some other way? What attracts its constituents to manifest in the way they do? Obviously, as we saw in trying to describe being
in chapter 7, "Being Qualities," there is a great mystery here. Yet the
attractors exist. Strange attractor seems as good a descriptor as any.

This discussion is not an attempt to marry science and spirituality. I
am not suggesting that God is a strange attractor. I am not suggesting
that a vital energy animates life that acts as a strange attractor—as do Sri
Aurobindo and Montessori. I am not attempting to state that the attractors contain meaning. I do not have those insights. I am only pointing
out that strange attractors have been known throughout human inquiry.
They are part of the store of human knowledge.

In Natural Learning Rhythms, the organizing principles are the
strange attractors. They are "intangible, yet within is form." They draw
the child to new levels of complexity.

The initial conditions for each stage are critical for well-being, as
they set the course for development. Still very important, but less so, are
the moments of entry into the new phases. This is great news, for it ful-
fills the promise that healing can happen many times in childhood. For
example, remedies applied during transitions often have the greatest
effect. Well-being can be restored. As just one example, I have found that
a new partner can be accepted as a parent if bonding occurs during the
transitions. The myth that the child's personality is formed or decided in
early childhood is debunked.

I shall refer to children and families that ride the wave of chaos and
emergence as being "in the flow." This expression is chosen with care.
The graph of a nonlinear equation appears as a sine curve, or wave.
Being in the flow is for Mihaly Csikszentmihalyi, of the University of
Chicago, nothing less than "transcendent health" for the individual and
for society.[120] Flow theory has inspired applications in everything from
understanding Japanese motorcycle gangs to creative writing to clinical
approaches to therapy.[121] Flow can be equated with optimal well-being
for children and families.

Csikszentmihalyi cites these characteristics of the flow experience:

- Clear goals and immediate feedback.
- The opportunities for acting decisively are relatively high, and
  they are matched by one's perceived ability to act.
- Action and awareness merge.
- Concentration on the task at hand.
- A sense of potential control.

- Loss of self-consciousness.
- Altered sense of time.
- Experience becomes autotelic, or worth doing for its own sake.[122]

With all due respect, this sounds like play.

Emergence occurs and what happens? Lag. The new order must, as Kordis and Lynch say, "be discovered and created. The discovery part is instantaneous. To know it is to *be* it. However, creating that future...takes time."[123]

Lag in natural child development occurs during the hesitancy phase and the beginning of the receptivity phase. In a family system, it takes time for all family members to acknowledge the new complexity.

Hesitancies serve the critical function of alerting the family that a major shift is taking place. In this lag it is time to mobilize resources, to contemplate new nourishments, and to allow attachment to the former way of self-organization to dissolve. Hesitancies call for reassuring intimacy—for connection in the midst of chaos.

Receptivity is the time for the child to absorb the new world that she now inhabits. Vulnerable, amazed, curious, and a bit overwhelmed and fearful, the child in the receptivity phase can be moody and precocious—at times pushing the family to change and at other times holding it back while she tests, examines, and learns how to appreciate her newly arrived capacities. It is only with the transition to trial and error and the realization of the meaning-making moment that the child fully actualizes the new complexity.

The lag must occur for the new world to emerge. It cannot be avoided. Yet hesitancies are often misunderstood in the family. Transition dynamics are intense. Receptivity is often hurried as parents have a difficult time understanding the vulnerability and the stops and starts as the child begins her new life. Therefore, the lag is often where the flow gets blocked.

In Figure 10-1, each stage is represented as a wave. The dotted lines represent the hesitancy and receptivity phases. The lag, obviously, is the dip.

Breakthrough occurs when the wave of the new stage is "above" that of the previous stage. This coincides with the arrival of the trial and error phase and the meaning-making moment. The downside of the wave is the fall toward equilibrium. The system is losing energy. A remedy is called for.

Figure 10-1–Emergence of Developmental Stages

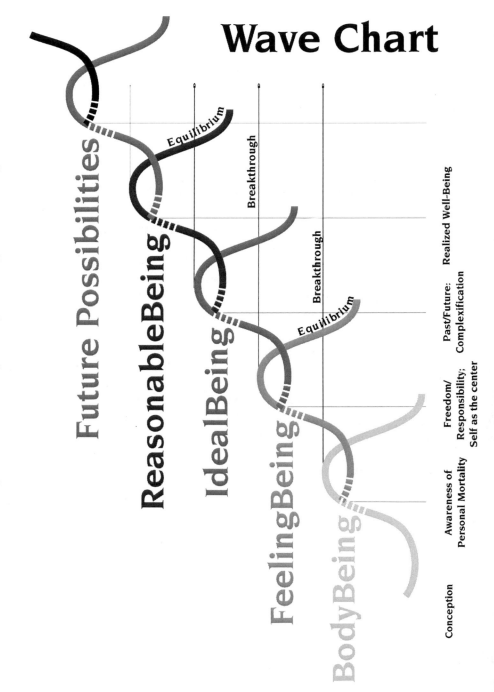

Wave Chart

Future Possibilities

ReasonableBeing

IdealBeing

FeelingBeing

BodyBeing

Equilibrium

Breakthrough

Breakthrough

Equilibrium

| Conception | Awareness of Personal Mortality | Freedom/ Responsibility; Self as the center | Past/Future: Complexification | Realized Well-Being |

The purpose of a remedy is to help the child rejoin the flow. The steepness of the ascent depends on how far down the wave the child has slid. The axiom is that the closer to equilibrium, the more closed the child and the fewer the avenues for intervention. A successful diagnosis depends on an accurate assessment of the child's position on the wave. How to accomplish this task is discussed in the next section.

We can now begin our exploration of dysfunction—blocks to the flow—and what to do about it. For a formal etiological statement of the Natural Learning Rhythms perspective on dysfunction please read this endnote.[124]

The Wave of Well-being

The first step in diagnosis is to locate the child's position on the wave. We can begin with this the following figure.

In Figure 10-2 , the wave represents any of the four developmental stages. The stage begins with the initial conditions at the lower left and then rides the wave through the stage to the bifurcation-chaos moment. The quality of that ride depends on the nourishments. The well-being wave at the top depicts a child flowing through a stage and the subsequent transition.

The second wave, "Dysfunction on the Way Down," shows a child who has not entered the dip. At first, momentum carries her up the wave. Soon, however, she has maximized the resources of that stage and starts to slide. At first, there will be whispers of difficulty. If there is no response, the child descends into alarm reactions. If there is no remedy, the descent moves to resistance, then to exhaustion, and finally to collapse. At any point, a remedy can be applied. However, the further down on the wave, the more precipitous the ascent back to the flow.

Lynch and Kordis call the period after the bifurcation and still on the ascent "doing more and more for less and less." During this time, a BodyBeing child, for example, might still draw attention to herself as the center of the world by overly emphatic exhibitions of behaviors that were praised when they were younger. An IdealBeing child might prove his loyalty through aggressive defense of his peer group, even at the risk of bodily harm. In each case, the child should have taken the dip and moved to the higher stage. They are doing more and more for less and less. That is a sign of difficulty. A response in this moment can allow reentry to the flow quickly.

Elders must keep in mind the developmental perspective in considering the five regions of dysfunction. For example, no one should expect BodyBeing children to have a wide scope of awareness of the feelings of

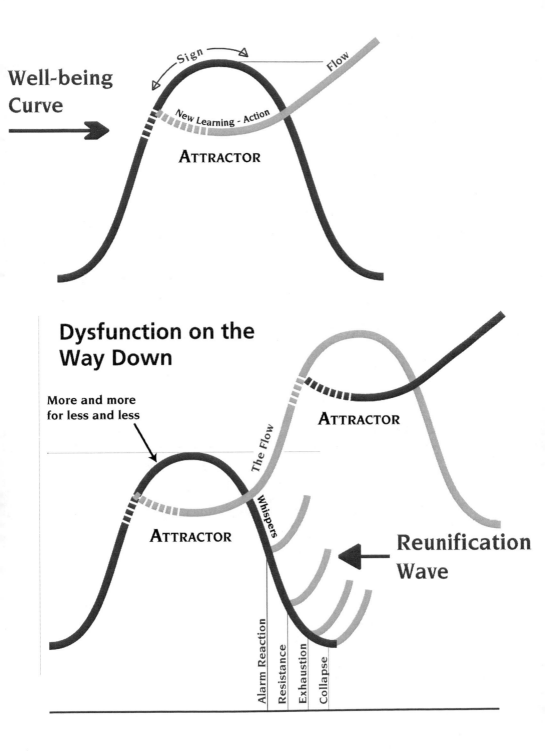

Figure 10-2—Well-Being Assessment

- The Limitations of Behavior for Diagnoses -

Behavior alone cannot definitively describe which degree of dys-function—whispers, alarm reaction, resistance, exhaustion, or col-lapse—the child inhabits. The behavior has meaning for the child in the context of her own world. It is not objective. For one child, apa-thy might be an alarm reaction; for another, it might indicate col-lapse. The distorted behavior is an arrow pointing to where the system—child and family—is coming unglued. It is very valuable for orientating toward the difficulty, but it is not sufficient for formulat-ing a diagnosis.

Grasping at behavior is a common mistake that elders make when they analyze childhood dysfunction. It leads to technique-based responses; they come from I-It. Remedies are relational; they live as I-Thou.

The work of diagnosis belongs to the people who know the child and the family. This usually means the parents. Counselors, thera-pists, and psychologists can help. Most, unfortunately, default to modifying the child's behavior, as is evidenced by the skyrocketing use of drugs to control children. If an insightful professional can be found, then she can aid the diagnostic process immeasurably.

others, or FeelingBeing children to consider the implications of their actions for their future. Generally, the five regions of dysfunction can be depicted in the following way.

Whispers refer to small actions that seem out of place and out of character. They often go unnoticed or are ignored. It is only when the dysfunction descends that parents recall the whispers and place them in their proper context. This highlights a cardinal rule of reunification: Always listen to that small feeling of disquiet that arises when a child acts in a way that you do not understand. Something is happening, and it pays a thousand times over to deal with the situation as a whisper rather than as a collapse. Your disquiet is a call to attention.

A whisper can be something as subtle as turning a shoulder away during a conversation. Some other common whispers include verbal complaints, unwillingness to cooperate, disregard of feelings, defiant acts that are not dramatic and have relatively modest consequences, minor disruptions of the family's schedule, contemptuous facial expressions, put-downs of relatives and friends of other family members, and taking delight in another's pain or embarrassment. These are just examples. The whisper arises in personal and family contexts. Its meaning can be derived only by those who are familiar with those contexts. As Josette says, "Every family is its own culture."

Alarm reactions are unmistakable. They often involve chronic repetition of a single behavior or set of behaviors that defy comprehension. Scarring, in which the child cuts a part of her body, is a trend among teen girls and is probably an alarm reaction by many of them. Alarm reactions can simply be a cry for attention. Chronic repetition usually surfaces when attention continues to be withheld or is given without developmental sensitivity. Behavior modification techniques often have short-term value, and then the reaction pops up again in a similar form.

Alarm reactions can include loss of enjoyment in favorite activities, intense sibling rivalry, hostility toward one parent along with fawning on the other, defacing property, pervasive cynicism and sarcasm, serial outbursts of temper, and public impoliteness. Again, these are just examples.

Whispers and alarm reactions can often be remedied by restoring the nourishments. Either the nourishment is missing or it is provided in a way the child cannot assimilate. The first step in all reunification strategies is to profile the nourishments and attempt to cure any deprivation. Otherwise, diagnosis is impossible. In my experience, about two-thirds of dysfunctions can be remedied through a restructuring of the developmental diet.

In resistance, the flow is dammed. Obviously, dysfunctional behaviors have rooted so deeply that the child now accepts them as normal. The discussion about her behavior is over. This is the way she is. She is indifferent to the consequences of her actions—to whether they are self-destructive or harmful to others. There may be a thrill in the resistance itself.

Resistance can include adherence to cliques and gangs, deliberate failure at socially approved activities, vituperative anger towards parent and authority, stymieing family schedules and activities, substance abuse, apathy, excessive fear or bravado, and refusal of the nourishments. Children mired in resistance often use revenge to justify their actions.

This list reflects some of the resistance behaviors I have seen. Any of the alarm reactions taken to extremes can also be resistance. Most parents recognize resistance, but few know how to respond. The child usually gets labeled as the problem, and therapy or some form of constraint is then imposed. The family system is forgotten. Parents have told me that when they have finally accepted the child's behavior as a family problem, feelings of failure and pain fueled their previous avoidance. I would add that the zeitgeist, with its maniacal adherence to the individual and separated child, supports that avoidance. The child is broken. Look at how he behaves. Let's fix him. What is his problem, anyway?

Resistance, unchecked, is ultimately exhausting. The tension and false self that must be maintained in order to resist wears the child down. Exhausted, some children become prey; some become predators. Some prey on themselves. They act as victims, then hate themselves for it and inflict self-punishment. The world is reduced to "for me or against me." Morality does not enter. Exhausted children feel cornered and have only the energy for fight or flight. It's a last-ditch effort to have some semblance of health. Fear underlies the region. Will life always be this way? Is there no way out?

Exhausted behaviors are often rife with hurt and subtle and overt violence. Self-hatred can erupt at any moment. Cynicism predominates. Abuse of their own body, gratuitous lying, pleasure in pain, cycling between massive doses of stimulation and dense lethargy, and allegiance to exhausted peers and causes represent some exhausted behaviors.

Whispers are rarely mistaken for exhaustion, but alarm reactions and resistance certainly are. In this book, we have also shown that healthy behaviors can be mistaken for dysfunction. If you weren't aware of Natural Learning Rhythms, then Alyssa's choosing the horror movies (chapter 4) could easily be interpreted as an alarm reaction, or, given the argument and her mother stomping off, resistance. Cranky Chris's (chapter 6) withdrawal and hostility to his teammates looks like resistance bordering on exhaustion.

Behavior indicates; it does not define. Diagnosis requires greater specificity.

Collapsing children see themselves as inadequate. Life is overwhelming, and closing down seems like the only safe option. Rather than fail, collapsing children often find a steady-state, flat-line persona that hovers just above equilibrium. After the drama of alarm, resistance, and exhaustion, collapse is sometimes considered an improvement, or at least an acceptable state of affairs, by parents and teachers. Collapsed children are hurt, have no response to the pain, and have no idea of how to get help. Everything they have tried has failed.

Sometimes, the descent toward equilibrium proceeds steadily; at other times, a new input might cause a temporary halt or reversal. A new teacher, for example, meets the child's needs and the child responds. Or the child grows into a stage that a parent can more easily nourish. Then I usually hear parents say that the child was "just going through a stage." This attitude is so dangerous. It ignores the family system and even carries a whiff that somehow the parents should be pitied. Perhaps they should be, but for reasons that are different from those they suspect.

A child may manifest alarm reactions in one environment and exhaustion or collapse in another. For instance, Lynn, fourteen, daughter of a violent alcoholic father, lived a collapsed life at home. Regimented and disciplined, she became the classic enabler. Controlled by fear, she behaved only in those ways that would not rile her father. He beat her if she didn't do well at school, so Lynn achieved good grades and was docile around the teachers. Alarm reactions did manifest at school, however. She sneaked cigarettes in the bathroom. She also jumped to the defense of any child who she thought was being treated unfairly by teachers or older students. The teachers overlooked these behaviors because she was a "good girl who did her work and didn't cause trouble."

All dysfunctional histories of which I am aware follow the sequence of whispers, alarm reactions, resistance, exhaustion, and collapse. I know of no child who skips a step on their descent. Remedies can be applied in all regions.

The Figure 10-3, "Dysfunction on the Way Up," illustrates the dynamics of dysfunction before the lag. In Figure 10-2, the child has already missed the lag and is out of the flow. Here, the child is in the flow and then bounces out. Getting back to the flow requires catching the wave on its ascent, not taking the dip, and reorganizing in the new stage. The regions and sequencing are the same. They are represented as an aggregate because, on the way up, the child can fall off the flow at any time.

Dashes are used instead of solid lines because it is easier to reestablish well-being during the ascent than after the lag has been missed. Often, only a very small dip and reorganization are necessary. Usually, a restructuring of the nourishments is all that is needed, especially in response to whispers and alarms. Catching a whisper on the ascent prevents an ocean of unnecessary suffering and expense.

Excesses and Deficiencies

With all due respect to the proverbial Italian mother who keeps telling her child to "eat, eat," developmental nourishments can be given in excess. The following pages give examples of both excesses and deficiencies for the key nourishments of each developmental stage. There is also a brief comment sketching a balanced "diet." Determining if a nourishment is given in excess or deficiency is a step toward reunification.

Figure 10-3–Dysfunction on the Way Up

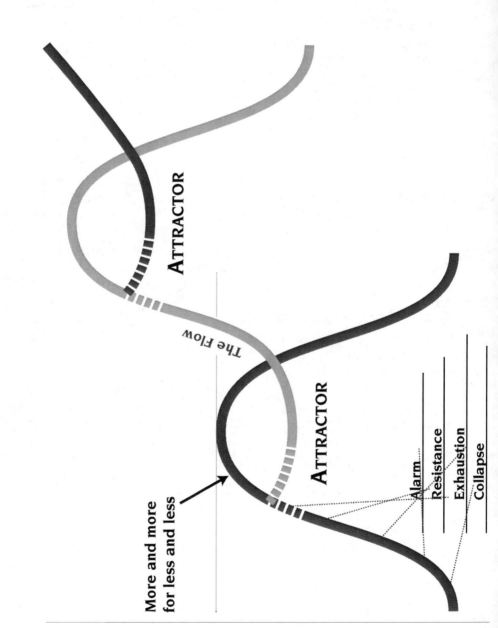

The last two sections of this chapter will combine all the steps into a coherent strategy.

As always, these are examples; you and your family will probably find others or modify them.

BodyBeing—Loving Touch

Excess

Holding, kissing, or confining to the point of smothering the child; commenting on everything she does to the point that your presence invades rather than supports; forcing the child to sit on your lap or cuddle when she does not want to; holding her when it is clear she wants to run and explore; pinching on the cheek and saying, "You're so cute," and similar actions; tickling her to the point she is hysterical.

Well-Being

Allowing the child to feel connected to warmth and security as a blanket of love; observing the child's body for signals that she has had enough or needs more; following an expansive "out" time with an "inward" and connected time that includes physical contact; using touch along with words to convey acceptance and rightness; allowing the child to crawl up on your lap whenever she expresses the desire for contact, even at work or in social situations.

Deficiency

Sparse physical contact; sparse physical reassurance; letting the child cry by himself for long stretches; leaving the child to himself frequently or in long stretches; using physical contact regularly for punishment, restriction, or control; time-outs, except on rare occasions; ignoring the security that touch transmits; pushing him away when he comes to sit on your lap, with comments such as, "You're too big for that now, big children don't need that any more"; giving the child food as a substitute for love and physical contact.

Excesses and Deficiencies for FeelingBeing—Feeling Mentors

Excess

Continually asking the child how he is feeling; didactically teaching right and wrong; controlling his behavior with ongoing evaluations of whether or not he behaved appropriately; comparing the child with other children or standards; frequently telling the child his efforts are not good enough; attempting to be perfect parents; overly criticizing one another as to who is the better parent; often asking the child to evaluate your parenting skills; overly critical of others.

Well-Being

Lifelong learner willing to explore, adapt, and implement; no standard of perfection; transparent about mistakes and ready to engage new ways of interacting; open about uncertainty in life; accepting that the child is learning how with to accommodate life's changes through your mentoring; honesty about limitations; unbending commitment; fairness with all children, not just your own; provide many social venues; support the child to feel all his feelings without judgment.

Deficiency

No feeling mentors of the same gender as the child (feeling mentor does not have to be spouse); lack of support for the child when he is being treated unfairly, unjustly, or unkindly; expecting the child to be reasonable; rationalizing and justifying inequality; sarcasm, especially toward other people; inconsiderate remarks about the ethnicity or customs of others; frequently subjecting the child to uncaring elders.

IdealBeing—Sensitive Respect

Excess

Taking over her ideals; directing how she should actualize her ideas; asking about every event in the child's life; too much control over how she should explore her freedom; commenting on every identity exploration; more than occasionally offering your ideas of how she can explore an identity; trying to be a member of her peer group; to become so identified with being a teenager yourself that you forget you are the parent and not a friend.

Well-Being

Inquire with the child; be interested in her ideals and help her find ways to explore them; co-create boundaries; reevaluate co-created boundaries regularly; be curious but not overly concerned about each identity (except those that are dangerous or those that appear to be alien to her core identity); allow room for exciting (but not dangerous) forays into freedom; eliminate lectures; no arbitrary punishments; match responsibility with freedom, i.e., taking care of the car with the freedom to use it as opposed to linking the car to taking out the garbage.

Deficiency

Undermining the child's security by saying such things as, "Not under my roof; if you want so much freedom go out and earn it yourself"; giving the child too much responsibility, i.e., unrealistic academic goals, excessive expectations around social norms, demanding inordinate financial contributions; using achievement of responsibility for control; competing with the child; taking the child's assertions personally; letting your fears limit the child's explorations; abandoning the child due to your aversion to their identity explorations.

ReasonableBeing—Recognition of Commitment

Excess

Pushing the child to investigate subject areas of your preference; pressing the child for large financial commitments; taking over the child's fact-finding work and continually drawing conclusions.

Well-Being

Allowing the freedom to choose areas of interest; dialoguing about the value and meaning of the chosen subject; helping to create opportunities for investigation and examination; exploration of ideological preferences; modeling tolerance for life and for the often tedious investigations that must be carried through before the value of the investigation can be realized; appreciating the importance of social life in the definition of self; recognizing the journey of self-discovery reflected in the investigation of their chosen field.

Deficiency

Showing no interest in the chosen field; becoming bored with or denigrating toward investigations that do not meet your standards; insisting that producing an income be part of the investigation; not attempting to understand the motivations for the child's choices; neglecting to support data collecting opportunities for the investigation; being defensive about your own point of view.

ReasonableBeing—Recognition of Equality

Excess

Romanticizing the past in order to establish equality; grasping for comradeship; interfering with the child's personal life and pushing for friendship with the child's peers; glorifying your heroes; corrupting dialogue to prove your point; insisting that the child be your equal.

Well-Being

Recognize that the child's search for meaning in life is as valuable as your own; be willing to support her search in every way you can; be incisive but not invasive in dialoguing about her interests; exercise patience while she works out the meaning of equality; share in family decisions; continue your own growth in self-knowledge; provide whatever financial support that you can without directing how it must be spent.

Deficiency

Intellectualizing on the feeling-based understanding of interconnectedness, i.e., "We're all one" or "All life is interconnected"; proselytizing and therefore trivializing; teaching equality through words, books, and songs rather than providing her with opportunities to directly experience it through travel, adventure, study, and self-exploration; making denigrating remarks about others; absenteeism, especially when you don't agree with the child's equality expression.

ReasonableBeing—Recognition of Achievement

Excess

Being competitive (no matter how subtly) and challenging the child's achievements; comparing one's own achievements with those of the child; extolling their achievements excessively; basking in the glory of the child's achievements; trying to direct the next achievement now that this one has been reached; synthesizing the child's understanding for her; placing the child in unwelcome social situations in which achievements are publicized or emphasized; interference with and interpretation of interpersonal relationships; naming ways the child must prove her achievements.

Well-Being

Acknowledge, acknowledge, acknowledge; engage in gentle, straightforward dialogue that allows the child's deepening awareness of maturity and which in no way defines it; support the expanding scope of interpersonal relationships; provide opportunities for the child to explore and critique people and activities that she deems relevant to her interest; provide opportunities for her to synthesize the results of her search, including with experts in her field and with you; communicate about your own interests and investigations.

Deficiency

Mostly omission: failing to see the child's maturity; failure to communicate appreciation of the child's maturity; inhibiting others from acknowledging the child; failing to provide opportunities to investigate; assuming the child has to prove the worth of their achievement to you; underscoring aspects of their achievement that do not meet your expectations, i.e., "how is that going to pay?"

ReasonableBeing—Recognition of Recognition

Excess

Becoming overly excited by their understanding and insights and then attempting either to direct them or to venerate them; overly praising the child; basking in reflected glory; pretending to understand the child when her understanding is beyond you; continually presenting the child with opportunities you believe are important but that she sees as peripheral; imposing your definition of substantive values.

Well-Being

Dialogue; simply support the creations of the child; if her investigation seems out of balance, help guide the child to uncover the root of her condition; let her guide you to the meaning and value of her moment; keep a sense of humor; answer all questions truthfully without adding moral lessons; support the exploration of substantive values such as truth, love, and meaning.

Deficiency

Simply missing this developmental moment; placing yourself in opposition to him; casting the child's explorations as "weird" or faddish; demanding that explorations must be relevant to the child's future or monetary success; neglecting the importance of investigating modes of knowing beyond reasonableness. (These modes are discussed in Appendix A).

Creating and Maintaining Healthy Boundaries

Though boundaries have been mentioned in various parts of this book, the discussion has been incomplete. Appreciating the importance of boundaries and having the confidence to set them is an important part of family well-being. Boundaries are a natural part of everyday life. Therefore, they are not considered a remedy. In their absence, dysfunction thrives, just as it does when the nourishments are missing.

The following dialogue took place when Josette sat with a group of parents to discuss boundaries. The "parent" voice is actually a combination of the remarks of three parents who sat on the panel with her and acted as the audience's voice.

Parent: Let's talk boundaries. There were at least a couple of times in every stage of development that you have described where there was a lot of friction about boundaries with my children.

Josette: Go slowly here. Your statement seems to imply that boundaries are intended to prohibit the child's actions.

Parent: Yes. Isn't that what a boundary is?

Josette: Not totally. Here we are in this room together. Or maybe we are in a car. In either case, what is the boundary?

Parent: The walls of the room or the body of the car.

Josette: And what are the walls doing?

Parent: They are keeping us in the room. They prohibit, to use your word, us from leaving.

Josette: What else are they doing?

Parent: Oh, I get it. They are keeping the rest of the world away.

Josette: And if they didn't do that?

Parent: Then we wouldn't be safe and able to have this dialogue. The room would be too crowded and noisy.

Josette: So boundaries serve to inhibit and to enable. It is very important to understand this. We, as adults, believe that we are stopping our children from doing something when we create a boundary. But if we create the boundary with developmental sensitivity, we can actually nourish optimal well-being.

Parent: But it often turns to friction because children want to do something and we won't let them. Therefore, we are inhibiting them.

Josette: Just because a child wants something does not mean that it serves well-being. It is natural for anyone to become frustrated when they want something they cannot have.

Parent: I can relate. But I have learned ways to deal with my frustration.

Josette: And that is part of what they are learning too. They have to learn how to manage themselves in each life stage. The new capacities and the new organizing principle bring new opportunities, and the child must learn how to use them well. Of course, there is going to be frustration.

Parent: If the frustration is part of learning the boundary, then why does it veer quickly toward conflict?

Josette: For the most part, because the boundary was not created with attention to developmental awareness. For instance, it is confusing to the BodyBeing child when the parent uses logic in making a boundary. The child does not fully understand the logic, and their confusion adds to the frustration and leads to desperation. The BodyBeing child cannot get what they want, and the communication is not in their language.

Parent: Which for the BodyBeing child is sensation. So you are saying that it would have to be a boundary that is communicated sensorially?

Josette: I am. It must be a sensation-based boundary.

Parent: Well, how do you do that?

Josette: I'll answer that in a minute. There is one more general point about boundaries that must be made before we turn to the specifics of each stage. First, answer this question: When do you think boundaries are made?

Parent: When the child wants to do something and you don't believe they should. Wait, that's too obvious. I know you're going to disagree...

Josette: Let me rephrase the question. When an adult is in relationship with the child, when aren't boundaries made?

Parent: I think I see where you are heading with this. Are you saying that there are implied boundaries in every interaction that we have?

Josette: Exactly. Providing the proper developmental nourishment is itself a statement about boundaries. It says that wholeness is the field that we play in together. Within that boundary, your family's unique expression of optimal well-being comes forward.

Parent: Surely you are not saying that the frustration disappears.

Josette: No, of course not. But the "adversarialness" does. Parents and children face life's challenges together. They both know that they are on the same side. They know that rightful place, trust, and autonomy will not be violated.

Parent: The first step in creating healthy boundaries is nourishing the organizing principle of the developmental stage that the child is in. Okay, that makes sense. And the second step?

Josette: The second step is to be developmentally attuned in making a prohibiting boundary. To use the child's language and to not ask them to behave beyond their capacities are the essential qualities of a healthy prohibitive boundary.

As we explore the specifics of creating healthy boundaries, we have to keep these things in mind: Every interaction within a family—obvious and subtle; explicit, tacit, and implied—is a boundary statement. Boundaries are critical for the way we see ourselves and carry ourselves in the world. Boundaries determine, in large measure, our social life and psychological well-being. Family is the matrix; the home is where we learn and practice boundaries.

Parent: How do you create a prohibitive boundary with a BodyBeing child?

Josette: It is, of course, a sensation-based boundary. Let's take a simple scenario. A four-year-old child goes into her house with mud on her hands. She sees a white wall and desires the sensory exploration of muddy hand on the white wall. Her father sees the child's intent and says, "No." He can see that his daughter is undeterred. Dad places himself in front of his daughter. He gets on his knees so there is direct eye contact. With love and caring, he firmly tells the child, "No." The child stops. Dad has become a mountain—immovable yet not taking the behavior personally. BodyBeing children are not testing our will; they are exploring the sensory world. By investing his body and intention in the boundary, Dad makes the sensory quality unmistakable. *My dad is not moving. This is a boundary I cannot cross.*

Parent: That's it? "No"? No explanation, no reason? Just "No"?

Josette: That's right, just "No." But "No" like a mountain says no. Also notice that he did not punish her, threaten her, or divert her to a more pleasant activity. And he never stopped loving her—never made her feel bad.

Parent: Okay, but what if the child persists? I know many a BodyBeing child who would.

Josette: So do I. If the daughter kept going for the wall, Dad—gently but firmly—can take the child to the sink and wash her hands. He should describe what he is doing with kindness, but with decisiveness. The child is exploring the sensation of muddy-hands-on-wall. She also is exploring the reaction-of-parents-to-muddy-hands-on-wall. In either case, the boundary must be clear and consistent—she should be reminded that she must wash her hands. The child should not be told that she is "good" or "bad." Simply, this is a boundary. Clean hands in the house. No rational explanation, no moral judgment. End of story.

Parent: Okay, that would work with some children. But I do know some who would push it even further.

Josette: So do I. Sometimes the frustration boils over into a tantrum. This presents an important learning opportunity for both child and parent. Rightful place must be maintained while the boundary is kept, and the sensory modality must continue to be used. Therefore, stay connected with the child; calmly tell her that she is loved and that she belongs with this family. If she will allow it, touch her lovingly. If touch is not accepted, continue to talk with her.

Parent: Some parents would just want to send that child away until she stops screaming.

Josette: That would be a mistake. Do not send the child away or threaten her. When the storm of the tantrum passes, welcome the child back and simply engage life again. After a few times, the child will realize that raising the sensation volume through tantrums does not work. Throughout, parent and child have remained connected. Reestablishing balance comes quickly and more easily with time. A tantrum is not a test of wills. Everyone gets frustrated from time to time and that frustration must be expressed. One of the only ways a BodyBeing child can express frustration is to amplify the sensations in the environment. The child must never doubt that she belongs with us. Our sensation boundary tells them that they are safe and secure. Tantrums become unnecessary when sensory boundaries are consistently maintained.

Parent: Why not yell at the child to get their attention or threaten them with a punishment?

Josette: There are two answers: The first is that to do so is a violation of rightful place. No one learns well when they are threatened. Second, sensory learning requires much repetition. If we create a sensory-based boundary several times, the child learns most efficiently because of the consistent example. When a child is threatened, they become afraid and do not learn as quickly or as well.

           Also, deals don't work. Do not make contracts or deals to create a boundary. A contract implies a perspective of the future that is beyond children this age. Many parents experience unnecessary family strife by doing some version of the following deal: "If you promise to clean up your room when we get home, then we can go to the park now." The child will agree, and of course upon return from the park the cleanup problem persists.

           And last, but certainly not least, negotiations simply don't work. Bribing the child by saying, "If you put the toys away now, then we can go the park," may work initially, but soon the child learns to demand a reward before any chore is done. Life becomes a constant series of negotiations, and the boundaries become ever more blurred. The child's sense of rightful place erodes.

Parent: What can I say to the child?

Josette: Words are toys for the BodyBeing child. She has neither the context nor the sense of the future that gives words the meaning that they have for adults. There is no point in relying on words to set boundaries with BodyBeing children.

Parent: But the child will often make the deal. They will agree to the conditions and even say the words back when asked.

Josette: Sure. But saying the words is not the same as understanding the words. The conditions and implications of contracts and negotiations are beyond children this age. If they agreed to a deal, they most likely did it because they sensed it would please the parent, or because there was an immediate sensory gratification. They do not have a moral stake in keeping their word. BodyBeing children play with words. They are not bound by them.

Parent: What a relief. I spend so much time trying to explain why I am making a boundary and I get so frustrated when they don't understand. You are saying I do not have to do that anymore.

Josette: No more. But you do have to provide the nourishments; and you do have to use the language of sensation; and you must be careful to see their explorations as appropriate and not as a battle of wills.

Parent: That sounds better than the frustration. What about the FeelingBeing child? How do you make boundaries with children in that stage?

Josette: Consider this scenario: Eleven-year-old Ken was skipping his chores. His parents' constant reminders were to no avail. Frustration built. Before it erupted, Ken's parents asked him if he felt that the chore distribution for family members was fair. It took patience and several attempts. Responding to the honesty and care, Ken communicated his feelings of unfairness in the family. His parents listened patiently, asked questions, and paraphrased to let Ken know that he was heard and understood. Children must be able to feel their parents are sincere and caring.

      To their surprise, Ken's complaint was that the chore list was handed down from the parents and not mutually decided. The actual chore was not the problem at all. After the parents finished listening to Ken, the solution appeared to be rather simple: Ken's parents agreed to mutual decision making in the future.

Parent: So the whole family was involved in creating the problem and in finding the solution.

Josette: Family-based boundaries are the best. Each member of the family has a responsibility to the others. The boundary works because of the trust in the family. Communication is paramount. The three rules of boundary setting with FeelingBeing children are communicate, communicate, and communicate. Even when the child holds an unnecessarily stubborn position, make sure they know that they are heard. Trustworthy people listen before they respond.

Parent: And if this doesn't work?

Josette: If there is communication but no agreement, then parents need to kindly, but firmly, set the boundary. A parent must take the time to explain that this boundary is their best attempt at fairness. Then the parent must simply hold the boundary.

Parent: And if resistance persists?

Josette: Often, when children this age are having trouble accepting a boundary, it works to perform the task together. For example, if your child does not do his homework, then do the homework with the child. Another option is to stay nearby and do your desk work at the same table as the child. If chores are not getting done, consider doing all the chores together rather than apportioning them. FeelingBeing children work best in community. Perceived isolation presents problems, and the child will often refuse to cooperate in order to have company. By doing things with others, the child learns about relationship and the family enjoys cooperation.

Parent: What about IdealBeing? I intensely dislike it when they present their disagreements in a personal way. Sometimes it feels like a blatant attack.

Josette: But it's not about the parent. It is an idealistic projection. If there is a disagreement, it is this stage's version of frustration. The child wants something that they cannot get. They have new capacities at their disposal. They are much more aware of the world, of their parents' strengths and faults. They have to examine family values and decide which ones are truly theirs. They are insecure, and they are surprised by their changes as much as the parent. Sensitive respect nourishes the child by not penalizing them for the challenges of their moment.

Parent: I can think of times when I have been very respectful of my teen and they still continued to aggressively challenge me. It felt like an attack.

Josette: That is a most difficult moment, no doubt. The teen's frustration is riled and he doesn't know how to handle it. He expects you to understand and doesn't believe that you can really help. He can barely hear what you have to say. In most cases, a good response is to slow things down.

Parent: What does that mean? How do you slow things down?

Josette: You inquire. You ask questions. You make sure that you understand every word that your teen is saying.

Parent: And they don't become annoyed?

Josette: They might, but not usually and not if you are careful. If the teen, for example, is screaming that you are locking them up by not letting them stay out late, ask them what "locking up" means. You will often get another aggressive answer, but it will probably let you know what their concern is. Don't get riled yourself. Really try to understand why the issue is so important to them. Do not advance your own position at this time.

Parent: That will take some practice.

Josette: Sure. But once you get the hang of it, you will save time and heartache.

Parent: When do you state your position?

Josette: Only after you are sure you understand everything about theirs. Paraphrase until the teen agrees that you do understand. Then say whether you agree or disagree.

Parent: It sounds like the same idea as the way to respond to tantrums.

Josette: They are similar in some ways. Don't give a child a chance to believe that they are not connected. They are part of the family. They are connected. All responses to all children should start with remembering that connection.

Parent: Sensitive respect for a teen. I certainly did not get that when I was that age.

Josette: Would you have liked it?

Parent: Very much. I had such a difficult time from thirteen to sixteen.

Josette: Offering sensitive respect to teenagers allows parents to share the teen's perspective and offer ideas and suggestions that the teen will find meaningful and useful. Sensitive respect gives the teen permission to explore a multitude of identities. It speeds them on their way to discovering their core identity. And it creates the medium in which they can evaluate those identities. Best of all, parents and teens are on the same side and the parent's voice is trusted and respected in turn. It also helps a parent understand the quickly changing nature of identity creation in teens.

There's more. Nourished by sensitive respect, the teen accepts the process of her development with a minimum of self-consciousness and the absence of guilt. Sensitive respect calls for engagement that serves the teen's exploration of many identities so she can develop an identity that is an expression of her core nature.

Parent: I can remember people ridiculing me when I was fifteen—telling me I was bad or wrong for whatever reason. I remember that just making me clam up. This seems like exactly the opposite of what you are saying here.

Josette: The opposite of sensitive respect is ridicule. Ridicule irritates the underlying insecurity and offers no support for learning how to self-govern. The teen feels foolish and defensive about their idealistic assertions rather than discovering their value for identity formation. Teens who are regularly ridiculed usually react with rebellion or apathy. Any ridicule-driven boundary damages the teen and the family as a whole.

Parent: It is obvious that teens value peer interaction highly. Is peer engagement a nourishment?

Josette: Yes, a very important one.

Parent: I find it easy to enjoy and support my teen when he is with peers I approve of. But there are times when I do not like the people that he is with. He really doesn't like it when I bring it up.

Josette: No, of course not. Perhaps he feels ridiculed for his choices. Remember, IdealBeing children want to take responsibility and explore freedom through ideals. First, you have to find out why those peers are important to him. What identity is he exploring and how do these peers embody it? What ideas do they represent? You will probably have more luck inquiring about the ideals and identities than you will if you make the actual peers he associates with the issue.

Parent: I have to admit I am afraid of the influence of some of these peers. What else can I do?

Josette: Become acquainted with the peers. It is not a matter of becoming friends but of opening the communication. You may find your fears unfounded. Or you may find new ways to talk to your child. You will certainly get more understanding of what the peers represent to your child. And do not forget co-creation.

Parent: So I would state my concerns and listen to his and then invite him to offer solutions? Always with sensitive respect, of course.

Josette: Yes, though with peers I would be careful not to imply that the child does not have free will. He has, after all, made the choice to be with that peer group even if you believe that they are influencing him more than he is influencing them. It is connecting to his choices, his identities, and his ideals that will lead to well-being.

Parent: I understand. Are there other nourishments?

Josette: Personal space. Teens need a place that they can govern.

Parent: So you wouldn't interfere in the way they kept their room.

Josette: We are going to talk about co-creation, not control. But successful boundaries with teens do depend on the parent clearly stating what is out of bounds. In my family, I would not allow food or wet towels to be left in their rooms. Other parents would have other values. But just because I name what is out of bounds, I am not saying what the rules should be. I expect the child will have some things that are out of bounds for me as well. One teen I know made it clear that he would not tolerate any outsider cleaning his room.

Parent: Okay, that makes sense. Back to the nourishments. We have sensitive respect, peers, and personal space. Anything else?

Josette: Sure. But I just realized something from our conversation. It is the difference between a boundary and a path. A boundary says these are the limits and let's see what we can create inside those limits. A path says that we have to walk the straight and narrow and that there is only one way to go. We are talking about boundaries.

Parent: That is a good distinction. It is the difference between co-creation and control.

Josette: Yes. The other nourishments for IdealBeing are challenges in the realm of success, the opportunity to express and act on ideals, and, finally, dynamic activities.

Parent: Do the challenges have to have a high possibility of success because of the insecurity?

Josette: Yes. Too much failure undermines autonomy, especially in the early part of the stage.

Parent: The need to live one's ideal is obvious. I really appreciated what you said about the connection between ideals, identity exploration, and discovering one's core nature.

Josette: And that is why parents have to avoid taking the teen's assertions personally. These are identity explorations directed toward self-discovery. This is a difficult journey—much more difficult than learning to walk or talk. Supporting identity exploration and avoiding ridicule with IdealBeing children is the responsible thing to do. And just by doing it, the parent has nourished freedom and responsibility in the teen.

Parent: When you said that the parent has to avoid taking the teen's assertions personally, it sounds like the first step in the healthy creation of prohibitive boundaries with IdealBeing children.

Josette: First and foremost.

Parent: And the next steps?

Josette: Here's an example of a parent using Natural Learning Rhythms. Fifteen-year-old Marie wanted to go to a party and "stay as long as I want." She would not say who would be at the party and reluctantly stated where the party would be located.

She wanted to be trusted and did not want her parents to pry. Her parents were naturally apprehensive.

Joan, Marie's mother, spoke her apprehension without making Marie wrong or bad. She knew that parental concerns are a legitimate and crucial part of co-creating boundaries with teenagers. "Young people do foolish things at late-night parties," Joan said. "I don't want you caught in the middle." Marie held her ground. Joan named drugs as her principal concern and discussed the possibility that Marie might find herself trapped or imposed upon. Marie held her ground; she felt she could handle herself.

This is the right time for each parent to acknowledge Marie's growth into responsibility and freedom. Marie's father, Robert, spoke to this. He told her that he was happy that she wanted more freedom—that it was a sign of her growing maturity. He agreed that the party could be one way that Marie expanded into greater freedom. Could she participate in co-creating a design that included more freedom while meeting the legitimate parental concerns?

Marie could and did. She suggested that she call every two hours to reassure her parents that she was all right. Joan thanked her for the suggestion. She said two hours seemed too long. How about every hour and a curfew of eleven o'clock? Marie said eleven was too early and that it would be embarrassing to call in front of her friends. Joan asked if she could call Marie more frequently. Marie said that she would put her cell phone on "vibrate" and that she would either answer it then or call within the hour. Then they agreed on a midnight curfew.

Parent: And if she broke the curfew or didn't call?

Josette: Well, what would you do?

Parent: We would talk!

Josette: About what?

Parent: About eroding trust and the importance of keeping your word, and the hurt feelings that come with a broken agreement.

Josette: In other words, about freedom and responsibility.

Parent: Yes. But I would feel betrayed and definitely not trust her as much. It would be hard for me to give her that much freedom again.

Josette: Yes, and your feelings and needs are an important part of co-creation. Responding to violations of boundaries by readjusting the limits is legitimate feedback and the responsibility of the parent. It's great to make your concerns known.

Parent: So you would suggest co-creating a new boundary relationship.

Josette: I would. And in this way parent and teen grow in freedom and responsibility together. And experience strongly suggests that it will take a few tries, but soon the respect for one another's needs will be accepted and folded into the boundaries without complaint.

Once again, this is a family-based boundary. Teens must be able to see their parents are sincere in hearing their voice in the governance over their life. Each member of the family has something to contribute for a mutually acceptable solution to be reached. The boundary works because the teen's self-governance is respected and she can feel ownership of the final decision.

Administering a Remedy—A Just Attitude

Dr. Robert Ornstein, a teacher at the University of California San Francisco Medical Center and Stanford University, and Dr. David Sobel, director of patient information at Kaiser Permanente, spend about twenty pages in their book *The Healing Brain* to extol the history and value of the placebo effect. In itself, a placebo has no medicinal value. It is inert and used either to serve as a control in an experiment or as a token to placate the patient. Yet throughout medical history, researchers have experimentally validated many times that patients taking a placebo heal quicker and more often than those who do not.

This is the placebo effect. Ornstein and Sobel suggest that the two reasons for the success of placebos are the patient's confidence in the person administering the placebo and faith in the institution certifying the procedure. They conclude, "The real import of the placebo is that it gives testimony to the fact that we have within us certain self-healing mechanisms, intrinsic healing systems, which can be mobilized by appropriate cures which foster a sense of positive expectancy."[125]

In Natural Learning Rhythms, relationship sets the stage for healing. Relationship implies an honest attempt to provide the nourishments, demands participation, and ensures that the remedy embraces the whole family. Relationship creates confidence. The child knows, *I am not alone. I am not bad. There is no stigma. We are all in this together. Together we can change.* The parent knows, *I am doing all that I can. I am staying connected with my child despite the severe challenge of dysfunction. We can do together what none of us could do alone.* Relationship sanctifies family as the place where healing occurs and the parent as the custodian of the healing knowledge. Remedies gain potency when the parents maintain an attitude of humor, humility, inclusion, and creative confrontation. This is a just attitude—fair, equitable, and honest. It prioritizes interactions and keeps the focus on the interpersonal exchanges—the locus of healing—while participating in the remedy.

Humor is the ability to laugh at oneself. It is poking fun at human limitations in the midst of the immensity of life. Humor never hurts anyone. Humorous people know when to be serious. Poking fun at the wrong time is not humor. The language historian H.W. Fowler points out that the purpose of humor is discovery and its field of action is human nature.[126]

Humility implies connection, as it is the surrendering of status along with the willingness to admit mistakes. Humility breaks down the barriers between family members and allows for open communication, a key element for more complex self-organization. Humor and humility are two of the secondary organizing principles of ReasonableBeing.

Being reasonable, which includes the ability to honor the various perspectives of family members, is the ground for inclusion. There also must be specific activities and behaviors that establish and maintain connection between the child displaying the dysfunction and the family. One way to promote inclusion is to maintain the family schedule and to allocate responsibilities to the extent the dysfunction allows. Also, it is a mistake to neglect the nourishments of the other children at home. They must have adequate opportunities to express and, if possible, redress their frustration with the impact of the dysfunction on their lives.

Creative confrontation means to never give a child a chance to believe that all is not interconnected, a maxim that Aldous Huxley and Gregory Bateson, each in their own way, held as the central aspect of relationship with children. The fact is that the child is a member of the family, the community, the species, life, and nature. Separation is false, though belief in it and acting as if it is true are heartbreakingly real.

Of the four components of a just attitude, creative confrontation is the most difficult for parents to uphold. The tendency is to send the child away. Typically, this results in a time-out for BodyBeing and FeelingBeing children and an ultimatum to "do it this way or leave" for the IdealBeing child.

Confrontation is the stumbling block. Many adults were wounded in confrontations with parents, teachers, and other authorities in their childhood and are loathe to confront their children. Natural Learning Rhythms uses the word *confrontation* according to the following definition from *The Oxford English Dictionary*: to bring people face-to-face to examine and elicit the truth. The word *creative* is a reminder to confront with tact and developmental sensitivity. Creative confrontation often calls for implementation of a boundary.

The Shadow

Every chapter except chapter 8, "Intelligence and Academics," contains important information about the shadow and IdealBeing children. It is during IdealBeing that children play with the shadow, and it is IdealBeing children who bring it to the family's attention. But the shadow takes root in all stages of childhood. When the children become parents, unresolved shadow issues continually enter the family dynamic. If these issues are so strong that they prevent dancing, then they become a block and must be dissolved in order to reunify the family. For example, my experience as a family consultant for more than twenty years strongly indicates that the many boundary issues that adults face in their marriages and workplaces have roots in unresolved shadow issues from their BodyBeing years.

As a FeelingBeing child, it was not safe for Jody to express the feelings of moroseness or of intuitiveness. If she was gloomy, her mother called her "mopehead"; if she expressed her intuitions, her father sternly demanded reasonable explanations. When she couldn't provide them, he called her stupid. Jody began using food as a buffer. When intuitiveness or moroseness arose, Jody would eat to soothe herself. As is typical in shadow dynamics, Jody repressed both the good and the bad feelings. She did not discriminate. That is the power of family values. The overriding need is family connection. Intuition did not have a chance when up against Dad's demands.

Jump forward thirty years. Jody is the parent of Lora, now ten years old. She has not resolved her shadow concerning food or the associated feelings. Lora feels those feelings and absorbs them as all FeelingBeing children do, but she has no place to express them. She feels that it isn't safe. As one would expect, Jody has difficulty supplying the nourishment of inspiration. Lora can also feel some hypocrisy in the way Jody tries to control her daughter's eating habits. Lora takes to stealing from her mother's purse to buy bags of candy. Jody finds out and gets very angry. No reason Lora offers is good enough. Punishment is meted out. Three years later, Lora is bulimic. The family comes to family camp. Jody is confused. How did they get here?

This is, finally, the right question. As always, the good questions lead to better questions. What remedies can help? How can they reunify?

Table 10-5—BodyBeing Dysfunctions/Remedies

- Rightful Place -

Well Being—I can find the power and strength to listen and respond to the sensation information I receive from my environment. I can do this in a way that allows my body to adapt with maximum integration and functioning in any environment.

Dysfunctions	Remedies
• Lack of enthusiasm for life • Not wanting to be touched • Stubborn or overly submissive • Extreme shyness or over-bravado • Overly territorial or underprotective of body, family, or home • Unable or unwilling to explore with all the senses • Unkind to peers and siblings • Exhibitionism • Inability to find safe personal space • Restlessness that cannot be satisfied, or a nervous physical habit • Ineptness in relation to navigating their own body and objects • Often unsure in nature • Cruel to animals or other children • Lack of interest in life • Cranky and difficult when learning new skills • Excessive whining and tantrums	• Reorganize family relationships; i.e., time with parents, supervised sibling time • Gardening • Pets • Eliminate all types of threats • Nonthreatening challenges • Guided exploration of exciting physical environments • Time playing with a sensitive older child • Shared responsibilities; i.e., building/cooking/handwork activities • Supervised play with small group of mixed-gender children • Quiet time in nature • Uninterrupted time with each parent in which the child chooses the activity (four and older) • Supervised time with younger children and infants

Table 10-5—BodyBeing Dysfunctions/Remedies, continued

- Boundary/Strength -

Well Being—I can make an accurate assessment of the sensory information in my world. With this information, I can make the appropriate adjustments as to when to start and stop.

Dysfunctions	Remedies
• Repeated incidents endangering the body • Lack of awareness of contact with themselves, environments, and others • Poor assessment of how and where objects are placed • Diminished curiosity • Clumsy and fear filled in nature • Unable to assess sensation values in everyday environment • Unwilling to leave primary support person even with safe loved ones	• Restructure the environment to include lots of safe and interesting sensory exploration opportunities • Reorganize family relationships; i.e., time with parents, supervised sibling time • Coordination games and activities • Reorganize flexibility parameters with any and all of the people in the child's life • Building, cooking, and handwork activities • Pacing the child and remarking on the physical boundaries in play, in nature, in the neighborhood • Supervised contact with animals • Challenging physical activities • Contact with the wild parts of nature

Table 10-6—FeelingBeing Dysfunctions/Remedies

- Trust -

Well Being—Connected to my feelings mentors, I learn to trust my own feelings and explore interpersonal relationships with others in my community.I assess the worthiness of a situation by the trust I feel.I can feel inspired.

Dysfunctions	Remedies
• Disrespectful of others' feelings • Cruel to people and things • Afraid in nature • Unable to make friends • Unable to approximate fairness for self and others • Untrusting of healthy mentors • Unable to feel inspired • Avoid most social contacts • Suspicious • Morbid • Find it funny when others hurt themselves • Often tense and unapproachable • Bullying or obsequious	• Repeated contact with an inspirational teen or elder • Additional mentors • Supervised peer play • Pace child in social situations • Review and modify all role models and mentors • Create opportunity to experience transcendence • Nature or wilderness games in small groups • Supervised time with younger children and infants • Cooperative games and activities • Relaxed, open conversations about death • Create opportunities for inspiration • Expose to different ethnicities, in their homes if possible • Much exposure to humor

Table 10-6—FeelingBeing Dysfunctions/Remedies, continued

- Reciprocal Cooperation -	
Well Being—I am connected to family, extended family, and community and the relationships are just. I experience my elders as feeling mentors and allow them to know my feelings. My world view has expanded to include my own death, the cycles of the natural world, and the possibility of feeling transcendence.	

Dysfunctions	Remedies
• Jealousy • Excessive hero worship • Lack of care or abuse of body • Excessive embarrassment in safe social situations • Senseless flash moods • Unable or unwilling to listen • Overattachment to parents • Wishing to be saved by an outside power; i.e., flying saucers, white knight on horse • Exhibitionism or overly self-consciousness • Cruelty or meanness • Unable to feel glory, wonder, and beauty • Insensitive to animals • Overly egocentric; still needing to be the center of attention • Unwilling to consider death • Objectifying nature; i.e., the rock tripped me • Unable or unwilling to cooperate • Lying • Stealing	• Involvement in charity work with mentors • Inspirational teenager or elder • Supply biological sexual information • Inspirational biographies • Pace child in varied social situations • Exploring plant and animal life cycles • Inspirational exploration stories • Accompanied travel to see other cultures • Contact with the less fortunate • Opportunity to experience transcendence • Quiet time in nature or with beautiful music or art • Supervised peer play • Supervised time with infants • Time in the wild • Nature stories and films • Relaxed, open conversations about death • Opportunities to engage myth and drama • Much exposure to humor • Opportunity to bring justice to an unjust situation, either personally or socially

Table 10-6—IdealBeing Dysfunctions/Remedies

- Autonomy -

Well Being—I project ideals as a way to inaugurate my journey to self-government. I explore identities as a way to connect to my core nature. I hurt no one, including myself, in this exploration. I value family but need to participate in the organization of the relationship.

Dysfunctions	Remedies
• Prolonged attachment to childhood and childish ways • Self-pity • Excessive need to prove independence • Bullying; obsequious • Prejudice • Hero worship • Ineffectual definition of personal space • Predatory in exploration of shadow • Identification with predator/prey • Immature sense of justice • Overly egocentric • Whining and tantrums • Little desire for personal freedom • Little desire to participate in ideals • Lonely or very low social life • Cynical about themselves, society, and life • Shunning parents • Destructive peer choices • Sarcastic • Cruel • Fun at the expense of others	• Challenges in nature • Difficult tasks with support to succeed • Apprenticeships with skilled elders • Challenging athletic activities • Opportunity for safe self-reflection and self-examination whether with trusted elder, in facilitated small groups, or in adventures with peers specifically designed for this purpose • Travel and exploration of natural wonders • Introduction to developmental psychology • Biographies and myths • Pacing by older, responsible teen in social interactions • Service work with other people from different ethnic backgrounds • Organized challenging, cooperative peer endeavors • Guidance in how to deal with ridicule and disrespect • Supervised care of the young • Charity work

Table 10-6—IdealBeing Dysfunctions/Remedies, continued

- Identity Construction, Personal Power, and Freedom -

Well Being—I accept that responsibility and freedom come together. I move to my core nature. I feel powerful and unique—that special something that makes me, me. I know I will do something great in life.

Dysfunctions	Remedies
• Violent or violating attitude toward people, objects, and institutions • Domineering behavior; bullying • Arrogance; lying • Defensive loyalty to family and institutions • Punishment of self and others • Self-righteous; delight in conquering • Excessive fear • Limp capitulation to an unwelcome decision without inquiry with the decision makers, usually parents, peers, or teachers • Friends are mostly FeelingBeing children • Careless with nature	• Apprenticeships and internships with caring yet challenging elders, including intelligent athletic coaches • Connection with global politics in the realm of ideals • Difficult challenges with support to succeed • Charity work • Guided adventures and adventurous travel • Caring for others, such as sick loved one or younger relatives • Introduction to new peers with new values in new environments • Educational opportunity out of the home; boarding school • Time in nature with competent and adventuresome naturalist • Expanded social venues and opportunities • Engaging entire peer group in project that accords with their ideals • Pointing out the link between freedom and responsibility whenever possible

Table 10-6–ReasonableBeing Dysfunctions/Remedies

- Interconnectedness, Humor, and Humility -

Well Being—I can see the fluid unity of life and the value of each part of it. I believe that by studying one part, I can get to know the whole better. I am capable of accomplishing things in a meaningful, mature way, especially in intimate relationship with others. I am able to laugh at myself. I see the humor in humans as the meaning givers in this universe of mystery enfolded within mystery. I am capable of understanding that many limits are self-imposed boundaries. I am humbled by the vastness and beauty of the universe. I seek and actualize substantive values.

Dysfunctions	Remedies
• Complete identification with peers • Excessive daydreaming • Lack of enthusiasm • Cannot leave home • Immature peer relationships • Obsessed with field of interest • Uncomfortable with sexual engagement or exploration • Unwilling to commit to thorough investigations • Mockery • Excessive sarcasm • Cynicism • Emphasis on answers rather than questions • Overly suspicious • Enjoyment of the difficulties of others • Overbearing pride or presumption • Overly competitive with self or others • Self-righteous and defensive of beliefs • Inability to inquire into life's meaning • Disrespectful in romantic relationship explorations • Fear of novelty and change • Unable to function in a wide variety of social situations	• Study of the nature of relationships • Examination into their areas of difficulty; i.e., loneliness • Placing and then pacing the child in situations where they must make critical choices and learn • Study of all modes of knowing • Opportunity to engage practices specifically designed to increase self-knowledge according to the child's proclivities • Encouragement and guidance in sexuality, including study of practices from around the world • Engagement in caring relationships that result in positive sexual experiences, with guidance if necessary • Time for solitude and reflection in nature • Opportunities for a rigorous examination of the natural world • Deep inquiry into self, including personal history • Time with masters in their fields of interest • Penetrating investigation into ethics, experiential and referring to the child's life if possible • Recapitulation of the child's life in which parents answer all her questions honestly • Exposure to genuinely humorous situations • Opportunity and support to take risks and explore • Contact with creative people • Multiple and varied cultural experiences, including service work with those of different ethnic backgrounds

Table 10-6–ReasonableBeing Dysfunctions/Remedies, continued

- Interconnectedness, Humor, and Humility -

Well Being—I am able to commit to what I have found to be true while maintaining a hypothetical and playful relationship to it. I can assess myself, my understanding, and others in the world. I know everything has its place and purpose and look for how it connects with everything else. I accept the awesome task of exploring and finding meaning in my world and so get a glimpse of the intrinsic nature of mind.

Dysfunctions	Remedies
• Out of balance beliefs; i.e., killing to prove one's point • Overly defensive of one's own opinion • Unable to evaluate social situations • Lack of initiative • Obsession with trying to make their world stable • Preoccupation with the dull and repetitive • Superficial and self-centered • Unable to see the value of others or of differing investigations • Rigid beliefs and prejudice • Compromise, including seduction (of all types) for social acceptance • Proselytizing • Repulsed by breadth of human endeavor and exploration • Overly dependent on intellect • Afraid of personal power • Afraid of chaos • Afraid of others • Preoccupied with security	• Exposure to new areas of study • Travel and engagement with other cultures • Contact with those engaged in emergent knowledge • Opportunity to play with systems creation in the field of their choice, guided if necessary • Opportunity to engage practices specifically designed to increase self-knowledge according to the child's proclivities • Encouragement and guidance in sexuality • Examination of the spectrum of psychology, including the transpersonal • Charity work • Guided simulations of decision-making process • Co-exploration of a project of the child's choice; i.e., science, music, art, ecology • Self-study, guided if needed • Exposure to genuinely humorous situations • Opportunity and support to take risks and explore • Multiple and varied cultural experiences • Time with masters in fields of interest with access to tools, data, and colleagues • Study of and experimentation with substantive values

Reunification is a family affair. Dissolving the shadow is an important step in the process.

Introduction to the Remedies

The remedy tables numbered 10-5, 10-6, 10-7, and 10-8, which immediately precede this section, assume that elders have made a considered attempt to nourish the child and that chronic dysfunction is still appearing. Therefore, the dysfunctions indicated do not refer to single or occasional instances but to recurring and long-lasting behaviors.

The dysfunctions and remedies will be readily recognizable to parents and teachers. These are the people with whom children interact every day. The approach is not aimed at therapists and is not intended to be compared with their diagnostic approach.

Dysfunctional behavior is treated as an arrow pointing to the block in the flow of well-being. A behavior or a combination of behaviors can cause a block. The remedies are not specific to the behaviors. For example, jealousy is one of the behaviors listed as a dysfunction in FeelingBeing. Remember, that means chronic jealousy, not sporadic episodes. Charity work is listed as one of the remedies. This does not mean that charity work is specifically designed to dissolve chronic jealousy. It is not a one-to-one correlation. Rather, charity work will deepen the child's appreciation of fairness and justice, two important FeelingBeing nourishments. Well nourished, trust strengthens and the symptom of chronic jealousy loses its purchase.

The suggested approach is to look over the dysfunction columns for the child's life stage to see if there is a match with observed chronic behaviors. If there is, do any of the others match as well? Are there others that the adult believes are connected? Then, the remedies should be examined. Do you feel intuitively that any stand out as useful? Why?

Dysfunction results in limited access to the depth of the organizing principle or secondary organizing principle. The remedies are designed to restore optimal access. The tables indicate the organizing principle or secondary organizing principle affected by the dysfunction. Any response that restores optimal access is a remedy.

Remedies are one of the steps in reunification. The last part of this chapter brings all the steps together. There will be a detailed case history of a successful reunification. There will also be step-by-step guidance, an algorithm, in how to create a reunification strategy.

All remedies affect the whole family; many call for action by members other than the child manifesting the dysfunction. When a remedy calls for a mentor, for guidance, or for supervision, the assumption is that the person filling the role will be familiar with Natural Learning Rhythms. In remedies that call for pacing, the assumption is that the elder will determine the rhythm of the remedy with developmental sensitivity.

The child is not dysfunctional; the child's behavior is a symptom of a dysfunction. As Alice Miller, Carl Jung, Alfred Adler, Gregory Bateson, and the renowned discipline of family systems therapy, and many, many others have pointed out, dysfunction is a family affair. Reunification addresses the dysfunction. Remedies respond to the symptoms. Observing the effects of the remedies helps refine the reunification.

Remedies that have been found to be particularly useful by many families are listed in more than one place. If any remedy strikes you as odd, then don't use it—there are many others. Undoubtedly, observant parents will notice dysfunctions that are not listed, or descriptions that are close to but not exactly what they see in their child. Likewise, the remedies will have to be modified, or new ones discovered, to fit the culture of the family.

As always, tables are meant to stimulate. Everything on them I have experienced firsthand during fieldwork. Every remedy has been tried by me, Josette, EnCompass staff, parents, or professionals with whom I have had long-term relationships. The remedies can do no harm; in fact, they usually do some good. If, for instance, charity work does not contribute to dissolving a block, it still brings the family closer and provides a meaningful experience.

Reunification

Reunification means the child and family reemerge in the flow. Since they have been mired in dysfunction, this seems like a new emergence. All the dynamics of emergence are at play.

There are nine steps to creating a reunifier. They are:

1. Determining the child's developmental moment, with a careful eye to transitions.
2. Identifying the dysfunctional behavior.
3. Profiling the child's nourishments, including the way boundaries are made, and excesses and deficiencies, then deciding how to respond.
4. Evaluating the effect of the parent's shadow; if it pertains to the behavior, then deciding how to respond.

5. Profiling just attitude, and if there is a problem, deciding how to respond.
6. Approximating the behavior's place on the continuum of whispers to collapse.
7. Choosing a remedy.
8. After three months, taking the results and going through the process again.
9. After six months, taking the results and going through the process again.

This list is an algorithm. Every step is equally important. They have to be taken in sequence, although sometimes steps 4 and 5 can overlap. It is only when steps 1 to 9 are completed that all the parts of the reunifier are present. The rhythm of implementation depends on the family schedule and resources. If possible, all responses should be carried out simultaneously. The results of steps 1 to 7 become a variable in step 8, and the results of step 8 become a variable in step 9. This process can be continued as long as necessary, with varying lengths of time between iterations.

Reunification emerges. All emergence dynamics are present. First, there is participation. All family members participate, each according to their developmental capacities and the requirements of the chosen responses. There is open communication about the reunification process and choices, as secrecy would poison the process.

Second, in fluid, dynamic systems, simple acts repeated many times lead to greater complexity. Third, the relations of the components are self-creating. They interact with each other and their environment to optimize well-being. They co-evolve. More complex self-organization occurs.

- Natural Learning Rhythms Saves Time -

Some parents have been intimidated by the nine-step process at first glance. That didn't last long. When the steps were taken in sequence, then reunification flowed. Parents quickly realized that the reunification process saved money and time. As the energy that was bound in the dysfunction was released, all family members prospered. Often, within three months, they spent less time on the chronic dysfunction and the adversarial tensions that surrounded it, and more time in meaningful learning together. They also saved a bundle on counseling costs.

Therefore, reunification wisely insists that the restoration of well-being reside in the relationships among family members. They must co-evolve. No part of the system can be isolated.

The system moves and changes through a series of bifurcation points. Each of these points represents a choice. When members of the family participate in the reunification process, each bifurcation, or choice, is up toward greater complexity. The system moves toward chaos. Life blossoms at the edge of chaos. It is a moment of new initial conditions. The reunification responses provide very favorable conditions. The family enters chaos. They are connected; no part is isolated. They take the dip together by investing the time and resources to become skillful in the reunification responses.

What will emergence look like? What will it be? The family cannot be certain. Predictions and agendas get in the way. Emergence is indeterminate. The algorithm must be run for the results to be known. All that can be said is that the family will rejoin the flow.

Reunification Case History—The Wyatts

I met the four Wyatts when they enrolled in the EnCompass Signature Program for Family Excellence. After some warm-up activities, the parents met to introduce themselves and to name their goals for the course. "We came in two separate cars," Carla said before even telling the group her name, "and I only wish we had four so everyone could travel alone."

Not a happy mom. "She's right," Peter, her husband, said. "It's hell in the car with those two kids."

"Interesting," Josette said dryly, "but it might be better if we started with your names."

By the end of that first weekend, I had a clear picture of the Wyatt household. Carla had lost touch with Kurt, her sixteen-year-old son. She resented that his interest in computers and photography occupied most of his time. She wanted him to be interested in the activities she enjoyed, such as family outings in nature. She heckled him about the subjects he had difficulty with in school. When disagreements erupted, Carla had little patience and was soon muttering comments like, "He's impossible. All he wants to do is have the last word." The arguments turned biting and bitter, and the family sunk into isolation.

Peter tried to help but was ineffectual. He entered the arguments too late, as he believed that they should "work it out together." Carla and Kurt then jumped all over him for his "stupid remarks." When his intervention only fanned the flames, he turned his attention to protecting their daughter, ten-year-old Vera.

Kurt sometimes took his frustrations out on Vera. If she approached him at the wrong time, he would snap at her. A couple of years earlier, he had welcomed her interest in computers and photography and had tutored her in their use. Now, he set up barbed wire around himself at those times. If she dared approach, he spitefully told her to go ask her father.

Vera was the proverbial good girl. She cooperated with everyone. When Kurt and Carla battled, she faded into the background. If it happened at home, she would just raise the volume on the TV. She did well in school, had many friends, and often acted the part of Daddy's little girl. Vera told Peter that she liked it when he protected her. After her mother's temper calmed, Vera would show up with a bright smile and the suggestion of a project that she knew her mother enjoyed doing with her. After Kurt was cruel to her, she rationalized his behavior with the thought that *He is having a tough time with Mom.* Sometimes, she cried at night in bed, alone, telling no one.

Carla and Peter wanted a technique—an answer—to make Kurt act better. They listened to the information about organizing principles and nourishments. As they said later, it made intuitive sense and they were desperate. The techniques they had tried had worked for a short while, but the problem returned, seemingly worse than before.

The next four weeks of the Signature course are conducted over the telephone. One night a week for an hour and a half, parents call the bridge line. The bridge line allows everyone to be in conference together. It is very convenient. The parents do not need child care. They can call from anywhere. During the bridge calls, parents receive detailed information about development, the organizing principles, and the nourishments. With the printed Natural Learning Rhythms information in front of them, they can follow the discussion easily. There is ample time for questions and answers. At the end of the month, there is a second weekend of whole family experiential learning. Parents fine-tune their appreciation and delivery of the nourishments.

Carla found herself challenged by the need to provide sensitive respect and engage her child's ideals. Peter could not imagine co-creating a boundary with Karl. Each of them maintained that Vera was "doing fine." On the second day, though, a mini-breakthrough occurred. Kurt helped Carla and Vera during one of the problem-solving initiatives. Surprised, she thanked him.

The EnCompass staff knew of Kurt's passions, of course, and had suggested that he make a photo journal of his experience in the

Signature Program. Computers were set up so he could polish his work. In the afternoon, quietly, Carla wandered over to the children's project area and looked at Kurt's work. Impressed, she went to find Kurt. Unfortunately, he was lambasting Peter and Vera. The fragile mood broke, but the possibility of well-being had been sparked.

Peter spent a long time considering reciprocal cooperation. He finally admitted that Vera's good girl was not an expression of well-being. Vera didn't trust her family; she managed them.

In the midst of a family game, Kurt was rude to Vera. She shuddered, then quickly put on a happy face. Carla and Peter saw it. They rededicated themselves to providing the FeelingBeing nourishments for their daughter. They profiled the nourishments available, and during the weekend, they tried to provide those that were missing. Vera responded, albeit sporadically. Twice she told Kurt to stop bothering her. Once she demanded her family finish playing the game and quit arguing.

The bridge line conferences resumed for the next four weeks. There was a class each week for each life stage. Generally, parents attended the class just for the stage of their child, but Carla and Peter decided to attend classes for all the stages. These classes thoroughly examined each stage, transitions, and the dance. Parents had many opportunities to experiment with nourishments and to ask questions.

At the end of the month, the Signature Program culminated in a three-day retreat for the whole family. Carla and Peter had good news and bad news. Carla had done an inquiry with her son about his attraction to computers and photography. She found out that Kurt's primary motivation was self-expression. He admitted that they had become a refuge for him as family relationships worsened. She asked if he would show her what he did. Kurt warily agreed. Carla was genuinely surprised at his level of expertise.

There were other similar experiences, but they happened infrequently. The arguments lessened, but they continued. Peter still did not know what to do. Also, he mistakenly believed that he should not take an interest in computers with Kurt so that "my wife and son can have a clear field." Both parents still felt personally attacked by Kurt.

Kurt did agree to go on a spring nature adventure with his class. While he didn't reach out to Vera, he no longer treated her badly.

Life between Vera and her parents was seemingly more difficult. She refused to do chores. She bristled but capitulated when Peter comforted her. She wanted her own computer. She told small lies. For Vera, unfairness was everywhere. Yet again, Peter and Carla revisited FeelingBeing nourishments. They saw gaps in honesty and justice and knew that their ability to be feeling mentors was compromised. But they did not know what to do. They were giving their best with both children.

Much had changed for the better, however. The sibling rivalry had all but disappeared. Carla and Peter were tuning in to Kurt's ideals. Kurt's interest expanded to include time in nature. Vera was shedding the good girl persona. Her actions were typical of a child returning to well-being. She needed some time to express the built-up poisons and to test the system to see if it was trustworthy. If her parents could dance with her, then the prognosis was good.

By most standards of normal, life at the Wyatt household was good. But they had had a taste of great and wanted to do more. They had experienced dance moments and saw the benefits. Carla was beginning to unlock aspects of her autonomy that had been conceded due to the interplay with her mother and older sister. Peter identified the existence of a block in his inability to connect with his son when Kurt was angry. He had no idea of its nature, but he wanted to get rid of it. They also had made the most important switch: They now knew that family is a source of joy and empowerment. They were apprehensive, for they understood they couldn't predict the emergent family organization. They were cautious, for there were still scars and open wounds. But the fear was gone. Given where they had started, the enticement of optimal well-being was a strange attractor indeed.

Peter and Carla Wyatt then decided to take the advanced Natural Learning Rhythms course on reunification. They had met the one requirement for the course by spending several months making their best attempts to provide the nourishments. Without that, diagnosis would always have been clouded by the possibility that the dysfunction was simply a lack of nourishment.

In the course, they deepened their understanding of optimal well-being and learned about the dynamics of change and emergence. The shadow, which they had encountered in the Signature Program, grabbed them. At the end of the course, they created their own reunifier.

Here is what they did:

Step One: The Child's Developmental Moment—Carla and Peter had a lively dialogue as to whether Kurt had passed through the meaning-making moment of IdealBeing or was in the midst of it. Based on his commitment to computers and photography and his availability, perhaps even desire, to share his work with Carla, they decided he had crossed into trial and error. Vera had definitely moved into FeelingBeing competency. Based on this analysis, Carla and Peter understood that they would have to choose powerful remedies, as the vulnerability of receptivity had passed for both children.

Step Two: Identifying the Dysfunctional Behavior—Using the remedies tables, Carla and Peter instantly agreed that Kurt shunned his parents and often aggressively exploited their weaknesses. Repulsed at first by the word *predator*, they eventually conceded that it fit Kurt. They believed that Vera's attachment to Peter was still a dysfunction, as she clung to him in times of stress and looked past Carla as a decision maker in the home. They added the inability to feel inspiration and to listen as additional concerns. Casting the behavior in naked terms shocked them at first and then spurred them to action.

Step Three: Profiling the Nourishments—Peter and Carla had done much of this work already. As they considered the nourishments again, Vera's need for inspiration stood out. Kurt had an excess of personal space, and it had turned into a way for him to keep out the family. Peter and Carla noticed other ways to modify the nourishments as well. Boundaries were still a problem. They had begun to ask Vera about fairness but lost patience when she didn't agree with them. They had tentatively broached co-creation with Kurt only to be rebuffed. As they spoke, they realized that Vera was watching their boundary decisions with Kurt carefully. From now on, they would insist on co-creation with Kurt and on fairness with Vera.

Step Four: The Parents' Shadow—Peter and Carla used the inquiry technique with one another to try to determine their shadow and the way it influenced the family. They remembered the admonition from the dance that if a parent cannot provide a nourishment, there is a very good chance they did not receive it as a child. In the seminar, they did an exercise in which they considered what aspects of themselves went into the shadow during their FeelingBeing and IdealBeing years. The results surprised them. Conflict had not been allowed in Peter's household. He couldn't even raise his voice without being sent to his room. He realized that he had learned to either be peaceful or avoid conflict. In a flash of insight, he saw that an aspect of protecting Vera was a reenactment of protecting himself. Obviously, this shadow obscured his ability to successfully interact with his wife and son during their conflicts. Peter said that he wanted to participate in the next conflict. He knew it would be very challenging and asked for Carla's help. She consented but only on the condition that Peter ask for Kurt's help as well. Peter gulped but saw the wisdom in the suggestion and agreed.

It seemed that more shadow work was needed for Peter. They decided that he would try counseling with a professional for a short while for the specific purpose of uncovering the shadow. It would be a financial strain, and they made the budgetary considerations to cover the costs.

Carla had realized during the Signature Program that the interactions with her mother and elder sister had led to a loss of autonomy. She was in continuing dialogue with them in an attempt to redress the imbalance. Happily, they were willing participants. One revelation startled her. Both her mother and her sister stated that her sister was the star of the family and Carla was often in the background. They casually commented that she was "such a good sport about it." At their words, Carla exploded into angry tears. Since that moment, she considered how her repression of her frustration influenced her parenting of Vera. Carla and Peter decided that she would start looking at the leadership qualities in her daughter and guarantee that Vera had the opportunity and support to actualize them.

Step Five: Profiling Just Attitude—Peter and Carla had lost their ability to find humor in their lives. They laughed at jokes and enjoyed banter with adults but were not able to laugh at themselves in the home and rarely laughed with the children. Carla also had a hard time admitting mistakes. They thought about inclusion and their wish for four cars. They traced their difficulty with creative confrontation back to the shadow work. In short, their attitude in the home was not conducive to healing. Given their resources and time, they hoped that their shadow work, as well as their other responses, would positively impact their attitude. They did want to laugh and enjoy life more. Peter suggested that they let the children lead them to humor. Why should the parents do all the work? Then Carla and Peter smiled, with a glint of love and respect in their eyes.

Step Six: The Continuum of Whispers to Collapse—Both children had been bouncing between resistance and collapse before the Wyatts joined the Signature Program. Peter and Carla acknowledged that the work they had done had halted the descent. They now tentatively agreed that the children now bounced between whispers and alarm reactions, with perhaps some resistance. This analysis left them both hopeful and concerned.

Step Seven: Choosing Remedies—Carla and Peter considered their remedy options very carefully. Which ones did the family need? Which ones would the children accept? Which ones did they have the time and money to actualize?

They chose three. The first was an original. They would have contact with people from different ethnic communities. After they became acquainted and were somewhat trusted, they would look for and engage opportunities to do service work in which both the people providing the service and the recipients were of mixed ethnic backgrounds. To concentrate on only service work would cast that ethnic group as victims and subtly promote prejudice. Carla, who had a Latino heritage, had experienced this attitude as a child. They planned to reach into other communities through the families of their children's friends as well as co-workers.

The need for inspiration had been highlighted time and again as Carla and Peter had gone through the process. It was a need for Vera and certainly for Carla, and so they decided that the two of them would go on inspirational adventures together. They planned one for the next month at a national park. Nature had always inspired Carla, and she delighted in the understanding that her inspiration could nourish her daughter.

Last, they chose to find Kurt a suitable apprenticeship. They would try to find a mentor who not only was skilled in computers and photography but also was willing and able to appreciate Kurt's developmental moment. Peter was somewhat afraid that this approach would take Kurt farther from the family, but he decided to proceed, as he knew there would be a reevaluation in three months.

Having made their decisions, the Wyatts would spend the next three months practicing to the best of their ability. Barring a catastrophe, they would not re-engage the decision-making process until then.

Step Eight: Revisit at Three Months: Two of the three remedies were winners. It had taken six weeks to find the master who would work with Kurt. She turned out to be a twenty-nine-year-old married entrepreneur, Tina, who had a thriving graphic arts business. Peter and Carla had not been looking for a female. Kurt had only been looking for a computer wizard. He had located her. Tina welcomed the idea of apprentices and accepted the responsibility of helping to guide the young man in life as well as the trade.

Carla reveled in the nature excursions. Vera, not a great fan of sweat and bugs, gladly went along to be with her mother, who, she said, "was much nicer out there." Kurt went occasionally, and he preferred to take challenging hikes with his father. A bit of competition had crept into their relationship, but it seemed a good thing and was often the subject for jesting. Peter's fear that the apprenticeship would pull Kurt from the family never materialized.

The Wyatts were having trouble making new acquaintances in different ethnic groups. Vera believed that their agenda scared people. "We want to be your friends so that we can do service together? I don't think so," she said, and everyone laughed. They held a family meeting and decided that they would volunteer to work with the elderly and infirm in their community.

The formation of prohibitive boundaries remained difficult. Neither child trusted the intentions of their parents at these times; the children anticipated that disagreement would quickly degenerate to disaster. Ironically, it was Carla's frustration with the lack of trust, and not the work to create the boundary, that set Carla off and confirmed the children's fears.

Peter suggested to Carla that they try to include everyone in the boundary. Carla, disbelieving, pointed out that Peter had yet to participate in a disagreement between her and Kurt. He claimed that he was now ready. Also, he wanted to take advantage of Vera's ability to assess the fairness in a situation. Carla tentatively agreed. Later, she told me that she soon realized it was the surrender of control that scared her. Her family was becoming empowered, and she worried what her new role would be. She reviewed her seminar notes. The fact of indeterminacy quieted her. She couldn't know, but staying in the flow did lead to more complex self-organization. She had to put her faith in her family and their intention to experience well-being.

Step Nine: Revisit at Six Months: When the Wyatts stopped and looked back as a family, the biggest change they saw was the arrival of just attitude. Of course, the children did not know it by that name. They knew that everyone joked on occasion and that everyone could admit they were wrong without fear. Vera made humorous comments every day about the current hot topic of the household: Carla was teaching Kurt how to drive.

Their confusion around the formation of prohibitive boundaries lessened but continued. Peter tried hard and stayed for the end, but his contribution noticeably slackened during controversy. Once, though, he became so involved that he lost his temper and yelled at his wife and child. When he finished, he looked around in amazement. Who did that? He started to shrink into his shell, afraid of his family's reactions. Again, he was amazed. They were smiling and they treated his ideas with respect. That evening, he discussed the event with Carla. She had only one comment for him: "What took you so long?"

Kurt's apprenticeship was a complete success. Serendipitously, he did not view girls as objects, which many of his friends did. Peter attributed his mature attitude to the relationship with Tina.

Nature adventures continued to call Carla. Sometimes she went alone. More often, she went with Vera. Vera asked if she could bring friends. At first, Carla was reluctant to give up her private time with her daughter. Then she remembered her goal to support the leadership skills in her child and decided to use the group time to collectively explore the issue. Before agreeing, she informed Vera of her intentions. Vera liked the idea, as did her friends. Carla gloried in the exchange with young girls. She became a mentor and now had assurance that her daughter would not be overlooked as she had been. The bimonthly excursions became a highlight of their time together.

The charity work did not spark any of them. This surprised me, as I have seen it be very effective for many families. While the Wyatts participated with good feelings and enjoyed helping others, it did not seem necessary to treat the activity as a remedy. They decided that they would continue as they saw fit but dropped it from their reunification plan.

The Wyatts' reunification strategy always stayed within the capacity of their available resources. They didn't try anything that would upset their financial stability or violate their family culture. They used their understanding to maximum advantage. For instance, they accepted that they would have to choose powerful remedies. They opened their eyes to the facts of the dysfunction and used them as a spur rather than as an excuse to collapse.

Always trying to reasonably approach their lives from the perspective of the needs of the family, they did simple things. Adventures in nature, finding an apprentice relationship, and counseling seem, from the outside, to be relatively insignificant in considering family healing. Yet, applied at the right leverage point and in a responsive environment, they had enormous effect. This is classic emergence dynamics.

They were honest, they persevered, they modified, and they stayed in open communication with one another. Carla agreed to include everyone in the making of prohibitive boundaries. Peter and Carla gambled that just attitude would come if they kept to the plan. Peter worked hard to stay engaged during conflict. As they looked back, the family realized that it was his engagement of hard work more than the results that endeared him to the family and deepened their intimacy. Carla danced with Vera and her friends in way she never anticipated.

The Wyatts have rejoined the flow. They are on their way. They had challenges, but they are facing them together as a family. Their reunification plan has now become their everyday life. They have the confidence to change it as needed. Both children are about to enter transitions, and new opportunities are certainly on the way. Life blossoms at the edge of chaos.

Reunification Assistance

To reunify, do the nine-step process. Minimally, the engagement will be a family tonic. Maximally, family life will flow.

There are a number of tables in this book to help with step 1, determining the child's developmental moment. The "Being Qualities" table provides the most detail, but the remedies tables in this chapter may be sufficient.

Go slowly with step 2. Think over all the child's behaviors before deciding which ones to address. Peter and Carla, for instance, felt that Vera's inability to listen was at the root of some of her more dramatic expressions. I have included behavior assessment tables for each stage in Appendix B, to help with this process.

Step 3 is the heart of the process. Detailed descriptions of the nourishments, with accompanying summary tables, are included throughout the book. There must be a concerted effort to provide the nourishment for three months before proceeding with reunification. Many reunification plans end here as the proper nourishments prove to be sufficient for returning to the flow. I have included nourishment assessment tables in Appendix C to help with this process.

Step 4 is for the parents. Several books are listed in the Bibliography that can help. Shadow work can be done with most therapists, especially with those from the Jungian persuasion. Shadow work is addressed in advanced Natural Learning Rhythms seminars, as the Wyatts experienced.

Step 5 requires care. Each of the four aspects of just attitude must be present in the home in some way. The atmosphere of trust is critical for the remedy to be potent.

Step 6 is a reality check. It brings the dysfunction into clear view. For the Wyatts, this was a crucial moment. They realized that delay brought the danger of imminent collapse.

Use the remedies tables as a starting place for step 7. Dysfunction can be defined only by the parents, for they know the family culture. The remedies must be modified to fit the available resources.

Diligent application of the first seven steps must occur before step 8. As with all nonlinear events, the results from the first run are a factor in the next. Inadequate data will undermine the chances for optimal well-being. The same sequence is true for step 9.

Cultural Evolution

By returning to the very sources of human development as we observe all the structures of consciousness, and moving from there towards our present day and our contemporary situation and consciousness, we can not only discover the past and the present moment of our existence but also gain a view into the future which reveals the traits of a new reality amidst the decline of our age.

—Jean Gebser

Chapter Eleven # SOCIAL JUSTICE

People whose integrity has not been damaged in childhood, who were protected, respected, and treated with honesty by their parents, will be—both in their youth and in adulthood—intelligent, responsive, empathetic, and highly sensitive. They will take pleasure in life and will not feel any need to kill or even hurt others or themselves. They will use their power to defend themselves, not to attack others. They will not be able to do otherwise than respect and protect those weaker than themselves, including their children, because this is what they have learned from their own experience, and because it is this knowledge (and not the experience of cruelty) that has been stored up inside them from the beginning. It will be inconceivable to such people that earlier generations had to build up a gigantic war industry in order to feel comfortable and safe in this world. Since it will not be their unconscious drive in life to ward off intimidation experienced at a very early age, they will be able to deal with attempts at intimidation in their adult life more rationally and more creatively.
—Alice Miller

By treating everyone with respect, you teach them to treat everyone with respect also, because the only effective teaching is by example.

Just as the most powerful provocation to violent behavior is disrespect, the most powerful means of preventing violence is universal respect.
—James Gilligan, *Preventing Violence*

Optimal well-being is the world of relationship and connection. Life's challenges are faced together; adversaries disappear. Spirituality lives as a daily experience. The aesthetic of each person finds meaningful expression. There is support for intellectual and academic excellence. Families realize their ability to prevent and remedy dysfunction. Optimal well-being means strong, centered, resilient families in which both children and parents develop new resources and make real contributions to each other and society.[127]

What, then, is the social value of families living in optimal well-being? How does Natural Learning Rhythms contribute to social justice?

A just society supports each of its members to self-create—to produce and continuously regenerate and realize the networks that produced them. The following corollary is also true: A society whose members have the opportunity to self-create will act justly. More succinctly, a society is just to the extent that its members have the opportunity to self-create.

The history of African-Americans is a case in point. It is not that optimal social justice has been achieved and racial prejudice has been eliminated. However, there is more opportunity for self-creation for African-Americans now than there was two hundred years ago, one hundred years ago, or even fifty years ago. Because of this, African-Americans have made magnificent contributions in all areas of American society—such as jurisprudence, civic government, ethics, the healing professions, and entertainment.

The increased opportunity for African-Americans to self-create has had a ripple effect that increases respect for all people. But most important, it has allowed neighborly contact, which has enriched the network of connections and therefore each person's opportunities to self-create. These interactions bring emotional security in that participants can interact successfully with those of diverse ethnicities. Their friendships have meaning and value. They can trust and be trusted. These neighborly contacts are a positive step toward social justice.

Trustworthy connection and interaction are the basis for participation in social justice. Participation exists when each person's contribution is recognized, appreciated, and engaged. Open communication among the participants brings feedback that allows ever more refined interactions. Then social self-creation occurs, and social justice emerges.

Once again, this is the dynamics of emergence. There will be self-organization at a greater level of complexity. The actual form of the new complexity cannot be determined but can be known only through participation.

A long list of social ills results from neglecting the importance of children for the emergence of optimal social justice. Some of these ills will be considered when we elucidate the children's contribution to social justice. One needs to be examined now: violence. When the link between the neglect of children and violence is established, the need to include children in any reasonable approach to social justice becomes obvious and imperative.

Violence

James Gilligan, first introduced in chapter 7, "Being Qualities," points out the futility of relying upon law and the traditional approach to morality as a response to violence.

> For the past four millennia, since the time of the first law-givers—Hammurabi and Moses, Drakon and Solon, Plato and Aristotle, Cicero and Justinian—humanity has been engaged in a great social experiment, testing the hypothesis that we could prevent violence, or at least diminish its scale and intensity, by labeling it "evil" and "criminal"; ordering people not to engage in it; and then, when they commit acts of violence anyway, retaliating with more violence of our own, which we call "punishment" and "justice." Now, four thousand years is long enough to test any hypothesis, and the results of this experiment have been in for a long time: this means of attempt to prevent violence, which I will call the traditional moral and legal approach, far from solving the problem of violence, or even diminishing the threat it poses to our continued survival, has in fact been followed by a continued escalation of the frequency and intensity of violence, to the point that the century we have just survived has been the bloodiest in all human history, with more humans killing other humans than in all previous centuries combined. Worse yet, we have now achieved, through a deliberate effort, the technological ability to kill everyone on earth...[which may happen] unless we can increase our ability to prevent violence far more effectively than we have done for the past four thousand years.[128]

Four thousand years. Gilligan is right. It does seem like it is time to try something different.

Gilligan worked for twenty-five years directing the provision of psychiatric services to Massachusetts prisons and the prison mental hospital. He has worked intimately with violent perpetrators, completed a comprehensive study of the research on violence, lowered recidivism, and instituted programs that dramatically reduced—and in some cases eliminated—violence in prisons. His insight that "violence is an attempt to achieve justice" is a clarion call to pay attention to the way that the feeling of injustice takes root in a person's consciousness. In his book *Preventing Violence*, Gilligan, after much deliberation, boils it down to a single word: shame. Where there is shame there is the feeling of injustice. Where there is the experience of injustice there is the desire for revenge. Revenge involves violence.

Shame is an experience, a gestalt, and it is very difficult to dissolve once it has taken root. That is why Gilligan emphasizes preventing violence, which means eradicating conditions that foster shame.

Gilligan has some insights that map into Natural Learning Rhythms beautifully. For instance, he points out that frustration does not cause shame and anger. Learning, no matter how challenging, does not lead to extreme anger. Insult, loss of self-esteem, and humiliation do.[129] In Natural Learning Rhythms, therefore, when a child of any age becomes frustrated with a task or while learning an appropriate boundary, the critical response is to simply maintain relationship and avoid making the child bad or wrong. Everyone becomes frustrated while learning; no one needs to be shamed for it.

Gilligan points out that social stratification is one of the principle causes of shame in America. After citing the research and his own fieldwork, he points out that there are many creative ways to equalize the distribution of resources. In addition to social and political measures, he ponders a society in which each person's work is enjoyable and creative. He then says:

> The play that infants and children engage in is clearly an inborn, inherent trait of human beings. Play has been called the work that children do, the means by which they acquire the skills and knowledge that enable them to develop and mature into adults. Play has also been described, when applied to adults, as simply another name for work that one enjoys. We could use the word to refer to unalienated labor, creative work, work that is an end in itself. I believe that the wish and the need to engage in this creative work/play is only conditioned out of human beings.[130]

Play, according to Gilligan, is the natural mode of work. Play does not lead to social inequities that result in shame. Play does not need violence to redress the insult of shame and loss of self-esteem. While Gilligan considers this as a possible future from the perspective of economic reform, Natural Learning Rhythms sees it as a likely result when play has been given its proper place in learning during childhood.

While there are multiple ways that shame has been heaped upon children, as we saw in the "Chauvinism" section of chapter 9, "The Dance," Gilligan concentrates on the most important and well known. Punishment of children leads to violent adults, and corporal punishment of children greatly increases the risk of adults perpetrating physical violence.[131] He also recognizes the chauvinism toward children and cites many instances of age discrimination by both government and religion.[132] Interestingly, Gilligan points out that all religions have numerous authoritative declarations about honoring the mother and father but absolutely none about honoring children. He seems to be in accord with Alice Miller's dictum that if one has been oppressed, then one will oppress others. The point cannot be overstated: Shaming children is a principle cause of the cycle of violence and revenge that permeates society. Social justice cannot be achieved until the shaming of children ceases.

Abolishing punishment does not mean eliminating boundaries in relation to children. Children naturally need and desire boundaries. The frustration that they experience while learning them does not lead to violent anger when those boundaries are created with developmental sensitivity.

Gilligan and Natural Learning Rhythms hold that respect, recognition, and appreciation will greatly reduce and perhaps eliminate shame. Natural Learning Rhythms, of course, shows that the key to accomplish this with children is developmental awareness. Gilligan speaks of the prison population. Listen to the compassionate yet non-sentimental regard with which he holds these people.

> Violent criminals are not violent because they are dumb, out of touch with reality, or unable to recognize hypocrisy, dishonesty and injustice when they see it. They are violent precisely because they are aware of the hypocrisy, dishonesty, and injustice that surrounds them.[133]

Of course, he does not suggest that society tolerate their violent behavior. But prisoners are not dumb. Neither are children. Children do not act disrespectfully because they are stupid or uncaring, but rather because they are sensitive—they are attempting to learn and grow and cannot abide the insult. Disrespect needs to be bounded, but the underlying cause—the shame, the insult, the wound to self-esteem—must be remedied or the disrespect will appear in a new form.

One of the most startling results of Gilligan's prison reforms is that prisoners—including rapists and other violent perpetrators—who achieved a college degree while they were incarcerated were much less likely to return to prison. Considering this and other research, Gilligan firmly believes that free higher education should be available to all as a way to prevent violence.

In addition, he believes that if prisons were oriented toward education and away from punishment, there would be significantly less recidivism. Prisons are already schools, he claims. Why not turn them from schools for teaching criminal behavior to schools for restoring self-esteem?

First, though, for this and all other responses to violence, Gilligan realizes that "we will have to renounces our own urge to violence—that is, punishment—and decide that we want to engage in educational and therapeutic endeavors instead, so as to facilitate maturation, development, and healing."[134]

In Natural Learning Rhythms terms, we have to dance. By engaging in relationships that emphasize well-being and not pathology, we can heal where we have been shamed and so not oppress others. Family then becomes the wellspring of community and social empowerment. Well-being becomes the operating mode of social life.

The Family

Until this point in the book, we have considered optimal well-being in children and how that leads to optimal well-being in all family members. Now we can look at the family as a social unit. From the perspective of society, what is the value and meaning of family?

The answer is obvious. The family is the source of emotional well-being. The priceless value of the family is that it is the source of emotional well-being.

Family may have been an important economic unit in previous historical eras. It may have been an important legal entity. And it may be that the great emotional value of family intimacy is a later, emergent phenomenon. As economic and legal interests lose their power and emotional intimacy prevails, the family is transformed. New complexity emerges. No one can deny how great it feels to love and to be loved—one taste and there is no turning to economic or legal justifications for accepting the responsibility of a family. That responsibility brings the unparalleled freedom to love and to be loved. One dad summed it beautifully at the end of a family retreat: "We have learned so much here, but one thing we should never forget. We have these children because they bring joy to our lives."

Family members know each other. The emotional learning and growth that occur in a family cannot be matched in any other social form. Family may have started for economic reasons—it may have evolved into a form for tribal continuity and then supported the privatization of wealth—but in the process something extraordinary and valuable happened: Emotional intimacy came home.

Gilligan is right when he connects shame, injustice, and violence. And he may be correct that resolving shaming situations such as inequity between rich and poor, gender stereotypes, and age discrimination is critical for preventing violence. Perhaps Gardner would add that education that does not respect a child's blend of intelligences adds to the shame. But the social form that has the most power to prevent violence is the family. It is not just the respect and care that family brings, but the awakening and realization of the intimacy, love, and self-knowledge that dissolves shame and reveals the harmfulness of shaming others.

Humans want and need emotional connection, and the family is the natural place to get it. Proof of this lies in understanding some of the dynamics of divorce. Lack of trust, not lack of economic potency or legal standing, leads to divorce. Most divorces are very expensive; almost all of them lead to lessened social esteem. Yet they continue to occur at a record pace in all sectors of society. Why? What is missing? The love has gone, the trust has gone, and with them the meaning of their life together has gone. Why stay married? Having supported many families during divorce, I have found over and over that the suffering centers on the sundering of relationship, not on the economic or legal ramifications.

For families who enjoy well-being, social justice is not an abstract utopian ideal, but an evolving natural expression of families living justly. The social reform that they might choose to engage is that which supports their family's well-being and helps to create the society in which they wish to live. Neither need be sacrificed. Self-knowledge and social knowledge are not actualized separately.

Can family be appreciated for its gift of emotional well-being? Can family be seen as a source of social vitality? It seems to me that such recognition and appreciation will occur only when we clearly see, as

Gilligan demonstrates, that social ills stem from the lack of emotional wisdom. Then the source of emotional learning and well-being will be given the support it deserves. That source, the family, will not be constrained by legal, economic, or religious definitions. Care and love will be the qualities by which a family is defined. Society will realize that taking steps to ensure that its people are emotionally well is the best investment it can make.

An important question for social justice arises. Who can see the importance of family as the source of society's emotional well-being? Who can rally perhaps the most extensive social reform in history so that education and resources are abundantly allocated to family support and thus establish emotional well-being as the social norm?

Gifts of the Children

The answer to the questions at the end of the last section, I believe, begins with appreciating the societal contributions of children. Those children who experience themselves as socially valuable throughout their childhood have the greatest likelihood of facilitating the transition to a socially just world. It will not be children who are seen only for the contribution they might make as adults or for their ability to learn cultural customs and skills. Such chauvinism sees the child as an adult-in-the-making, not a child-as-she-is. The child is an It, and her contribution is viewed according the anticipated gains she may one day bring to society. It will be children seen as Thou, whose social importance is acknowledged in each moment of their lives, that will bring about the transformation of the family for maximum social good.

BodyBeing—Happiness and Bonding

Josette and I once attended a barbecue with the extended family of a couple who are wealthy philanthropists. About fifteen people were there, including their two granddaughters, ages four and six, respectively. As we were chatting, the girls rushed in and announced that the trampoline had been set up and could Grandpa and Grandma come see the new tricks, "pretty please." With a big smile, off they went.

There is nothing unusual about this scene. Variations occur thousands of times every day in homes throughout the world. Elders feel honored; children feel connected. Generational continuity is established. The elders commit to the young; the young love the elders. Society lives.

Perhaps you have experience such a moment yourself. What draws you? Is it economic or survival advantage? Or is it something else?

When our hosts returned, they were beaming. Josette asked about the performance. "It was the usual," Grandma said with a laugh, "energy bouncing everywhere. That nonsense is the reason we give money to children's programs. No one should be deprived of that."

I politely asked what she meant by "that."

"That is their energy, their power, their sense of self. They are giving everything they have. They want to be with us. They care about us. This is the way they show it. I win in every way. I received the bounty of their gift and I get to affirm what is strong and meaningful in them. That establishes the ground for a long life together." She stopped, considered, appraising me. A minute passed during which she was obviously weighing different answers. "Look," she finally said, a slight forcefulness covering a deeply held sentiment, "the bottom line is happiness. Happy people make for a great world."

They do. No question about it. And few things bring as much happiness as the simple innocence, joy, discovery, acceptance, and exuberance of BodyBeing children. Everyone agrees that the pursuit of happiness is an unalienable right, and here are BodyBeing children right in the middle of providing it.

BodyBeing children accept the elders in their lives. This simple acceptance has far-reaching consequences. It bonds children to parents.[135] For most families the bond happens effortlessly, as it naturally should. That bond bonds society. It is that critical first step in which there is complete acceptance that one's well-being is connected to the well-being of others. Crucial for rightful place, the bond develops throughout the BodyBeing years and throughout life. It provides the basis for trust and is a sterling example of interconnectedness in every stage of life.

Parents bond to the children as well. The uncritical acceptance by the child is very difficult to refuse. In perfect tandem, parents feel fulfilled when they unconditionally accept the child. They have accepted a responsibility that includes the eternal freedom to love. This moment serves for many as the actualization of substantive values crucial for optimal well-being in ReasonableBeing. It is a dance step. Socially, it is a commitment to have a world where the child can live in well-being.

Generally, BodyBeing children are not appreciated for this gift, because elders assume they do not know what they are doing. Yet, using their language of sensation, they clearly communicate their need for loving touch. Their bodies relax and open when they are secure and warm. Their wonderful curiosity flourishes in sensory-rich environments. If there is deprivation, the child shows dissatisfaction. Careful observation reveals that the child is communicating continuously and in great detail though their body. Soon words appear and are used to the same effect. The bond established at birth, reinforced through infancy, is now spoken. They know how to bond and sense its great importance. They are letting us know that they know, if only we know how to receive the information.

What they do not understand, of course, is the larger social impact of their capacity for acceptance and bonding. For that matter, neither do reasonable people understand the social impact of their new system, the Internet. Simple, small steps lead to complex emergence that cannot be predicted throughout life, not just during BodyBeing.

It is chauvinistic to ignore the contribution of BodyBeing children because we don't understand the nature of their knowledge or their form of communication. Devaluation of a people because their values and symbol systems do not match those of the dominant culture is the same type of chauvinism that pervaded cultures for many years. It creates an "us" and a "them" and is the highway for condescension and imposition.

Exuberance, discovery, and curiosity bring happiness to the world. They also bring the joy of play, a social value that when restored to its natural place has the potential to bring work and life into balance. Throughout this book, I have debunked the fear that playing at life would be a threat to survival in that necessary and creative work would be neglected. The opposite argument could more easily be defended. Working without play equals excessive stress, which is a grave threat to individual and societal survival.

Finally, there is the innocence of the BodyBeing child. Anyone with half a heart sees that innocence and desires a better world. I am not speaking of a dewy-eyed romanticism that sees children as more pure or spiritual. Nor do I hold that children are born a blank slate, waiting and available for parents and society to write upon. As parents with more than one child know, children arrive with individual propensities and predispositions. Yet their innocence is a powerful invitation to participate. It opens the field for whatever influence the parent and society might have. It clearly states, Here I am, present and dependent. I am your child and the incarnation of society. How will you relate?

FeelingBeing–Crucible for Social Justice

After a recent talk I gave at an exclusive private school, Martha, the school psychologist, took a moment to express her appreciation. "I was so happy to hear you speak about FeelingBeing," she said. "I have been insisting that we give these children every opportunity to talk together about their social life and about their concerns for the way the school is run. Not everyone around here has agreed with me and I have been searching for a way to justify my position."

I am always delighted to meet a "natural," a person who knows children and is unwilling to let a lack of reasons get in the way of expressing that knowledge. Naturals are always delighted when they encounter Natural Learning Rhythms and especially seem to appreciate the description of FeelingBeing. Nevertheless, I had to make sure that Martha was not referring only to the girls, for I have seen many schools blindly reinforce the myth that girls are more gregarious and social than boys. That prejudice becomes a self-fulfilling prophecy that is preyed upon by advertisers and toy companies.

"Oh, no," Martha said, "we would never separate our children that way. There are children who talk more than others, but just about everyone is interested. And the results can be seen throughout the day. We have fewer problems with cliques than I have seen in other schools. Boys and girls play together on the playground. And the thing that I am most proud of is that our children will ask one another for help with their schoolwork."

"That should be sufficient to convince your colleagues of the value of your approach."

"Yes, but it is the ability of the children to talk through conflict that is the most convincing. Now, though, I have the developmental information I need as well." Martha then said something I have heard from naturals many times: "I was really never comfortable talking about children of this age as "tweens." It has a disrespectful tone. It feels great to give this stage a name and the consideration it deserves."

Extended family, school, and home communities are crown jewels of the social environment of FeelingBeing children. They explore interpersonal dynamics as they learn how to decipher their own feelings and the feelings of others. They embody society. Their most extraordinary gift is that they are creating society as they live. Adults have only to observe them carefully to see how social relationships form.

Martha intuited this and so insisted that her school give the children a large interpersonal field in which to grow and learn. Her observations lent meaningful direction to the way she mentored the children toward a just school community. Significantly, she saw her protection of their right to talk about their interpersonal concerns as important mentoring.

- An Early Lesson -

Twenty years ago, when I was running nature class, parents began to approach Josette and me for family consultations. One of the families presented us with a difficult problem, and I spent the better part of two days contemplating the situation. Friday arrived, and with it the class. During the hike through the forest, I hung back, pensive. The children felt my concern, and when we stopped for snack, they asked me about it. I thought about their capacity for fairness and decided to ask for help.

Disguising the identity of my clients, I told the children about the case. It involved a child who had been with a friend when the friend stole money from a girl in their class. Though the child had not himself stolen the money, he was blamed for not stopping his friend and then for not telling the teacher. Compounding the problem, his mother and father disagreed as to whether their son deserved to be reprimanded. She believed that stealing was wrong and that her son should at least have reported it if he couldn't stop it. The father admired his son's loyalty to his friend and didn't like the idea of one child tattling on another. The family was in disarray, and the school was going to render its judgment the next Monday.

The class considered the issue for some time. Twelve children were in attendance, and each position had its adherents. Then eleven-year-old Sally said that it wasn't fair that the boy didn't know whose rules to follow. Stephen, twelve, jumped in: "Yeah, you mean his parents or his teachers, right?" And then everyone in the class, including me, saw the problem at the same time. It was as if a flash of understanding passed through us. All at once, everyone had something to say and a consensus soon emerged. How could the boy have done differently? The values of his parents were not aligned with those of the school, or even with those of each other.

The problem was with the adults, not the boy. They couldn't agree. He was in a double bind. He had conflicting value systems as models. It wasn't fair to judge him by the school's standards when his parents were more important in his life.

On Monday, I shared this perspective with the parents. They were able to feel the conflict in their son and participate in the tension with him. They went to the school meeting united and firmly told the authorities that they would take the responsibility of ensuring that their son would not do it again.

I had learned a great lesson. Consult FeelingBeing children, especially those in trial and error and competency, for help in resolving interpersonal dilemmas.

As they embody the creation of social relationships, so FeelingBeing children reflect the society in which they live. They absorb the feelings of others and focus on the mentorship of the trusted elders in their life. Therefore, careful observation of FeelingBeing also yields direct information on the current social moment. Adults can use this information to restructure their own relationships toward a more just society.

FeelingBeing children have innate capacities for fairness, justice, and ethics. They engage social situations in order to develop these capacities. Their world view of social justice is developing in the context of interactions within the family, extended family, and community. This is the moment. The window for social justice is open. Here, as with BodyBeing, is the gift of acceptance and availability, only this time the field is social justice itself.

In this window exists the most obvious, simple, and direct opportunity for social justice. It is to treat the FeelingBeing child with social dignity and respect—to deliberately appreciate the social gift that is their being and to provide the field in which they can play and optimally develop their natural capacities. That field is not world politics or a particular social cause, but rather the everyday world of interpersonal dynamics.

Fairness pertains to the outcomes of a specific event. Martha insists that when the children converse, they center on a particular issue. The issue can change during the conversation as long as everyone agrees to the change. At some point, as Martha and I and others have seen many times in our fieldwork, the fairness of the situation will be considered. Rarely will the children debate the future consequences of a decision. While they will take relevant recent history into consideration, abstracting the events of early childhood is usually not seen as germane. Rather, their deliberations on fairness will be in the moment and situationally bound. So, for instance, when they were trying to decide who should be first for a horseback-riding lesson, a group of FeelingBeing children agreed that it should be a particular boy because he "had a hard time with his brother and needed to feel better."

Justice refers to the capacity to discern whether people are emotionally engaging with others appropriately and whether they are engaging with situations appropriately. Justice is the connection to the larger society. In this context, feelings about a social issue can be explored. For instance, walking through the different sections of a city and asking the children to record their perceptions in art or poetry allows them to feel the inequities of living in poverty without enlisting them in a cause or asking them to digest complex political issues that are beyond their capacities.

Ethics is the capacity to relate—to feel I-Thou. Ethical people intend well-being for the community. Ethics is defined as the "science of morals," and morals are those social customs that call forth quality of character. FeelingBeing children living in optimal well-being are nourished, not needy. They live in psychological abundance, in being, and not in deficit. Through reciprocal cooperation, they continually bring responsible ethics to the community and society. They cooperate in the spirit of trust, and trust is the cornerstone of character.

As always, self-creating depends on the relationship of the components of the system. When those relationships, or connections, occur in the medium of open communication, when they have the greatest opportunity to interact without negative outside influences, then the system lives optimally through regeneration, realization, and more complex self-organization.

Fairness, justice, and ethics are the components of social justice in FeelingBeing children. Open communication among them requires a conscience that is able to feel all their feelings without prejudice. As Carl Rogers said, a person with an open conscience (italics are mine)

> is able to experience all of his feelings, and is afraid of none of his feelings; he is his own sifter of evidence, but is open to evidence from all sources; he is completely engaged in the process of being and becoming himself, and *thus discovers that he is soundly and realistically social*; he lives completely in this moment, but learns that this is the soundest living for all times.[136]

In the "Values" section of chapter 5, "Spirituality," the importance of an open conscience was described. With support to feel all her feelings the child's conscience can assess their value and so activate the full spectrum of their natural ethical capacity. Trust and reciprocal cooperation result. Trust has nothing to do with perfection or infallibility, but with confidence that actions taken that feel wrong can be rectified without shame or blame. Repression is minimized and so shadow behaviors such as prejudice, pornography, and most forms of violence have no purchase.

Social justice cannot develop when concepts of right and wrong, and good and bad, are imposed upon conscience. A nonlinear system is reduced to a linear one. Equilibrium sets in. Social justice becomes rutted in attitudes that have less and less to do with regeneration, realization, and self-organization and more to do with defending the status quo. Development and evolution slow down. The rationalizations and justifications for injustice increase. As Gilligan points out, every violent act seems justified to the perpetrator. And he was writing only about the criminally violent. It is now clear that rationalizations and justifications are the currency of those without a fully functioning conscience, in whom ethics, justice, and fairness have been corrupted and have little to do with well-being for themselves or others.

Each family is its own culture, and each child develops to maximize well-being within that culture. Therefore, each FeelingBeing child will have his own unique expression of social justice. It will take the entire stage to develop, and every phase provides a social gift along the way. The naive magnification of social rules and customs during receptivity reveals hypocritical behaviors that often pass unnoticed by others. One mother, for instance, told me that she did not realize that she was always late to her in-laws' home for dinner but always insistent that the family arrive on time when they were visiting her parents until her nine-year-old pointed it out. The openness to inspiration in trial and error creates the field in which humans meet for the arts and for spiritual purposes. By competency, the FeelingBeing child has realized his unique appreciation of fairness, justice, and ethics as they have value in his family, school, and community. Ignoring this capacity leaves society bereft of the gift, and the child is confused, angry, and sometimes shamed for suggesting that he might have the just response when it opposes that of a person in authority.

Optimal well-being for FeelingBeing children promotes the actualization of social justice. This life stage is the leverage point for creating a just society. This is at once a cause for optimism and heartbreaking. So little awareness and resources are devoted to FeelingBeing; so many resources in every sphere of human endeavor are wasted because of this neglect. Can our society at least begin to appreciate the social contribution of FeelingBeing children? Can we allow them the moment to engage the feelings attendant to fairness, justice, and ethics? Can we resist subverting their development and eschew imposed morality? Can we accept their trust as a sacred gift and cherish it through relationship?

IdealBeing—Loyalty and Liberty

Typical of the black-and-white nature of the age for both children and parents, IdealBeing children are either richly rewarded for their societal contribution or vilified. If the contribution matches social norms and mores, there is reward; if it highlights the shadow, there is vilification. This confusion, which adds to the misperception of teenagers, stems from elders evaluating their contribution based on results rather than understanding the contribution itself.

The first right of an autonomous person is the right to choose. Few people cling to this right more stubbornly and more capriciously than the IdealBeing child in the phase of receptivity. The right to choose is defended against every assault, reasonable and otherwise. Every parent with a child in this phase knows this. How often have we stood by with a better way to do something, hearts hurting as we watch the child struggle yet completely unwilling to take our advice? Many parents find this difficult to bear, as I did until I realized that stepping into the right to choose is the first step on a long, perilous journey and one that is absolutely necessary for human society and evolution. I can think of no way to ease into it. You either take responsibility for choosing or you don't. Once you do, then the learning is in the playing and struggling with it. Underneath the choices themselves, the right to choose is affirmed time and again by IdealBeing children.

The right to choose is the basis of a democratic society. It is representation in taxation, checks and balances in civic government, and the definition of liberty itself. The right to choose translates easily into the right to vote. The question can only be asked, not answered: How would society change if children had adequate time to develop the right to choose through the meaning-making moment of IdealBeing before they were praised or ridiculed for those choices? Boundaries must be maintained, of course, but herding receptive IdealBeing children onto the path of narrowed choices through praise, blame, shame, or withholding the love and support they need undermines their ability to take the responsibility that naturally arises with the right to choose. That basic principle of liberty—the right to choose—becomes tainted with social preferences. This insult reverberates through society. People are believed to have the right to choose only if they belong to the dominant religion, or economic approach, or gender, or sexual orientation, or race.

Nourishment during the meaning-making moment brings the conviction to the IdealBeing child that she can do great things, that her actions do matter, and that she will have a significant and meaningful future. Trial and error begins, and with it comes a fierce loyalty to the chosen ideals. At the same time, an abrupt winnowing of ideals occurs; only a few become the focus. Loyalty to those ideals becomes an ideal in itself. Loyalty is a matter of honor and dignity.

The child knows that peers are necessary to accomplish the ideals, and so loyal peers take on added importance. Often people with tangential skills who rally the group around an ideal—such as cheerleaders, flag wavers and color bearers, equipment managers, and accomplished communicators—are as important as the highly skilled members. Disloyalty by any member to the team, gang, club, or peer group is often treated as treason with subsequent punishment and excommunication.

For many people, the loyalties imprinted during IdealBeing trial and error and competency last a lifetime. They either stand up to ReasonableBeing scrutiny or they are never examined. If a loyalty is left unexamined, the shadow of it eventually appears. For example, patriotism can turn into corrupt politics, friends may be betrayed, business acumen putrefies to greed, and religious zealots become autocratic.

Generally, in my experience, the degree to which a loyalty has been examined is reflected in social tolerance. Those loyalties that are scrutinized tend to be seen more playfully. When we find enjoyment and meaning in playing in the field of a loyalty, there is no need to impose it on others as the path to a perfect society.

Loyalty is a word that binds in so many ways. Derived from the Latin word for law, *loyal* originally meant faithfulness in carrying out legal obligations. When it is under the aegis of autonomy, loyalty is a commitment simultaneously to trust and to meaning: trust in that the chosen ideal is worthy; meaning in that the loyalty amplifies the value of that ideal. In the spirit of the secondary organizing principle of freedom, healthy IdealBeing children defend each person's right to be loyal to their ideals. Loyalty is a more complex expression of the bonding of BodyBeing and of the just and fair community of FeelingBeing.

Loyalty degenerates into blind allegiance or rebellion when the results of the loyalty become a currency to be traded for social acceptance. A good team player becomes the star and, seduced by adulation and other presents, forsakes the team for his own glory. A teen, loyal to the idea of an equal-opportunity America, raises his voice against injustice and is branded a rebel. In the first instance, the result fit the norms of society; in the second, it exposed the shadow. In both cases, well-being was undermined. The magnificent IdealBeing social contribution of loyalty, crucial for social continuity and social justice, has been reduced to the normative value of the ideal itself. The child then attaches to the ideal—the star in the first example and the rebel in the second—and becomes numb to the complexities of the world. Development is blocked; the initial conditions for ReasonableBeing are suboptimal. Doubt that naturally arises in contacting the complexities of the world decays into confusion. When confusion hits, there is a grasping for the ideal. Other loyalists are there to confirm that this is the way out of the confusion. College recruiters promise fame, sex, and money; gang leaders promise fame, sex, and money. The doubt is never grappled with. The ideal becomes the right way, the way of the true believer. Loyalty and ideal are wedded; inquiry becomes very difficult.

Examples of this abound in our society. How many athletes or sports franchise owners appreciate the history and social implications of the game they play and for which they have been so richly rewarded? How many rock stars follow through on working to resolve the social issues many of their songs decry? How many soldiers question the meaning and purpose of war, and of the war they are fighting? How many religionists question the meaning of spirituality and take into account that every culture has produced saints and sages before proselytizing that their religion is superior? Where is the loyalty of corporate executives to their employees, of sports team owners to their fans? How many polluters and arms traders understand that they are damaging themselves with their wasteful actions? How many environmentalists feel the fear of losing employment when they demand an end to clear-cutting?

Loyalty is a human capacity that develops in the service of ideals. Athletic coaches, clergy, and teachers have recounted story after story of the loyalty of teenagers to furthering the goals of their organization. During IdealBeing, loyalty is a prime support for the child who sees herself as capable yet still lacks the experience to accurately assess which ideals best fit her core nature and are viable in society. Loyalty provides the courage and perseverance to follow the chosen ones and find out their value.

A secondary importance of loyalty is that it provides an additional filter in connecting with and evaluating peers. IdealBeing children see one another as serving a common ideal and can select peers with greater care and perspective. Inquiry by a respectful adult that enables the child to link her chosen ideals, her newfound confidence in her personal power, and her peer choices can be one of the most effective ways to co-create boundaries with IdealBeing children.

By the competency phase, the IdealBeing child has solidified a sense of self and, with recognizable loyalty, has invested that self in the chosen ideal. Nested in this investment is the journey to the child's core nature. They have confidence, due to the meaning-making moment, that they can find value and purpose in life.

With the rapids of the perilous transition to autonomy having been successfully navigated, the IdealBeing child experiences a radically novel freedom to express their ideals. Respect and care appear in those whose ideal is interpersonal relationships and romance, willingness to practice long hours and increased ability to appreciate the subtleties of the game appear in the loyal athlete, and leaps in understanding appear in those IdealBeing children committed to intellectual pursuits. The responsibility that comes with this freedom is never seen as a dull obligation or a burden.[137]

The purity of expression by the competent IdealBeing child provides an unending source of creative, contemporary ideals that infuse society with keen vigor and vivacity. From the perspective of social justice, it does matter whether these ideals match social norms or arise from the shadow. The gang ideal, for example, contributes as much to social justice as the armed forces ideal. Both arise from the warrior response to injustice. Each calls forth powerful loyalty and membership responsibility. Each contains profound messages about the quality of social life. Each suggests ways that, were they related to in optimal well-being, would improve social life dramatically. It's as if these children continually scrub society clean of entrenched beliefs that would inhibit social self-organization into greater complexity.

ReasonableBeing—The Meaning of Social Justice

A just society supports each of its members to self-create—to produce and continuously regenerate and realize the network that produced them. The corollary is also true: A society whose members have the opportunity to self-create will act justly. It is the connections and relationships that determine the quality of those networks. As the organizing principle of ReasonableBeing is interconnectedness and the secondary organizing principle is systems creation, we can expect children in this life stage to make significant contributions to social justice. They do not disappoint.

After completing her journey, Joanna, introduced in the "Eruptions of Wisdom—Meaning-Making Moments" section of chapter 5, "Spirituality," experienced what she called "the shock of my life. I had always been aware of the injustice of prejudice and poverty, but I had never connected them to my life. I had some money and I wasn't prejudiced, or so I thought. Also, I felt so open, so connected that I thought I could handle anything life threw my way."

Joanna had come to visit on her way to accepting the position as program coordinator for a nonprofit organization dedicated to supporting Latino women. She had graduated from Stanford and was enrolled in an on-line masters program in nonprofit management offered by Indiana University. I had fixed her a cup of tea, and Josette had asked her the reasons for her career choice.

"Then I went to Mexico for the summer to help rebuild homes damaged by a tropical storm. As soon as I arrived, I sensed something was wrong." Joanna's eyes slid to her hands. She seemed far away. When she looked up, remembered pain held her fast. With a slight shake of her head, she refocused on us. "In my heart, I knew that I knew nothing about Mexicans or about poverty. I felt a sham. Did replacing the tin on the roof of their homes mean I was really helping, or really connected? And I saw my own prejudice. It wasn't that I thought Mexicans were lesser people but that I thought I knew something about their struggles. I couldn't even speak their language. I was trying to do good and was condescending enough to believe that when I did the people should be appreciative."

The openings that Joanna experienced during her earlier journey were a step toward interconnectedness. She could not have been so humble and sensitive were it not for the work she had done. Yet, like so many of us, Joanna believed that she would be able to meet any situation with her newfound awareness. It did resolve many of the issues that had plagued her. But she emerged into greater complexity, which included more complex challenges.

Joanna, with the ReasonableBeing perspective of connection with the previous stages, sensed she was out of place. Clear of conscience, she felt all her feelings without judging herself. Her identity as a nonprejudiced person crumbled. Genuine interconnectedness called for much more than fixing a roof and going home. Joanna had encountered a new awareness of suffering. Kindness wasn't enough; empathy wasn't enough. Joanna had to reach deeper.

"I was stunned but not devastated. I went to work on the roof while tolerating my irritation and ambiguity. I said little and tried to observe my Mexican hosts closely. On the surface they were generous and kind, but I sensed what I can only call a bewildered anger underneath. I'm sure none of the other volunteers noticed.

"By the third day, I understood. Poverty, hurricane, well-outfitted Americans, a grind-it-out past and a grind-it-out future, and yet an honest dignity and sense of gratitude for the help confounded our hosts. I am giving it a description, but it is a feeling and I doubt that they would agree with my description. It doesn't matter.

"I couldn't speak to it, and it frustrated me. What could I do? Superficially, things were going well, but I saw there wasn't a real connection. The project ended; nothing changed. I left with many thanks given and taken but a grave dissatisfaction. In a new way, I loved all the people involved. I really have no other word for it, though maybe compassion is as good. I don't mean anything like romantic love. It was a deep, committed caring. I was so touched. They all tried so hard and gave so much. But it wasn't enough. It wouldn't stand a more difficult test; it wouldn't endure. At once I wanted to help and I knew that I couldn't figure out what to do.

"As I reflect on my position it really is uncertain. No thought or concept or strategy has the power to connect in a really meaningful way. There has to be some deeper way to connect.

"So here I am. There is not much else to do. Life has thrown me towards the Latino community, but it could be towards anyone. I can't pretend that the connection lies in the action, such as fixing the roof. So off I go to try to understand by going deeper." Unexpectedly, Joanna giggled. Her face shined with happiness. "Who knows where it will lead?"

Joanna embodies many of the contributions that ReasonableBeing children living in well-being bring to society. She questions her actions and does not merely buy in to social approbation as sufficient justification for them. She wants to know for herself. She seeks meaning in the moment. If it is not present, she wants to know why and is willing to examine everything, including herself, to find out.

Labor has meaning for Joanna. It is not just a commodity. As a statement of who she is and what she holds dear, labor must meet the stringent criteria of substantive value. Without some aspect of love, truth, or beauty—without at least a hint of I-Thou—an alarm sounds. Why do this? What's missing? How can this action, this labor, tie in to meaning? Does this labor accord with who I am and the future I intend?

Tolerance plays through each of Joanna's choices. She acknowledges her confusion and tries to understand it, not push it away. She observes more acutely when awkwardness appears in her social interactions. In other words, tolerating the subtle yet pervasive dysfunction in the situation did not lead to withdrawal, but to deeper, unobtrusive penetration. Ambiguity could not force her out of her connection with the others. She even resisted the impulse to fix the problem when she understood its roots, as she saw that she had not made the necessary commitment to have sufficient standing in the community.

Finally, the tolerance gave way to ReasonableBeing wisdom. Joanna called it love or compassion. I prefer the word *compassion*, though not used according to the dictionary definition. Rather than referring only to the emotion attendant to the suffering of others, which is adequately covered by the pathos words—pity, sympathy, and empathy—spiritual phi-losophy couples the emotion with insight. Knowledge of the needs of the moment for optimal well-being emerges. Action follows quickly and sometimes coincidentally. Compassion is, as Joanna said, not founded in thought, though it may appear there. In Joanna's case, compassion meant exploring a more inclusive way of participating. She has no need for surety as to where this will lead. The energy for action is not the antic-ipated result, but rather the realization of the necessity.

What could be more natural? With a firm sense of rightful place, Joanna sensed something was amiss. With a keen ability to trust and an open conscience, she deciphered her own feelings and the feelings of those around her. Self-governing, Joanna chose her actions with respect for herself and her co-workers. Aware that interconnectedness is never absent, she summoned patience and tolerance. Enriched by the mean-ing-making moment, Joanna knew that there are modes of knowing beyond reasonableness. As Joanna is drawn to substantive values, com-passion naturally emerges.

At this point, choice disappears. All the anxieties around balancing the pros and cons of various options dissolve. The necessity of the moment is obvious and the work required is accepted without resistance, though it may be quite difficult. The quatrain of William Blake quoted earlier bears repeating:

> Love seeketh not Itself to please,
> Nor for Itself hath any care.
> But for another gives its ease,
> And builds a heaven in hell's despair.

Joanna emerged into her vocation, her calling. Only through partic-ipation can she know the depth and breadth of meaning her vocation will have for her. As she gigglingly reminded us, the open-endedness is a source of happiness, not tension. Having found her vocation, Joanna will be entrusted with more complex problems to solve. Her social contri-bution will touch many lives.

Summary—The Unalienable Right to Life, Liberty, and the Pursuit of Happiness

What can guarantee social justice? Concerned social justice theorists have tackled this question. Two of the best are Fritzjof Capra and Csikszentmihalyi. Capra believes that teaching children the principles of ecology, particularly sustainability, will lead to a just society. He does not specify how this teaching should take place. Csikszentmihalyi, holding that the experience of flow will lead to a just society, suggests that groups of people interested in maximizing flow band together in small cells to support one another. Children will be become socially just citizens if the whole person should be emphasized in education. A good way to start this, according to Csikszentmihalyi, is for grassroots movements to take over school districts and incorporate the work of Howard Gardner. A detailed assessment of the approaches of Capra and Csikszentmihalyi can be found in this endnote.[138]

Natural Learning Rhythms suggests a new approach: Include children in the social justice discourse. Celebrate their gifts to society. Parent and educate them with dignity so that their natural capacities for social justice have the right environment in which to flourish. Natural Learning Rhythms asks the question, what kind of society would result if the adults enjoy optimal well-being in their childhood?

While noble in attempt, legislating the protection of human rights cannot succeed until the human capacities for social justice are nourished. The wisdom to organize society to guarantee those rights resides in each of us throughout our lives, not just when we are adults. In fact, aspects of that wisdom are part of each life stage. That is the key to social justice. Children who experience social justice throughout their lives, within developmental capacities, will naturally become socially just adults.

The capacities for life, liberty, and the pursuit of happiness live in every human being, children included. BodyBeing children embody happiness, FeelingBeing children embody social justice, IdealBeing children embody liberty, and ReasonableBeing connects all of these qualities into social systems that include tolerance and meaning.

Every stage deepens connection, understanding, and appreciation of life. BodyBeing begins the social process with bonding, play, and innocence. FeelingBeing moves to a new level with ethics, justice, and fairness. Together, they establish the foundation of belongingness and interpersonal relationship, so necessary for social membership. IdealBeing builds on this by insisting on the right to choose and the importance of loyalty. This establishes individual liberty, a powerful addition to social membership. A citizen belongs and therefore enjoys the right of freedom of choice.

These are the qualities—bonding, play, innocence, ethics, fairness, justice, right to choose, and loyalty—that ReasonableBeing children get to play with. They add interconnectedness, tolerance, and meaning, and the realization dawns that life, liberty, and the pursuit of happiness must include all people. It is not whether a person participates, but how. Participation, in which each person's contribution has been recognized, appreciated, and engaged, becomes a societal norm. That appreciation of social justice becomes an initial condition for the adult transitioning out of ReasonableBeing.

Democracy is a cradle for the development of social justice, as it provides sufficient freedom to relate to children in optimal well-being. Undoubtedly, new forms of democracy will emerge as children who grow in well-being assume decision-making positions in society. For now, we can rejoice in the opportunity to dance with our children. Relationship with children that honors their social contributions creates optimal conditions for an eminently wise social system to naturally unfold.

Chapter Twelve	MISCONCEPTIONS

A sin of omission...can be like the rusty head of a hatchet buried in the heartwood of a tree—it eventually finds the teeth of a whirling saw blade.

—James Lee Burke

Here's a teaching story told in many cultures. I first heard it from a Tibetan man visiting my home and have subsequently found versions in the Hebrew, Persian and Native American traditions.

One dark night, two men were sitting in a quiet cottage in the country enjoying their evening tea. One of the men, tired from a day's labor, started to nod off. His friend rose to lock the door and thought he heard a rustling noise outside. After rousing his friend, they decided to investigate. Stepping outside into a night lit only by starlight, they saw a long, coiled *thing* lying in the tall grass.

They jumped back, looked at each other, and ran for their shovels. Taking no chances, they vigorously chopped at the thing with the shovels' sharp edges. It moved each time they struck and only when they had severed several pieces did they feel content and safe. Tired but satisfied, they retired for the night.

In the morning, they went out to investigate. They had successfully destroyed a long, thick rope.

Many people guess the end of the story and laugh it off. It even seems a bit trite—a commonplace occurrence not worth its formal standing as a teaching story. But this attitude overlooks an important point.

It was *always* a rope. It was *never* a snake. One can perhaps laugh it off when just a ruined rope is the result of a misconception. It is much harder when the result is the wounded consciousness and well-being of a child, and therefore of a family, a community, and a society.

Conception is a powerful word. It has two distinct etymological roots. The first, "to take in," refers to taking the seed into the womb, to engendering, to pregnancy. The second, "to abstract," refers to the mind's creative abilities. This, according to *The Oxford English Dictionary*, is the common current usage: "To form a mental representation or idea of; to form or have a conception or notion of; to think of, imagine." Conception is the origin of that which comes to life. It is the moment of creation of a new form.

Therefore, a misconception means that the view or belief is false or inaccurate from its beginning. And if it is false at its origin, it can never be true. The rope will never be a snake.

Moreover, the further the misconception gets from its origin, the more myths it needs to sustain it. For instance, with the misconception that the locus of development is in the child and not in the relationship, the fiction must be maintained that dysfunctional behavior is the child's problem. This plague leads to greater and greater isolation of the child and the adult. After a while, many believe that the isolation is good—that each person must solve their problems on their own, and that failure to do so is proof of unworthiness. Superiority myths take hold; the norm becomes that some people are more sacred than others. Superior people deserve superior rights. The myth that defending the superiority is a sacred duty takes hold. Anyone who fails to do so is a traitor. Sadly, the original misconception has contributed to the belief that the group should use valuable resources to defend its superiority rather than enjoying the well-being of relationship.

Misconceptions about Child Development

In order for a new paradigm to be legitimate, it must dissolve significant misconceptions and their seemingly intractable problems. Natural Learning Rhythms is an expression of the new paradigm of an ontological epistemology of children. Table 13-1 lists some of the misconceptions that have been revealed by Natural Learning Rhythms about children and families. Their dissolution has composed the body of this book. The left side of the table names the misconception; the right side states where the principal relevant information can be found. Chapter titles are in italics.

Table 13-1—Misconceptions About Child Development

Its a Misconception to	Chapter and Section
1. see the child as separate from the family, the community, or the unfolding wholeness of life.	Chapter 3, *Ontological Epistemology*; chapter 5, *Spirituality*, section, "Recognizing Wisdom"; this chapter, *misconceptions*, section, "The Misconception of Separation"
2. assume that the child sees herself as separate or immature.	Chapter 5, *Spirituality*, section, "Recognizing Wisdom"; this chapter, *Misconceptions*, section, "The Misconception of Separation"
3. hold expectations that are different than developmental capacities.	Chapter 8, *Intelligence and Academics*, section, "Assessing Academic Strengths and Weaknesses"; chapter 9, *The Dance*, section, "The End of Chauvinism"
4. view knowledge as a currency.	Chapter 3, *Ontological Epistemology*, section, "Genetic Epistemology"
5. assume pathology without first understanding the developmental moment and the well-being that may be coming forth.	Chapter 1, *Author's Voice*; chapter 2, *A Brief Overview of Natural Learning Rhythms*
6. believe that the child's personality is determined in the early years of life.	Chapter 5, *Spirituality*, section, "Values"
7. mistake struggle and frustration for dysfunction or proof of separation.	Chapter 5, *Spirituality*, section, "Eruptions of Wisdom—Meaning-Making Moments"
8. support verbal-linguistic and logical-mathematical intelligences more than any other intelligence.	Chapter 8, *Intelligence and Academics*, section, "Multiple Intelligences"
9. place the locus of development in the child and not in relationship.	Chapter 5, *Spirituality*, section, "Relationship"
10. connect boundaries only to prohibition.	Chapter 10, *Reunification*, section, "Creating and Maintaining Healthy Boundaries"
11. neglect the shadow in considering the motivations of teens.	Chapter 4, *Play*, section, "IdealBeing"
12. attempt to change dysfunctional behavior rather that reinvigorate well-being.	Chapter 10, *Reunification*, section, "A Brief Recapitulation of Optimal Well-Being"

Table 13-1–Misconceptions About Child Development, continued

It's a Misconception to	Chapter and Section
13. respond to dysfunction without including the whole family.	Chapter 10, *Reunification*, section, "Reunification"
14. ignore the meaning that children make of their lives.	Chapter 5, *Spirituality*, section, "Eruptions of Wisdom–Meaning-Making Moments"
15. devalue the importance of the little events, the day-to-day interactions, that are the bedrock of development.	Chapter 3, *Ontological Epistemology*
16. believe that, at any age, boys like to play only with boys and that girls like to play only with girls.	Chapter 5, *Spirituality*, section, "Nourishing FeelingBeing
17. attend to presumptions about whether humans are born good or bad, or have just dropped in from heaven or from hell.	This chapter, *Misconceptions*, section, "The Misconception of Separation"
18. think that sibling rivalry is natural.	Chapter 10, *Reunification*, section, "Reunification"; this chapter, *Misconceptions*, section, "Divorce and Blended Families"
19. countenance the chauvinism that adults bring upon their children.	Chapter 9, *The Dance*, section, "The End of Chauvinism"
20. behave as if behavior or mental map making describes a child's nature.	Chapter 3, *Ontological Epistemology*, section, "Genetic Epistemology"
21. anticipate growth and maturity to occur in steady progression.	Chapter 6, *Transitions*, section, "NonLinear Dynamics"; Chapter 10, *Reunification*, section, "At The Edge of Chaos"
22. disregard the child's awareness of death and his own mortality.	Chapter 5, *Spirituality*, section, "Nourishing FeelingBeing"
23. depend on rewards and punishments.	Chapter 4, *Play*, section, "Trust"
24. confuse a sensation with a feeling.	Chapter 4, *Play*, sections, "Play and BodyBeing," "Play and FeelingBeing"

Table 13-1–Misconceptions About Child Development, continued

It's a Misconception to	Chapter and Section
25. expose BodyBeing and FeelingBeing children to the troubles in the world.	Chapter 7, *Being Qualities*, section, "Freedom and Responsibility"
26. make ReasonableBeing children pay for higher education.	Chapter 7, *Being Qualities*, section, "Freedom and Responsibility"
27. fail to prioritize emotional intimacy as a core value for the family.	Chapter 11, *Social Justice*, section, "The Family"
28. de-emphasize the importance of children for the optimal well-being of the family and society.	Chapter 11, *Social Justice*, section, "Gifts of the Children"
29. expect developmentally consistent behavior during transitions.	Chapter 6, *Transitions*
30. assume that the dynamics of open systems-evolution and emergence-do not apply to child development.	Chapter 10, *Reunification*, section, "The Wave of Well-Being"
31. impose adult standards on the child's expression of spirituality.	Chapter 5, *Spirituality*, section, "Recognizing Wisdom"
32. undervalue play.	Chapter 4, *Play*
33. teach conscience, ethics, and morality didactically.	Chapter 5, *Spirituality*, section, "Recognizing Wisdom"
34. accept the role of police-person.	Chapter 5, *Spirituality*, section, "Recognizing Wisdom"

What use does understanding these misconceptions have in daily life with children? As is indicated by the chapter and section references in Table 13-1, this critical question has been answered throughout this book. Still, experience has shown that these misconceptions are deeply rooted in the mythology of our culture. They also have burrowed their way deep into our psyches; to dissolve them requires effort. Will my child suffer socially and academically if I insist on a curriculum that speaks to his unique blend of intelligences (#8)? Will my friends and relatives ridicule me if I coddle my six-and-a-half-year-old during a hesitancy (#21)? How should I react when friends and relatives violate his developmental moment (#3)?

These and many similar challenging questions face us daily when we are living a life dedicated to optimal well-being in children and families. In order to provide additional insight and fortification, additional applications to everyday situations in life with children are discussed in the following sections.

Media

The controversy over the effect of television on the young has been the subject of much research over the past decade. Those interested in the results can consult the American Academy of Pediatrics website or the numerous other sources available through a simple search on the Internet. I have found the work of Dr. Jane Healy to be particularly useful, but I shy away from endorsing any research-based position. It is simply too easy to skew the results by preselecting which categories are measured and by statistical sleight of hand. Also, every family is its own culture. While the way in which children are exposed to the media is important, unless it is terribly out of balance it will not determine whether well-being exists in the family. That depends on the nourishments. If the daily diet of developmental nourishments is close to the right mix for the child, then the family is dancing. Everyone grows together.

Over the years, Natural Learning Rhythms has provided many families with sufficient insight for them to make judicious decisions about the media. The best direction for each family can be discerned through appreciation of child development.

BodyBeing children mediate the world through sensation. If, for the moment, the content of a program is set aside, what are the sensory qualities of television? Rather than answer this question, I suggest that you sit in front of the television for two hours with your eyes closed and notice the effect it has on your body. This is a simple, reasonable experiment, valid because the sensory mode still lives in each of us.

Now, do the same experiment with your eyes open in front of early morning cartoons. Maintain your attention on the sensory input. At first, the colors and sounds dazzle. Do you notice the changes in the intensity of sound and color, and the speed at which the images change? What bodily reactions do you have?

BodyBeing children do not mediate the sensory input. They absorb it. They are attracted by pleasant sensations and repulsed by unpleasant ones. New sensations deserve exploration. Excitement is both new and pleasant. If the program has continual sensory excitement, then the child will keep watching. In addition, BodyBeing children learn through repetition. That is why Road Runner can keep running into the wall and not lose his audience. Excitement, repeat, excitement, anticipate, repeat is a rhythm to which BodyBeing children are attuned. Like any pleasure-seeking creature, they will return over and over to the source of excitement in hopes of another jolt. This behavior can easily turn to addiction, and older BodyBeing children who have watched too much television can be easily bored without constant sensory stimulation.

The content of the program matters little. *Sesame Street* is better than the news, but it still depends on violence and contrived excitement to entice the child. While Oscar the Grouch is of greater sensory appeal than Dan Rather, he nevertheless is not there in the flesh, and he is not engaged in body-centered relationships. The education content of *Sesame Street* is well intended, but it is still abstract for the child, whether the teacher is a bird or a person. At least the characters play with words, which is always appealing to BodyBeing children.

FeelingBeing children engage the content of an event. They feel the relationships of the people, connect to the feelings implicit in their concerns, and, by trial and error, they can decipher the social rules at play. Words are more than toys and place definers, as they were for BodyBeing. Words convey tones and hues. They demand personal involvement and the risks attendant to any relationship. Words and images paint a captivating gestalt, beckoning children to throw in their chips and relate to family, community, friends, and life.

Therefore, the content of the media is very important for FeelingBeing children. The story counts, and counts mightily. The media to which we expose children is nothing short of a statement of our mentoring. Allowing the children to watch a particular movie, story, or sporting event—and the accompanying commercials—endorses the relationships, ethics, and values of that show. It creates the boundary of

- Restricting Media for BodyBeing -

Elizabeth and Charles attended a family retreat with their two-year-old daughter, Julia, and their six-year-old son, Robert. They had heard of the Natural Learning Rhythms view on BodyBeing and the media at a lunchtime talk I delivered for Nike employees. At one of the parent forums, someone asked about the media and children. Elizabeth immediately asked to tell of her experience with her children. First, she described her and Charles's experiences with the TV-watching exercises described above.

"It started us thinking, and we began to observe our own sensations while watching adult programs after the children were in bed. One night, the late news came on with pictures of the results of terrorist activity. I became tense. My shoulders bunched, my jaw tightened, and I seemed to prepare for a fight. It was subtle, of course, but it was there. *Oh, no,* I thought. I have watched the news with the children in my lap. Sure, I was bouncing them on my knee, but there was no way I wasn't tensing at the same time. What was the sensory message in that?

"That was one thing, but there was another. After looking at Dr. Healy's work, I realized that excessive media might well be implicated in aggravating ADHD. At the time, several of Robert's teachers at school were telling us to get him tested. We resisted because we did not want a diagnosis strapped on our son and because we could not find any reliable long-term research on the drugs they were suggesting. While we thought about it, we decided to eliminate television and computers. We also regulated his diet more carefully and, as Natural Learning Rhythms implies, we increased his physical activity dramatically. Every morning, we did fun exercises together. If he had no friends to play with later in the afternoon, one of us would go bike riding with him.

"I am no expert on ADHD, nor would I dare give advice on our experience. But I can say this: The symptoms disappeared. We did not have to face that difficult choice. Something we did nipped it in the bud."

acceptable stories and contexts and invites the children to experiment with relationships in the same playing field as the one they have just witnessed.

The news and world events present a unique challenge. FeelingBeing children develop their values within the matrix of family, friends, and community. They do not have a global geopolitical perspective. Yet the news and the many references to it throughout television continually draw children to the tension surrounding events that are beyond their ken. While exposure can be minimized, it cannot be contained for most children. In addition, schools routinely include world events as part of the curriculum and use media to reinforce their teaching.

The best response is, as always, to nourish the organizing principle. This calls for feeling mentorship. Each parent can discover the best way to do this with their child. One caveat: Do not impose morality on the child. She still must discover her own ethics. A good example of this was given in the section "A Walk Through the Table" in chapter 7, "Being Qualities," in which I recommended to parents that they help the child look at her own anger as a way to understand the first Gulf war.

With the Internet and the increasing availability of images of sexuality in television, including and perhaps especially commercials, FeelingBeing children are bombarded with messages about gender objectification. Projections of desire and fantasy fill the airwaves; there is precious little about the complexity of relationship between males and females. Moreover, the Mattel myth—so named because it sells lots of products—that children want to play only with others of the same gender pervades the media. It does require an extra effort to provide FeelingBeing children with many opportunities to have mentored interactions with members of the other gender, and of varied ethnicities, to offset these stereotypes.

Bringing the child's feelings to the fore while they are engaging the media invigorates well-being. While you are watching a video together, use the "stop" button and take time out to discuss the characters. Try to guess what will happen. Take the time to relate a personal story from your life that is somehow connected to the story. Ask the child if they have an experience that matches that of one of the characters. The same approach can be taken in reading a story.

Live performances, if they are done well and are not too advanced for the age, can satisfy part of the need for stories. The range of feelings is experienced more directly. The collective experience of the audience becomes part of the event. Live performances are often more memorable than those that are watched on electronic media and can provide a touchstone for many conversations for quite some time.

IdealBeing children, with their intriguing task of learning to self-govern, use the media to explore and express identities. As they need a large, though not unlimited, field in which to do this, there really are few out-of-bounds media events. Each family is its own culture, and each must decide on boundaries. Severe limitation, however, will most likely result in rebellion or in repression and subsequent domination by a long shadow.

- IdealBeing, the Media, and Sex -

Many IdealBeing children fantasize about sex. With the ready availability of the entire spectrum of sexual activities available on the Internet, and to a lesser but still significant degree on television, IdealBeing children can use the media to make their fantasies explicit.

Also, IdealBeing children in the receptivity phase are often shy about sex and particularly shy about their fantasies. At the same time, they are most vulnerable to prurient imprints that match their hidden shadow desires. Also, given the general ignorance and neglect of FeelingBeing in American society, sharing their fantasies with trusted parents rarely occurs. Turning to private or peer group pornography, unfortunately, is often their response.

Each family must choose how to meet this challenge. Ignoring it is a choice, but it leaves the entire responsibility with the teen. As always, IdealBeing boundaries work best when they are co-created. Navigating this moment successfully will draw the family closer, but it may take several tries before that is accomplished. Nevertheless, it is well worth the effort. Healthy sexuality is of prime importance for optimal well-being throughout life.

The media provide one of the better opportunities for parents to appreciate the ideals of their teen. Which media do the teen choose? Why? Inquiry during a video can lead to open discussion of the values of the teen and society. Issues such as social justice, parenting, and the connection between freedom and responsibility naturally come up. Playing at predicting the ending of a movie often reveals interesting perspectives on character and plot. Everyone gets to play critic. There are no wrong comments, and lively debates need never descend into arguments.

Divorce and Blended Families

Divorce ruptures families and traumatizes children. No child expects divorce. In those few cases in which a teen agrees that divorce is the better choice, the hurt still pervades. A good analogy might be to a serious car crash. Everyone is shaken to the core. The wonderful resilience of humans suggests a decent recovery with the proper response.[139] This section provides a spectrum of responses for families to apply when they are suffering divorce, or when they are relating to other families and children who are going through a divorce or are recovering from one. It should be used in conjunction with all the information in chapter 10, "Reunification."

Many adults remarry after a divorce. The new, blended families can take on a dizzying array of configurations. As just one example, consider the blended Fried family, which for simplicity's sake I will call Family A. The Frieds then had two children in their new marriage. It was the second marriage for Sam and for his new wife, Marcie. She had two children from her previous marriage, Family B. Sam's first wife had a daughter from a previous liaison. Despite the difficulties in the marriage, Family B in this example, the father and his stepdaughter bonded. She came for extended stays with the new family. Marcie's former husband remarried, and his wife came with a child. They then gave birth to a new child. This is Family C. This means that ten children from four households will be interacting as siblings and cousins according to a dizzying array of visitation schedules.

In the old days, we used to chart the relationships among all the influential family members. I recall starting with a sheet of paper and successively moving to legal pads, easel pads, and white boards. At first, we used solid and dotted lines to indicate the affinities among the people. We then added color, loops, thick and thin lines, and finally several degrees of thickness with color coding for each degree. A fat red dotted red line had one meaning; a skinny red dotted line another. As you might guess, we do not chart anymore. We couldn't afford the stationary supplies.

Here are the variables that need to be considered in blending Family A, the new Fried family:

- Ages and stages of the children.
- Degree of friendliness/animosity between the parents and their exes
- Children's academic life, including intelligences and schools
- Children's unique challenges, such as disabilities or amount of time single-parented
- Various visitation schedules
- Divorce decrees as to financial and legal obligations (medical, education, religion, travel)
- Primary and secondary sibling relationships
- After-school activities
- Friends of the children who are outside the family
- Ability of the adults to honestly communicate with one another
- Changes in employment and income of each household

- Divorce May Be Necessary -

Some seminar participants have taken my unflinching recognition of the traumas attendant to divorce to imply that I condemn divorce. Actually, I do not. If the love is gone, then the love is gone. In private consultations, I do everything I can to see if there is something there that can be resurrected. If there is, then the effort to resurrect it is a valuable nourishment for the children. Staying connected in the midst of challenges serves children of all ages. If no genuine effort is possible, then well-being cannot flourish and, difficult as it is, divorce is the better choice.

Fortunately, there are simple, direct ways to optimal well-being in spite of this formidable list. You may well be able to infer them from the reading that you have already done. I will review them in the next section.

For Divorcing and for Blending Families

The following discussion is designed to awaken and nourish optimal well-being. It is not just to help families maintain the peace or meet social norms. Natural Learning Rhythms centers on the greatness inherent in each of us. While they are quite challenging, divorce and blending families can be an opportunity for intimacy, intelligence, and insight.

Family is the field in which we play to develop intimacy, and it is the crucible for learning relationship. All too often, parents forget this while they are in the throes of a divorce or in the process of blending families. The relationships with the children become reduced to logistics: Are the children safe? Did they get their meal? Did they get to school on time and with their homework? These are important concerns, but if they become the focus of the family at the expense of developing intimacy, then they become a detriment. In other words, the priority remains recognizing and responding to the whole child, not managing her behavior.

It is critical to take advantage of the learning opportunities of the moment. How do we stay connected during adversity? How can we participate in one another's suffering and joy without violating developmental guidelines? How can we make sure that we end up on the other side together?

The Alexandrian blow that slices through the Gordian knot of divorce and blending families is to place the well-being of the children first. This brings order to the unfolding dynamics. The well-being of the children is the one priority that all interested parties can agree on. And it satisfies the parents' principle concern, which was eloquently stated by a mother at a recent seminar: "I am only as happy as my unhappiest child."

I know this is hard to do. The emotional upheavals, the logistical tangles, the surprises from lawyers and exes, the confusion of the children as to what is a dad (or a mom, or a sibling), the varied responses from schools and extended family, and the unfamiliarity with the parenting style of the new spouse—as well as any combination of these—are demanding and often overwhelming.

Based on my experiences with families, I have found it to be invariably true that if the needs of the child are met, the family will flourish. If they are not, the family will falter. There is no other way to keep all the parts connected, stepfamilies included. Even with a commitment to placing the children first, two conditions must be met, or the antipathies of the adults will probably interfere. First, there has to be some agreement on the nature of well-being in children. Early on in our work, Josette and I recognized this as a valuable contribution of Natural Learning Rhythms. Second, there must be patience and dedication. It will take time and effort to appreciate well-being and to become familiar with the new circumstances that follow from divorce and blending families.

Classic Dilemmas

The children cannot understand the complexities of the parents' concerns during divorce or blending. Neither the animosity between the divorcing parents nor the romance between the new parents mitigates the suffering of the children. "That's fine for them," fourteen-year-old Nancy told me, referring to her father's remarriage in another state, "but it doesn't mean that I have my dad back."

No one can bring her dad back. Divorce is annihilation of the familiar and the secure. But someone can provide Nancy with sensitive respect by connecting to how her ideals have been impacted. When I did this, she, like many other IdealBeing children, spoke of her confusion about marriage and the viability of long-term relationships. She had the ideal that the future would bring that perfect, enduring love. She had few resources and less perspective on how to respond. Fortuitously, both sets of parents agreed to put the children first. Using inquiry, books, movies, and co-creating schedules, they helped Nancy gain new perspective on her own power and resourcefulness.

The effect on children of the traumas of divorce and blending families is complex and somewhat inscrutable. BodyBeing children will often show their reaction in their bodies or in some sort of sensation-based disruption. However, they tend to move on to new sensations fairly rapidly. All the same, unresolved underlying familial anxieties register. The careful observer might see tensions gradually developing in the child's body.

Then FeelingBeing arrives. The tension and pain often find expression in a fresh melancholy. The comment of the FeelingBeing child who told Josette that she didn't know there could be so many kinds of love might be recast to say that she didn't know there were so many kinds of sadness. In the vulnerability of FeelingBeing receptivity, the child may feel lonely or isolated, whereas a year earlier, during BodyBeing competency, she was happy and vibrant.

The following are examples of attempts to align the child's natural learning rhythms with the challenges of divorce and blending families. There are as many examples as there are families and children. Each family is its own culture; each will have its unique expression. Whatever that expression may be, the same principle holds: Place the child first by providing the developmental nourishments.

The family structure is changing radically. What's at stake for the children? What are some of the common pitfalls and critical challenges?

Threat poisons rightful place for BodyBeing children. Forgetting that absence of security is a threat and being overwhelmed by logistical demands, parents sometimes leave BodyBeing children with insensitive or impersonal caretakers. More often, parents recognize the threat to security of the suddenly missing parent or the suddenly appearing new "family." But many go too far in the other direction. They forget flexibility. Without flexibility, without time to move in BodyBeing time, there is little opportunity for the child to explore boundaries. Balancing security with flexibility so that the inexorable curiosity of BodyBeing children can play with boundaries is necessary for rightful place. When parents take the responsibility to make sure that BodyBeing children do not get lost in the craze of family restructuring, they enjoy the freedom to start a new life within the matrix of well-being.

Justice for FeelingBeing children refers to the quality of the relationships among people in the family, extended family, and community. That, along with their surrounding environment, is the FeelingBeing world. Within that, justice is global. Fairness, on the other hand, refers to a specific situation. It asks that the response of the moment feel right. Divorce and blending families call both fairness and justice to the fore. The questions become: Is this interaction (among any and all family members) just? Does it contribute to a world view that is just? Does this feel right to the child? Has fairness for all concerned been considered?

The dangers of degenerating into hypocrisy are great for divorcing parents. There is the triple-edged sword of the negative feelings about the former partner, the desolation of love lost (or the realization that it hadn't really been found), and the fear of loss of time with the children. It becomes all too easy to slip into badmouthing the ex and to overly criticizing the stepparent despite the stated intent of support. FeelingBeing and IdealBeing children are hypersensitive to the new relationships, especially the one between their biological parents, who, for the first time in the lives of the children, are not living together.

Parents who are often overwhelmed need to get outside help. If the overwhelm remains bottled up, it can detonate in the family. An explosion is not secure, flexible, fair, just, or respectful. A taut wariness in the children often results. Also, if outside help is needed and is not sought, parents may "adultify" the child. They tell the child of problems beyond his capacities and start to depend on the child for understanding. This leads to more tension. The child, out of his depth, takes on the additional burden of trying to help, or he retreats and loses faith in the parent's stability.

If the overwhelm centers on relationships with the children, then an experiential learning program—founded on well-being and including the whole family—is much more valuable than therapy with the child. In a family retreat, for example, there is no social stigma and no family member is singled out as a problem. Strengths are celebrated. Family dynamics come to the fore in the context of activities. When friction flares, there is adequate time and space to work through it. Parents have time for reflection and experimentation with approaches that are designed to reinvigorate well-being. Facilitators are both male and female and include teen apprentices, who add vital feedback for parents and children. Many children have remarked at the end of a program that they were grateful they weren't "therapized," as my young friends contemptuously put it.

IdealBeing children need sensitive respect, wither if ridiculed, organize their world to optimize autonomy, and support processes that they co-create. The tightrope that must be walked, therefore, is inviting their participation without surrendering control. IdealBeing children do not have the perspective to determine their own visitation schedule, for instance, but they certainly deserve to understand the basis for it and to suggest different options. They have the right to demand time for peers and to pursue their ideals. Patrick, a sixteen-year-old, justifiably insisted that the visitation schedule accommodate his soccer tournaments. His parents justifiably insisted that time with each of them and with his siblings were important for all of them. Together, they reworked the summer schedule so that all needs could be accommodated.

In their newly awakening search for identity, many IdealBeing children will seek out an estranged parent. They are not seeking reasons for the separation but clues as to who they are. Some will want to spend additional time with the less familiar parent. Reorganization of physical custody may be useful at these times.

Sibling relations throughout divorce and blending are subtle. Sometimes, siblings mimic the parents' arguments in an attempt to resolve them. At other times, they fight as a show of support for a chosen parent. Most often, however, fights indicate that they are lacking developmental nourishment. Whatever the motivation, the contentiousness is a form of either alarm or resistance and calls for family reunification.

If at all possible, siblings should live together. This applies even to siblings who have trouble with one another. Staying connected during conflict is central to intimacy. It establishes rightful place, wins trust,

- The Problem of Conflicting Values -

Jennifer, who had been a single mom for two years and had just started a new family, asked the question that almost all parents in her situation ask: "What do I do when our family commits to placing the child first and my ex's does not?" Unfortunately for Jennifer, there is little she can do to influence the other family. If they shared similar values, they probably would not have divorced. She can ask and suggest that they agree on a parenting approach. Other than that, all that she can do is nourish optimal well-being when the children are with her.

Such conflicts erode the child's stability. It is not so much that the child has to integrate more than one value system, but rather the hostility of the mentors for one another and an implied allegiance to one or the other that cripples many children. It is a tragedy. Great fortitude is called for to ensure optimal well-being in these circumstances.

I do have some experience with families in Jennifer's dilemma reentering the flow. The key seems to be that the new siblings in the blended families receive proper developmental nourishment whenever possible. They then learn to respect one another and support one another when they are together. That family becomes a powerful matrix. There are fits and starts and bumps in the road, but with the whole new family on the same page, the children thrive and steadily integrate well-being as their natural way of living.

increases confidence for autonomy, and maintains interconnectedness. Also, in the throes of difficulties, children often establish compensatory bonds. They nourish one another, to the best of their ability, to make up for the inevitable oversights intrinsic to the turmoil of radical changes in family structure.

The natural differences in the attention to rules during play between BodyBeing and FeelingBeing children can be a surprising source of conflict in blending families. While children from these stages often enjoy playing together, their interactions can quickly deteriorate when the BodyBeing child ignores the rules. Care should be taken not to expect them to entertain each other for long periods of time or too often.

Similar protection should be offered when the mix is IdealBeing children with FeelingBeing children. The teen's need to self-govern leaves them without empathy for the cooperative, family-embedded, relationally sensitive nature of FeelingBeing. They view it with disdain, no doubt in part because that is exactly what they are casting off.

All of the above remarks are intended to help divorcing and blending families emerge into greater complexity. Therefore, all the dynamics of emergence are implied. Small changes can have large effects as the new complexity emerges. Care should be taken, if possible, with the way divorce and potential new partners are introduced. That care, as always, is to meet the children within their developmental capacities. Critical moments also exist during major shifts in family structure, such as when a parent moves out, a new relationship is consecrated, new siblings begin to live with one another, a new baby enters the family, or one of the children enters a transition between life stages.

On a lesser scale, each switch from one household to the other is a moment of new order for the child. These times are commonly difficult for children. Some strategies that might help include switching during daytime, especially with younger children, and ensuring that the child has all they need at the other house. Also, it helps to not linger during the switch. It is not a good time to work on other mutual concerns.

Gradually but inexorably, a family that is engaging well-being will move to the edge of chaos. A bifurcation will occur in which the opportunity to emerge into greater complexity appears. At this point, the family will probably hesitate. Security and trust will need to be reaffirmed. The family will enter the dip. It is a time when all that they have practiced is called upon.

Have you ever had a moment when everything seemed a bit brighter and clearer? When nothing seemed out of place? When colors were richer and sounds more distinct? It's not that anything out there has changed. A veil has dissolved—a veil that wasn't even recognized until it disappeared. It's as if the atmosphere has become more transparent.

That is emergence into the flow. In families, it appears as open communication, mutual support and enjoyment, the absence of adversaries, and the willingness to meet challenges—including those of divorce and blending families—together.

The Misconception of Separation

Children are life; life includes children. Children are family; family includes children. Children are society; society includes children. Children are conscious; consciousness includes children. It is impossible to describe one without the other. Children are interconnected always and everywhere. They live in the matrix of family, of life, of nature, and of Nature. To place them elsewhere, such as trapped in a psychology of separateness, is a misconception. There may have been compelling historical reasons for doing this, as the disciplines of cultural anthropology and depth psychology suggest. There may also have been compelling historical reasons for believing that the earth is flat, that the liver is the seat of intelligence, and that God intends that people of color should be slaves. The simple unadorned facts are that the earth is round, the brain is the seat of intelligence, and God intends for no person to be a slave. It is also a fact that our humanness is nothing less than interconnectedness with family, society, life, and consciousness.

Interconnectedness affirms human uniqueness. It is the network of processes—the relationships—that is the essential unit of life, that is the locus of self-creation. Each of us has a unique network, and each of us has unique relationships. There was no "you" before, and there will never be another "you." The same is true for each and every child.

Interconnectedness does not refer only to sharing the same family or the same planet. Relationship does not refer only to the experiences humans share. It runs much deeper than that.

Interconnectedness lives in human consciousness. When we care for a child, we are caring for consciousness itself, for human life to emerge into greater awareness. Caring for a child is a singular spiritual opportunity, in which the responsibility for self-creation and self-knowledge is present in the relationship. A profound ontological question arises: How do we see the being of the child? Is she separate and doomed to a life of suffering, or is she connected and emerging into richer, more complex relationships with self and her world? Are the struggles in her life proof of separation or opportunities for greater self-awareness? Does he love, have values, and make meaning in each life stage, or is he a bundle of confused, immature behaviors wandering through the world cut off and alone?

Sages and saints continually bring attention to the truth of interconnectedness in consciousness. From a simple insight such as the pattern that connects to the following couplet, the message is clear: Humans share in the great experiment of life and evolution, share in the knowledge of personal mortality, and share in the opportunity for love.

As the river gives itself to the sea,
What's inside of you lives inside of me.
    —Kabir, *The Kabir Book*, translated by Robert Bly

The misconception of children as separate is at the root of so much unnecessary suffering. When children are seen as fallen, sinful, or tainted with bad karma, then life becomes a chore to make up for the transgression. Attention goes to the perceived evil, and parenting and education are dedicated to rooting it out. For example, BodyBeing children exploring boundaries becomes a test of wills; IdealBeing children learning to self-govern are seen as pathetically naive and selfish. In education, schools exist to perpetuate the dominant cultural values, whether of the Puritanical allegiance to Christianity or the corporate allegiance to math and science. Otherwise, it is believed, the child may give in to cruelty or self-indulgence and not become a productive member of society. In this mindset, the child is there to be molded, and her contribution only counts when she becomes an adult.

And so condemned to a life of separation before they were born, the child becomes anxious. Will I do evil? Will I succeed? The child creates personas—masks that she hopes are passports to acceptability—to inclusion rather than separation. Lost is the opportunity to develop personality, her unique natural expression. Self-creation constrained by the suboptimal relationships of her network leads to degeneration rather then emergence. Childhood becomes a problem to be solved. Adulthood becomes a time of recovery from childhood or the continuation of the masked life that began with the misconception of separation.

The consequences of this misconception are ominous. Throughout his book *The Atman Project*, Wilber does not mention the importance and value of relationship. This is the central mistake of separatists' child development paradigms: They believe that development happens in the child and not in relationship. He seems to ignore Bateson's point that context provides definition. Two entities, the child and her-world-at-the-moment, come into existence together, in relationship. And the context that they create depends on their "double description." It is never one or the other. Moreover, the feedback between systems ensures that this double description dynamically evolves.

For Wilber, the nature of the ego changes to meet developmental challenges in response to the unseen guidance of Atman. Ego in itself is unreal, a "separate self-sense," full of suffering and dissolved only in transpersonal awareness. It is a cosmic sleight of hand, an illusion embedded to destroy illusion. As an illusion, the ego suffers until it dissolves at the moment of fulfilling its cosmic, superconscious purpose. And because the ego is seen as separate, the child is considered to be an individual on his or her own journey to awakening.

In Natural Learning Rhythms, a principle function of the ego is to serve as the locus of relationship. The changing nature of the ego calls forth more complex relationships. When the ego enjoys optimal well-being, when the relationships in the child's life nourish the organizing principle, then wisdom that is infused with spirituality—wisdom that allows all family members to actualize their potential—shines. This makes no comparison between a child's capacities and an adult's.. It simply states that there is an awareness that children can live and that this awareness fully and unconditionally deserves to be known as spiritual awareness.

Development is not an individual climbing towards spiritual heights, but the unfolding of being. Every instance of being is an instance of relationship. Does this ontological perspective place most of the previous work in development in a different context? Yes. Natural Learning Rhythms is a giant (and not the final or ultimate) step of a new paradigm. Either the previous work must be updated to include relationship and wisdom or it must be relegated to the status of the "special case," as Newtonian physics is when quantum mechanics and the theories of relativity are included.

As with every other capacity, spiritual capacities become more complex, more inclusive, as we age. This does not make them more spiritual. Consciousness, as Wilber and other spiritual philosophers know, is—to use the succinct phrase of metaphysician Ernest Holmes—"open at the top." Spirituality is about being, being who you are in the deepest way available.

The answer to separation is relationship. Let's listen to Martin Buber once more:

... the world of senses does not need to be laid aside as though it were illusory. There is no illusory world, there is only the world...Only the barrier of separation has to be destroyed. Further, no "going beyond sense experience" is necessary; for every experience, even the most spiritual, could yield us an It...For everything that has ever been devised and contrived in the time of the human spirit as precept, alleged preparation, practice, or meditation, has nothing to do with the primal, simple fact of the meeting (of I-Thou).[140]

One of the most startling statements about this meeting comes from the *Bhagavad Gita*. The *Gita* is a specific section of the epic poem, the *Mahabharata*, which tells the story of the great warrior Arjuna and his brothers. At the moment of the *Gita*, Arjuna must lead his army in an attempt to regain their kingdom, from which they had been exiled. Krishna, God incarnate, is Arjuna's charioteer. Just before the battle is to begin, Arjuna becomes desolate and despondent. He must fight against his teachers, friends, and family. He cannot see the point and turns to Krishna for advice. The rest of the *Gita* is Krishna's answer.

The first third of the *Gita* includes answers to Arjuna's questions about life, death, fear, and duty, along with specific practices that lead to self-knowledge. The second third describes profound mystical experiences. The last third tells how to live a life in which the spiritual truths can be actualized. Though short in length, the *Gita* is a comprehensive and compelling document to aid freedom. Then, at the very end, Krishna tells Arjuna:

Abandoning all supports take refuge in Me alone.
Fear not; I will liberate thee from all sins.

Arjuna is amazed. Krishna says that all Arjuna must do is love Him completely. Arjuna cannot believe it. Krishna holds his ground. An incisive commentator on the *Gita*, Sri Krishna Prem (born Ronald Nixon, he was raised in England and spent his adult life in India) offers this perspective:

For this ultimate Being of His is not to be approached through philosophic knowledge; that leads to the experience of Him as undifferentiated Brahman; nor through yogik meditation; that leads to the experience of a Consciousness that dwells, luminous but yet impersonal, within the hearts of all. Rather, it is to be approached by a power which dwells in that most apparently limited and entangled of all things, the human personality as such...

It is only against our personal background, only because we stand all the time on a firm basis of personal feeling, that we are able to enjoy the adventure into impersonality. A world devoid of personality would be, not merely a poorer world, but an infinitely poorer world. Hidden in the very heart of our personal[ity] is the mystic Jewel...the innermost treasure of man, Sri Krishna's richest and innermost being, approachable alone through personal surrender and personal love.[141]

That is the ego that is loving and lovable. It is not an ego bound by developmental deprivation and therefore in defensive reaction. It is an ego enjoying optimal well-being—an ego participating without reserve in the pattern that connects. And that ego's love for spirit, for being, in relationship, does not participate in separation.

Little children are no closer to the "spirit world," to use Steiner's phrase, or to "hell realms," to use Wilber's phrase, than anyone else. They are children, here, as they are, available to know and to be known. It is an unnecessary imposition to see them through a speculative separatist lens. It denies relationship. Here is the child. See her as she is. It is all right here.

William Blake uttered the inspired aphorism, "Eternity is in love with the productions of time." There is no instance of existence when love is absent from life. That relationship is love, pure love, in every moment. That love lives as the two-at-once, as Bateson so clearly told us in the "Spirituality" chapter, not as the two-as-one; it is their natural and inevitable relationship. The illusion of separation is neither necessary nor natural, but only a searing ontological mistake.

Questions

The ultimate questions are now before us: Is our future best secured by awakened people living in optimal well-being or by technology? By children respected throughout their lives or by politics and other social institutions? By speaking the children's language or by insisting that they speak ours? By dancing or by rearing? Is freedom realized through recognizing the responsibility to cherish each child or through wars? Through spending on the education that each child needs or on bombs? Through relationship with children or through arguing about special interests?

The questions are ours. The responses will determine the quality of our world for an era.

I do see one very probable outcome when children grow in optimal well-being. Psychology will become the most important discipline of human inquiry, for it looks directly at human consciousness. Psychology will shed its vain and unnecessary pretense to be a science and unabashedly delve into the whole of human nature. Anthropology and brain science will be its principle supports. Human responsibility and freedom will emerge to allow a world in which all people play with compassion and wisdom.

Appendix A NATURAL LEARNING RHYTHMS AND THE EVOLUTION OF CONSCIOUSNESS

Man occupies the crest of the evolutionary wave. With him occurs the passage from an unconscious to a conscious evolution.

— Sri Aurobindo

The following question comes up in almost every program: What happens after ReasonableBeing? What are the dynamics, characteristics, and qualities of the next life stages? It is a reasonable question and reflects the sincerity and acumen of the questioner. All reasonable people, able to see the different ways that the child organized her world in previous stages, easily infer that there are more complex modes of knowing.

In the past, Josette and I have avoided the question for three reasons: First, the question does not pertain to the immediate concerns of children and families. Second, so many adults have to spend valuable time and energy reclaiming well-being and wisdom from a deficient childhood that attention to other possibilities seems a distraction. We therefore direct the questioners to the dance and to reunification. This leads directly to the third reason: The life stage after ReasonableBeing can be known only through participation.

Everyone has their own intimate knowledge of the four stages of childhood, and parents, teachers, and child-oriented professionals have an immediate and daily need to understand these stages as deeply as possible. Relationship with these stages is the key to well-being in the person, family, community, and society. Not everyone, however, shares similar experiences in adult development. The mystery deepens as the complexity unfolds. As more people enter or attain well-being in adulthood, there will be greater understanding about the organizing principle of its life stages.

There are intimations, however, and this essay plays with them. Some parents and child caregivers may find this extraneous and for that reason it is an appendix and not a chapter. While it will extend Natural Learning Rhythms to a wider perspective and attempt to peek a bit into possible futures, it is not necessary for appreciating and applying Natural Learning Rhythms to current relationships with children.

For those who wish to play in the field of consciousness evolution, the rules are simple. There can be no violation of the dynamics of emergence. Well-being is in bounds; pathology is out of bounds. This chapter is not concerned with the culture of deficit, though there is no denial of its existence or potency. If the culture moves down to less complexity because of the weight of the deficits, then, given the explosive resources currently available to humans, there isn't much of a future worth considering. If evolution moves to greater complexity, then appreciation of the being, as opposed to the performance, of children will be absolutely necessary. No other than a population who danced with well-being during childhood could steward such a world.

Consciousness and Culture

The word *culture* first referred to the cultivation of the land. By 1510, culture came to include cultivation of the intellect through education; by 1805, it referred to the intellectual side of civilization. Now it is defined as a gestalt. Culture is, according to *The Oxford English Dictionary*, "the sum of the language, customs, beliefs, and art considered characteristic of a particular group of people at a certain stage of its development or history." And as a gestalt, it is whole and unified and its evolution cannot be predicted from its individual elements, even when they are considered together.

Culture, then, emerges from the consciousness of people. It is the collective expression of consciousness of a given era. The manifestations of culture in social organization—the arts, language, and beliefs—point to the consciousness from which they originated. When we examine these manifestations carefully, we can draw inferences that indicate the underlying consciousness of the people. If we compare the cultures of societies of a given epoch, we can discern the evolution of consciousness as reflected in culture.

It is an exciting and admittedly hypothetical investigation. In undertaking it, we must bear in mind that consciousness is not an "it." A mystery lives in the heart of existence, and we play to participate, not to pretend we have come upon ultimate answers.

Amazingly, in the 1950s—before nonlinear dynamics and before the articulation of autopoiesis and emergence—two students of consciousness stepped forward to describe the evolution of consciousness. One, Pierre Teilhard de Chardin, was a Jesuit priest and paleontologist who sought to integrate science and religion into a unified view of the purpose and future of humanity. Personally castigated and his writings forbidden by the Church, de Chardin's view would eventually influence many young priests to bring science and evolution to their faith.

The other, Prussian-born Jean Gebser, wandered through Italy, France, and Spain studying philosophy, writing poetry, and meeting with some of the leading intellectuals, artists, and thinkers of the times. Eventually settling in Switzerland, he became friends with Carl Jung and taught for many years at Jung's institute. His meticulous research on culture informs his approach to the evolution of consciousness.

These two men set the stage for a host of cultural evolutionists, most notably Ken Wilber. Wilber's approach, called integral psychology, looks at the evolution of consciousness as the integration of four realms—social, physiological, cultural, and conceptual. He also makes the invaluable contribution of synthesizing the works of other students of the evolution of consciousness, such as the biologist Erich Jantsch, the philosopher Jurgen Habermas, and the sage Aurobindo.

De Chardin, Gebser, and Wilber each has a different starting place for his inquiry into consciousness evolution; each employs a different research methodology; each looks to culture for important clues; and each comes to remarkably similar conclusions. As we explore their work, the principles of the evolution of consciousness will become clear. I will then turn to Natural Learning Rhythms and show the relationship between it and evolutionary consciousness. In the process, the question of what stages come after ReasonableBeing will be considered.

Pierre Teilhard de Chardin

Paleontologists study extinct and fossil humans, animals, and plants in order to ascertain the history of organic life. In *The Phenomenon of*

Man, de Chardin carefully describes his scientific findings. De Chardin had an inquiring mind, and the record of life's origins stimulated important questions: What is the nature of matter? What is the difference between life and nonlife? In life, what is the difference between human and nonhuman? In humanity, are there any differences between humans of different eras? If so, what are legitimate ways to mark the differences? These questions suggest that de Chardin was interested in the nature of being. Paleontology and religion were the avenues he used to pursue his quest. It might be apt to describe him as an ontological paleontologist priest.

Two observations dominate de Chardin's approach: unity and increasing complexity. As he succinctly summarizes his understanding, "*Union differentiates*. In every organized whole, the parts perfect themselves and fulfill themselves."[142] Evolution is the overarching process of this differentiation.

> Is evolution a theory, a system or an hypotheses? It is much more: it is a general condition to which all theories, all hypotheses, all systems must bow and which they must satisfy henceforward, if they are to be thinkable and true. Evolution is a light illuminating all facts, a curve that all lines must follow.[143]

De Chardin carefully traces evolution, beginning with the inorganic world and ending in the mind of humans. In looking at crystals, for instance, he notices that they link themselves in a particular way. Over time, this concatenation provides the energy by which they self-organize to greater complexity. Amazingly, he put this idea forward at least a dozen years before Ilya Prigogine won the Nobel Prize for demonstrating molecular self-organization, a demonstration that laid the foundation for nonlinear dynamics, and showed that the forces of change, growth, and evolution were much deeper than Darwin's theory of natural selection suggested.[144]

To help the reader appreciate the full meaning of evolution, de Chardin points to "the within" of things. In this, de Chardin is in league with the great cosmologists, sages, saints, and philosophers who have recognized that some type of consciousness infuses all things. Here are the words of the renowned Indian sage Aurobindo, which, as Ken Wilber's research shows, also could have come from Alfred North Whitehead or Leibniz.

Life evolves out of Matter, Mind out of Life, because they are already involved there: Matter is a form of veiled Life, Life a form of veiled Mind.[145]

The within is the compressed, encoded consciousness that evolves through all forms to greater complexity. This idea raises that eternally worthwhile question: How is this known? Wilber, like all students of the evolution of consciousness, sees humans as the most complex form of evolved organism. Inquiring into how he could know the within of a cell or molecule, he realizes that cells and molecules are part of us. "That is, nothing in the preceding stages of evolution can be ultimately foreign to us since they are all, in various degrees and ways, in us, as part of our very being."[146]

De Chardin offers an elegant summation: "The *within, consciousness* and then *spontaneity*—three expressions for the same thing."[147] *Spontaneity* refers to complexity, self-organization, and emergence. We know the within because it is part of our being. This is the very definition of ontological epistemology—knowledge emerges in being, as being. Therefore, it seems we may refer to de Chardin, and the host of sages, saints, philosophers, cosmologists, evolutionary biologists, and people of this level of awareness as ontological epistemological paleontologist spiritual adepts. Or maybe, following the lead of Fourth Way teacher Gurdjieff—whose definition of conscience appears in the "Values" section of chapter 5, "Spirituality"—we should just call them *awake*.

These two forces—union, which is the within, and differentiation, which is evolution—operate unceasingly in all forms. This concept can easily be rephrased according to the definition of autopoiesis. Each entity, dynamically charged through the interaction of union and differentiation, produces and continuously regenerates and realizes the networks that produced them; it is self-making, self-creating.

Union and differentiation operate throughout evolution. This implies that autopoiesis applies to consciousness itself. All forms, never losing their unique wholeness, also live as one interconnected self-creating network in which the enfolded consciousness self-organizes to greater complexity.

According to de Chardin, humans are aware of the fundamental dynamic of union and differentiation because

In the last century and a half the most prodigious event, perhaps, ever recorded by history since the threshold of reflection has been taking place in our minds: the definitive access of consciousness to a *scale of new dimensions*; and in consequence the birth of an entirely renewed universe, without any change of line or feature by the simple transformation of its intimate substance...

What makes and classifies a "modern" man is having become capable of seeing in terms not of space and time alone, but also of durations, or—it comes to the same thing—of biological space-time; and above all having become incapable of seeing anything otherwise—anything—*not even himself.*

This last step brings us to the heart of the metamorphosis.[148]

De Chardin then quotes evolutionary biologist Julian Huxley: "Man is nothing else than evolution become conscious of itself."[149]

As consciousness reflects upon itself through the agency of humanity, harmony—reflected in the interconnected unity—becomes apparent. "The frontiers between pairs of opposites [such as natural and artificial or physical and moral] tend to vanish."[150] De Chardin provides three examples to demonstrate this harmony.

Unity of structure connects social phenomena and biology into a single culture...in the formation and dissemination of languages, in the development and specialization of new industries, in the formulation and propagation of philosophic and religious doctrines...

The social phenomenon is the culmination and not the attenuation of the biological phenomenon.[151]

Unity of mechanism refers to mutation as the driving force of change in both biological forms and in "the ramifications of institutions and ideas which interlace to form human society." De Chardin points out that curiosity and invention, natural characteristics of human consciousness, lead to mutations in all spheres of human endeavor, including self-perception and self-knowledge. He concludes that "the spirit of research and conquest is the permanent soul of evolution."[152]

Unity of movement, the third example, points to the rise and expansion of consciousness throughout evolution.

Man is not the centre of the universe as we once thought in our simplicity, but something much more wonderful—the arrow pointing the way to the final unification of the world in terms of life. Man alone constitutes the last-born, the freshest, the most complicated, the most subtle of all successive layers of life.[153]

De Chardin's name for this awakening consciousness is the *noosphere*. According to *The Oxford English Dictionary*, *nous* is from Greek philosophy and refers to mind, intellect, and intuitive apprehension. The noosphere is the realm of mind where the immensities of time and space are accepted as fact and thus allow insight into duration. The mind capable of this perspective, this scope, can see the whole of evolution and the immensity of the galaxies, intuitively apprehend their importance, appreciate unity and the attendant harmony, and become open to a more complex future.

> Really I can see no coherent, and therefore, scientific, way of grouping its immense succession of facts but as a gigantic psycho-biological operation, a sort of *mega-synthesis*, the "super-arrangement" to which all the thinking elements of the earth find themselves today individually and collectively subject.[154]

Humans who apprehend the mega-synthesis live in the new evolutionary form, the noosphere.

> We are faced with a harmonized collectivity of consciousness equivalent to a sort of super-consciousness. The idea is that of the earth not only becoming covered by myriads of grains of thought, but becoming enclosed in a single thinking so as to form, functionally, no more than a single vast grain of thought on the sidereal scale, the plurality of individual reflections grouping themselves together and reinforcing one another in the act of a single unanimous reflection.[155]

De Chardin acknowledges that the noosphere will seem ridiculous to the common person, "but to a mind become familiar with the fantastic dimensions of the universe it will, on the contrary seem quite natural, because it is simply proportionate with the astronomical immensities." The noosphere brings a world of social harmony and the unleashing of unused powers. In other words, to "a spirit of the earth."[156]

A spirit of the earth with all humanity organizing the world according to the noosphere is the encoded possible future of life on earth. But a mega-synthesis is a cosmological statement. De Chardin, to complete

380 | APPENDIX A

380 | APPENDIX A

his understanding, must move beyond humans and earth. He does not disappoint.

> Thus under the influence of these two factors—the essential immiscibility of consciousnesses, and the natural mechanism of unification—the only fashion in which we could correctly express the final state of a world undergoing psychical concentration would be as a system whose unity coincides in a paroxysm of harmonized complexity.[157] This paroxysm of harmonized complexity is the Omega point.
>
> By its structure Omega, in its ultimate principle, can only be a distinct Centre radiating at the core of a system of centres; a grouping in which personalization of the All and personalizations of the elements reach their maximum, simultaneously and without merging, under the influence of a supremely autonomous focus of union.[158]

There are four qualities to Omega: autonomy, actuality, irreversibility, and transcendence. Autonomy means that Omega is both the source and the culmination and therefore, while operating through evolution, it stands completely free of it. Actuality means that Omega exists and has always existed. Irreversibility means that evolution must culminate in Omega. There is no going back. And finally, transcendence states that Omega is not an "It" and cannot be defined.

> The medium in which Omega actualizes is love.
>
> Considered in its full biological reality, love—that is to say, the affinity of being with being—is not peculiar to man. It is a general property of all life and as such it embraces, in its varieties and degrees, all the forms successively adopted by organized matter.[159]
>
> Love is beyond conventional relationships.
>
> Love in all its subtleties is nothing more, and nothing less, than the more or less direct trace marked on the heart...by the psychical convergence of the universe upon itself.[160]

At the same time, the dynamics of romantic love reveal the universal power of love:

> At what moment do lovers come into the most complete possession of themselves if not when they say they are lost in each

other? In truth, does not love every instant achieve all around, in the couple or the team, the magic feat, the feat reputed to be contradictory, of "personalizing" by totalizing? And if that is what it can achieve daily on a small scale, why should it not repeat this one day on world-wide dimensions?[161]

De Chardin concludes that "A universal love is not only psychologically possible; it is the only compete and final way in which we are able to love."

The breadth of de Chardin's insight—from inorganic molecules to Omega—is breathtaking. Yet, questions arise. Are there any stumbling blocks? Can it really be that the future is encoded and all we have to do is sit back and wait for the noosphere and then take off toward Omega?

De Chardin realizes the enormity of participating in a world of duration, of billions of light-years, of nanoseconds, and of trillions of life forms evolving through billions of years. He realizes the difficulty in accepting the implied paradox that the only constant is change—that change is a substantive value which endures. Even his Catholic church, even his Jesuit order famed for its intellectual acumen, cannot abide his insights. De Chardin is not jumping from the observable material world to God as almost every religion does. He is showing the evolution of consciousness and that spiritual greatness is inherent in the process. Humanity is the hinge. Through reflective participation, humanity becomes the locus in which spirituality becomes aware of itself, becomes conscious. This is a long way from waiting for heaven and a savior. Awakened spiritual responsibility and freedom are the human birthright, ready to be actualized through entry into the noosphere and beyond.

In letting go of belief in conventional religion, letting go of the idea of finite space and time, letting go of the notion of a finished, stable universe, we run the risk of becoming unmoored, adrift, directionless, and weighted with extreme feelings of isolation. At the same time, having glimpsed the fact of durable time and space, of the inevitability of evolution, and of the increasing complexity of consciousness, de Chardin insists that there is no turning away. If we do, then we will have denied the very source of our energy and greatness.

Even on stocks of material energy, even under the spur of immediate fear or desire, without the taste for life, mankind would soon stop inventing and constructing for a work it knew to be doomed in advance. And, stricken at the very source of

382 | APPENDIX A

the impetus which sustains it, it would disintegrate from nausea or revolt and crumble into dust.

Having once known the taste of a universal and durable progress, we can never banish it from our minds any more than our intelligence can escape for the space-time perspective it once has glimpsed.[162]

If evolution has led us to this moment, then evolution has only greater consciousness in store for us. It is in us; we are the conscious agents of evolution. Acceptance of the reality of durable time and space, of the immensity of the universe, and the fact of consciousness express-ing itself though evolution brings the reality of the noosphere. This awakening is the answer to the threat of isolation that comes with the first realization of the vastness of the universe, a ReasonableBeing capac-ity.

One more obstacle, the fear of death, must be dissolved in order for us to enter the noosphere. Fear of death implies that life is finite and bounded, and it confuses individuality with personalization. Interestingly, de Chardin does not refer to the concept of the soul, but to "the essential immiscibility of consciousnesses, and the natural mecha-nism of unification" in order to dissolve this fear. Evolution depends on the sovereignty of each of its constituents. Grasses do not turn into flow-ers, though flowers may be a more complex life form. They stay grasses and as grasses participate wholly in the biosphere and in evolution. As for humans, each of us is included in the larger whole exactly because the consciousness within the forms is incapable of mixing. Humans do not dissolve in the All; we participate in it. That participation does not end. To suggest that it does denies Omega—denies the infinite space and time obvious in evolution, in reflective consciousness, and in conscious evolution.

Jean Gebser

Culture reflects the consciousness of the people of an era. Jean Gebser, using an array of cultural examples, describes the structures of human consciousness.

"The initial archaic [consciousness] structure is zero-dimensional..." It is a time of undifferentiated identification, in which humans moved through the world dreamless and silent. No known artifacts of this era could possibly exist as humans moved seamlessly as the world, not with the world. Gebser asserts the existence of archaic consciousness based on ancient myths that were created in a later era.[163] For instance, many creation myths point to a type of Garden of Eden of blissful nondifferentiation. Also, sages who have probed to the depths of their own consciousness have described archaic structures, often as deep dreamless sleep. Like most students of consciousness evolution, Gebser holds that all that humans have ever been is present and within us. Therefore, the reports of reliable consciousness explorers have great value, especially if similar reports come from people of different societies.

Etymologically, *perspective* means to inspect or look through. First applied to the science of optics, perspective was adopted by the visual arts to describe depth and distance. The Enlightenment thinkers expanded the definition to include the mental outlook over time. Gebser repeatedly uses all three connotations of perspective—inspection, depth, and outlook—to assess the consciousness during the successive cultural eras. Accordingly, the archaic consciousness, with no differentiation between being and nonbeing,[164] has no perspective; perspective never arises. Zero-dimensional implies that time and space do not enter consciousness—that there is no perspective.

The magic structure of consciousness begins with the movement from identity to unity, to being with the world. Magic is a one-dimensional existence in which consciousness is confined to points, parts, or details, "in which the part can and does stand for the whole." The world, confusingly accidental, "as we experience dream events in sleep," must now be confronted and mastered.

> Man replies to the forces streaming toward him with his own corresponding forces: he stands up to Nature. He tries to exorcise her, to guide her; he strives to be independent of her; then he begins to be conscious of his own will. Witchcraft and sorcery, totem and taboo, are the natural means by which he seeks to free himself from the transcendent power of nature, by which his soul strives to materialize within him and to become increasingly conscious of itself.[165]

Will comes forward as impulse and instinct, a powerful natural merging in which the magical person believes that her reality is the only possible reality. Every entity of the part—from the sun to the grass to the hunted animal to the person to the group—is taking the only action it can. There is very little responsibility or freedom. In this sense, the magical person is egoless.

Gebser calls the magic structure *preperspective*. Everything resolves to the part; there is no outside space and time. Everything outside the point, the single part, is unreal. There is no depth to consciousness.

Gebser's analysis of the cave paintings of many different societies, particularly the depiction of the hunting ritual, provides compelling evidence for his description of the magical person. It also highlights the startling fact that all magical representations of human faces have no mouth. The magical world is not verbal; it is merged, and Gebser attributes well-established parapsychological phenomena, such as telepathy, to magical consciousness. Accompanied by a comprehensive etymological discourse on certain critical terms such as "magic" and "forest," Gebser makes a compelling case for designating magical as a distinct era in human consciousness.[166]

He then attends to the next structure to consciousness.

> Just as the archaic structure was an expression of zero-dimensional identity and original wholeness, and the magic structure an expression of one-dimensional unity and man's merging with nature, so is the mythical structure the expression of two-dimensional polarity.
>
> While the archaic structure led to the unity of the magic structure by a loss of wholeness and identity, providing a gradually increasing awareness of man's individuation, the liberating struggle against nature in the magic structure brought about a disengagement from nature and an awareness of the external world. The mythical structure, in turn, leads to the emergent awareness of the internal world of the soul; its symbol is the circle, the age-old symbol for the soul. The individuated point of the magic structure is expanded into an encompassing ring on a two-dimensional surface. It encompasses, balances, and ties together all polarities, as the year, in the course of its perpetual polar cycle of summer and winter, turns back upon itself.[167]

This new polar world is simultaneously verbal and silent. Its muses are silent and invisible, but they work through humans to produce such articulate and nuanced works as *The Odyssey*. It is the world of opposites and cycles, the seen and unseen, the said and the unsaid—each polar opposite necessary for interpersonal values to emerge from the nonpersonal magical world. And with consciousness of the polarities and cycles comes consciousness of time.

The great cosmological images in the early myths are the soul's recollection of the world's origination. In later myths, the soul recalls the genesis of earth and man, reflecting the powers of light and darkness in the images of the gods. Slowly the timeless becomes temporal; there is a gradual transition from remotest timelessness to tangible periodicity. This ambivalent relation between time and timelessness, which defies our rational understanding, once again finds its expression in the polarity of the mythical structure, for both forms simultaneously exist and complement each other.[168]

For the first time, humans can self-reflect. I am here, the world is out there; cycles unfold independently of me; and so with this infinite world, there is an I—there is an emergent consciousness, which I call the *psyche*, the soul. Dream time counts, as does the unconscious. Myth vacillates between the polar opposites of the divine and the natural, and humans identify with each as they try to place themselves in the increasingly complex world.

While there is time in this two-dimensional world, there isn't a coherent realization of space. The mythical entities—the soul, for instance—are often located in the elements, particularly in water, which has the properties of vast mystery, rejuvenation, and reflection.[169] Any aspect of the psyche can be anywhere, and the personifications of the psyche—the mythical gods and demons—occupy whatever space allows them to fulfill their respective mythical roles. The things of the world, however, have a definite temporal quality. They occur in the cycles and rhythms of the natural world. This two-dimensionality, this plane of time free-floating in space and intersecting it according to the dictates of the psyche, is *preperspective*. Without fixed spatial locations, perspective cannot be ascertained.

According to Gebser, by 1500 the concretion of space did become normative in human consciousness. This development is reflected in the explosion of art that captured all the nuance of depth and distance. Gebser offers further support for this assertion through careful etymological and historical inquiry into the word *mental* and the kinds of activity called mental in different eras. While the birth of genuine perspective can be seen as far back as the myth of Athena and in cognate myths from around the world, magic, and primarily myth, had a much stronger grip on human consciousness. Since that time, however, perspective has been trying to break through. Gebser points out that every attempt to insist on the law, and the wrath that accompanies disobeying it, are attempts to bring thought and deliberation to the vacillating, irrational soul.

> What is fundamental here...is the first intimation of the emergence of directed or discursive thought. Where mythical thinking, to the extent that it could be called "thinking," was a shaping or designing of images in the imagination which took place within the confines of the [two dimensional] polar cycle, discursive thought is fundamentally different. It is no longer polar-related, enclosed in and reflecting polarity from which it gains its energy but rather directed toward objects and duality, creating and directing this duality, and drawing its energy from the individual ego.
>
> This process is an extraordinary event, which is literally earth-shaking; it bursts man's protective psychic circle and congruity with the psychic-naturalistic-cosmic-temporal world of polarity and enclosure. The ring is broken, and man steps out of the two dimensional surface into space, which he will attempt to master by his thinking. This is an unprecedented event, an event that fundamentally alters the world.[170]

Among his many examples, Gebser cites Western religion as an example of the arising of rational thought and accompanying perspective. Moses' God is wrathful and other; it is blasphemy to even say God's name, and mythic gods are heresy. Jesus accepts Moses' God completely. Moses and Jesus claim direct contact with God—Moses through the burning bush and his time on the mountain, Christ in his heart of hearts. There is no mythic intermediary. To escape the polarity of the soul, Moses gives the law; Christ not only accepts the law but also walks on water, or symbolically, on the soul. They have transcended myth. Their teachings call for discursive thought in order to discern the right and moral course of action, but their actions were (and in many instances, still are) interpreted according the prevailing magical and mythic structures. I might add that a similar dichotomy occurs in Buddhism. The first lines of the Dhammapada, the only book believed to actually have been authored, at least in part, by Buddha, begins with an appeal to the mind:

> Creatures from mind their character derive,
> Mind-marshaled are they and mind-made.[171]

Yet the religion that bears his name is replete with references to miracles, Buddha's various forms in his supposed reincarnations, and psychic personifications of gods and demons.

Judeo-Christian religion also brought the notion of redemption, a thinking construct that, as Gebser points out, allows the person to change the past. The wrong has been righted and is no longer a wrong. This concept frees the person to concentrate on the future, which is the self-centered desire of this mental construct. Direction and the right to choose the future are reclaimed from the gods. Human agency has radically increased.[172]

The use of wrath to insist on direction carries the long shadow of patriarchy, enforcement through dominance, and mistaking power and information for knowledge. It insists on the right and denies the left; it prefers persuasion but relies on intimidation. It is, in Gebser's word, one-sided. "The one-sidedness is to be found in the identification of rightness with directionality and judgment."[173]

Duality—in which the polar opposites are torn apart, abstracted, measured, and compared—dominates the mental realm. Anything can be pulled apart and opposed. The thesis has an antithesis. Direction is a choice, and the individual is present to make it. Add the ability to abstract, the crowning achievement of the mental realm, and a profound perspective on change and growth becomes obvious. The thesis and antithesis interact to form a synthesis. This synthesis becomes the new thesis; the fact and inevitability of evolution are simply and naturally present.

It is also the birth of philosophy, of the ability of an individual to hold thought constructions as supreme in deciphering the world. The responsibility for happiness and connection now falls directly to each person. It is not ascribed to the gods, or to God, but to human interpretation and understanding. Philosophy replaced myth just as myth replaced magical merging as the way to apprehend our place in the universe

Symbolically, the dot of magic transformed to the circle of myth. Now, the circle transforms to the triangle of rational thought and representation. Also, the characteristic attributes of magic—impulse and instinct—gave way to the mythic attribute of imagination. In the mental realm, imagination is supplanted by abstraction. Consciousness has metamorphosed from nonperspective to preperspective to perspective. It has self-organized to the greater complexity of organizing time and space, and then abstracting many of the laws implicit therein. It has come to locate itself in space and time and call itself *I*. Consciousness can now know itself as rational.

How, according to Gebser, do these new structures of consciousness come about?

> To explain this in rational terms we must suppose that the power of a possible manifestation itself creates an organ able to manifest this power...In other words, the components in us that are to enter our mental awareness also create the preconditions for their own effective realization.[174]

This remarkable passage, written matter-of-factly and without emphasis in the early 1950s, presages the discovery of autopoiesis by the biologists Maturana and Varela. We produce and continuously regenerate and realize the networks that produced us; we are self-making, self-creating.

Gebser takes a next step. The responsibility, and attendant freedom, for realizing our inherent possibilities resides in each of us. Chance and luck can only set the stage.

> But chance and destiny are merely the agencies which release the intensities in ourselves that are ready for manifestation. It is these intensities that cause the decisive events to "happen by chance" or "destine" these events for us. These intensities manage the chance and destiny so that the possibilities for their own manifestation occur. In a word, we are our chances and destiny.[175]

There is widespread agreement among evolutionists that structural change occurs in leaps and not as one smooth continuum. Mutations bring the possibility of the leap, and favorable initial conditions and subsequent nourishments allow its fruition. Gebser applies this approach to the structures of consciousness:

> A true process always occurs in quanta, that is, in leaps or, expressed in quasi-biological and not physical terms, in mutations. It occurs spontaneously, indeterminately, and, consequently, discontinuously. Moreover, we become aware of such presumably invisible processes only when they have reached sufficient strength to manifest themselves on the basis of the cumulative momentum.[176]

There is no "why" for mutations. They arise and if, to use Gebser's term, they are intensified, then they prevail. As they are intensified, they become "components in us which enter our mental awareness and create the preconditions for their own effective realization." A latent possibility, inherent in our being, is now actualized.

With the new actualization—the new complexity—comes new possibilities. We integrate more of who we are and more of the world simultaneously. In other words, we inhabit more niches in both the environment and in consciousness. Six hundred years ago, most Westerners believed that life had existed for only six thousand years, that the stars were nearby, and that humans were the center of the universe. Medicine resolved to bloodletting and herbs, with corpse dissection a capital offense. Public communication was conducted through edict, gossip, and church books. Under the ocean and outer space were the stuff of myth and imagination, not locations for exploration. Art was two-dimensional, not three-dimensional. Philosophy, and especially spiritual philosophy, had greater insight cosmologically, but in practical terms it had very little to say about the specific dynamics of life on earth. Agency did not belong to each of us. Humans were controlled by the nature, by the gods (fate), or by an unapproachable God whose capriciousness had to be accepted on faith.

Six hundred years is a very, very short time for biological evolution, which measures physical structural change. The great gift that Gebser brings is that consciousness evolution is measured by the intensifications in time. Archaic consciousness had no notion of time. Magical consciousness is aware of time only at the point of contact. Time outside of that point does not exist. According to the hunter, the deer presents itself and existence is only that moment. There is no other time sense. Mythical time, finally, acknowledges the observable natural cycles. The rest of time and space is left to the imagination; the stars are nearby.

Each successive consciousness structure is an intensification of time. With perspective, with the awareness of space *and* time, humans are able to play with time—to bind it and expand it, to use time as a variable in their experiments. The time it takes to do something is mostly determined by human agency. How long, for instance, does it take to see and speak with someone in India? Only a few seconds if a videophone is used. How far away is the moon? What does it mean to live "clear across the country," a phrase that was common thirty years ago? For the evolution of consciousness, six hundred years ago is forever, or the blink of an eye.

Perspective has brought greater freedom in all material endeavors, has revealed more of the dynamics of life and consciousness, and has given us broader insight into our psyches and our place in life. Now that human agency has been established, the following questions naturally arise: Can we apply this new freedom in a responsible way for cultural evolution? Can we accept Gebser's dictum that we are our own chance and destiny?

Every structural change in consciousness has a weakness in which the mutation can take root. It is easy for us to look back and see the problems with magical and mythic structures. What is the weakness in the mental-rational-conceptual realm? And what mutation is afoot and how can intensification of that mutation occur? In short, according to Gebser, what is the next era in the evolution of consciousness?

The first problem resides in the nature of mutation.

Mutational periods are times of disturbance and even destruction. That fact that a given vessel—in this case man—is compelled or enabled to realize an additional possibility of the world causes first of all a shake-up of the previously existing, habitual, vital-psychic-mental order. The resultant disorder, if it is not mastered on the strength of insight into the occurring mutation brings on chaos rather than a restructuration and novel constellation of reality.[177]

Therefore, understanding, preparation, commitment, and courage are required. No one can stand back and let it happen. In his personal comments to the reader at the beginning of Part Two of *The Ever-Present Origin*, Gebser clarifies the necessary disposition.

What is come?...As in any crisis there are two possible answers to the question of its outcome: demise or transition. It is my hope [that this book helps] solve such an alternative in a positive way. To be sure this requires co-operation; for this reason the book itself has been written in such a way as to require a certain participation of the reader. Anyone who takes to heart the solution to our problems, and who has not forgotten that we partake every moment of our lives in the originary powers of an ultimately spiritual nature, will be willing to participate in this task. [This] is addressed to those who do not wish to forfeit in their lives the humility and dignity that are only then granted to us when we recognize spiritual values...the strengths of origin, and our own strength in bringing this origin to effectivity are the factors that will decide our fate.[178]

Mutations are new, unknown. Clinging to the known—preferring the familiar, resisting the paradoxical truths that change is constant and that change is a substantive value—is a tenacious obstacle. Fear of death is the most common clinging. As Krishnamurti points out, we are less afraid of the unknown than of letting go of the known.

Adding to the difficulty is the requirement of participation. It would be challenging enough if we knew that our entire way of organizing the world was going to mutate and that we had to just endure it and learn to live with it. Gebser, though, insists that we have to choose it, or the outcome will be demise. Awareness of spiritual origination, appreciation of the evolution of consciousness, and courage to participate provide optimal conditions for success. "It is the coming-to-manifestation itself which is effectual."[179]

The challenges of mutation and participation without remembrance of spiritual origin can lead to the belief that humanity is isolated and, to use Gebser's word, lost. Interdependency on interpersonal, planetary, and cosmic scales is forgotten. A person thus "restricts his ties to his past, which is then lost in uncertainty. At the same time he also forfeits his future, the mirroring of his past. The loss is even greater, since the present, as he understands it, necessarily becomes irrelevant: a nothing, a nowhere, the impalpable point of severance and forlornness."[180] In short, lost people must rely on memory, concepts, quantification of time, and their own projections to organize their world. As Gebser says, lost people suffer from time anxiety.

Lost people can be found everywhere in our society. The shadow of the mental era informs their actions. Alienation in labor, lack of respect for life and the environment, belief in patriarchy for family and society, and adherence to the supremacy of the rational mind, with the attendant failure to appreciate and integrate all the realms of consciousness, provide the conditions for demise. Gebser only wishes to point this out, not dwell on it. However, the consequences are dire if the lost ones dominate.

It is an understandable error of our present-day rationality to think that the uncontrollable frenzy of events could be contained by power, agreements, compromise, reform, or revitalization. In such instances it is always assumed that man is himself the shaper of the future. And anyone who indulges in this mistaken anthropocentric belief, this illusion proceeding from rational hubris, should be resigned to "the end with terror." He would be correct in only one respect: an end is approaching, namely the end of his epoch. And since he is unable to free himself from the confines of his three-dimensional, conceptual world, this is tantamount to an "an absolute end."[181]

It is the integration of all previous structures of consciousness that will allow the new consciousness to emerge. Gebser calls it integral consciousness. This integration will result in the realization that time "represents an aspect of the element of intensity which constitutes the world." Gebser is referring to the within. "We are contrasting this in-tensive element with the ex-tensive spatial-material phenomena..."[182] In other words, time is a critical aspect of human consciousness. Intensifying it leads to greater complexity. Integration of those structures already present—archaic, magic, mythic, and rational—leads to time-freedom, which Gebser states, " is the conscious form of archaic, original pre-temporality." He then elucidates how time-freedom happens and the inevitable positive outcome:

Time-freedom can be realized by achieving each of the previous time-mutations from archaic pre-temporality. By granting to magic timelessness, mythical temporicity, and mental-conceptual temporality their integral efficacy, and by living them in accord with the strength of their degree of consciousness, we are able to bring about this realization...

As such, time-freedom is not only the quintessence of time, but also the conscious quintessence of all previous temporal forms. Their becoming conscious...is also a liberation from all of these time forms; everything becomes present, concrete, and thus integrable present. But this implies that preconscious origin becomes conscious present; that each and every time-form basic to the one-, two-, and three-dimensional worlds is integrated and thereby superseded.

This also means that we perceive the world in its foundations and are not exclusively bound to its vital, experiential, and conceptual forms. To adduce just one example: we no longer observe the world only from a fixed perspective, but perceive it as aperspectival and unfixed...Anyone able to realize and thus concretize the three previously basic temporal forms already consciously stands in four-dimensionality...

In—or rather through—time-freedom, the foundations or bases become transparent right down to the original and pre-conscious pre-temporality. Time-freedom, in its conscious form, is the fourth dimension; it is an integrative dimension.

A as prefix means *not*. The *aperspectival* consciousness structure does not rely on perspective for knowledge. It has all the time qualities of the previous consciousness structures available to it. It is, as Gebser says, the conscious form of pre-temporality. To clarify this point, Gebser states that origin does not mean beginning and the present does not equal the moment. Likewise, the sum of preperspective, unperspective, and perspective does not equal aperspective. Origin refers to spiritual awareness and is ever present. It is never not-here; it is never not-there. Presence does not reduce to a discrete moment in time, but, by virtue of its connection to origin, includes all the times of the structures of consciousness. Aperspective is a mutation and cannot be known or predicted by previous structures.[183]

The aperspectival consciousness structure adds a new, transparent dimension to truth. The whole is now realized, as it is, and not as just a representation or conception. The integration of the all the structures of consciousness awakens wholeness. Separation has ended.

Gebser finds considerable evidence for the existence of aperspectival consciousness. In Picasso's paintings, for instance, "time itself has been incorporated...When we look at this drawing, we take in at one glance the whole man, perceiving not just one possible aspect, but simultaneously the front, the side and the back. In sum all of the various aspects are present at once."[184] Similar, careful analysis of other visual artists, architects, musicians, and poets support the same point.

Science provides substantial additional evidence. Here is physicist Amit Goswami on some of the paradoxical findings from quantum mechanics which imply aperspectival consciousness:

- A quantum object (for example, an electron) can be at more than one place at the same time (the wave property).
- A quantum object cannot be said to manifest in ordinary space-time reality until we observe it as a particle (collapse of the wave).
- A quantum object ceases to exist here and simultaneously appears in existence over there; we cannot say it went through the intervening space (the quantum jump).

- A manifestation of one quantum object, caused by our observation, simultaneously influences its correlated twin object—no
  matter haw far apart they are (quantum action at a distance).[185]

Einstein found the equation e = mc², which revealed space and time
as a single intensification, space-time. It also allowed humans to unleash
atomic energy, certainly a quantum leap up from fossil fuels.

Gebser provides more examples from biology and other sciences. He
then turns to psychology and makes his most telling points from the
work of his colleague Carl Jung. Freud opened the door by acknowledging the importance of dreams and brought respectability to magical and
mythic information. Jung included dreams and went much further. His
work on the symbols in dreams connected myth to philosophy. His
description of archetypes and of the collective unconscious reestablished
the interdependence between terrestrial and cosmic life. The connections are intensive and present in the human psyche.[186]

Gebser moves to philosophy, noting Henri Bergson's insight that
"time is an invention or it is nothing at all." Interestingly, he also points
out that Edmund Husserl, the father of the highly influential school of
phenomenology, emphasized that transparency is revealed in the relationships among phenomena, rather than the phenomena themselves.[187] Gebser then mines the fields of jurisprudence, sociology, and
economics to demonstrate the existence and influence of aperspectival
consciousness.

While the avant-garde in all of these disciplines has begun to establish the aperspectival structure, it "will not be fully valid so as long as it is
not lived in daily life."[188] Echoing Gilligan, he believes that revaluing
labor as an expression of oneself and not as a commodity is one way to
actualize time-freedom. It can also be known by placing care and compassion for the *whole* before individual desire. Contact is then made with
spiritual origin. Aperspectival labor and spirituality energize the positive
outcome in human beings who are aware of interdependence and naturally engage in transparent and lucid freedom, in the truth of wholeness,
as it is actualized in everyday life.

Ken Wilber

Ken Wilber agrees with many of the insights of de Chardin and
Gebser. There is a within of things; the intensification of the within
energizes mutations that result in quantum leaps in the structures of consciousness. These leaps are defined principally by changes in the order-

ing of time. While each new structure of consciousness is radically different from the one preceding it, taken as a whole, evolution is seen as nothing less than consciousness becoming aware of itself through the agency of life and, especially, through humanity. Our within includes consciousness of the spiritual, the ever-present origin, the way in which the whole becomes known.

Wilber names the new consciousness structure *vision-logic*. Though unique in some significant ways, some of which I will explore shortly, it shares many of the essential qualities of the noosphere and the aperspectival. A synthesis occurs in which the whole, taken as a whole, is revealed as an organizing principle. Neither earth nor the sun nor humans are the center of the universe. Arbitrary dualities, such as social versus biological (nature versus nurture), dissolve. Cultural and physical evolution interweave as the creative evolution of consciousness, of our ever-present origin, of the pattern that connects.

It is a powerful understanding backed up by extensive research. No one does a better job of synthesizing the extraordinary and compelling contributions of philosophers, sages, saints, biologists, anthropologists, psychologists, and physicists than Ken Wilber. If we add the artists as Gebser suggested, we have to extend the category of the awake to anyone who participates in their discipline as emergent and therefore unequivocally lives with the whole as their organizing principle. Yet it is utterly baffling that these three men do not see children as whole, or of perhaps greater importance, appreciate that children see themselves as whole. Despite Wilber's attempt to include children, which shall be examined shortly, none of them sees though the child's eyes or feels through the child's heart.

Wilber makes several important contributions that either have been neglected or have not been fully developed by others. In order to substantiate the interrelatedness—the essential participation—of all events, Wilber specifies a four-quadrant scheme that includes, in his word, "everything." He labels the quadrants "interior-social," "exterior-social," "interior-individual," and "exterior-individual." By cross-correlating the events in each quadrant, he lends exquisite detail to the evolution of consciousness. As just one small example, he dissects the magical structure of consciousness. The interior-social aspect is defined by all members of the group holding the same magical beliefs. The exterior-social groups that support this are tribes that live in villages. The interior-individual aspect is the appearance and development of concepts. The exterior-individual expression is the arrival of the complex neocortex. Simply put, the magical structure of consciousness manifest in all four quadrants. None are superfluous; each enhances the others. Readers wishing for greater detail should read his *A Brief History of Everything*.

Of great importance, Wilber includes child development in his appreciation of the evolution of consciousness. Using Piaget's model, he correlates the life stages of children with the structures of consciousness. For example, following the lead of Joseph Campbell, renowned for his work in bringing the meaning of myths to public awareness, Wilber holds that pre-operational and concrete operational thought are the basis of mythical consciousness. They arise together. The existence of one automatically implies the other.[189]

That Wilber has used Piaget's model, with its severe limitations as described in chapters 3 and 4 of this book, should not obscure the provocative questions he has raised: Does child development recapitulate consciousness development? Is there a one-to-one correlation between the life stages of children and the successive expressions of consciousness?

De Chardin sees the noosphere as the structure of consciousness that is the next link on the way to Omega, to the inevitable "paroxysm of harmonized complexity." There is a purpose, a telos, in evolution—to actualize Omega. Gebser does not take a stand on telos. It may or may not be operating. Certainly, though, there is evolution of consciousness and the arrival of the aperspectival structure of consciousness.

Wilber holds that telos is implicit in evolution.

> Limited contexts find resolution, not by anything that can be done on the same level, but only by transcending that level, by finding its deeper and wider context. Deeper and wider contexts exert a pull, a telos, on present limited contexts.
>
> And that is the truth common to all Omega-point theorists...They always point to ways beyond our preset perceptions, and assuming their contexts are genuine, they are right: we will never be happy until we, too, can live with a larger horizon...
>
> And a final Omega point? That would imply a final Whole, and there is no such [whole] anywhere in the manifest existence. But perhaps we can interpret it differently. Who knows, perhaps, telos...moves the entire Kosmos and God may indeed be an all-embracing chaotic attractor, acting, as Whitehead said, throughout the world by gentle persuasion toward love.[190]

Exhaustively examining spiritual traditions from around the world and yet writing with admirable restraint, Wilber suggests structures beyond vision-logic that, though the evidence is esoteric, nevertheless seem undeniable. He calls these realms the transpersonal, or the *theosphere*.

> The evidence, though still preliminary, strongly suggests that, at a minimum, there are four general stages of transpersonal development, each with at least two substages (and some with many more).[191]

Wilber describes these stages in chapters 12 and 13 of *A Brief History of Everything*. Even in these deeper structures, the same dynamics are at play.

> Each of these stages follows the same patterns and shows the same characteristics as all the other stages of consciousness evolution...each possesses a new and higher sense of self existing in a new and wider world of others, with new drives, new cognitions, new moral stance and so forth; each possesses a deep structure (basic defining pattern) that is culturally invariant but with surface structures (manifestations) that are culturally conditioned and molded.[192]

But whether we are considering vision-logic or the theosphere, it all begins with reasonableness, as Wilber points out when he considers the teachings of the great sages and saints.

> Their teachings, and their contemplative endeavors were (and are) transrational through and through. That is, although all of the contemplative traditions aim at going within and beyond reason, they all start with reason, start with the notion that truth is to be established by evidence, that truth is the result of experimental methods, that truth is to be tested in the laboratory of personal experience, that these truths are open to all those who wish to try the experiment and thus disclose for themselves the truth or falsity of the spiritual claims—and that dogmas or given beliefs are precisely what hinder the emergence of deeper trust and wider visions.
> Thus, each of these spiritual or transpersonal endeavors...claims that there exist higher domains of aware-

ness, embrace, love, identity, reality self, and truth. But these claims are not dogmatic; they are not believed in merely because an authority proclaimed them, or because sociocentric tradition hands them down, or because salvation depends upon being a "true believer." Rather, the claims about these higher domains are a conclusion based on hundreds of years of experimental introspection and communal verification. False claims are rejected on the basis of consensual evidence, and further evidence is used to adjust and fine-tune the experimental conclusions.

These spiritual endeavors, in other words, are purely scientific in any meaningful sense of the word, and the systematic presentations of these endeavors follow precisely those of any reconstructive science.[193]

It is remarkable that de Chardin, Gebser, and Wilber insist that the process starts with reasonableness and that the transition to the new, deeper consciousness structure has considerable challenges. I am not equating the noosphere with either the aperspectival or vision-logic. Wilber does not ascribe the depth to vision-logic that Gebser does to the aperspectival. Therefore, though Wilber's summary of the challenges describes the transition from vision-logic to the transpersonal, it is applicable to the shift to the aperspectival or to the noosphere.

As vision-logic adds up all the possibilities given to the mind's eye, it eventually reaches a dismal conclusion: personal life is a brief spark in the cosmic void. No matter how wonderful it all might be now, we are still going to die: dread...is the authentic response..., a dread that calls us back from self forgetting to self-presence, a dread that seizes not this or that part of me (body, or persona, or ego, or mind), but rather the totality of my being-in-the-world. When I authentically see my life, I see its ending, I see its death; and I see that my "other selves," my ego, my personas were all sustained by inauthenticity, by an avoidance of the awareness of lonely death.

Wilber poses this question: "Is there any meaning in my life which will not be destroyed by the inevitable death awaiting me?" First, he describes how the question would never occur in magic or mythical consciousness. He then returns to the fundamental challenge.

No, that question arises from a self that knows too much, sees too much, feels too much. The consolations are gone; the skull will grin in at the banquet; it can no longer tranquilize itself with the trivial. From the depths, it cries to gods no longer there, searches for a meaning not yet disclosed, still to be incarnated. Its very agony is worth a trillion happy magics and million believing myths, and yet its only consolation is its relenting pain—a pain, a dread, an emptiness that feels beyond the comforts and distractions of the body, the personal, the ego, looks bravely into the fact of the Void, and can no longer explain away either the Mystery or the Terror.[194]

How would a child nourished in optimal well-being respond to the challenges of the transition from ReasonableBeing to the next consciousness structure? Neither de Chardin nor Gebser has anything to say about children and families. Wilber does not consider family and the way it might effect human development. He uses Piaget's scheme of cognitive development, a scheme that does not include the child's capacity for love, aesthetic, meaning, relationship, or awareness of death. Piaget notes only the growth in the child's information processing and her subsequent adaptations. There is no way a child viewed in such a limited, separatist way can be prepared for the quantum leaps in the structures of consciousness that are inherent in human development.

Natural Learning Rhythms begins to respond to the glaring omission of children and families from the cited discourses on the evolution of consciousness.

Disclaimer

I am a student of consciousness in children and only secondarily a student of the broader field of the evolution of consciousness. While I greatly admire the perspicacity of de Chardin, Gebser, Wilber, Aurobindo, and their peers, and am deeply impressed by their conclusions, I do not assert that the life stage after ReasonableBeing is the aperspectival, the noosphere, vision-logic, or the theosphere.

Natural Learning Rhythms is based primarily on fieldwork—on being with children in their everyday lives, and especially in their family life. Verification proceeds through observations of oneself and the children, and cross-correlation with the findings of skilled colleagues. Verification includes learning how to participate with children—to enter their flow—and directly experience their natural expressions. Most important, verification comes from the many families who have been able to successfully implement Natural Learning Rhythms in their homes. The same standards that Wilber suggests for "any reconstructive science" apply to Natural Learning Rhythms. It starts with reason. Validity arrives with tests and experimentation. Anyone can try the experiment. Its conclusions are the result of intense, honest inquiry and experience.

Therefore, Natural Learning Rhythms is not based on theories of the evolution of consciousness. It is not trying to mold itself to that paradigm. Natural Learning Rhythms stands directly on its value as a powerful and meaningful way to actualize optimal well-being in children and families, irrespective of any overarching theory.

Nevertheless, it fits very well. Similar synchronicities have occurred throughout my experience with Natural Learning Rhythms, though not with so extensive and profound a field as the evolution of consciousness. For instance, there is the correlation between rapprochement, discovered by the cognitive psychologist Margaret Mahler, and hesitancies. There is the correlation between the American Academy of Pediatrics calling for severe restriction of television for children below seven and the insistence of Natural Learning Rhythms that, irrespective of content, television is not a healthy sensation for BodyBeing children. There is the correlation between students of consciousness evolution pointing to more complex life stages and the characteristic of ReasonableBeing to realize and value modes of knowing beyond reasonableness.

Natural Learning Rhythms lends as much support to the field of the evolution of consciousness as it derives from it. Natural Learning Rhythms supplies the crucial component of the evolution of consciousness in children. Without that, all suppositions about what adults must do to access deeper structures beyond reasonableness are suspect. Is the obstacle to a deeper structure of consciousness really "dread" for a child free from the constant reinforcement of separatism? How does optimal well-being in ReasonableBeing affect the transition to the next stage? What can be known about an adult without appreciation of her childhood? What if everyone were dancing?

Beyond ReasonableBeing

The language of ReasonableBeing is dialogue, which literally means to "cut into meaning." ReasonableBeing complicates and ultimately supplants IdealBeing through intensification of the awareness of time. Incisive apprehension of systems is the ReasonableBeing child's modus operandi. For the healthy ReasonableBeing child, everything is subject to examination.

ReasonableBeing children question death. What is the meaning of death? How does it affect our choices in life? What does religion/spirituality/philosophy have to say? Is it valid? How does facing death influence values and ethics? What is the relationship of love to death? Any dialogue that ignores death is not reasonable.

Death instigates the search for substantive values. It brings to consciousness the one question, consistently at play, which pulverizes the rock to reveal the diamond: Does this engagement—whatever it is—allow participation in substantive values?

Here is a summary list of the ReasonableBeing characteristics just described:

- Meaning
- Awareness of the intensification of time
- Apprehension of systems
- Questioning death
- Substantive values

Every one of the qualities of being that are necessary to actualize the next higher stage—the stage after ReasonableBeing—is built into our long, playful childhood. This is our nature, our genius, our being.

ReasonableBeing children have a conscious perspective on the organizing principles of the previous developmental stages. If they have lived in well-being, then they know rightful place, trust, autonomy, and interconnectedness. They know where they belong and how to belong and so cannot get lost. They trust themselves and the universe. They have felt the immensity of death and also the immensity of inspiration and transcendence. Death is not dreadful but a call to relationship. They self-govern and have accepted challenges, struggles, and frustration as natural in life. They have the experience of their previous transitions and have the confidence the meet the demands of further transitions. They are interconnected; they are aware that relationships and not objects or things determine development. Change, though challenging, is a substantive value. Participating in the flow brings emergence into greater complexity. Though they realize they cannot predict the next stage, they know that, met with the proper nourishments, it will bring deeper belongingness, trust, autonomy, connection, and something new—something that will increase transparency, that will awaken even a deeper knowing. Isolation, a concern during the receptivity phase of ReasonableBeing, dissolves.

The rumblings of a new stage begin during the phase transition from trial and error to competency in the current stage. And in that last phase transition of childhood, between trial and error and competency in ReasonableBeing, the inclusive perspective of the vastness of the universe coupled with the complexity of its inherent systems encounters the certainty of change coupled with the knowledge of ever more complex modes of knowing. It is a clash of cosmic proportions. What lies out there? I mean really *out* there? And what is in here? I mean really *in* here?

Given this rumbling, can we discern any of the qualities of the new stage? It will probably be more inclusive and more transparent. Can you imagine trying to explain an electron microscope or the Hubble telescope to a person who believes that a god of lightning controls all things electronic? The transparency, the time intensification, would be too much. They would have but three choices: grow, concretize a myth, or babble incoherently. While the nature of the transparency of the new stage cannot be known without participation in the new stage, the trend toward transparency seems to be a fact of development.

So does the trend toward inclusion—toward seeing the relationships among all things as the basis for self-creation. If this is so, then the emphasis will turn toward nourishing being rather than judging performance. A greater sense of the whole person will emerge. Talents and intelligences will take their rightful place as expressions of being and lose their preeminence as the criteria of character. Actualization of the new stage will not depend on the magnified expression of a given talent. It will be the end of the tortured artist, the wounded healer, the mad scientist, and the martyred saint. We will know greater genuineness, greater authenticity, and greater wisdom.

But who will be prepared for such a life? They will be children who have been nourished, who know optimal well-being, who have not had separatism imposed upon them through mythical concepts like original sin and bad karma, and who therefore can actualize ReasonableBeing. It all starts with reasonableness. It all starts with those who have known themselves as whole and so will embrace the ever-emerging wholes that form the substance of their natural learning rhythms.

I do not know if child development recapitulates the evolution of consciousness. It is an intriguing idea.

For the moment, let's play with the notion as if it were true. BodyBeing's self-perception of "I am the center of the world; the world is an extension of my body" could certainly be seen as embodying the magic structure of consciousness. The child is embedded in the moment. The egocentricity of the stage should never be construed as egotism, for the child merges with her world. She and the world move identically.

FeelingBeing children love myth. The classic myth motif of facing death and returning a hero to the community aptly mirrors the awareness of personal mortality at the beginning of FeelingBeing and the opportunity for transcendence during the meaning-making moment. The arrival of their free-flowing imagination has the lack of fixed space that Gebser holds as central to the mythical, nonperspective consciousness structure. They are connected to the time sense of the cycles of nature.

IdealBeing seems to express a mix of the mythical and mental structures of consciousness. Time has certainly intensified; the child is sure there is a future in which he will have greater freedom and for which he will have to take greater responsibility. But his idealistic projections have mythical attributes. It is an age of honor and chivalry, of projected greatness and wells of despair. Time intensity has started, but the complexity of the mental structure arrives only with ReasonableBeing.

The key to the aperspectival structure of consciousness is time-freedom. Time-freedom is achieved through integration of all previous temporal forms. This integration is one of the great capacities of ReasonableBeing. Time-freedom is one of the natural outcomes of optimal well-being in ReasonableBeing.

And while we are playing, let us not forget the dance. Dancing adults who have had less than optimal parenting can become whole by nourishing their children in each life stage. In doing this, they integrate the time quality of each developmental stage. By dancing, they enter the aperspectival consciousness structure. Once they are healed, they live in optimal well-being. The adult can now play with the transcendence dance. Might this allow participation in the theosphere/noosphere that Wilber and de Chardin describe?

Appendix B BEHAVIOR
ASSESSMENT
TABLES

Table B-1–BodyBeing
Well-Being in Children up to 8 Years of Age

Check	Developed capacity of rightful place (belonging):
	Enthusiastic for life
	Receptive to loving touch
	Open innocence to people
	Able to communicate needs
	Able to explore with his/her senses
	Kind to peers
	Able to find safe personal space
	Kind to animals with a natural curiosity
	Towards-life attitude
	Openly curious when learning new skills
	Other observations:

Check	Developed sense of boundaries
	Pro-life explorations (never puts his/her own life in danger)
	Appropriately protective of body
	Aware of his/her contact with others in the environment
	Aware of contact with objects in the environment
	Able to enjoy nature
	Able to assess sensation values in everyday environment
	Willing to leave primary support person if the environment and people are safe
	Able to navigate the physical environment safely with his/her body
	Other observations:

Table B-2—FeelingBeing
Well-Being in Children 9 through 12 Years of Age

Check	Developed capacity of trust	Check	Developed capacity of reciprocal cooperation with others
	Respectful of the feelings of others		Able to feel good about the success of another
	Able to show caring for people and things		Able to function in groups and share leadership
	Able to enjoy nature and feel a sense of awe		Personal care for his/her body: Relaxed in safe situations
	Able to make new friends		Able to listen
	Able to trust his/her own feelings		Able to assist others when needed
	Able to assess and trust the feelings of others		Confident to try new things
	Able to approximate fairness for self and others		Able and willing to participate cooperatively
	Trusting of healthy mentors		Kind to others and sensitive to animals:
	Able to communicate their feelings		Curious about death as a natural part of life:
	Able to feel inspired		Other observations:
	Pro-life explorations (never puts his/her own life in danger)		
	Other observations:		

Table B-3—IdealBeing
Well-Being in Teens 13 through 18 Years of Age

Check	Developed capacity of autonomy
	Able to make responsible choices
	Able to define and enjoy personal space
	Able to leave childhood behind
	Able to express his/her ideals
	Able to co-create boundaries
	Understands the responsibilities that go along with freedom
	Able to make new friends
	Able to stay connected with family
	Good sense of humor (not at others' expense)
	Faith in his/her own abilities to navigate a variety of social environments
Other observations:	

Check	Developed capacities of identity construction, personal freedom, and personal power
	Able to play with symbols and abstractions
	Healthy personal care and hygiene
	Open, curious attitude toward others and new things
	Able to take responsibility and tell the truth
	Able to take constructive criticism and learn
	Kind toward others
	Respectful attitude toward objects and institutions
	Able to form identities and experiment with them (without over-identifying)
	Able to engage in discussion with adults, parents, and peers
	Able to access friendships with peers
	Confident to learn new things
Other observations:	

Table B-4–ReasonableBeing
Well-Being in Young Adults 19 through 23 Years of Age

Check	Developed capacities of interconnection, humor, and humility	Check	Developed reasonable capacity to act with intention, be incisive, commit in relationship, organize a relationship to systems creation
	A developed sense of self that can be questioned and modified		Able to openly explore ideology and drop what is not appropriate
	Interested in substantive values		Able to express an opinion and be open to hear the opinions of others
	Able to describe the meaning of his/her interests		Able to evaluate social situations
			Able to relate to life with initiative
	Comfortable to make appropriate boundaries (say no) if something does not feel appropriate		Accepting of change as a part of life
			Able to see the value of others or of differing opinions
	Able to openly communicate and engage another's point of view		Able to stand as an individual in social situations
	Able to engage new questions		Able to examine beliefs openly and allow others to have their own beliefs
	Able to laugh at oneself and find humor in life		Able to engage meaning in life with some depth
	Able to trust in the mystery of life		Able to handle personal power appropriately in a variety of social situations
	Able to function in a wide variety of social situations		Able to make a commitment to find meaning in life
	Able to consider connections and systems		Able to play with symbols and abstractions
	Other observations:		Other observations:

NOURISHMENT ASSESSMENT TABLES

Table C-1–BodyBeing

Describe how these nourishments are supplied (or not supplied) for your BodyBeing child. Also consider whether the nourishments are supplied in excess or deficiency.

(Key Nourishment) Loving touch People who are affectionate and lovingly touch with an attitude of acceptance.	
Security Safety and well-executed boundaries.	
Warmth Warmth of heart as well as warm, textured environments.	
Flexibility Time for the child to experience the world slowly and repetitively, if necessary, and to have varied environments to explore. It is an attitude as well as an action.	
Textured sensory learning tools Toys and tools that nourish sensation exploration with sensation-based learning.	

Table C-2–FeelingBeing

Describe how these nourishments are supplied (or not supplied) for your FeelingBeing child. Also consider whether the nourishments are supplied in excess or deficiency.

(Key Nourishment) **Feeling mentoring** Elders able to share feelings honestly, without an ulterior motive, speak the language of feelings, and remember that the child is always feeling.	
Fairness An opportunity to be with people and in situations free from favoritism.	
Justice Appropriateness in relationships between people and between people and their environment.	
Caring Exposure to people who express their caring in a way the child can understand.	
Honesty Exposure to people who are reliable and live without deception.	
Adventure Exposure to unusual, wild, exciting, and inspirational experiences.	
Adaptability Exposure to people who are able to change and adapt with a good attitude to a wide variety of relationships and situations.	

Table C-3–IdealBeing

Describe how these nourishments are supplied (or not supplied) for your IdealBeing child. Also consider whether the nourishments are supplied in excess or deficiency.

(Key Nourishment) Sensitive Respect Support the child's search for environments that support his or her core nature with respect for the identities that are "tried on" during this search.	
Challenges in the realm of success Co-create opportunities for social and academic challenges that fully engage the child's ideals. Provide support with a high chance of success; otherwise, insecurity can take hold and can "lock" the child into an identity.	
Adventure and active activities Provide opportunities for enough adventure and active activities in forms that match the child's individual disposition.	
Peer sensitivity Respect the child's choice of friends and provide exposure to a wide social mix that allows for exploration of identity construction.	
Personal space Respect the child's need for private and personal space. "Knock before entering."	
Opportunity to express ideals Values are the foundation of all ideals. Provide the child with environments that allow the child to identify with their own ideals as they change, thus stimulating the formation of new values.	
New identity exploration opportunities Honor the child's search for wider social circles. Provide environments and educational options that expose the child to an array of identities to try on and choose from.	

Table C-4–ReasonableBeing

Describe how these nourishments are supplied (or not supplied) for your ReasonableBeing child. Also consider whether the nourishments are supplied in excess or deficiency.

(Key Nourishment) Mature recognition *Recognition of commitment*—recognition of the individual's ability to commit through time *Recognition of equality*—any reasonable inquiry is honored as valid and equal to others.Recognition of achievements-recognition of the individual's ability to discover substantive values. *Recognition of recognition*—recognition of the individual's ability to self-observe and be responsible for the construction of meaning in life.	
Comparison Support for and engagement in the comparison of systems of thought to other systems of thought.	
Experimentation Co-creation of environments that allow for the examination of interests without condescension.	
Recapitulation Willingness to go over the individual's life, year by year, and review, summarize, and recapture life from a reasonable perspective.	
Investigation Incisive inquiry into thoughts or ideas.	
Discernment Support for the individual's ability to perceive and act with good judgment. Recognition of the individual's ability to distinguish himself or herself.	

BIBLIOGRAPHY

Airasian, P.W. (1991) *Classroom Assessment*. New York: McGraw Hill.

Ames, L.B.H., and Carol Chase. (1985) *Your Seven Year Old: Life in a Minor Key.* New York: Delacorte Press.

Ames, L.B.H., and Carol Chase. (1989) *Your Eight Year Old: Lively and Outgoing.* New York: Delacorte Press.

Assagioli, R. (1971) *Psychosynthesis*. New York: Penguin.

Aurobindo, S. (1960) *The Life Divine* (second edition, volume III). Pondicherry, India: Sri Aurobindo Ashram Press.

Aurobindo, S. (1962) *The Human Cycle, The Ideal of Human Unity, War and Self Determination* (volume IX). Pondicherry, India: Sri Aurobindo Ashram Press.

Aurobindo, S. (1976) *The Synthesis of Yoga* (sixth edition, third impression, 1984 edition). Pondicherry, India: Sri Aurobindo Ashram, Publication Department.

Barbour, J.B. (2000) *The End of Time: The Next Revolution in Physics*. Oxford; New York: Oxford University Press.

Bateson, G. (1972) *Steps to an Ecology of Mind: Collected Essays in Anthropology, Psychiatry, Evolution, and Epistemology*. San Francisco: Chandler Publishing Company

Bateson, G. (1979) *Mind and Nature: A Necessary Unity* (first edition). New York: Dutton.

Bateson, G., and M.C. Bateson. (1987) *Angels Fear: Towards an Epistemology of the Sacred*. New York: Macmillan.

Belenky, M.F. (1997) *Women's Ways of Knowing: The Development of Self, Voice, and Mind* (tenth anniversary edition). New York: Basic Books.

Bly, R. (1977) *The Kabir Book*. Boston: The Seventies Press.

Bohm, D. (1981) *Wholeness and the Implicate Order*. London; New York: Routledge & Kegan Paul.

Bohm, D. (1994) *Thought as a System*. London; New York: Routledge

Bohm, D., and J. Krishnamurti. (1985) *The Ending of Time*. San Francisco: Harper San Francisco.

Briggs, J., and F.D. Peat. (1989) *Turbulent Mirror: An Illustrated Guide to Chaos Theory and the Science of Wholeness* (first edition). New York: Harper & Row.

Brown, L.M., and C. Gilligan. (1992) *Meeting at the Crossroads: Women's Psychology and Girls' Development*. Cambridge, Massachusetts: Harvard University Press.

Brown, W.C. (11 July 2003). *Hormones of the Reproductive System: Females*. Retrieved August 2003, from *users.rcn.com/jkimball.ma.ultranet/BiologyPages /S/SexHormones.html*.

Buber, M. (1958) *I and Thou* (second edition). New York: Scribner.

Burman, E. (1994) *Deconstructing Developmental Psychology*. London and New York: Routledge.

Cadwell, L.B. (1997) *Bringing Reggio Emilia Home: An Innovative Approach to Early Childhood Education*. New York: Teachers College Press.

Cameron, A. (1986) *Daughters of Copper Woman*. Vancouver, British Columbia: Press Gang Publishers.

Capra, F. (1996) *The Web of Life: A New Scientific Understanding of Living Systems* (first Anchor Books edition). New York: Anchor Books.

Chamberlain, D. (1988) *Babies Remember Birth* (volume 2003). Los Angeles: Jeremy P. Tarcher, Inc.

Cotton, R. C. and M. Lillian. (1990) *Children's Death Concepts: Relationship to Cognitive Functioning, Age, Experience with Death, Fear of Death, and Hopelessness*. New York: Lawrence Erlbaum Associates.

Coveney, P., and R. Highfield. (1991) *The Arrow of Time: A Voyage through Science to Solve Time's Greatest Mystery* (first American edition). New York: Fawcett Columbine.

Csikszentmihalyi, M. (1988). *Optimal Experience: Psychological Studies of Flow in Consciousness*. Cambridge: Cambridge University Press.

Csikszentmihalyi, M. (1993) *The Evolving Self: A Psychology for the Third Millennium*. New York: Harper Perennial.

Del Prete, T. (1990) *Thomas Merton and the Education of the Whole Person*. Birmingham, Alabama: Religious Education Press.

Dewey, J. (1929) *Democracy and Education: An Introduction to the Philosophy of Education*. New York: The Macmillan Company.

Dreikurs, R., and V. Soltz. (1964). *Children: The Challenge* (first edition). New York: Duell, Sloan & Pearce.

Eckhart, M., and M. Fox. (1980) *Breakthrough: Meister Eckhart's Creation Spirituality, in New Translation*. Garden City, New York: Doubleday.

Edmunds, A.J. (1902) *Hymns of the Faith (Dhammapada)*. Chicago: Open Court.

Erikson, E.H., and S. Schlein. (1987. *A Way of Looking at Things: Selected Papers from 1930 to 1980* (first edition). New York: Norton.

Feifel, H. (1959) *The Meaning of Death*. New York: Blakiston Division, McGraw-Hill.

Forbes, S.H. (1999) *Holistic Education: An Analysis of Its Intellectual Precedents and Nature*. Unpublished. Submitted for the degree of Doctor of Philosophy, University of Oxford, Oxford.

Fowler, H.W. (1926) *A Dictionary of Modern English Usage*. Oxford, London: The Clarendon Press; H. Milford.

Froebel, F. (1909) *Education by Development*. New York: D. Appleton and Company.

Gardner, H. (1983) *Frames of Mind: The Theory of Multiple Intelligences*. New York: Basic Books.

Gardner, H. (1991) *The Unschooled Mind: How Children Think and How Schools Should Teach*. New York: Basic Books.

Gardner, H. (1999) *Intelligence Reframed: Multiple Intelligences for the 21st Century*. New York: Basic Books.

Gatto, J.T. (1992) *Dumbing Us Down: The Hidden Curriculum of Compulsory Schooling*. Philadelphia: New Society Publishers.

Gesell, A., F.L. Ilg, L.B. Ames, and G.E. Bullis. (1946) *The Child from Five to Ten*. New York and London: Harper & Brothers.

Ghose, A. (1974) *The Future Evolution of Man: The Divine Life upon Earth*. Wheaton, Illinois: Theosophical Publishing House.

Gilligan, C. (1982) *In a Different Voice: Psychological Theory and Women's Development*. Cambridge, Massachusetts: Harvard University Press.

Gilligan, C., and J. Bardige (editors). (1988) *Mapping the Moral Domain: A Contribution of Women's Thinking to Psychological Theory and Education* (seventh edition (1994), volume 2). Cambridge, Massachusetts: Harvard University Press.

Gilligan, J. (1999) *Violence: Reflections on a Western Epidemic*. Philadelphia: Jessica Kingsley Publishers.

Gilligan, J. (2001) *Preventing Violence*. New York: Thames & Hudson.

Gleick, J. (1988) *Chaos: Making a New Science*. New York: Penguin.

Goswami, A. (1993) *The Self-Aware Universe: How Consciousness Creates the Material World*. New York: G.P. Putnam's Sons.

Hawking, S.W. (1988) *A Brief History of Time: From the Big Bang to Black Holes*. Toronto; New York: Bantam Books.

Hawking, S.W. (2001) *The Universe in a Nutshell*. New York: Bantam Books.

Hoffman, L. (1981) *Foundations of Family Therapy: A Conceptual Framework for Systems Change*. New York: Basic Books.

Hoffman, L. (2002) *Family Therapy: An Intimate History* (first edition). New York: W.W. Norton.

Holt, J.C. (1981) *Teach Your Own: A Hopeful Path for Education*. New York Delacorte Press/Seymour Lawrence.

Holt, J.C. (1995) *How Children Learn* (revised edition). Reading, Massachusetts: Addison-Wesley.

Huizinga, J. (1955) *Homo Ludens: A Study of the Play-Element in Culture*. Boston: Beacon Press.

Huxley, A. (1945) *The Perennial Philosophy* (first edition). New York and London: Harper & Brothers Publishers.

Huxley, A. (1962) *Island*. New York: Harper & Row.

Jirâasek, J.E. (2001) *An Atlas of the Human Embryo and Fetus: A Photographic Review of Human Prenatal Development*. New York: Parthenon Publishing Group.

Johnson, S. (2001) *Emergence: The Connected Lives of Ants, Brains, Cities, and Software*. New York: Scribner.

Jung, C.G. (1964) *The Development of Personality* (second print, with corrections). New York: Bollingen Foundation; distributed by Pantheon Books.

Jung, C.G. (1977) *The Collected Works of C.G. Jung* (R.F.C. Hull, translated, volume 17). London: Routledge & Kegan Paul.

Kabat-Zinn, M., and J. Kabat-Zinn. (1997) *Everyday Blessings: The Inner Work of Mindful Parenting* (first edition). New York: Hyperion.

Koestler, A. (1959) *The Sleepwalkers: A History of Man's Changing Vision of the Universe*. London; New York: Arkana.

Korzybski, A. (1948) *Science and Sanity: An Introduction to Non-Aristotelian Systems and General Semantics* (third edition). Lakeville, Connecticut: International Non-Aristotelian Library Publishing Company, Institute of General Semantics.

Kozol, J. (1991) *Savage Inequalities: Children in America's Schools*. New York: HarperCollins.

Krishna Prem, S. (1988) *The Yoga of the Bhagavad Gita*. Longmead, England: Element.

Krishnamurti, J. (1953) *Education and the Significance of Life*. New York: Harper & Row.

Krishnamurti, J. (1973) *Beyond Violence*. New York: Harper & Row.

Krishnamurti, J. (1975) *Beginnings of Learning* (first edition). New York: Harper & Row.

Krishnamurti, J. (1981) *Letters to the Schools*. Madras; New Delhi: Krishnamurti Foundation India; Sole Distributors, B.I. Publications.

Krishnamurti, J. (1996) *Total Freedom: The Essential Krishnamurti* (first edition). San Francisco: HarperCollins Publishers.

Krishnamurti, J. (1999) *This Light in Oneself: True Meditation*. Boston and London: Shambhala Publications.

Kuhn, T.S. (1996) *The Structure of Scientific Revolutions* (third edition). Chicago: University of Chicago Press.

Lemann, N. (1999) *The Big Test: The Secret History of the American Meritocracy* (first edition). New York: Farrar Straus and Giroux.

Lewin, R. (1993) *Complexity: Life at the Edge of Chaos* (first Collier Books edition). New York; Toronto: Collier Books; Maxwell Macmillan Canada; Maxwell Macmillan International.

Liebschner, J. (1992) *A Child's Work: Freedom and Play in Froebel's Educational Theory and Practice*. Cambridge, United Kingdom: Lutterworth Press.

Lowenfeld, M. (1967) *Play in Childhood*. New York: John Wiley & Sons.

Luvmour, J., and B. Luvmour (1993) *Natural Learning Rhythms: How and When Children Learn*. Berkeley, California: Celestial Arts.

Luvmour, B., and J. Luvmour. (1990) *Everyone Wins: Cooperative Games and Activities*. Philadelphia: New Society Publishers.

Luvmour, J., and B. Luvmour. *Metamorphosis: A Guide to Family, Individual and Community Awakening through Rites of Passage*. Unpublished manuscript.

Lynch, D., and P.L. Kordis. (1988) *Strategy of the Dolphin: Scoring a Win in a Chaotic World* (first edition). New York: Morrow.

Mahdi, L.C., and F.M. Little (editors). (1987) *Betwixt & Between: Patterns of Masculine and Feminine Initiation* (third, 1988 edition). La Salle, Illinois: Open Court Publishing Company.

Mahdi, L.C., and M. Meade. (1996) *Crossroads: The Quest for Contemporary Rites of Passage*. Chicago: Open Court.

Mahler, M.S. (1975) *The Psychological Birth of the Human Infant: Symbiosis and Individuation* (first paperback edition). New York Basic Books.

Marshak, D. (1997) *The Common Vision: Parenting and Educating for Wholeness*. New York: P. Lang.

Maslow, A.H. (1968) *Toward a Psychology of Being* (second edition). New York: Van Nostrand Reinhold Company.

Maslow, A.H. (1971) *The Farther Reaches of Human Nature*. New York: The Viking Press.

Matt, D.C. (1995) *The Essential Kabbalah: The Heart of Jewish Mysticism* (first edition). San Francisco: Harper San Francisco.

Maturana, H.R., and F.J. Varela. (1980) *Autopoiesis and Cognition: The Realization of the Living*. Dordrecht, Holland; Boston: D. Reidel Publishing Company.

Miller, A. (1983) *For Your Own Good: Hidden Cruelty in Child-Rearing and the Roots of Violence*. New York: Farrar Straus Giroux.

Miller, A. (1984) *Thou Shalt Not Be Aware: Society's Betrayal of the Child* (American edition). New York: Farrar Straus Giroux.

Miller, R. (1992) *Educational Freedom for a Democratic Society: A Critique of National Goals, Standards, and Curriculum*. Brandon, Vermont: Resource Center for Redesigning Education, 1992.

Miller, R. (1992) *What Are Schools For? Holistic Education in American Culture* (second revised edition). Brandon, Vermont: Holistic Education Press.

Miller, R. (2002) *Free Schools, Free People: Education and Democracy after the 1960s*. Albany: State University of New York Press.

Montagu, A. (1971) *Touching: The Human Significance of the Skin*. New York: Columbia University Press.

Montessori, M. (1966) *The Secret of Childhood* (S.J.M. Joseph Costelloe, The Creighton University, translation). New York: Ballantine Books.

Montessori, M. (1995) *The Absorbent Mind*. New York: Henry Holt and Company.

Mooney MD, S.B., and Linda C. Guidice, MD, Ph.D. (June 11, 2002). *Endocrinology of Pregnancy*, chapter 13. *www.endotext.com/female/female13/female13.htm*.

Mooney MD, S.B., and Linda C. Guidice, MD, Ph.D. (June 11, 2002). *Placental Peptide Hormones: Pituitary-like Hormones*. *www.endotext.com/female/female13/female13_2.htm*

Moore, K.L., and Persaud, T.V.N. (1993) *The Developing Human: Clinically Oriented Embryology* (fifth edition). Philadelphia: Saunders.

Nakagawa, Y. (2000) *Education for Awakening: An Eastern Approach to Holistic Education*. Burlington: Vermont: Foundation for Educational Renewal.

Ornstein, R.E., and D.S. Sobel. (1987) *The Healing Brain: Breakthrough Discoveries about How the Brain Keeps Us Healthy*. New York: Simon and Schuster.

Ouspensky, P.D. (1949) *In Search of the Miraculous: Fragments of an Unknown Teaching*. New York: Harcourt Brace Jovanovich.

Oxford CD-ROM (Firm). (1996) *The New Shorter Oxford English Dictionary* (version 1.0.3., Windows). Oxford: Oxford University Press.

Pearce, J.C. (1977) *Magical Child*. New York: Dutton.

Piaget, J. (1951) *Play, Dreams, and Imitation in Childhood*. New York: Norton.

Piaget, J. (1977) *The Essential Piaget*. New York: Basic Books.

Plotinus, Mackenna, S., and J.M. Dillon. (1991) *The Enneads* (abridged edition). London; New York: Penguin.

Porter, E., J. Gleick, and J. Russek. (1990) *Nature's Chaos*. New York: Viking.

Ravitch, D. (2000) *Left Back: A Century of Failed School Reforms*. New York: Simon & Schuster.

Rogers, C.R. (1983) *Freedom to Learn for the 80's.* New York: Macmillan Publishing Company.

Rogers, C.R., and W.B. Stevens. (1971) *Person to Person: The Problem of Being Human*. New York: Pocket Books.

Sadker, M., and D.M. Sadker. (1994) *Failing at Fairness: How America's Schools Cheat Girls*. New York; Toronto: C. Scribner's Sons; Maxwell Macmillan Canada; Maxwell Macmillan International.

Seidel, S. (1991) *Five Phases in the Implementation of Portfolio Assessment in Classrooms, Schools and School Districts*. Paper presented at the Harvard Graduate School of Education.

Sells, M.A. (1994) *Mystical Languages of Unsaying*. Chicago and London: The University of Chicago Press.

Shah, I. (1973) *The Exploits of the Incomparable Mulla Nasrudin*. London: Pan Books.

Siegel, D.J. (1999) *The Developing Mind: Toward a Neurobiology of Interpersonal Experience* (first edition). New York: The Guilford Press.

Siegel, D.J., and M. Hartzell (2003) *Parenting from the Inside Out: How a Deeper Self-Understanding Can Help You Raise Children Who Thrive*. New York: J.P. Tarcher/Putnam.

Sogyal, Gaffney, P., and A. Harvey. (1992) *The Tibetan Book of Living and Dying*. San Francisco: Harper San Francisco.

Spring, J.H. (1998) *American Education* (eighth edition). Boston: McGraw-Hill.

Steiner, R. (1995) *The Kingdom of Childhood: Seven Lectures and Answers to Questions Given in Torquay*, August 12-20, 1924. Hudson, New York: Anthroposophic Press.

Steiner, R. (1996) *The Education of the Child and Early Lectures on Education*. Hudson, New York: Anthroposophic Press.

Steiner, R. (1996). *Rudolf Steiner in the Waldorf School: Lectures and Addresses to Children, Parents, and Teachers, 1919-1924*. Hudson, New York: Anthroposophic Press.

Steiner, R. (2000) *Practical Advice to Teachers*. Great Barrington, Massachusetts: Anthroposophic Press.

Stern, D.N. (1985) *The Interpersonal World of the Infant: A View from Psychoanalysis and Developmental Psychology*. New York: Basic Books.

Stern, D.N. (1990) *Diary of a Baby*. New York: Basic Books.

Strauss, R. (1999) Self and Possible Selves during the Transition to Fatherhood. *Journal of Family Psychology*, 13(2): 244–259.

Talbot, M. (1991). *The Holographic Universe* (first edition). New York HarperCollins Publishers.

Tzu, L. (1972). *Tao-te Ching* (Gia Fu Feng; English, Jane, translation). New York: Vintage Books, A Division of Random House.

Turner, V. (1989) *The Ritual Process: Structure and Anti-Structure* (sixth edition). Ithaca, New York: Cornell University Press.

Vygotsky, L.S. (1962) *Thought and Language* (Eugenia Hanfman and Gertrude Vakar, translation): Cambridge; Massachusetts Institute of Technology.

Vygotsky, L.S. (1978) *Mind in Society*. Boston: Harvard College.

Waldrop, M.M. (1992) *Complexity: The Emerging Science at the Edge of Order and Chaos*. New York: Simon & Schuster.

Wickes, F.G. (1927) *The Inner World of Childhood*. New York: Signet Books.

Wiggins, G.P. (1993) *Assessing Student Performance: Exploring the Purpose and Limits of Testing*. San Francisco: Jossey-Bass.

Wilber, K. (1977) *The Spectrum of Consciousness* (second Quest edition, 1993). U.S.A., London; Quest Books.

Wilber, K. (1995) *Sex, Ecology and Spirituality: The Spirit of Evolution*. Boston: Shambhala.

Wilber, K. (1996) *The Atman Project: A Transpersonal View of Human Development* (second edition). Wheaton, Illinois: Quest Books, The Theosophical Publishing House.

Wilber, K. (1996) *A Brief History of Everything* (first edition). Boston: Shambhala.

Wilber, K. (2000) *Integral Psychology: Consciousness, Spirit, Psychology, Therapy* (first paperback edition). Boston: Shambhala.

NOTES

1   Bohm, *Wholeness and the Implicate Order*, p. 21.
2   This well documented principle is one of the bedrocks of quantum mechanics. It shows that matter, at its essence, is either a particle or a wave, but not both. Moreover, the determination of which it is comes is known through the influence of the person observing it. See Goswami, 1993, for more.
3   Huizinga, 1955.
4   Lowenfeld, 1967.
5   Froebel, 1909.
6   Stern, 1985.
7   We will use case histories throughout this book rather than the technique of correlating large numbers of individual observations of various children. That technique attempts to quantify results and "prove" its theories scientifically. There are a number of problems with that approach. First, there are no objective observations. Dr. Margaret Lowenfeld, a careful researcher of play in children, understood the problem well. She realized that the human mind cannot grasp what is wholly unfamiliar to it, is more apt to see what it has already noticed, is unable to see what it has not been trained to accept, and unconsciously distorts what it hears and sees, according to its own prejudices. She also observed that children tend to tell adults what they want to hear. She bridged these difficulties by banning note taking in the presence of children and limiting interactions to those the children initiated. When the play period ended, staff recorded the events as objectively as possible and then subjected themselves to rigorous cross-referencing and group critique that had the stated intention of revealing prejudices. Some of her insights are included in Chapter 4, "Play."

8   Maria Nagy had noted this in 1948. See Feifel, 1959.
9   Peat, F.D. (1987). David Bohm 1917–1992 [*Omni* magazine article]. Retrieved March 12, 2002, from *www.fdavidpeat.com/interviews/bohm.htm*, p. 9.
10 See the meticulous work of Dr. Jane Healy for a reasonable exploration of the effects of TV on children.
11 Luvmour, Luvmour et al., 1990.
12 Huizinga, 1955.
13 *www.acs.appstate.edu/~davisct/nt/jung.html#shadow LINK DOESN'T WORK*
14 Korzybski, 1948.
15 Goswami, 1993.
16 This story is condensed from the original format. For the full version see Shah, *The Exploits of the Incomparable Mulla Nasrudin*, p. 23, "How Nasrudin Created Truth."
17 Wisdom in this sense is similar to Bohm's "implicate order."
18 Siegel, 1999.
19 Krishnamurti, 1953, p.29.
20 Krishnamurti, 1953, p.46.
21 Krishnamurti, 1953, p.62.
22 Maslow, 1968.
23 Forbes, 1999.
24 Rogers, pp. 123–124.
25 Krishnamurti, 1953, p.64.
26 Bateson, 1979.
27 Montagu, 1971.
28 Montessori, 1995, pp. 61–62.
29 Montessori, 1995, p. 74.
30 Wickes, 1927.
31 Ouspensky, 1949.
32 Zweig and Abrams, 1991.
33 Bohm, 1994.
34 Bohm, 1994.
35 Bohm, 1994.
36 Wilber, 1996.
37 Siegel, 1999.
38 Although it is not a topic intensively researched, there are studies that indicate that FeelingBeing children who believe the teachings of their church cope less well with the death of a loved one than children brought up without religion. As stated by C. Randy Cotton and Lillian M. Range in *Children's Death Concepts: Relationship to Cognitive Functioning, Age, Experience with Death, Fear of Death, and Hopelessness*, "...a religious belief in an afterlife may thus have contributed to these children's misunderstanding about death's cause or inevitability."
39 Jirâasek, 2001.
40 Mooney MD, 2002 and Giudice MD.

41 Strauss, 1999.
42 *www.marchofdimes.com/professionals/681_1158.asp.*
43 Mooney MD, 2002 and Giudice MD.
44 *www.cis.mcmaster.ca/inabis98/komisaruk/kristal0542/index.html.*
45 Moore, 1993.
46 Stahlman and Gray in Kretchmer, 1987, p.303.
47 While I admit to being simply a student without wide experience in research in this field, I have not come across any information on the effect of contractions on the fetus and particularly the role the sensations of touch play in guiding the fetus through the birthing process.
48 Cotton, 1990.
49 Ken Wilber makes the point that the very nature of a whole is that it is incomplete. There is no pure "wholeness." Life is open-ended, and the desire for a final state is an imposition on what is. For this reason, following Koestler, he adopts the term "holon." His long exegesis of holons in *Sex, Ecology and Spirituality* is well worth reading. One important point (p. 40) is that holons have four fundamental capacities: self-preservation, self-adaptation, self-transcendence, and self-dissolution. Froebel also knew of this fundamental law. As he is less well known, and as educators so rarely get credit for seeing and actualizing what philosophers later elaborate, a short quote is in order: "But, since the developing educator is, as well as the pupil, a manifold part-whole of the all-life...he carries within him, though in manner peculiar to himself, the general laws of the whole, and especially the laws of development of the whole, and hence brings them to his own recognition and consciousness." *Education by Development* (p. 27).

  Thus the whole that is BodyBeing is but part of the bigger whole of child development. It contains its own limitation, which allows for self-transcendence (greater complexity) and ultimately self-dissolution.
50 Goette, Carla. Chattanooga Funeral Home, Chattanooga, Tennessee, runs a support group for bereavement with children. Her work is used by school districts in Georgia. The following is from *wwww.bartow.k12.ga.us/psych/crisis/achilds.htm.*
  Ages six to nine:
  • begins to understand that death is final
  • can understand a more detailed description as to why/how the person died
  • views death in a violent sense—often personified as a skeleton or monster that comes after you
  • may feel death is contagious
  • looks for natural explanations
  • acts as a literal and concrete thinker
  • has concern for peers
  • denies the death happened
  • fears that other loved ones will die

Ages nine to twelve:
- begins to understand the possibility of her own death
- sees death as final
- feels intense emotions of anger and guilt
- displays interest in the physical aspects (biological processes) of dying
- may express concerns about the future effect of the death on her (especially regarding finances and lifestyle)—more future oriented
- withdraws from others and tries to hide her feelings

51 Feifel, 1959.
52 Gesell, 1946.
53 Ames, 1985.
54 Ames, 1989.
55 Nurses, who are also primary workers in the field, come to the same conclusion. See *www.nursingceu.com/NCEU/courses/goodgrief/*.
56 Joseph Chilton Pearce noted the same phenomena in *Magical Child*.
57 Steiner sees the new stage beginning at six with the change of teeth. Piaget has it somewhere around seven with concrete operational thought. Natural Learning Rhythms suggests that these sensitive observers are noticing the first glimmerings of the new stage. However, the organizing principle is still primarily that of the previous stage. The glimmerings are there to herald the coming change and to prepare child and parent for their arrival. One sign, whether it be a physiological change or a cognitive one, is not sufficient to define a life stage. As this chapter demonstrates, it is the emergent whole from the constellation of changes that indicates which organizing principle reigns.
58 Coveney, 1991.
59 Coveney, 1991; Talbot, 1991.
60 National Longitudinal Study on Adolescent Health (1998), *Strong School, Family Ties Protect Teens from Violence, Drugs, Suicide, and Early Sex.* *www.nichd.nih.gov/about/cpr/dbs/pubs/ti8.pdf.*
61 Marshak, 1997.
62 Mahler, 1975.
63 Steiner, 1995.
64 Steiner, 1996; Steiner, 1995.
65 Spiritual adepts have faced the problem of attempting to describe emergent knowledge from time beyond memory. In his erudite and incisive study of the way venerated saints and sages have spoken about their insights, Michael Sells's book *Mystical Languages of Unsaying* makes the compelling point that "in order to claim that the transcendent is beyond names I must give it a name: the transcendent."lxv Offering in-depth analysis of the writings of Plotinus, John the Scot Eriugena, Ibn Al-Arabi, Marguerite Porete, and

Meister Eckhart, Sells talks of three responses to the problem of naming transcendence.

The first response is silence. The second response is to distinguish between ways in which the transcendent is beyond names and ways in which it is not...The third response begins with the refusal to solve the dilemma posed by the attempt to refer to the transcendent through a distinction between two kinds of name. The dilemma is accepted as...unresolvable; but this acceptance, instead of leading to silence, leads to a new mode of discourse. This discourse has been called negative theology.

Sells than describes the tact his subjects have taken.

Apophasis is the common Greek designation for this language. Apophasis can mean "negation," but its etymology suggests a meaning that more precisely characterizes the discourse in question: apo phasis (un-saying or speaking-away). The term apophasis is commonly paired with kataphasis (affirmation, saying, speaking-with). Every act of unsaying demands or presupposes a previous saying.

In other words, every time they give a descriptor of the transcendent, they negate it as soon as possible. The first line of *Tao-te Ching*, states that "The *Tao* that can be named is not the eternal *Tao*" and then in a masterful bit of apophasis offers eighty-one sutras that attempt to name it. Sells offers a Buddhist example:

...the Mahayana Buddhist Vimalakirti Sutra, which asserts that "all constructs are empty," and then playfully turns that statement back upon itself with the assertions that "the construct that all constructs are empty is empty," and "the construct that the construct that all constructs are empty is empty is empty."

I am reminded of one of the greatest lines in spiritual philosophy. Nagarjuna, who brought Buddhism from India to Tibet, had the following dialogue with a spiritual seeker:

Seeker: All is one! One means Not-Two!

Nagarjuna: Yes. Not-Two and Not-Not-Two.

Why have these influential mystics chosen apophasis?

Rather than pointing to an object, apophatic language attempts to evoke in the reader an event that is—in its movement beyond structures of self and other, subject and object—structurally analogous to the event of mystical union.

In Natural Learning Rhythms terms, they are trying to engender participation. They know that the word is not sufficient. They know that an experience that is not unsaid will turn into dogma. They know that knowledge is not information and not a currency but must be realized in the bones. Those who refuse their apophatic language wish only to download their ideas, a type of separation the mystic will not allow.

In the end, Sells offers the word *mystery* as a "referential openness onto the depths of a particular tradition, and into conversation with other traditions. Yet as elusive as it is, mystery is in principle accessible to all."

What is true for mystery is certainly true for being. To paraphrase the *Tao*, the being that is merely the sum of the being qualities is not the being of your child.

66 Gilligan, 1999.
67 Miller, 1983.
68 Ravitch, 2000.
69 Miller, 1992.
70 *www.nd.edu/~rbarger/www7/puritans.htm.*
71 Kozol, 1991.
72 Spring, 1998.
73 *www.nd.edu/~rbarger/www7/latingra.html.*
74 Miller, 1992.
75 Ravitch, 2000.
76 *www.tncrimlaw.com/civil_bible/horace_mann.html.*
77 *rbarger/ww7/ord17857.html.*
78 Miller, 1992.
79 Ravitch, 2000.
80 *rbarger/ww7/ord17857.html.*
81 Lemann, 1999.
82 Ravitch, 2000, p. 70.
83 Ravitch, 2000.
84 Miller, 1992.
85 Ravitch, 2000.
86 Spring (pp. 244–245) Miller, R. (1990, pp. 99–120), and Ravitch, (pp. 169–170) share this interpretation of Dewey's view of experience.
87 Spring nicely summarizes the multicultural movement (pp. 146–166). YEAR
88 Dewey, 1929.
89 Miller (pp. 99–120) argues this throughout. He would also object to one definition for progressive education. Spring, (pp. 245–245) agrees that Dewey and child-centered do not belong together.
90 Spring, 1998.
91 Gatto, 1992.
92 Ravitch, 2000.
93 Miller, 2002.
94 Gardner, 1999.
95 Gardner, 1991, p. 105.
96 Gardner, 1983.
97 Gardner, 1983.
98 Gardner, 1983.
99 Reading comprehension is the subject of much research. Numerous studies support our claim that children in FeelingBeing comprehend differently

than those in BodyBeing. This implies a different context in which information is understood. One excellent study, "The Role of Metacognition in Reading and Studying," has the following pithy observations: "Young children have different ideas of what it means to skim. For example, Myers and Paris (1978) report that sixth graders understand that the purpose of skimming is to pick out the informative words, whereas second graders think they skim by reading the easy words. These different skimming strategies reflect conceptions of reading as meaning-getting and word-decoding, respectively."

100 Repeatedly, we have had difficulty finding research on the brains of nine-year-old children. The brain evolves in relationship to its environment. Much more needs to be done in order to coordinate brain activity and child development. See the nine-year-old brain at
www.loni.ucla.edu/~thompson/JAY/Growth_REVISED.html.

101 Cadwell, 1997.

102 www.apa.org/pi/parent.html.

103 Jung, 1954, pp. 78-79.

104 Maturana and Varela, 1980.

105 Maturana and Varela, 1980, p. xxix.

106 Waldrop, p.234.

107 Wilber, 1995, p.47.

108 Gleick, p. 24.

109 Gleick and Porter, Nature's Chaos, has beautiful pictures and excellent explanatory text illustrating self-similarity in nature.

110 Plotinus, 1991.

111 Ouspensky, 1949.

111 Godman, "God and the Godhead," The Mountain Path, 31(3 & 4), 1994, pp. 183-188.

112 Assagioli, Psychosynthesis, has a collection of this insightful holistic approach to psychotherapy.

113 Mandala, by Jose and Miriam Arguelles, describes not only the universality of mandalas, but also their hidden significance, which is nothing less than a depiction of the Great Chain of Being.

114 As this quote by Robert Ornstein in his introduction to Chapter 1 in The Evolution of Consciousness shows, Rumi had specific knowledge of the Great Chain: "Originally you were clay. From being mineral, you became vegetable. From vegetable, you became animal, and from animal, man." Aurobindo reminds us of something similar when he tells us that Vedic philosophy has always included the idea that life is inherent in inorganic matter.

115 See Matt, The Essential Kabbalah. His excellent diagram opposite page 1 is a mandala as well.

116 See Soygal Rinpoche, The Tibetan Book of Living and Dying, as well as the classic by Evans-Wentz, The Tibetan Book of the Dead.

117 Wilber, 2000, pp. 197-217.

118 Gleick, p. 175.

119 Wilber, 1995, p. 74.

120 Csikszentmihalyi makes this point in many places in his writing. See particularly Part II, "The Power of the Future" in *The Evolving Self*.

121 Csikszentmihalyi, M., and I. Csikszentmihalyi (editors), *Optimal Experience: Psychological Studies of Flow in Consciousness*, contains articles on sociological, historical, and psychological applications of flow theory.

122 Csikszentmihalyi. 1993, pp. 178–179.

123 Kordis and Lynch, p. 171.

124 Here is a formal etiological statement of the Natural Learning Rhythms perspective on dysfunction.

In each developmental stage, the child perceives the world through a primary mode of perception. During each stage, the organizing principle, and much of the resulting perception, is sensitive to specific input. This input feeds, nourishes, and allows connection with the depths of the organizing principle of that stage. These nourishments, therefore, are essential input to enable well-being. When elders allow the child access to well-being, she gains a greater perception of her own identity as a unique expression of wholeness. In each stage, the child, as a self-organizing system, reaches a limit sufficiently far from equilibrium and moves to a new stage—a new level of complexity.

If these nourishments are provided inappropriately for a stage, in either excess or deficiency, the mind is thwarted and detoured from its complete access to well-being. Consequently, the identity and sense of self at the stage are distorted, dissociated, and disconnected, lacking integration and wholeness. This disconnected self expresses its identity accordingly in behaviors and modes consistent with the inappropriate nourishments provided. The malnourished self goes into protective mode, loses contact with the depth of the organizing principle, and expresses this separation as dissonant behavior. The developmentally driven aspects, or primary qualities, of self are thus disjointed and dissociated—or disowned altogether.

Malnourishment of the psyche interferes with the flow of the life energy that creates, manifests, and heals. Once the interference is reduced, the flow is innately reestablished in its connection to well-being. The connected self expresses the flow of life energy as integrated wholeness and unity—as a "sum greater than its parts"—and all parts are fully acknowledged as essential and necessary.

In order to facilitate the reconnection to well-being, the suffering self is provided with events and experiences that are designed to reduce interferences to the flow of life energy. In effect, experiences are provided that nurture well-being by supplying the nourishments in ways that are assimilable and palatable. These nourishments modify our perception of ourselves and our world.

Separation is a disruption or interference in the flow; connection is an expression of the flow.

125 Ornstein and Sobel, p. 87.

126 Fowler, 1926.

127 EnCompass brochure "From Good to Great."

128 Gilligan, 2001, p.7.

129 Gilligan, 2001, p. 33.

130 Gilligan, 2001, p. 105.

131 Gilligan, 2001, p. 48.

132 Gilligan, 2001, pp. 47–49.

133 Gilligan, 2001, p. 101.

134 Gilligan, 2001, p. 118.

135 In the 1960s, John Bowlby's research showed that the bond is critical for psychological well-being for the child. Without the bond, the child is unable to attach to meaningful people and events in their lives. This tendency increases as they get older and becomes more pronounced in the teen years. There is a wealth of good literature on attachment parenting and bonding for those interested.

136 Rogers, 1983, p. 290.

137 The same quality of excellence usually does not appear when the IdealBeing child is not engaged in their field of interest. There, with little meaningful connection to the importance of the endeavor, the child will do only what is necessary to get by, or less. Self-motivation hinges primarily on expression of the ideal and only secondarily on other activities.

138 Other insightful researchers have considered the implications of complexity and emergence for social justice. I will briefly review the work of two, Fritjof Capra and Mihaly Csikszentmihalyi, as representative of the field. They embody two of the dominant approaches to social justice. Capra approaches the issue from the perspective of the biosphere, and Csikszentmihalyi approaches it from the perspective of the psychology of the individual. Both have received much praise and spawned additional research based on their theories. Their work is scholarly and yet accessible to the lay reader. I have not, however, conducted an exhaustive survey of the field and do not wish to suggest that Capra and Csikszentmihalyi have covered all perspectives.

Capra came to public attention with his first book, *The Tao of Physics*, in which he correlated many of the surprising conclusions of quantum mechanics with Eastern spiritual philosophy. He enriched the perennial philosophy by drawing science in to it. Not only did the sages and saints of many of the cultures of the world agree on the essential characteristics of spirituality, as the perennial philosophy demonstrates, but science, the queen of the West, was now substantively linked as well. Capra had laid a plank in the bridge towards a unified appreciation of human consciousness. His next book was eagerly awaited.

In *The Web of Life*, Capra links complexity, autopoiesis (self-creating), and living systems. His perspective emphasizes the self-organization in cells, phyla, all living systems, and evolution itself. So far, so good. At the end of the book, Capra posits how human society can be organized to maximize ecological well-being for all life.

> We need to revitalize our communities—including our educational communities, business communities, and political communities—so that the principles of ecology become manifest in them as principles of education, management, and politics.

While acknowledging that human societies have unique considerations, such as self-awareness, Capra insists that the ecological principles that have sustained life for three billion years should guide human society. He calls these principles ecoliteracy.

The first principle is interdependence:

> Understanding ecological interdependence means understanding relationships. It requires the shifts of perception that are characteristic of systems thinking—from the parts to the whole, from objects to relationships, from contents to patterns. A sustainable human community is aware of the multiple relationships among its members. Nourishing the community means nourishing those relationships.

The second principle is open communication so that nonlinear feedback loops are not restricted. The third is flexibility, so that extreme stress does not overtax the system. Socially, flexibility means the avoidance of fixed moral guidelines. Instead, people should use conflict resolution tools in which the resolution depends "on context" and avoids rigidity. Unfortunately, the specific tools are not mentioned, nor is who gets to define the context. Also, the question remains unanswered of whether the insistence that there be no fixed moral guidelines is, in itself, a fixed moral guideline.

Last, ecoliteracy asserts that the principle of diversity must be maintained:

> In human communities ethnic and cultural diversity may play the same role [as biological diversity]. Diversity means many different relationships, many different approaches to the same problem. A diverse community is a resilient community, capable of adapting to changing situations.
>
> However, diversity is a strategic advantage only if there is a truly vibrant community, sustained by a web of relationships...If the community is aware of the interdependence of all its members, diversity will enrich all the relationships and thus enrich the community as a whole, as well as each individual member.

Capra's work is an excellent synthesis of the dynamics of emergence and its application to the biosphere. His principles are correct and clearly articulated. Yet he is studying nature and life and completely overlooks the fact that those same principles that lead to sustainability and emergence are transparent in human life and development. How could we be here if they weren't? How can he speak of "the interdependence of all its members" and leave out children and families? What kind of diversity is that? Furthermore, conflict resolution tools cannot even solve the problems of divorce. How can they work for ethnic cleansing?

Hurting adults make hurtful decisions. Understanding the web of life will not convert people to follow the principles of ecoliteracy. As Gilligan said, acting unjustly is not the result of stupidity. It is the result of shame and pain. It can never be redressed by new information. Information is not knowledge.

Csikszentmihalyi, introduced in "The Edge of Chaos" section of Chapter 10, "Reunification," formulated flow theory to describe psychological well-being. In terms of society, Csikszentmihalyi recognizes that justice depends on the moral quality of the people. He quotes John Adams, second president of the United States, to show that the Constitution is viable only to the extent that moral quality prevails. Given conscientious ethics, he says, a good society

> ...makes it possible for each person to develop the skills necessary to experience flow in socially productive activities. At the same time, it guards against anyone's exploiting the psychic energy of another person for his or her own advantage. There is a constant watch for oppression and parasites. According to this perspective, freedom does not apply to *doing*, but to *being*. Each person is free to develop a self to the utmost level of his potential complexity, but not curtail another person's freedom to do so.

The "most urgent task" on the way to creating the good society is to develop a curriculum "that will make each child aware, from the first grade on, that life in the universe is interdependent."

Csikszentmihalyi is not concerned primarily with children, though he does have some useful insights for education:

> If we wish to have a society in which freedom coexists with responsibility, we must ensure that the environment in which young people grow up provides complex experiences...
> ...what is common to these ideals [of Aldous Huxley and Plato] is that they emphasize the training of the whole person, building on spontaneous interest and potentialities, and they stress risk and responsibilities, while making possi-

ble a joyous experience of growth. For instance Plato understood that it didn't make sense to expect children to grasp abstract ideas until they had learned how to control their bodies in athletic exercise, and until they learned about order through the rhythm of music and other forms of sensory harmony.

With all due respect, this sounds like play.

An example of progress in this regard is a public school that has turned away from the conventional curriculum and embraced one based on multiple intelligences. This kind of educational effort has the added benefit of coming from the grassroots, "where enthusiasm and commitment are strongest, [and] that new solutions are likely to emerge."

The next step to the good society is the creation of "evolutionary cells," which are small groupings of people who have the common interest of allowing maximum flow. Csikszentmihalyi spends several pages outlining the functions of the members of such a cell and the tasks the cell would engage. Emergence dynamics would allow these cells to self-organize at greater levels of complexity. They would become the "fellowship of the future" and eventually transform society.

In his work on the individual's psyche, Csikszentmihalyi has admirably extended the work of those pioneers—Abraham Maslow, Carl Rogers, Roberto Assagioli, and further back, Carl Jung and Alfred Adler, among others—who championed the importance of optimal psychological well-being. Thankfully, he at least includes children, albeit marginally, in the social justice discourse. But, alas, it is only to teach children, not to learn with them. It is only to impart the curriculum, not to develop relationship. How can anyone integrate interdependence when it is taught didactically and with little regard for the developmental language of the student?

Csikszentmihalyi identifies grassroots actions as necessary for a good society. He calls for parents and teachers to change schools and adults to organize into flow-oriented cells. This approach may be effective, but the most potent grassroots opportunity takes place every day in every family. It is the interaction between parent and child. There are no state guidelines that need interfere. That relationship is not necessarily subject to historical influences, either personal or cultural. It is possible to simply dance. In the dance, the natural abilities for creating social justice are optimized.

I agree with Csikszentmihalyi and John Adams that democracy depends on the moral quality of its people. While I am in awe of the American social experiment, I cannot pretend that social justice has been achieved here. Prejudice remains strong, soldiers come mostly from the poorer classes and the young, health care is over-priced and not available to all, the environment is seen as a commodity, political expediency is often an excuse to ignore human rights, and the gap between the rich and the middle class gets wider and wider. It does not seem that, by itself, the social institution of democracy is sufficient to guarantee social justice.

139 There are many good works on resilience in children. A good place to start an inquiry into resilience is the journal article "Fostering Resilience in Children" by Bonnie Bernard at *resilnet.uiuc.edu/library/benard95.html*.

140 Buber, 1958.

141 Prem, 1988, p. 186.

142 de Chardin, 1975, p. 262.

143 de Chardin, 1975, p. 219.

144 Greater complexity, after all, has little to do with sexuality and much to do with consciousness, of which sexuality is but an aspect.

145 Aurobindo, 1974, p. 25.

146 Wilber, 1995, p. 109.

147 de Chardin, 1975 p. 57.

148 de Chardin, 1975, p. 219.

149 de Chardin, 1975, p. 221.

150 de Chardin, 1975, p. 222.

151 de Chardin, 1975, p. 223.

152 de Chardin, 1975, p. 223-224.

153 de Chardin, 1975, p. 224.

154 de Chardin, 1975, p. 244.

155 de Chardin, 1975, p. 251-252.

156 de Chardin, 1975, p. 252-253.

157 de Chardin, 1975, p. 262.

158 de Chardin, 1975, p. 262-263.

159 de Chardin, 1975, p. 264.

160 de Chardin, 1975, p. 265.

161 de Chardin, 1975, p. 265.

162 de Chardin, p. 232.

163 Gebser, 1984, pp. 43-44.

164 The correlates nicely with Bateson's comment that it is the difference between being and non-being that allows consciousness of being. See the "Relationship" section of Chapter 5, "Spirituality."

165 Gebser, 1984, p. 46.

166 Gebser, 1984, pp. 45-60, 162-173.

167 Gebser, 1984, p. 66.

168 Gebser, 1984, p. 66.

169 Gebser, 1984, pp. 70-71

170 Gebser, 1984, p. 75.

171 Edmunds, 1902, p. 1.

172 Gebser, 1984, pp. 83-85.

173 Gebser, 1984, p. 85.

174 Gebser, 1984, p. 250.

175 Gebser, 1984, p. 250.

176 Gebser, 1984, p. 37.
177 Gebser, 1984, p. 295.
178 Gebser, 1984, pp. 279–280.
179 Gebser, 1984, p. 300.
180 Gebser, 1984, p. 296.
181 Gebser, 1984, p. 299.
182 Gebser, 1984, p. 304.
183 Gebser, 1984, pp. 294–295.
184 Gebser, 1984, p 24.
185 Goswami, 1993, p.8.
186 Gebser, 1984, pp. 393–402.
187 Gebser, 1984, pp. 406–409.
188 Gebser, 1984, p. 530.
189 Wilber, 1995, pp. 236–252.
190 Wilber, 1995, p. 78.
191 Wilber, 1995, p. 279.
192 Wilber, 1995, pp. 277–278.
193 Wilber, 1995, p. 265.
194 Wilber, 1995, pp. 263–264.

ABOUT THE AUTHOR

Ba Luvmour pioneered whole-family experiential learning and has led hundreds of seminars for parents and educators in Natural Learning Rhythms (NLR). He has co-authored books on NLR-related topics and spoken at national and international conferences.

Ba and his wife Josette founded EnCompass (*www.EnCompassFamilies.org*), a non-profit dedicated to using NLR to enable optimal well-being in children and families. As Executive Director, he has overseen EnCompass' growth since its inception in 1985. His responsibilities include networking, fundraising, board development, program facilitation and research. Contact him through *www.BaLuvmour.com*.

Ba and Josette live in Portland, OR.

Sentient Publications, LLC publishes books on cultural creativity, experimental education, transformative spirituality, holistic health, new science, ecology, and other topics, approached from an integral viewpoint.
Our authors are intensely interested in exploring the nature of life from
fresh perspectives, addressing life's great questions, and fostering the full
expression of the human potential. Sentient Publications' books arise
from the spirit of inquiry and the richness of the inherent dialogue
between writer and reader.

Our Culture Tools series is designed to give social catalyzers and cultural
entrepreneurs the essential information, technology, and inspiration to
forge a sustainable, creative, and compassionate world.

We are very interested in hearing from our readers. To direct suggestions
or comments to us, or to be added to our mailing list, please contact:

SENTIENT PUBLICATIONS, LLC
1113 Spruce Street
Boulder, CO 80302
303-443-2188
contact@sentientpublications.com
www.sentientpublications.com